LYSIMACHUS

LYSIMACHUS

A study in early Hellenistic kingship

Helen S. Lund

London and New York

First published 1992
by Routledge
11 New Fetter Lane, London EC4P 4EE

Simultaneously published in the USA and Canada
by Routledge
a division of Routledge, Chapman and Hall, Inc.
29 West 35th Street, New York, NY 10001

© 1992 Helen S. Lund

Typeset in 10/12pt Garamond by
Witwell Ltd, Southport
Printed and bound in Great Britain by
TJ Press Ltd, Padstow, Cornwall

British Library Cataloguing in Publication Data
Lund, Helen S.
Lysimachus: Study in Early Hellenistic Kingship
I. Title
938

Library of Congress Cataloging in Publication Data
Lund, Helen S. (Helen Sarah)
Lysimachus: a study in early Hellenistic kingship/Helen S. Lund.
p. cm.
Includes bibliographical references and index.
1. Lysimachus, King of Thrace, c. 361–281 BC.
2. Greece–History–Macedonian Hegemony, 323–281 BC.
3. Macedonia–History–Diadochi, 323–276 BC. 4. Thrace–Kings
and rulers–Biography.
I. Title
DF235.48.L97L86   1992
938'.08'092–dc20
[B]
92–2796
CIP

ISBN 0–415–07061–9

For my father

CONTENTS

ACKNOWLEDGEMENTS

Since this book started life as a doctoral thesis, I would like to thank, first of all, my supervisors, Mrs Amélie Kuhrt and Professor Michael Crawford, for their invaluable advice, constructive criticism, help and encouragement; also Dr Susan Sherwin-White, whose teaching first inspired my interest in the Diadoch period; for their help with specific problems, my thanks go to Dr M. J. Price, Dr Zosia Archibald and Dr Tom Blagg. Finally I must say thank you to James Lund and Hilary Marsh for their interest, support and practical assistance over the past five years.

ABBREVIATIONS

PERIODICALS

AJA	*American Journal of Archaeology*
A. J. Phil.	*American Journal of Philology*
ANSM	*American Numismatic Society: Museum Notes*
Ath. Mitt.	*Mitteilungen des Deutschen Archäologischen Institutes Athenische Abteilung*
BCH	*Bulletin de Correspondance Hellénique*
CQ	*Classical Quarterly*
CR	*Classical Review*
CRAI	*Comptes Rendus de l'Académie des Inscriptions et Belles Lettres*
CSCA	*California Studies in Classical Antiquity*
GRBS	*Greek, Roman and Byzantine Studies*
HSCP	*Harvard Studies in Classical Philology*
JEA	*Journal of Egyptian Archaeology*
JHS	*Journal of Hellenic Studies*
JNES	*Journal of Near Eastern Studies*
JNFA	*Journal of Numismatics and Fine Art*
JOAI	*Jahreshefte des Österreichischen Archäologischen Institutes*
JRS	*Journal of Roman Studies*
Mus. Helv.	*Museum Helveticum*
Num. Chron.	*Numismatic Chronicle*
PCPS	*Proceedings of the Cambridge Philological Society*
REA	*Revue des Etudes Anciennes*
REG	*Revue des Etudes Grecques*

Rev. Phil.	*Revue de Philologie*
Rhein. Mus.	*Rheinische Museum für Philologie*
Riv. Fil.	*Rivista di Filologia*
SCIV	*Studii si Cercetari de Istorie Veche*
Symbol. Osl.	*Symbolae Osloenses*
TAPhA	*Transactions of the American Philological Association*
YAYLA	*3rd Report of Northern Society for Anatolian Archaeology*
ZPE	*Zeitschrift für Papyrologie und Epigraphik*

COLLECTIONS OF INSCRIPTIONS

BMI	*British Museum Collection of Ancient Greek Inscriptions* vols I (Attica) and III (Priene, Iasus and Ephesus) (ed. E. Hicks)
GHI	*A Selection of Greek Historical Inscriptions* (ed. M. N. Tod)
IGBR	*Inscriptiones Graecae in Bulgaria Repertae* 4 vols (ed. G. Mihailov)
IG II²	*Inscriptiones Graecae* vol. II, pt. 1 (Inscriptiones Atticae Aetatis quae est inter Euclidis Annum et Augusti Tempore) (ed. U. Koehler)
IG XII	*Inscriptiones Graecae* vol. XII Supplementum (Inscriptiones Graecae Insularum Maris Aegaei praeter Delum) (ed. F. Hiller von Gaetringen)
I. Milet.	*Das Delphinion in Milet* Pt. II *Die Inschriften.* (ed. A. Rehm)
Inschr. Claz.	*Die Inschriften von Erythai und Klazomenai* (eds H. Engelmann and R. Merkelbach)
Inschr. Eph.	*Die Inschriften von Ephesos* (vols XIV and XV of *Inschriften Griechischer Städte aus Kleinasien*) (ed. C. Borker, C. and R. Merkelbach)
Inschr. Eryth.	*Die Inschriften von Erythrai und Klazomenai* (vol. I of *Inschriften Griechischer Städte aus Kleinasien*) (ed. H. Engelmann and R. Merkelbach)
Inschr. Iasos	*Die Inschriften von Iasos* (vol. XXVIII,

	1 of *Inschriften Griechischer Städte aus Kleinasien*) (ed. W. Blümer)
Inschr. Ilion	*Die Inschriften von Ilion* (vol. III of *Inschriften Griechischer Städte aus Kleinasien*) (ed. P. Frisch)
Inschr. Lampsakos	*Die Inschriften von Lampsakos* (vol. VI of *Inschriften Griechischer Städte aus Kleinasien*). (ed. P. Frisch)
Inschr. Tralles.	*Die Inschriften von Tralleis und Nysa* (vol. XXXVI, 1 of *Inschriften Griechischer Städte aus Kleinasien*) (ed. F. B. Poljakov)
I.Perg.	*Pergamon: Altertumer von Pergamon viii. Die Inschriften* (ed. M. Fraenkel *et al.*)
I.Priene	*Inschriften von Priene* (ed. F. Hiller von Gaetringen)
ISE	*Iscrizione Storiche Ellenistiche* 2 vols (ed. I. Moretti)
OGIS	*Orientis Graeci Inscriptiones Selectae* (ed. W. Dittenberger)
RC	*Royal Correspondence in the Hellenistic Period* (C. B. Welles)
RIJG	*Recueil des Inscriptiones Juridiques Grecques* (ed. R. Dareste, B. Haussoullier and Th. Reinach)
SEG	*Supplementum Epigraphicum Graecum* (eds various)
Syll³	*Sylloge Inscriptionum Graecarum*, 3rd edn (ed. W. Dittenberger)
Titul. Lyc.	*Tituli Lyciae linguis Graecis et Latinis conscripti* (vol. II of *Tituli Asiae Minoris*) (ed. E. Kalinka)

COLLECTIONS OF LITERARY FRAGMENTS, ETC.

ABC	*Assyrian and Babylonian Chronicles* (ed. A. K. Grayson)
FHG	*Fragmenta Historicorum Graecorum* (ed. C. Muller)
FGrH	*Die Fragmente der Griechischen Historiker* (ed. F. Jacoby)
LBAT	*Late Babylonian Astronomical and Related*

Texts (ed. A. J. Sachs)

PAPYRI

P.Oxy.   *The Oxyrhynchus Papyri* (Egypt Exploration
Society) (eds various)

OTHER

PW   *Pauly's Realencyclopaedie der Classischen
Altertumwissenschaft* (ed. G. Wissowa)

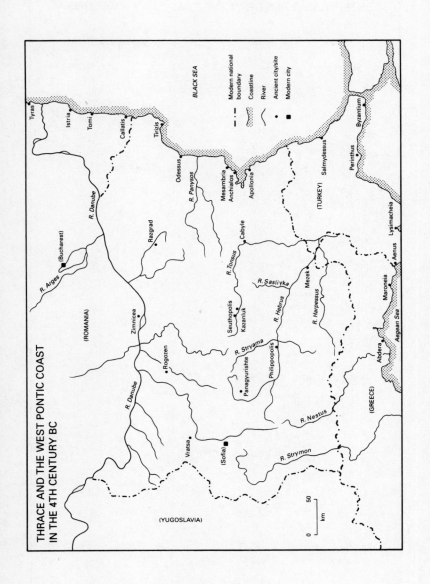

THRACE AND THE WEST PONTIC COAST
IN THE 4TH CENTURY BC

BLACK SEA

Modern national
boundary
Coastline
River
Ancient city/site
Modern city

Tyras
Istria
Tomi
Callatis
Tirizis
Odessus
Mesambria
Anchialos
Apollonia
Salmydessus
Byzantium
Perinthus
Lysimacheia
Aenus
Maroneia
Abdera

R. Danube
R. Panysos
R. Arges
(Bucharest)
Razgrad
Cabyle
R. Tonsus
R. Sasliyka
Seuthopolis
Kazanluk
R. Hebrus
Mezek
R. Harpessus
(ROMANIA)
Zimnicea
R. Stryama
Philippopolis
Rogozen
Panagyurishte
(TURKEY)
Aegean Sea
R. Danube
R. Nestus
(GREECE)
Vratsa
(Sofia)
R. Strymon

(YUGOSLAVIA)

50

km

0

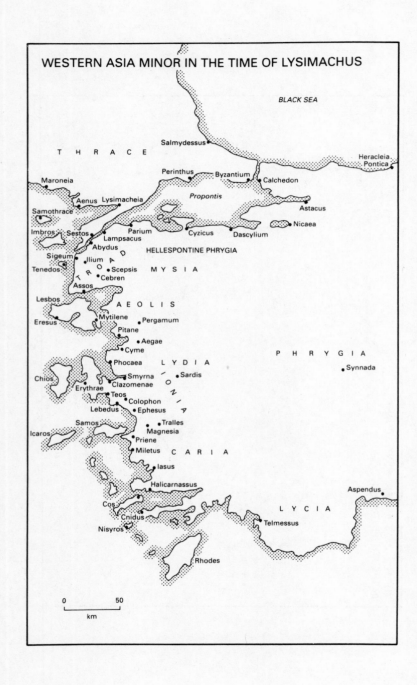

WESTERN ASIA MINOR IN THE TIME OF LYSIMACHUS

BLACK SEA

T H R A C E

Salmydessus

Heracleia
Pontica

Perinthus   Byzantium   Calchedon
Maroneia   Propontis
Aenus Lysimacheia
Astacus
Samothrace
Nicaea
Imbros   Sestos   Parium   Cyzicus   Dascylium
Lampsacus
Abydus   HELLESPONTINE PHRYGIA
Sigeum   Ilium
Tenedos   Scepsis   M Y S I A
Cebren
Assos

Lesbos   A E O L I S

Mytilene   Pergamum
Eresus   Pitane
Aegae
Cyme   P H R Y G I A

Phocaea   L Y D I A   Synnada
Chios   Smyrna   Sardis
Erythrae   Clazomenae
Teos   Colophon
Lebedus   Ephesus
Samos   Tralles
Magnesia
Priene
Icaros   Miletus   C A R I A

Iasus

Halicarnassus   Aspendus

Cos   L Y C I A
Cnidus   Telmessus
Nisyros

Rhodes

T
R
O
A
D

I
O
N
I
A

0   50
km

1

THE ROAD TO BABYLON

Family background, early career and 'character'

On 10 June 323 BC Alexander the Great lay dead in Babylon. Among the Companions mourning at his bedside was Lysimachus, son of Agathocles.[1] When the regent Perdiccas redistributed the empire's satrapies after Alexander's death, Lysimachus received the territory of Thrace. By 284 BC he ruled an empire embracing Thrace, the West Pontic coast, Macedonia, Thessaly, most of Anatolia, Heracleia Pontica and its Paphlagonian realm. His power had reached its zenith.

Probably in the following year his greatest enemy Demetrius Poliorcetes, taken prisoner by Seleucus, king of Syria, in 286 BC, drank himself to death, an ignominious end for one who had worn the diadem and been hailed by the Athenians as the only true god.[2] If, however, immortality is conferred through fame, then Lysimachus lost his last battle against Demetrius, whose exploits and excesses are preserved for us in the biography of Plutarch. There is no comparable record of Lysimachus' life.

Information, from literature, on Lysimachus' career is restricted to scattered notices in the narratives of the Alexander and Diadoch historians, themselves mostly preserved in the works of later historians and epitomators. Then there are Plutarch's biographies of Lysimachus' more favoured contemporaries, the work of geographers and travel writers like Strabo and Pausanias, chroniclers like Porphyry of Tyre. Finally, a string of anecdotes survives in the writings of Athenaeus, Diogenes Laertius, the moralising works of Plutarch, Seneca and other Roman writers. Some of these may go back to contemporary authors like Duris or Cleitarchus.[3]

Both the passage of time and the possibility of bias in the sources used by these late writers lead to distortions and some conflict of evidence. The literary evidence on Lysimachus is fragmentary and often suspect. This, together with the fact that written history is

1

essentially interpretation rather than 'fact', makes it improbable that an examination of this material will lead us to the 'real' Lysimachus. All that can be attempted is to discern the various traditions that developed about him and the motives that inspired them. If major themes emerge which cannot be attributed to a single source tradition, then this is the closest one can get to a 'true' portrait.

What then do the literary sources say about his background, his career before and after 323 BC, his relationship with Alexander and his personal character?

FAMILY BACKGROUND

Though Pausanias and Justin describe Lysimachus as Macedonian by birth, the patronymic 'son of Agathocles' used by Arrian, and Porphyry's description of him as 'Thessalus', have led to his father being identified as the Thessalian whom Theopompus describes as an intimate friend of Philip II. Less flatteringly, he is also dubbed a *penestes* (serf) who owed his position to *kolakeia* (flattery). Evidence for Theopompus' consistent hostility to Philip and his circle, however, suggests that this should be taken with a pinch of salt. It is, moreover, a favourite trick of the literary sources to label as 'parasites' men whom the epigraphic evidence shows as generals and diplomats of considerable importance.[4] As Theopompus himself admits, Agathocles shared in Philip's councils and was sent by him to 'deal with the Perrhaebi and take charge of affairs in that area'.

Since Arrian, in the *Indika*, names Lysimachus among the trierarchs from Pella in Macedonia, the simplest solution to the problem is to assume that Agathocles was rewarded for his services with estates at Pella. Presumably the family was swiftly assimilated into Macedonian society, with Agathocles' sons growing up with the status of Macedonians. Both Lysimachus and his brothers enjoyed a prominent position in Alexander's circle; this fits well with the picture of their father as a favourite at the Argead court. The arguments put forward by Merker, challenging both the idea of Lysimachus' Thessalian origin and his connection with Theopompus' 'parasite', do not seem to be conclusive.[5]

If Lysimachus' forebears were Greek, there is little suggestion that this proved a millstone round his neck; the anti-Greek prejudice apparently encountered by Eumenes of Cardia is conspicuous by its absence. On the contrary, *c.* 285 BC Lysimachus, at war with Pyrrhus over Macedon, 'contrived to subvert Pyrrhus' principal supporters . . .

reproaching them for having chosen as their master a man who was a foreigner'.[6]

Born some time between 361 BC and 351 BC, and therefore roughly contemporary with Alexander, Lysimachus was probably Agathocles' second son. His elder brother Alcimachus was already active as a diplomat and administrator in the first years of Alexander's rule. Honoured, perhaps, with *proxenia* at Athens in a decree of 336 BC, two years later he turns up in charge of an army, empowered by Alexander to 'liberate' the cities of Ionia and Aeolis.[7]

Agathocles, it seems, was rich in sons. Lysimachus had at least two other brothers. Autodicus' link with Lysimachus is assured by the king's later dedication of a statue of his sister-in-law Adaea. He looked set to follow in Lysimachus' footsteps, with promotion to the Bodyguard at Triparadeisus in 321 BC. Philip, Agathocles' remaining son, is known only for his dramatic death in Alexander's arms, exhausted by an attempt to keep pace, on foot, with a cavalry pursuit of Sogdian rebels, and by the fight that followed. Both Justin and Curtius tell the tale: for Curtius, devotion to Alexander inspired Philip's persistence in this gruelling feat, despite Lysimachus' attempts to dissuade him; as Justin tells it, it was his elder brother whom Philip was trying to emulate. If the circumstances of Philip's death are accepted as historical, then of the two, Curtius' version is preferable; certainly his presentation of Lysimachus, as one who clearly did not think 'the world well lost for love', even Alexander's, contrasted with Philip's romantic idealism, is quite consistent with other evidence which presents him as a hard-headed pragmatist. Justin's account is rendered suspect by its context – a passage devoted to extravagant praise of Lysimachus. It is, moreover, uncannily similar to a story in Appian where Lysimachus' powers of endurance are stressed as a preface to the famous legend of Alexander staunching Lysimachus' wound with his diadem.[8] This suggests that its source is propaganda post-dating Lysimachus' achievement of kingship, *c.* 305–4 BC.

ALEXANDER'S COMPANION

At first sight, evidence for Lysimachus' career with Alexander, limited as it is, falls into two main categories. Some references hinge mainly on his relationship with Alexander; since these may well be the product of literary traditions with specific motives for presenting both Lysimachus and Alexander in a certain light, their value for an assessment of character is clearly questionable. Others seem only to underline his prominence as a member of the social and military élite, but even these cannot always be taken at face value. Ever since Ptolemy's historiographic halo became tarnished,[9] it has been recognised that information in the Alexander Histories on his future Successors must be seen in the light of the propaganda which they later circulated. Another source of distortion for the events of Alexander's life-time is the apologetic tradition embedded in Ptolemy and Aristobulus, Arrian's main sources, once regarded as above suspicion.

The various titles by which Lysimachus is described give some indication of his role on Alexander's military staff. There is, however, surprisingly little information as to how, when and why he achieved this position. Arrian, using Aristobulus, names him among the seven *somatophylakes* of Alexander. The term has two meanings in Arrian, designating both the King's Footguard and the small group of officers who formed Alexander's personal staff; Lysimachus' aristocratic background and the context in which the terms are used make it clear that both *somatophulax* and the synonyms used by Porphyry and Arrian, *doruphoros* and *hypaspistes*, refer to his membership of the latter body. Reaching its maximum number of eight with Peucestas' promotion in 325 BC, the Bodyguard included such luminaries as Hephaistion, Perdiccas and Ptolemy. Membership implied service at Alexander's side, with men appointed to commands in another theatre of war, or to a governorship being replaced.[10]

Glimpses of the Bodyguard in action are disappointingly rare. Arrian's account of the army split over the Succession in 323 BC places them among 'the cavalry', with Lysimachus standing in the second rank, after the *megistoi*, Ptolemy, Perdiccas and Leonnatus. Lysimachus' presence at Alexander's side in pursuit of the Sogdian rebels in 328 BC might suggest that the Bodyguard normally served with Alexander in the field. Perdiccas and Hephaistion, however, seem to have held major cavalry commands concurrently with membership. Ptolemy's leadership of Alexander's crack corps – the hypaspists, Agrianes and archers – on a special mission during the siege of Sangala supports the view that in practice the Bodyguard had a fairly flexible role in Alexander's army. Since Lysimachus is singled out among those wounded at Sangala, it is possible that he took part in Ptolemy's mission which certainly seems to have borne the brunt of the fighting. Since, however, his name is listed under the total number wounded in the whole operation this cannot be regarded as certain.[11]

4

Evidently a member by 326 BC, the date when Lysimachus joined the Bodyguard is unknown. Since his promotion is not mentioned, Heckel suggests he was a member from the start of the Asian campaign, perhaps even appointed by Philip. Though Agathocles' position at court would probably favour his sons' promotion, this idea perhaps lays too much stress on 'aristocratic affiliations'. Entry to a body whose prestige is reflected by the key positions taken by its members after 323 BC, and which implied service close to Alexander's person, must surely have been determined primarily on ability. A simpler explanation may be that Ptolemy, writing an Alexander-centred history,[12] while naturally concerned to record his own achievements, was not quite so scrupulous about recording each and every promotion as it occurred during the campaign.

This raises the question as to whether Lysimachus' relatively infrequent appearance in the Alexander Histories can be ascribed to Ptolemy deliberately obscuring the achievements of a rival Successor. Though others may have found themselves victims of the Lagid eraser, Lysimachus probably did not. Though he is, for example, omitted from the group of notables whose brides at the Susa weddings of 324 BC are named, this is not Ptolemy's work – Arrian cites Aristobulus as his source at the beginning of the passage.[13]

On the contrary, Ptolemy is the source for the very occasions when Lysimachus is singled out. Lysimachus squeezes into the first boat making the hazardous crossing of the Hydaspes – with Alexander, Ptolemy, Perdiccas and Seleucus. This seems almost too good to be true, although the suspicion that Ptolemy later inserted himself and his fellow Successors into suitably prominent positions may be lessened by Perdiccas' inclusion. Lysimachus' wound at Sangala has already been mentioned.[14] There seems no good reason to doubt the historicity of this event. The complete omission of Lysimachus from Diodorus' book on Alexander, probably drawn largely from Cleitarchus, lends support for Ptolemy's innocence. Unless one assumes that Cleitarchus – admittedly pro-Ptolemaic[15] – expunged Ptolemy's rivals even more thoroughly than Ptolemy did himself, it must be accepted that Lysimachus only reached military prominence in the latter years of the expedition, during the Indian campaign.

Socially, his membership of the close circle around Alexander is suggested by his presence at Medeius' fatal dinner party in Babylon. Though the details given in the *Liber de Morte Testamentumque Alexandri* are unreliable as the product of later propaganda,[16] the author carefully excludes Lysimachus from the supposed poisoners of

Alexander, rather than simply denying his presence there; this may suggest that his attendance was a known fact. The historicity of his part in restraining Alexander in the famous quarrel with Cleitus, along with Leonnatus, Ptolemy and Perdiccas, might be questioned. Does Curtius' account reflect the Bodyguard's own apologia, fabricated to exculpate Alexander? In Arrian, whose source is generally seen as Ptolemy, Alexander is likewise restrained by companions, but they remain anonymous. Though possibly Curtius added the names to flesh out his account, the sensational treatment of the whole episode and the emphasis on the inebriation of all concerned suggests a source like Cleitarchus. This tends to reduce the likelihood of apologia. Whether Arrian's account derives directly from Ptolemy may also be doubted – the emphasis on heavy drinking and Alexander's non-Greek excesses hardly fits an apologetic source. As proof of Lysimachus' prominence at court, it hardly matters whether the story is fabricated or not. What is important is that the apologists clearly regarded him as a plausible candidate among those restraining the enraged king.[17]

IMAGES OF LYSIMACHUS

Lysimachus the Lion-tamer

One of the most striking of several images of Lysimachus which emerge from the literary evidence, this presentation is interesting for its focus on his relationship with Alexander. Its source is a group of stories which centre on a confrontation with a lion. The details vary – in some cases Alexander orders Lysimachus to be thrown to or shut up with the beast; the Roman moralisers, composing their treatises on *Clementia* or *Ira*, snapped this story up, as an illustration of the corrupting effects of power and the excesses of tyrants. Justin's version is the fullest; apparently following his source, Trogus, verbatim,[18] he connects the episode with the death of Callisthenes. Lysimachus, the philosopher's disciple, intervenes to put Callisthenes, brutally tortured by the bloodthirsty Alexander, out of his misery; thus he turns the tyrant's rage upon himself, leading to the famous meeting with the lion.

How credible is this story? Clearly it emanates from a tradition which aims to present Alexander, particularly in his latter years, as the archetypal megalomaniac tyrant. Though it would be naïve to deny that Alexander, or his Successors, ever treated their subordinates with brutality, the existence of similar stories directed against monarchs, including Lysimachus himself, might suggest that certain themes – such as the caging of men with or like beasts – came to form a stock-in-trade for the literary treatment of autocrats.[19] The historicity of the individual incident therefore becomes questionable. Nor is it necessarily proven by Plutarch's tale of Lysimachus regaling Demetrius' envoys with the story of Alexander's wrath. Lysimachus may have boasted of a lion-killing, but such unguarded denigration of Alexander before the envoys of his greatest enemy is hardly consistent with his well-attested concern to display veneration for Alexander.[20]

The sensational details, particularly in Justin, where Lysimachus thrusts his hand into the lion's mouth and tears out its tongue, and the emphasis on Alexander's anger in several sources, suggests Cleitarchus, popular among Roman readers in the late Republic and early Empire, as a possible source. Alternatively, the theme of a public spectacle involving men pitted against beasts, which seems to owe more to Roman gladiatorial shows than to anything in Greek life, may have originated in the Roman period. Neither Arrian nor Diodorus include the story: Curtius rejects it as a *fabula*.[21]

Though the likelihood that Alexander was responsible for hurling Lysimachus to the lion seems slim, it is probable that some version of a 'lion story', with Alexander as witness to Lysimachus' heroic feat, was current in the latter's life-time. Justin's version occurs in the context of an encomium where Lysimachus is praised for his *virtus* and the *magnitudo* of his *animus*. The stress here on his pre-eminence over his fellow Diadochs contrasts strikingly with the judgement of Arrian and Diodorus that Lysimachus was a figure of secondary importance. Almost certainly this encomium was composed in Lysimachus' life-time; the incentive for such a work after his death, with no heir left to promote it, does not seem strong.[22]

Justin's treatment of the lion episode emphasises Lysimachus' intimacy with Alexander. Duly impressed by Lysimachus' courage in handling the lion, Alexander consequently considers him *carior*; the comparative implies a previous affection. A similar stress in Pausanias' account on the respect and honour accorded Lysimachus by Alexander may suggest a common source. The same positive motifs occur also in Curtius' account of a lion hunt at Bazaira, an event which Curtius, significantly, sees as the core of truth underlying the later legend of Lysimachus in the Lion's Den. Here Lysimachus comes into conflict with Alexander for aiming at a lion which the king feels is his rightful prize. Interestingly, Alexander here seeks to emulate Lysimachus' own exploit – the single-handed killing of a lion in Syria which almost lost him his life. Despite the theme of competition, this story is favourable to Lysimachus without being overtly hostile to Alexander, who may be guilty of impetuosity but not of *ira*; he is, moreover, praised for his speedy dispatch of the lion. Suggesting by its tone a rivalry for excellence between men on equal and intimate terms, this passage is consistent with what else is known regarding Lysimachus' public stance towards Alexander.[23] It is likely, then, that more than one version of a 'lion story' circulated in the Diadoch period, probably emanating from Lysimachus' own court; the anti-tyrant twist, which in some versions makes the contest a punishment inflicted by Alexander, may have been added later.

Is there any historical basis for this legend of Lysimachus the Lion-killer? Though the survival of similar stories about Craterus and Perdiccas raises the suspicion that this image is merely the product of heroic propaganda, its most likely historical context is the Syrian hunt mentioned by Curtius. This has been identified with a hunt at Sidon in 332 BC; the historicity of this event may gain support from the depiction of a lion hunt on the Sidonian sarcophagus thought to belong to Alexander's protégé King Abdalonymus.[24]

The value of the lion-taming episode, then, lies in its revelation of a literary tradition which aimed to emphasise both Lysimachus' heroic strength and courage and a relationship with Alexander of equality and sufficient intimacy to allow rivalry and even the occasional dispute. Neither Lysimachus' abilities nor his friendship with Alexander are in doubt, but the encomiastic stance of Justin's source makes it likely that these features are exaggerated.

Philosopher-king

The link that Justin makes between Lysimachus and Callisthenes, presenting the future king as the philosopher's devoted pupil, taking moral inspiration from his master's 'excellence', is merely one part of a tradition which suggests that philosophy had a major influence in his life. This is made explicit in the encomiast's summing up of Lysimachus' character – *ut animi magnitudine philosophiam ipsam . . . vicerit.*[25]

Justin's evidence alone is not sufficient for credence in 'Lysimachus the philosopher'. Goukowsky argues that Trogus' source wished to present Lysimachus as the philosopher-king idealised in Hellenistic kingship theory, identifying that source as Onesicritus. The identification is supported both by Onesicritus' description of Alexander as a 'philosopher in arms', and an anecdote in Plutarch which shows Onesicritus established at the Thracian court, reading his History to Lysimachus.[26] In the context, then, of an encomium composed by Lysimachus' own court historian, Justin's assertion of a link between the two men is untrustworthy.

Quite plausibly, Lysimachus did have some intellectual interests. Arrian describes him as a pupil of the Indian sophist Calanus; the philosophers Hipparchia, Crates and the 'atheist' Theodorus were entertained at his court; Pliny makes a fleeting reference to his interest in botany. Is this enough to make Lysimachus a philosopher-king? Royal entertainment of philosophers need not prove a burning passion for their art. Intellectuals clearly formed part of the desirable trappings of the Hellenistic monarch's entourage and Ptolemy I, in particular, is shown fervently and not always successfully courting learned men.[27] The best evidence for a real interest in philosophy on Lysimachus' part is the connection with Calanus, since Arrian's source seems to be quite independent of the panegyric tradition found in Justin; the details of Calanus' death in Arrian are quite distinct from those in Plutarch, who clearly is using Onesicritus and Chares. Arrian's source may be Ptolemy, prominent in the episode, the pro-Ptolemaic Cleitarchus or even Duris.[28]

Against this, however, two pieces of evidence explicitly refute the idea of Lysimachus the sage. Firstly, Carystius of Pergamum refers to Lysimachus' expulsion of philosophers from his kingdom. Second, Justin's picture of Lysimachus as Callisthenes' pupil clashes with Plutarch's reference to hostility between the philosopher and 'men like Lysimachus and Hagnon' who objected to his pose as an opponent of tyranny. The value of Carystius' evidence is hard to assess; though the extant fragments of his work hardly inspire confidence,[29] it should be remembered that they are preserved out of context, in Athenaeus' *Deipnosophistae*; Athenaeus' selection may create an unbalanced picture of Carystius' writings. Plutarch's evidence is more important; his source is probably Chares, an eye-witness for events at Alexander's court and generally considered reliable. Berve wished to argue that 'Lysimachus' here designates not the future Diadoch, but Alexander's tutor. Plutarch, however, conveys a picture of court faction with Alexander's tough Macedonian friends ganging up against the previously obsequious Callisthenes, striking fashionable philosophical poses. In this context, the tutor, a timid and

9

elderly man, seems a far less likely associate for Hagnon, best known for his silver-studded boots and other flashy accessories, than our hero. The fact that 'Lysimachus' here is given no title is no argument in favour of the tutor; in the *Aexander*, Plutarch twice designates the tutor by title ('the Acarnanian', 'the Pedagogue') and once refers to 'King Lysimachus' for an incident after 305–4 BC; the fourth reference to 'Lysimachus' is the one in question.[30]

On balance, while philosophic interests on Lysimachus' part cannot be entirely rejected, there are strong reasons to suppose that Justin's emphasis on philosophy as a guiding force in his life is at least exaggerated.

The ruthless tyrant

Certainly, if character is reflected in action, accounts of Lysimachus' career after 323 BC reveal a man whose character is far from that of the intellectual. Though clearly capable, when necessary, of subtlety and cunning,[31] the personality which emerges is tough, pragmatic and ruthless.

For example, Lysimachus exchanges his beloved and politically useful wife, Amastris, for the still more useful Arsinoe. This is unexceptional for the period, but the sequel shows how thoroughly he had imbibed the philosophy that sentiment must always come second to political advantage. Fifteen years later, he finds it convenient to rekindle the ashes of his love for Amastris, supposedly the victim of matricide, taking up the avenger's sword against his stepsons to seize the valuable city of Heracleia Pontica. His son-in-law Antipater is dispatched when he objects to Lysimachus ceding his Macedonian inheritance to Demetrius in a time-buying manoeuvre; his wife Eurydice, Lysimachus' own daughter, is imprisoned. Lysimachus gains Paeonia through a pretended restoration of King Audoleon's heir Ariston; the commander who betrays Amphipolis to Lysimachus loses not only his promised reward but also his life. A courtier, Telesphorus, who unwisely cracks a joke at Arsinoe's expense, finds himself caged like an animal and horribly mutilated into the bargain. Potentially rebellious allies, the Autariatae, are massacred in their thousands; Lysimachus offers a considerable financial incentive to Seleucus to dispose of the conveniently captive Demetrius Poliorcetes; finally he orders the execution of his eldest son Agathocles.[32]

Some of these episodes are certainly worth taking seriously. Memnon's account of events at Heracleia is based on the contemporary historian Nymphis. Though the latter's reputed impartiality is probably overstated, there seems little reason to doubt his account here. Exploitation of dynastic struggle by a stronger power is a familiar theme, and Nymphis' record of the initially positive reaction in Heracleia to Lysimachus' rule diminishes the likelihood of distortion. Justin and Porphyry describe Lysimachus' murder of Antipater in very similar terms, suggesting a common source clearly independent of that used by Justin for the encomium of XV.3; there is no attempt to justify or exculpate Lysimachus. Though Diodorus confuses the issue, making Demetrius responsible for Antipater's death, it is difficult to reconcile this version with the general narrative of events of 294 BC.[33]

Assessment of the three stories told by Polyaenus is more difficult. No sources are cited and the book's stratagem framework means that incidents are presented out of their historical context. The loss of Diodorus' narrative for the years after 301 BC, and with it a possible 'control' for the Amphipolis and Paeonia episodes, exacerbates the problem. None of these stories is implausible in itself. The exploitation and discarding of protégés is paralleled by Lysimachus' and Demetrius' treatment of Cassander's heirs and by Polyperchon's use of Alexander's bastard son Heracles in 309 BC. Similarly the use and subsequent disposal of traitors is not uncommon. Pirates who aided Lysimachus' recapture of Ephesus *c.* 286 BC were then given a speedy departure 'since they had proved untrustworthy to their friends in Ephesus'. Whether or not moral standards were thus tardily recalled seems to have depended on the circumstances and interest of those involved; among the 'traitors' who flourished under their new masters are Docimus, the city founder, and Lysimachus' own *gazophylax* Philetaerus. The context for the Autariataean massacre is probably an incident in 302 BC recorded by Diodorus; while Polyaenus' source seems to have greatly increased the numbers involved and added a massacre where Diodorus, presumably using Hieronymus, records simply a desertion to Antigonus, wholesale killing of rebellious troops as a punishment or an attempt to prevent defection is not unheard of in this period.[34]

There remains the Telesphorus story, elaborated by Seneca with much emphasis on the mutilation and *fames et squalor et inluvies corporis*, and concluding with a neat moral twist – he who inflicted the punishment as much resembled a beast as his unfortunate victim. Found only in the Roman moralising tradition, it is typical of the anecdotal evidence for life at the Diadochs' courts. Found mainly in

Athenaeus' *Deipnosophistai* and the Roman moralisers, much of this evidence must be treated with caution, since the likelihood of anti-monarchic propaganda is strong. The repetition of certain themes, or actual stories, with reference to several individuals – autocratic rulers seem particularly prone to such treatment – suggests the build-up of a certain 'convention', which diminishes the value of such stories for the assessment of an individual. The Telesphorus story is a case in point; its similarity to the tales of cruelty attributed to Alexander and in particular its repetition in Plutarch, in a completely different context with another protagonist, tend to reduce its credibility.[35]

The joker

On a lighter note, jests and verbal repartee are a recurrent theme in anecdotes showing Lysimachus among his intimates at court. The king mocks gently at Onesicritus' wilder flights of fancy, asking wryly, when Onesicritus comes to the story of Alexander and the Amazon, 'And where was I then?' His sneers at Demetrius' enslavement to his mistress, the appropriately named Lamia, are not so gentle. He enjoys a joke with his friend Philippides and indulges in rough horseplay with his 'parasite' Bithys, stuffing a wooden scorpion down his front and getting stung in return by a request for a talent! He endures abuse at the hands of Ptolemy's court jester Sotades, but loses his sense of humour when Demetrius' toadies dub him *gazophylax*; these treasury officials were traditionally eunuchs.[36]

Lysimachus is not alone in attracting stories which involve jesting and repartee. Other monarchs – notably Philip II and Antigonus the One-Eyed – also joke and are the butt of jokes. Demetrius the Besieger is likewise known for his ready wit. Certain tales – notably one which might be called 'The Parasite's Request' – where a king resists or submits to a request for money, are repeated sufficiently often to raise the suspicion of a 'conventional story'.[37]

Other stories relating to Lysimachus have no exact parallel; their value as evidence for an individual character trait may gain support from the fact that while the Antigonids likewise feature as men of wit, stories of this kind are less frequently attached to Ptolemy I, while Seleucus and Cassander seemingly attract none at all. This might be explained by the chance survival of evidence and associated factors. Plutarch's choice of Demetrius as a subject for biography tends to favour the survival of Antigonid anecdotes. Both Plutarch and Athenaeus, it seems, drew heavily on Duris of Samos and his brother

Lynceus, a frequent guest at royal symposia. The brothers' residence in Athens under Antigonid rule might also explain a preponderance of anecdotes centred on the Antigonids and, by extension, their great enemy Lysimachus.[38]

This solution, however, is only partial. Since Duris probably wrote also on Seleucid affairs, then if Seleucus I had attracted 'joke' anecdotes, these should have been available to our sources. As for Cassander, he had effectively preceded Lysimachus as the great bugbear of the Antigonids. One might therefore expect him to be the butt of similar stories, at least for the period between 307 BC and his death in 297 BC.[39]

In conclusion, while some of the stories may be 'conventional', in the sense of their indiscriminate application to several individuals, others seemingly are not. Though the authors of such anecdotes, like all good dinner party raconteurs, may well have improved on their material, there seems no good reason to reject outright the idea that Lysimachus was a man who enjoyed an engagement of wits as much as one with weapons.

LYSIMACHUS, HIERONYMUS AND DURIS

Before embarking on an analysis of Lysimachus' career after Alexander's death, it is worth considering briefly one last aspect of his image in literature, namely the thesis that the major contemporary source for the period, Hieronymus of Cardia, was hostile to Lysimachus, while Duris of Samos was his apologist.[40]

The source for Hieronymus' supposed hostility to Lysimachus is Pausanias; though the context of this statement has provoked a sceptical reaction among modern scholars as to its reliability,[41] it is worth looking at the relevant sources to ascertain whether this accusation is in any sense justified. If negative bias does exist, what form does it take – omission, understatement or deliberate distortion?

Examination of the literary sources for Hieronymean hostility to Lysimachus is complicated by a number of factors. First, since Hieronymus' account focuses on events in which he was personally involved and on the figures of his patrons, Eumenes and the Antigonids, events like Lysimachus' Thracian campaigns are likely to suffer. Second, Diodorus must have compressed his sources to fit the scale of a universal history; his complete omission of Antigonus' war with Seleucus after 311 BC, known from the Babylonian Chronicle series, strikingly illustrates the distortion that can arise from epitomising.[42] Then there is the loss of Diodorus' narrative, except for a handful of fragments, for the period after 301 BC, the very moment when Lysimachus embarks upon his programme of imperial expansion. Finding Hieronymus in Plutarch, our main source for that period, is complicated by the biographer's method of drawing on stories which clearly come from several sources, within one chapter. Though blatantly 'pro-Antigonid' passages are generally ascribed to Hieronymus, with Duris responsible for those rather less flattering to Demetrius, some grey areas remain. Other factors also add to the difficulty of a neat source analysis. It is probable that Hieronymus himself was critical of one side of Demetrius' character. Then there is the question as to how far moralising passages on the greed for power, the destructiveness of ambition, etc. represent Plutarch's own contribution.[43]

Bearing these difficulties in mind, a detailed examination of Diodorus, the fragments of Arrian's *Successors*, and those passages in Plutarch likely to derive from Hieronymus[44] prompts the following conclusions. Hieronymus may certainly be guilty of understatement in his treatment of Lysimachus. For example, the founding of Lysimacheia, one of Lysimachus' major achievements and an important expression of his claim to kingship, is passed over in one sentence. The tone throughout is dry and factual; Lysimachus' exploits are not described in detail or made heroic in any way, while he himself remains very much a two-dimensional figure. There are some negative statements; for example, in the context of the Rhodian siege in 305–4 BC Lysimachus is described unflatteringly as 'secondary in reputation'; his victory against Seuthes in 323 BC is described as 'uncertain'; Lysimachus admits that he miscalculated in embarking upon the Getic campaign; Seleucus' fear and distrust of Lysimachus in 286 BC are stressed. An assessment of the historical situation, based on other evidence, suggests, however, that such statements represent no more than the truth. Hieronymus does, moreover, fail to exploit heaven-sent opportunities for hostility; Lysimacheia's foundation, for instance, does not prompt the bitter outpouring on the fate of Cardia which Pausanias' remarks might lead us to expect; similarly, though a spokesman for the Antigonid 'liberators', Hieronymus fails to seize the chance to attack Lysimachus afforded by Demetrius' recovery of Ephesus from him in 302 BC and its 'restoration to its former status'.[45]

On the positive side, Lysimachus' successful crushing of the Pontic cities' revolt is covered in some detail, as are the victories, both military and diplomatic, of his campaign in 302 BC against the

Antigonids; the effect of these successes on Antigonus are made clear. On two occasions, moreover, Lysimachus receives direct praise; Cassander's practice of calling on him for aid is ascribed not only to Lysimachus' territorial proximity but also to his *arete*. Threatened with capture by the Getae *c.* 292 BC, Lysimachus nobly rejects the advice of his *philoi* to abandon his men and save himself. Unless one assumes the sudden intrusion of another source into Diodorus' narrative, it seems reasonable to suppose that Hieronymus was fair-minded enough to admit the undoubted qualities of a man whom he personally disliked, just as Lysimachus himself reputedly admired the ships built by his great enemy Demetrius.[46]

What of the claim that Lysimachus had in Duris an apologist who was not above outright falsification of events to put his patron in a better light? The two main arguments for Duris as Lysimachus' creature are Lysimachus' toleration of Duris' tyranny in Samos and Duris' consistent hostility to Demetrius, Lysimachus' great foe. The claim that Duris falsified events rests on one incident: Lysimachus' defeat at Amphipolis in 287 BC, recorded by Pausanias, supposedly using Hieronymus, but omitted by Plutarch, whose source is assumed to be Duris.[47]

Arguments against each of these theses may be summarised briefly as follows.[48] The idea that Duris thanked Lysimachus for 'supporting' his tyranny with a glowing literary profile is undermined by the probability that Duris' family likewise ruled Samos under the Antigonids.[49] If Duris was hostile to one set of 'protectors', why should he be any more positive towards their successor?

Indeed, if one looks for praise of Lysimachus in Duris, it is not easily found. Evidence is generally ascribed to Duris on the basis of certain 'hallmarks', reflecting his preference for a 'tragic' style of history, his stress on *mimesis* (dramatic representation) and *hedone* (entertainment value). These include: an emphasis on costume and disguise, use of quotations from tragedy and images and similes from the theatre, an emphasis on the luxury and decadence of kings. Since Diodorus probably did not use Duris for his books on the Diadochs, most of the evidence comes from Plutarch. Shipley cites two pieces of evidence: the presentation of Lysimachus as a wit in chapter 25 of the *Demetrius*, and a touching story of Lysimachus' dog hurling itself onto his funeral pyre. Though the aim of the second tale might perhaps be sympathetic, the fidelity of animals – Alexander's horse, Xanthippus' dog – is a well-known literary theme. To cite the *gazophylax* story as a positive treatment of Lysimachus is most curious. In a slanging match between the two kings, Lysimachus' sneer at Demetrius' mistress Lamia is parried by Demetrius' insult to Lysimachus' wife. The preceding passage, where Demetrius' *philoi* toast Lysimachus as 'the treasurer' (*gazophylax*), is ascribed to Phylarchus, but may well derive ultimately from Duris. Here Lysimachus is not only dubbed a eunuch, but unlike the other kings who are similarly insulted, he is unable to laugh it off. If Phylarchus also drew on Duris for the other anecdotes which cast Lysimachus in a distinctly unflattering light, then the idea of Duris as Lysimachus' spokesman becomes increasingly doubtful. Returning to Duris himself, Lysimachus escapes neither the general criticism of arrogance directed at Alexander's Successors once they become kings nor the judgement that the kings who followed Alexander were only poor imitations of their master.[50]

Duris' hostility to Demetrius and in particular to his supporters in Athens need not reflect his position on Lysimachus' payroll. Rather it may be ascribed to his belonging to Samos' ruling family in the last years of the fourth century BC, when the Antigonid 'protectorate' seems to have implied close supervision of the island. A history of troubled Athenian/Samian relations may also have played its part; an Athenian cleruchy for over forty years, Samos was restored to the Samians by Alexander's Exiles Decree of 324 BC. Perdiccas upheld the exiles' cause after Alexander's death, but Polyperchon's brief regency revived the threat of renewed Athenian control. Like any self-respecting Samian, Duris may have feared that Stratocles and his faction might prevail upon their Antigonid patrons to give Samos back to Athens.[51]

As for the Amphipolis incident, faith in Pausanias as a superior source is misplaced. Relying on sources which are often no more than *logoi*, Pausanias' digression on Lysimachus is rife with error and shows little regard for chronology. Plutarch's source is unlikely to be undiluted Duris (the pro-Pyrrhan tone of much of this section suggests an Epirote source such as Proxenus of Thebes), nor need his omission of the Amphipolis defeat reflect apologia. While Lysimachus may well have been worsted at Amphipolis, perhaps in a clash with the garrison commander Andragathus, it seems unlikely that he and Demetrius met face to face; the rapid loss of morale among Demetrius' army with the news of Pyrrhus' capture of Beroia is hardly consistent with a recent victory on the scale that Pausanias suggests.[52] Plutarch's focus in this chapter is on Demetrius' dramatic loss of Macedon. If Demetrius was not involved in Lysimachus' early defeat, which was not in any case decisive for the final outcome, then Plutarch's omission of it may be ascribed to the biographer's selectivity. Without further examples of discrepancy between Duris and another 'superior' source covering the same event, this episode is insufficient to support the idea of consistent pro-Lysimachean distortion in Duris.

CONCLUSIONS

Analysis of the surviving literary evidence for Lysimachus' early career and 'character' yields the following conclusions. Family background and personal ability combined to give Lysimachus a head start on his career with Alexander. Though certainly a member of the élite, in both military and social terms, it is possible that he only achieved real prominence in the last years of Alexander's reign. Even then he seems to have remained in the 'second rank' among Alexander's generals, profiting from being on the spot at Babylon in 323 BC to receive a satrapy.

In terms of 'character', the literary sources present Lysimachus through a series of images; he is in turn Alexander's devoted friend, a mythic warrior hero, a philosopher, a comedian, a ruthless man driven by ambition. Plausibly there is a core of truth underlying most of these images, but the distorting effect of propaganda, be it Lysimachus' own, that of his rivals or of a later anti-monarchic tradition, is undeniable. These images tell us more about ideas of kingship, both in the Diadoch period and later, than about an individual man.

If Lysimachus was the target of negative bias on the part of Hieronymus of Cardia, this seems to manifest itself mainly in understatement. It is unlikely that Hieronymus fabricated incidents which place Lysimachus in a less than ideal light. There is, furthermore, little evidence to support the belief that Duris of Samos wrote as Lysimachus' apologist.

So far the emphasis has been on literary evidence, but the men of letters do not, of course, tell the whole story. The early Hellenistic age sees kings and cities publicise major policy decisions on stone; coins and statues, representing both 'real' and 'ideal' images of royalty, also commemorate victories and benefactions; shrines, cities and monumental tombs reflect their founders' aspirations to immortality. Public inscriptions,[53] coins, sculpture, painting, city ruins and other archaeological finds serve to complement, supplement and/or correct the evidence provided by the literary sources. The contribution made by this evidence for an understanding of Lysimachus' career will be made clear, where it is relevant, in the following chapters.

2

THRACE AND PONTUS

Cum inter successores eius provinciae dividerentur, ferocissimae gentes quasi omnium fortissimo adsignatae sunt (Justin XV.III.15.).

The glowing terms in which Justin describes the assignment of Thrace in 323 BC to Lysimachus may be suspect, given the panegyric context in which these lines appear. Nevertheless, the record of events in Thrace in the years immediately preceding his appointment supports the idea that he was chosen primarily for a military reputation which may have compensated for a lack of previous experience in government.[1]

MACEDONIAN RULE IN THRACE AND ON THE WEST PONTIC COAST

The first years of Macedonian rule in Thrace are ones of triumph. Profiting from dynastic rivalries which had split the powerful Odrysian kingdom into three realms, in 341 BC Philip II finally forced the strongest of these princes, Cersobleptes, to admit defeat. This action concluded a series of campaigns which brought under Macedon's rule the area between the Nestus River and the Haemus mountains. Philip maintained control through a network of Macedonian colonies, urban centres constructed on existing fortified sites which probably doubled as garrison towns. In addition he installed or retained those indigenous rulers who could be trusted to be compliant. An obligation to provide troops for Philip's army and payment of tribute were probable conditions for their 'rule'.[2]

The effectiveness of this arrangement in south-eastern Thrace is supported by the fact that Alexander's Thracian expeditions in 340 BC and 335 BC were directed not against Odrysians, but against the Maedi in the Rhodopes area and the Triballi in the north-west, beyond the

19

Haemus range. Alexander's victory served to reinforce the Macedonian presence between these mountains and the Danube, an area where Philip's influence seemingly took the form of alliances, both with Getic chieftains and Greek cities, rather than the formal control achieved in the south. With the river as a natural boundary between Macedonian territory and the tribes beyond, Alexander's foray to the further bank is best seen as a demonstration of strength, aimed at securing this 'frontier' before his departure to Asia, rather than an attempt at conquest beyond the river.[3]

Famed for its mercenaries in the fifth century BC, the value of Thrace as a recruiting ground for Alexander is demonstrated by the presence of Thracians on his Asian campaign. The Agrianes, included in Alexander's crack corps, represent the fruit of his friendship with the dynast Langarus, underlining the value for Macedon of exploiting rivalries between indigenous rulers. Frontinus suggests that Alexander saw recruitment as a method of culling Thracian strength at home; perhaps he aimed also to strengthen Thracian loyalty to himself through shared military experience, glory and victory's profits. On the administrative front, Alexander's reign sees the appointment of the *strategos* in Thrace. Effectively governor by virtue of his military and administrative powers, he was officially subordinate to Alexander's regent in Europe, Antipater.[4]

With Alexander's protracted absence in Asia, Macedon's record in Thrace ceases to be a cause for pride. One *strategos*, Memnon, saw Thrace as a source of troops with which to assert himself against Antipater. His successor, Zopyrion, launched an ambitious and possibly ill-advised campaign against the city of Olbia; it ended in his death and the annihilation of his army at Scythian hands *c.* 325 BC. The first *strategos'* ambition and the second's incompetence created unsettled conditions in Thrace which were fully exploited by the man who was to prove Lysimachus' chief opponent in the early years, the Odrysian dynast Seuthes III.[5]

LYSIMACHUS, SATRAP OF THRACE

When the regent Perdiccas made Thrace a separate satrapy in 323 BC, his first aim, it is said, was to diminish Antipater's authority. Whatever the truth of this, Lysimachus' satrapal appointment was surely justified in terms of military security; in Thrace, Seuthes III's rebellion gained fresh impetus from Alexander's death, while the threat of war in Greece would keep Antipater fully stretched. As satrap of Thrace, Lysimachus faced the task of restoring Macedon's prestige in a region which constituted the empire's northern 'frontier' against the barbarian tribes beyond, and provided a vital land link between Macedon and the Asian satrapies.[6]

The extent of Lysimachus' satrapy is the object of some dispute; most literary accounts suggest that it comprised the West Pontic coast as well as Thrace, though it is unclear whether the Greek *poleis* there were officially included. Pausanias' estimate is more conservative: 'After Alexander's death, Lysimachus ruled over the Thracians who are neighbours to the Macedonians, those whom Alexander had ruled and Philip before him. Well, these did not comprise a great part of Thrace.'[7]

Although Pausanias' aim of disparaging Macedonian achievement in order to highlight the subsequent Roman conquest may suggest some distortion, Arrian supports the idea of a more limited territory. Drawing on the reliable Hieronymus, he defines the satrapy as 'Thrace and the Chersonese and the peoples bordering the Thracians on the coast of the Euxine Pontus as far as Salmydessus'. The suggestion that this represents the actual territory still under Macedon's control, as opposed to a 'paper satrapy' delineated by the other sources, and that Lysimachus' task was to transform the ideal into the actual, is attractive.[8]

THE NATURE OF THE EVIDENCE

Before discussing the extent to which Lysimachus succeeded in meeting this brief, it must be noted that the literary evidence for his rule in Thrace is very sparse. Diodorus' account of the first clash with Seuthes breaks off abruptly; apart from the army numbers, there is no detail concerning battle sites, terrain, tactics, disposition of forces, etc. The literary tradition then falls silent on Lysimachus' activities in Thrace until the revolt of the West Pontic cities in 313 BC. There is almost no direct information as to Lysimachus' administration, nor do we know the site of his headquarters before Lysimacheia's walls rose in 309 BC.

Past attempts to account for Lysimachus' actions, particularly for the first decade, have therefore resorted to a reconstruction of events. Underlying these hypotheses are certain preconceptions; the relationship between Macedonian and Thracian is automatically conceived as that of ruler and subject.[9] In recent years, the dangers of this method have been fully exposed; excavations in modern Bulgaria have revealed and are still revealing a wealth of numismatic and archaeological finds which necessitate a reassessment of 'the Lysimachean conquest' and the nature of early Hellenistic Thracian society.

This non-literary evidence suggests that the period coinciding with Lysimachus' reign saw a remarkable growth of urbanisation and Hellenisation among the aristocracy. At present the bulk of the evidence comes from south-eastern Thrace, but finds from north-eastern Bulgaria, including those from a new site at Sboryanovo, suggest similar developments among the Getic tribes there. It is reasonable to suppose that the aspirations of the Thracian dynasts which prompted their active co-operation in this process[10] must also have affected the nature of their relations with the Macedonian rulers in Thrace. This is supported by the evidence for the career of Lysimachus' first great foe, the Odrysian Seuthes III.

SEUTHES III AND THE ODRYSIAN RENAISSANCE

This enterprising individual first takes the stage in 331 BC, when an Athenian inscription honours Rhebulas, son of Seuthes; another son, Cotys, already enjoyed Athenian citizenship. The text is fragmentary and the precise context of this Odrysian diplomacy therefore uncertain. Some see Seuthes as striving to win Athens' support for Memnon's revolt in which he took an active part, but this implies that when Memnon made terms with Antipater he was able to secure not only his own continued authority but also that of his Thracian associates. More plausibly, Seuthes may have hoped to profit from Memnon's rebellion without actually committing himself to action. Archibald sees his approach to Athens as an attempt to tap new sources of support, reflecting Thracian disillusionment in the wake of Memnon's return to the fold; certainly Curtius suggests that Seuthes bided his time until 325 BC when Zopyrion's defeat signalled the right time for revolt.[11]

With sons old enough to represent him diplomatically, Seuthes was at least 35 years old in 331 BC. Perhaps a protégé of Philip II, he has been linked with Cersobleptes' branch of the Odrysae; possibly he is to be identified with the brother or cousin whose fund-raising efforts for Cersobleptes are recorded by Polyaenus.[12] By 323 BC it is likely that he was already established on the site near modern Kazanluk which was to form the nucleus of his city, Seuthopolis. Though Philip's conquests had forced a shift north from the original seat of Odrysian power, probably centred on the River Artiscus near Mezek, in economic and strategic terms the new site could hardly be improved. A lofty position, with the waters of the Tonsus on three sides, made the fortified city easy to defend. Fertile terrain supporting an agricultural economy combined with a flourishing trade along the Tonsus and Hebrus rivers with Greek cities on the coasts of Thrace and Asia Minor and in mainland Greece. Finds from the city include Athenian black-glazed ware and a large number of Thasian amphora stamps.[13]

Seuthes' motives in taking the offensive against Lysimachus on his arrival in Thrace have been linked with the threat posed to this trade by the prospect of renewed Macedonian control over the Hebrus route and the West Pontic cities which now constituted Seuthes' main markets. This assumes, however, that Lysimachus was in a position to garrison the Pontic cities as early as 323 BC, something which is far from certain.[14] Though commercial factors may have played their part, the aspirations which the evidence from Seuthopolis reflects suggest that Seuthes' claim to revive the Odrysian kingdom as an independent power on an equal footing with the realms of the Successors was the main issue at stake.

Past Odrysian kings had exerted considerable influence both in Thrace and the Greek-speaking world beyond. Teres' conquest of the region between Salmydessus and the Bosphorus followed the Persians' expulsion from Europe. By 429 BC, Sitalces ruled an empire comprising all the tribes south and south-east of the Nestus–Danube line and planned to invade Macedon with a vast army. Seuthes I promoted expansion towards the Thracian Chersonese and commanded 800–1,000T p.a. in revenues.[15] Cotys I's deal with Philip II fixed the Odrysian frontier at the Nestus Valley; he captured most of the Thracian Chersonese, threatening Athenian control of the Propontis – probably marking the zenith of Odrysian achievement. It has also been suggested that he promoted a policy of tribal union with Getic and Triballian chiefs in the north and north-west. Holding onto the Chersonese, his most powerful successor Cersobleptes allied himself with Athens against Philip II until his deposition in 341 BC. By contrast with less than two decades of firm Macedonian control, Seuthes III had behind him a glorious heritage of over a century of Odrysian achievement.[16] That he was conscious of this is almost certain. In an aristocratic society wedded to the manly pursuits of warfare and hunting, which has apparently left no trace of any literary tradition, the likelihood of an oral tradition heroising the past is strong. This theory gains some support from Xenophon; Seuthes II displays knowledge of the legendary exploits of his ancestors and an interest in Odrysian genealogy.[17]

Small wonder then that Seuthes III saw Alexander's death and the prospect of schism in his empire as a golden opportunity to re-establish the Odrysian kingdom. What then were the resources which he could muster for the attempt?

THE ODRYSIAN ARMY

At his first encounter with Lysimachus in 323 BC, Seuthes' army numbered 20,000 infantry and 8,000 cavalry. Though small compared to Sitalces' force of 150,000 in 429 BC and merely a fraction of Strabo's estimate of Thrace's total military resources under Roman rule, it considerably outnumbered Lysimachus' forces. Evidence from Seuthopolis supports the idea that the Odrysae themselves formed the bulk of the cavalry, with infantry recruited from other tribes; the aristocratic glorification of the horseman particularly associated with the Thracians from the Homeric King Rhesus onwards is everywhere apparent. Apart from the Thracian cavalier, featured on the reverse of Seuthes' coinage, the main frieze on the *tholos* tomb at nearby Kazanluk depicts four-horse chariots at full speed, while the Samothracian cult of the Cabeiroi, attested at Seuthopolis, is centred on twin horsemen.[18]

Though Seuthopolis' population has not been calculated, the city's relatively small geographical area (5 hectares) and the spacious layout of its houses has suggested that residence there was restricted to the aristocracy and merchant classes. Beyond the walls, there were further settlements whose inhabitants made a living from agricultural labour; though these may have provided Seuthes with some infantry, the high numbers recorded by Diodorus seem to imply the recruitment of neighbouring tribes.[19] The precise extent of Seuthes' kingdom is uncertain, but Arrian's description of Lysimachus' Thracian satrapy together with coin hoard evidence and other finds suggest that his influence was restricted to the middle and upper reaches of the Tonsus, extending west perhaps as far as the Stryama River and east to the Sasliyka. By the end of the fourth century BC at least, an independent dynast ruled at Cabyle, *c.* 100 kilometres to the east.[20] A likely source of infantry is the tribes of the Haemus mountains, but whether this reflects a short-term alliance formed explicitly to repel the Macedonian threat, or a longstanding bond, perhaps one of dependency upon Seuthes, is unclear. In terms of influence further afield, there is as yet no evidence comparable to that which seems to link Seuthes' ancestors in guest-friendship with Triballian and Getic chiefs.

Though the literary evidence is sparse, tomb finds and vase-paintings give some idea of the kind of army which Lysimachus faced in 323 BC. The fourth-century Thracian warrior attired himself for battle in a composite cuirass of iron strips faced with bronze rings and a crescent-shaped iron collar; helmets found at Pletena in the Rhodopes include both Chalcidian and Phrygian types. The highest-ranking soldiers added greaves to this ensemble, but the elaborate silver-gilt examples from Vratsa and Aghigiol, masterpieces of Thracian art, are strictly for the parade ground. The use of bronze armour, knives and arrow-tips similar to Macedonian ones dated to the reigns of Philip and Alexander and of the Greek *xiphos* reflect a readiness to absorb influences from abroad, but home-grown weaponry such as the famous Thracian *rhomphaia* still kept its appeal. Though this has been identified as a long pike, of the sort found at Pletena, Sekunda argues that it was a sickle-spear used, probably by the mountain tribes, to disable cavalry opponents by cutting through the horses' legs. If correct, then this section would make the Thracian army effective at close-quarters against cavalry, once the javelin-throwers, slingers and archers had loosed the artillery which made Thracian mercenaries so prized by the Greeks.[21]

THE CONFLICT OF 323 BC – LYSIMACHUS MEETS SEUTHES

With an army of this calibre, superior numbers and advance preparation, Seuthes' hopes of victory were probably high; Hieronymus confirms this, judging that Lysimachus' decision to face Seuthes in a pitched battle was risky. In one sense, the gamble paid off; Diodorus ascribes the Macedonian victory to their troops' superior courage. If the battle site is correctly identified as the Thracian plain, then the greater discipline and experience of the Macedonian phalanx and cavalry on favourable terrain may explain a victory against heavy odds. Its cost was, however, high in terms of Lysimachus' already limited manpower, nor was it in any sense decisive.[22]

Diodorus records preparations for a second conflict, but all details have been lost. Previously it was assumed that Seuthes' disappearance from the literary evidence for the next decade must imply his subjection by Lysimachus,[23] but the discovery of Seuthopolis under the waters of the Tonsus has necessitated a radical reassessment of Seuthes' status, his relations with Lysimachus and the whole concept of Macedon's 'conquest of Thrace' in the Diadoch period. Coin hoards from the city and nearby, with types ranging from Philip II to Demetrius II, show that the city was established and continued to flourish during Lysimachus' 'rule'. Overstruck coins of Cassander and Lysimachus among Seuthes' own issues show that the Odrysian, whom Diodorus describes as *Basileus* in both 323 BC and 313 BC, was able to issue coinage without interruption from *c.* 330 BC to 297–5 BC.[24] These coin-types and other material evidence from Seuthopolis say much about Seuthes' aspirations to Hellenisation, which in turn may help to define his status in relation to Lysimachus.

HELLENISATION IN THRACE

The receptivity of the Thracian aristocracy to cultural influences both from the Greek world and the Near East is already reflected in fourth-century burial finds. Thracian-made *phialai* (libation bowls) patterned with scales, or decorated with lozenge- or almond-shaped bosses, reflect Achaemenid influence; silver bowls from the Rogozen hoard replicate the form of metalware found in western Asia Minor. The Panagyurishte treasure, a magnificent drinking set in gilded silver, the bulk of which is dated to the late fourth or early third century BC, reflects a taste for Greek mythology, with scenes showing the Judgement of Paris and the exploits of Heracles and Theseus. The style, however, mixes Greek, Graeco-Achaemenid and Thracian elements.[25]

Seuthopolis likewise reflects its founder's aspirations towards Hellenisation. While retaining as its core the traditional *tyrsis* (fortified palace) of the Thracian ruler, Seuthes' city is purpose-built on the model of the early Hellenistic cities of Greece, Asia Minor and Egypt, with streets laid out in the grid plan developed by Hippodamas of Miletus. Its *agora* and spacious houses built in the *pastas* and *prostas* styles are typical of late classical/early Hellenistic cities throughout the Greek world. The so-called Great Inscription from the palace suggests that Seuthes employed a Greek secretariat, and Greek graffiti on pottery and dedications support the belief in widespread literacy in Greek among its élite population. All this proclaims Seuthes' ambition to build a city which would echo in its sophistication, if not in scale, the cities of the Successors. By the end of Seuthes' reign, Macedonian influence on art and architecture can also be discerned in the vaulted tombs at Kazanluk and Koprinka; the use of stucco and warm red paint on their wall-paintings and the five-zone decoration scheme of the *tholos* tomb are likewise hallmarks of Macedonian art.[26]

As city-founder, Seuthes cuts an impressive figure. The enduring settlement of Seuthopolis, its strategic strength and prosperity and the evidence for the military forces which Seuthes continued to have at his disposal suggest a status rather different from the vassalage or enforced 'alliance' which was assumed to be an automatic and necessary consequence of Lysimachus' 'conquest' of south-eastern Thrace. How did Seuthes achieve this enviable position and on what sort of terms?

THE FIRST SETTLEMENT WITH SEUTHES

All details of Lysimachus' second clash with Seuthes in 323 BC are lost, but one might reasonably suppose that this too was indecisive or even that Lysimachus suffered defeat. In either case, a continued struggle for the Thracian hinterland may well have seemed too expensive in terms of money and men, deciding him to concentrate his energies elsewhere.[27] Nothing suggests that Seuthes had any financial or military obligations to Lysimachus. Presumably some kind of deal was made which recognised Seuthes' right to rule over the area of the upper Tonsus. Seuthes' eagerness for the accoutrements of Hellenisation may have facilitated a settlement, together with the recognition that a period of peace would bring increased prosperity.

The similarities between the Macedonian and Thracian aristocracies, a shared preoccupation with horses, hunting, drinking and warfare may be another factor which helps to explain the idea of an agreed settlement between Macedonian satrap and Thracian dynast.[28] In terms of background and shared enthusiasms the gap between Lysimachus and Seuthes was probably far narrower than is assumed by the traditional picture of 'Thracian barbarians' conquered by Macedonians whose claims to Hellenisation made them culturally superior.

To the best of our knowledge, the settlement worked for ten years; there is no mention of further Odrysian incursions into the Macedonian part of Thrace. If the construction of his new city kept Seuthes busy in the period after 323 BC, finally, however, it seems that recognition of his independence and possession of an economically and culturally flourishing kingdom did not satisfy his ambitions.

When the Greek cities on the West Pontic coast rebelled against Lysimachus in 313 BC, he joined them.

SEUTHES AND THE REVOLT OF 313 BC

Seuthes' decision to participate in the revolt need not represent a response to actions of Lysimachus nor need it reflect any longstanding link with the Greek cities of the Black Sea coast; rather it should be set in the wider context of the Diadoch wars. In particular, the policy of Antigonus the One-Eyed is an important factor. By 315 BC he was master of Asia Minor and, so Hieronymus says, aiming to reunite Alexander's empire by appealing to the sympathies of the Greek cities in his rivals' kingdoms. In instigating revolt among the West Pontic cities and providing them with financial and military aid, Antigonus' primary aim was not conquest of Thrace as such, but provision of a route for attack on Macedon. Accordingly, Seuthes may have hoped to profit from Lysimachus' defeat by the extension of his influence in south-eastern Thrace, perhaps over the area round Mezek, Odrysian territory before Philip's conquest. Only a major stake of this sort would have justified risking what he already had. The substantial support and alliance offered by Antigonus,[29] which increased the rebels' hope of victory, surely constituted a major factor in influencing his decision.

Hoddinott's discussion of the events of 313–12 BC ascribes a complex and double-dealing role to Seuthes, identifying his army with the 'Thracian' allies of the cities who 'changed sides' during a military clash with Lysimachus, after the latter had recaptured Odessus and Istria. Since Seuthes is subsequently found blocking the Haemus passes against Lysimachus on his march south to confront Antigonus' general Pausanias, this construction demands that he changed sides once again after his initial capitulation.[30] To make this acceptable, either the pliable Thracians of Diodorus' account must represent only a section of Seuthes' army, or we must assume that the Odrysians, following their submission to Lysimachus, were able to return south sufficiently fast to beat Lysimachus to the Haemus passes. Neither explanation seems very satisfactory.

New archaeological evidence and a closer look at Diodorus' terminology, however, suggest a different identity for these faint-hearted Thracians. The description of them as 'neighbours' of the West Pontic cities and their appearance alongside a Scythian army suggest rather that these Thracians occupied territory in the Dobroudja area itself.

Excavations at Cape Kaliakra between Callatis and Odessus on the Black Sea coast have revealed traces of a fortified Thracian settlement, dated to the Hellenistic period, identified as Tirizis and connected by its nomenclature with the Thracian tribe of the Terizoi. That the settlement goes back at least to the Diadoch period is suggested by Strabo's reference to a treasury established by Lysimachus at Tirizis.[31] It seems likely, then, that the Terizoi are the Thracians who capitulated to Lysimachus in 313 BC and that their continued dependence on him permitted his establishment of a treasury in this region of the Pontic coast.

By contrast, Seuthes' status seems to have been little altered by his part in the revolt. Seuthopolis continues to flourish and the dynast continues to issue his own coinage, with the finest examples, types VI and VII, dated to the period after 305–4 BC when Lysimachus had assumed the diadem. The Great Inscription from Seuthopolis shows Seuthes' family still in power at the end of the fourth century BC.[32] This is more comprehensible if his part in the conflict of 313 BC is restricted to the hard-fought battle described by Diodorus, where the Macedonian victory was again marginal, than set against the background of defeat and repeated treachery which Hoddinott assumes.

Lysimachus had proved once more his ability to defeat the Odrysians in battle, but again victory had proved costly in terms of resources. It is likely that by now Lysimachus was looking to extend his power beyond Thrace;[33] this, combined with the problems posed by Seuthes' military strength and his highly defensible city, may explain why he might prefer to make a deal with Seuthes rather than fight another round.

THE SETTLEMENT OF 312 BC

On this occasion, it is possible that Lysimachus' settlement with Seuthes was clinched with a marriage alliance; active in the campaign of 282 BC to 281 BC is Alexander, whom Pausanias describes as Lysimachus' son by an Odrysian woman. Since there is no mention of him among Lysimachus' male kinsmen in earlier campaigns, it may be better to see him as the child of a marriage in 312 BC rather than one in 323 BC.[34] In return for his Odrysian bride, Lysimachus may have given a daughter in marriage to Seuthes. Prominent in the negotiations recorded in the Great Inscription from Seuthopolis, dated to the last years of the fourth century, is Berenice, Seuthes' wife or widow and mother of his four sons. Her Macedonian name suggests that she is the daughter either of Antigonus or Lysimachus. Mihailov argued for a marriage alliance in 313 BC between Seuthes and Antigonus, citing the minority status of her sons which may be implied by Berenice's dominant role in the negotiations and a possible reference in l.10 to future grandsons. Rightly objecting to the idea that a marriage alliance between Seuthes and Antigonus could survive after Lysimachus' victories in 313–12 BC, Burstein links Berenice with Lysimachus, but dates her marriage to Seuthes earlier than 313 BC, based on the active role played by her sons in the Great Inscription.[35] There is one possible problem in accepting this; since Lysimachus' first attested marriage, to Nicaea, comes only in 321 BC, who was Berenice's mother?[36] An alternative solution is to combine Berenice's link with Lysimachus with a late date for the wedding;[37] a marriage alliance between Lysimachus and Seuthes in 312 BC is just as likely as one in 323 BC, since Seuthes' position does not appear to have changed substantially. In this case, it could be argued that the action involving Berenice's sons takes place in a formal, ritual context in which minors might take part as a symbol of their future authority.

It is reasonable to suppose that the failure of Antigonus' grand plan, his own defeat and perhaps advancing years convinced Seuthes that it would be wise to stay quiet for the future. Whether Lysimachus demanded a formal guarantee of this as the price of continued rule over his prosperous kingdom on the Tonsus is unknown. Although the very limited nature of the literary evidence inclines one to caution, there is nothing to suggest any further confrontations with Lysimachus after 313 BC. The possibility that Seuthes' dynasty, around the turn of the century, faced troubles of its own, which precluded any further incursions upon Macedonian preserves, may have been a contributing factor.

SEUTHES, SPARTOCUS AND ODRYSIAN DECLINE

The Great Inscription shows that by the end of the fourth century BC an independent dynasty flourished at nearby Cabyle, while the state of affairs within Seuthes' own household did not bode well for the future. With four male heirs of minor status and the queen as regent, there was strong potential both for outside intervention and dynastic struggle. The contemporary parallels of Thessalonice in Macedon and Amastris at Heracleia Pontica, both murdered by ambitious sons tiring of maternal regency, may be instructive.[38]

Clearly there was some kind of crisis at Seuthopolis towards the end of Seuthes' reign; the negotiations recorded in the Great Inscription involve the release by Seuthes' family of Epimenes, a miscreant who had taken sanctuary in the temple of the Great Gods, into some kind of bond-service with Spartocus, the dynast at Cabyle. Based on Epimenes' suppliant role, his Macedonian name, and a formula in l.2 assuring the reader of Seuthes' good health, Mihailov proposed a context of unsuccessful conspiracy (by Lysimachus?) to assassinate Seuthes. It does, however, seem unlikely that Epimenes, if guilty of attempting so grave a crime, would be allowed to escape with his life. Alternatively and more prosaically, the reference to Seuthes' physical well-being may simply denote a legal precedent for Berenice's actions, in the form of an undertaking made by her husband while still in good health.[39] The precise context for the Great Inscription remains, for now, obscure; certainly a recent suggestion that it records not the handing over of a human suppliant, but the transfer of executive power at Seuthopolis to Spartocus is quite untenable, both on linguistic and historical grounds.[40]

While this idea of Spartocus as Seuthopolis' new master is untenable, there is some reason to believe that towards the end of the fourth century BC Seuthes began to feel the squeeze as other dynasts established themselves in south-eastern Thrace. Apart from Spartocus, whose coin legends, more ambitiously than Seuthes' own, proclaim him *basileus*, coins were issued by other Thracian rulers who may be contemporary with these two. There is Skotoskos, possibly based at Aenus; other contenders are Sroios and Adaeus. The rarity of these coins, however, and the uncertainty as to their dates suggests that it is probably over-bold to see them as firm evidence for the 'erosion of Lysimachus' power' over the Thracian hinterland; from the Macedonian point of view, the rise of rival dynasts who might preoccupy and curb the expansionist tendencies of a ruler like Seuthes may have been no bad thing. As has been seen, Alexander was able to turn the rivalry of neighbouring dynasts to his own advantage.[41]

Similarly, it is important not to exaggerate Seuthes' own influence – he has, for instance, been credited with setting up the *strategia* in Thrace.[42] Though his military and economic resources, the duration and strong defences of his city and his ability to direct his own foreign policy all seem to proclaim his independent status, his sphere of action was apparently limited to the area immediately in the vicinity of Seuthopolis. His coinage is restricted to bronze, implying a circulation that was mainly local.[43] Though this need not imply obedience to Macedonian strictures against coining in precious metals, if the purpose of this coinage were in part the diffusion of 'propaganda', promoting loyalty to the Odrysian house, then its impact was limited. In economic terms, Seuthes' coinage presents no competition to the Macedonian royal issues. As regards kingly image, Seuthes seems to follow in the footsteps of the Diadochs, rather than innovating or anticipating their actions. Though Diodorus calls him *Basileus* with reference to events in 323 BC, the evidence from Seuthopolis gives no support to the idea that his claim to royalty predated that of the Successors by more than fifteen years. The title appears neither on his coins nor in the Great Inscription. Similarly the belief that Seuthes outdid the Diadochs in claiming for himself the stature of god on earth in his life-time seems ill-founded.[44]

After their appearance in the Great Inscription, the fate of Seuthes' family is uncertain. Though some scholars have identified Seuthes' son Sadala with a dynast honoured by Mesambria who seems to enjoy some measure of control over the city, the date of the decree is much disputed and firm arguments for a date early in the third century are lacking. The link between a fragmentary inscription (from Philippopolis?) praising an unknown honorand and his brothers, and the sons of Seuthes is still more tenuous.[45]

Whatever the fate of Seuthes' dynasty, his city became vulnerable to attack in the mid-third century BC and was destroyed by fire and sword. The Celts, whose degree of penetration into southern Thrace seems, on the basis of recent research, to have been overestimated, are not the certain culprits. The inferior nature of the settlement which followed until the city's inundation in the last decades of the third century BC suggests that Seuthopolis never recovered its former status.[46] It is reasonable to suppose that the death of Seuthes III, architect of the Odrysian renaissance, was followed by a period of political uncertainty, with the dynasty perhaps troubled both by internal strife and by pressure from neighbouring rulers in southeastern Thrace.

In conclusion then, it seems likely that Lysimachus achieved a working arrangement in south-eastern Thrace whereby the effective independence of dynasts like Seuthes and Spartocus in the upper Tonsus area was the price paid for continued peace and control of the region outlined by Arrian for 323 BC. Nevertheless, the military objective of regaining the ground lost during Alexander's reign had not been achieved and Lysimachus could be accused of failing to show the promise which may have prompted his appointment. Lack of success in the south was, however, offset by important gains else-

where. Some time between 323 BC and 313 BC Lysimachus took control
of the Greek cities on the West Pontic coast.

LYSIMACHUS AND THE BLACK SEA CITIES

Whether these cities formed part of the 'official satrapy' of Thrace is
uncertain; Justin, Curtius and Porphyry talk vaguely of Pontic regions
and peoples; there is no specific reference to *poleis*. Since they
certainly do not fall within the 'actual' Macedonian territory outlined
by Arrian, their appearance in 313 BC, garrisoned by Macedonian
troops, must represent a solid gain for Lysimachus in the extension of
his authority, as well as breaking new ground for Macedonian rule in
this region.[47]

For Philip II, the West Pontic cities' importance lay primarily in
the stranglehold they gave him over Athens, commanding as they did
a major grain route to Greece. With his usual blend of belligerence
and diplomacy, Philip concluded alliances with Odessus and Apollonia, but took up arms against Istria in tandem with the Scythian king
Atheas. Whether this amounts to Macedonian 'possession' of the
Dobroudja region is, however, doubtful. There is no evidence to
suggest that the cities were subject to the kind of supervision imposed
on Philip's League of Corinth 'allies'.[48]

The condition of the West Pontic cities under Alexander is still
more shadowy. Justin's description of Zopyrion as *praefectus Ponti*
has prompted ambitious claims; without support from a more reliable
literary source or inscriptions, this seems a rather slight foundation
for belief in the idea of Macedonian administration of the Dobroudja,
let alone Alexander's division of the West Pontic region into
administrative wards under a *strategos*. Possibly one might infer a
stable situation on the West Pontic coast in Alexander's reign from
the fact that Zopyrion's target in 325 BC was Olbia rather than these
cities, but this may imply simply the existence of amicable relations
rather than Macedonian control.[49]

The means by which Lysimachus acquired the cities is unknown;
Saitta's assumption of a long hard war following Lysimachus' 'subjection of the Odrysai' usefully accounts for the otherwise empty years of
Lysimachus' first decade in Thrace, but there is no evidence to support
it. Though garrisoning might suggest subjection rather than voluntary alliance, this is not an inevitable conclusion; Diodorus' narrative
shows that cities might be garrisoned as a 'protective measure' – in
319 BC the satraps of Lydia and Hellespontine Phrygia garrison their

cities only in response to Antigonus' aggression.[50] Faction, which often facilitates foreign occupation throughout the history of the Greek *poleis*, may also have played its part. A pro-Macedonian party might represent a legacy of Philip II's reign or an expression of discontent with the current regime. Istria, at least, seems to have suffered political upheaval within the recent past and was to experience it again later in the third century BC.[51]

Saitta's theory of a long, tough fight may spring in part from a mistaken belief in the cities as a united federation, reflected in his use of the economical but anachronistic term 'Pentapolis'. The date of origin for the Pontic *koinon* is much disputed but most scholars connect it with Roman domination of the West Pontic coast. Though proxeny and citizenship decrees reflect communication between cities later in the third century BC – Dionysopolis grants citizenship to a man from Odessus, Mesambria honours a teacher from Callatis – nothing suggests a formal federal association at the end of the fourth century.[52] Pippidi's belief that the revolt of 313 BC sees the first united stance of the West Pontic cities gains support from Diodorus' narrative which reflects the evident fragility of this union.[53]

The date when Lysimachus installed his garrisons is likewise unknown; it is not impossible that Macedonian forces took up residence only in 315 BC in response to the threat posed by Antigonid liberation propaganda. If one favours an earlier date, then the garrisons may represent a justifiable precaution against Thracian attack; alternatively, hostilities between the Diadochs themselves may have prompted Lysimachus to take such a security measure. Though control of the Pontic grain route was perhaps less significant than in the days of Athenian freedom, the power to hinder or facilitate grain shipments to the cities of mainland Greece still had value. With it, Lysimachus could aid his ally, Cassander, or cause difficulties to his Antigonid foes, as these two parties disputed the possession of mainland Greece. Conversely, if the cities fell into enemy hands, Lysimachus could find himself open to attack from the rear. Antigonus' proclamation of Greek freedom and autonomy in 315 BC and the part he played in the revolt of 313 BC reflect a recognition of Lysimachus' potential vulnerability in this area.[54]

What, then, did possession of the West Pontic cities represent for Lysimachus in terms of military and economic advantage? Strategically, control of the cities provided him with naval bases and a maritime route to the southern Black Sea coast and Paphlagonia. In 302 BC, Cassander's brother Pleistarchus used it to bring troops from

Odessus to Lysimachus at Heracleia Pontica; he commandeered 120 ships from Odessus for the crossing, reflecting the cities' great value to Lysimachus as a source of warships. Evidence for Istria's war fleet comes from an inscription recording the dispatch of ships to an ally, Apollonia, for war against Mesambria. Though post-dating Lysimachus' reign, it is probable that the city possessed a fleet throughout its history. At Callatis, an inscription of the Hellenistic period honours a citizen for equipping a warship at his own expense.[55]

Commercially, too, the West Pontic cities were an attractive acquisition. Archaeological finds in the regions of Callatis, Istria and Tomi reflect the cities' role as intermediaries in a thriving trade between the *poleis* of mainland Greece and the Aegean area and communities in the Thracian interior. Amphora stamps from Callatis indicate a high level of imports from Thasos, Heracleia Pontica and Rhodes from the mid-fourth century BC, continuing through the third.[56] An oared ship on Callatis' bronze coinage and the worship of Poseidon and Castor and Pollux at Istria underline the importance of maritime trade for the cities' prosperity. Dionysus' appearance on coins and an early(?) third-century reference to the festival of *Dionysiois Zenikois* point to Callatis' domestic wine industry. At Istria, fish from the Danube and Peuke rivers represented a major source of revenues; still more lucrative was the slave trade for which the city was famous.[57]

For Lysimachus, the cities of the West Pontic coast represented a rich prize. How, then, were their fortunes affected by his arrival on the scene?

LYSIMACHUS' GOVERNMENT OF THE WEST PONTIC CITIES

Lysimachus' reputation as a miser, combined with the evidence for garrisons in the cities, has led to the belief that he squeezed these prosperous *poleis* dry, subjecting them to harsh government.[58] One restriction upon autonomy does not, however, presuppose a host of others; as will be seen, in the context of the Successors' wars, garrisons were an indispensable military precaution. While this background of constant warfare also makes it likely that the cities lost the freedom to pursue an independent foreign policy, loss of internal autonomy and fiscal oppression need not automatically accompany Macedonian occupation.[59] Diodorus' reference to the 'recovery of autonomy' with the revolt in 313 BC does not in itself warrant such an assumption; removal of the garrisons might have been enough to prompt such a statement, particularly when Hieronymus, keen to promote Antigonus' 'liberation programme', is the likely source. Odessus, at least, was allowed to maintain her considerable war fleet under Lysimachus' rule, even after the revolt. Though Istrian texts do reflect economic hardship, loans from wealthy *proxenoi* and financial pressure applied by foreign rulers, these belong to the later Hellenistic period. The oppressors are Getic chieftains, not a Macedonian king.[60] As yet no comparable evidence has surfaced for the period of Lysimachus' rule. It is possible that the cities, particularly if they had offered resistance at Lysimachus' approach, were required to pay tribute (*phoros*); there is, however, no evidence to confirm this.[61] Memnon's reference to a common frontier between Tomi and Callatis by 261 BC led Pippidi to suggest that Lysimachus organised the territory around the cities into defined *chorai* worked by *laoi*. While Lysimachus' provisions for Priene *c.* 283/2 BC may perhaps serve as a parallel, reflecting his concern for the efficient exploitation of the cities' *chorai*, it is equally possible that the Greek colonists themselves, like their fellows in Asia Minor, were responsible for conquest of the land around their cities and the harnessing of its indigenous peoples as a workforce. Exploitation of the Pedieis at Priene and the Mariandynoi at Heraclea Pontica, for example, clearly pre-dates the arrival of the Hellenistic kings.[62]

Insofar as it is possible to gauge 'general levels of prosperity', there seems little reason to suppose that Lysimachus' reign was a period of economic hardship for the West Pontic cities. Indeed, Callatis' rise to a leading position among them has been dated to the last years of the fourth century BC. Among individual citizens, at least, there is substantial evidence for wealth and the opportunities for cultured leisure which it affords. Callatis' necropolis boasts terracotta statuettes from Attica of remarkable artistic quality, dated to the Diadoch period; a third-century epitaph from Mesambria betrays the influence of Homer's *Iliad*; burial finds from Tomi's Hellenistic necropolis include gold jewellery, bronze mirrors and fibulae and an athlete's strigil. In the mid-third century BC certain Istrian citizens were in a position to make loans of 1,000 and 2,000 staters.[63]

Evidence of this sort, however, must be handled with care. Tomb finds may represent only the very finest possessions of the rich rather than items in everyday use by the majority of the inhabitants. Furthermore the significance of evidence for great individual wealth in relation to general levels of prosperity is uncertain. For the

Marxist-Leninist historian, such riches in the hands of individual citizens must imply impoverishment of the masses.[64] Alternatively, the wealth which has bestowed upon these substantial citizens a kind of immortality may reflect a boom in commerce which would benefit men engaged in production and exchange at all levels of society.

Though specific evidence for Lysimachus' fiscal oppression of the West Pontic cities is lacking, the traditional belief in his imposition of high taxes upon them persists, finding its origin presumably in a series of anecdotes proclaiming him a miser and in particular one where the 'flatterers' of Demetrius, in 302 BC, dub him 'Treasurer' (*Gazophylax*). As will be argued at greater length in later chapters, the value of this evidence as proof of Lysimachus' accumulation of great wealth from taxes in the early part of his reign is doubtful; if anything, the insult's thrust seems to be that in the first half of his career Lysimachus was unable to throw money about in the way that kings were expected to.[65] Burstein, for one, sites the origins of this caricature in a period of 'fiscal austerity' imposed upon Lysimachus by his satrapy's limited resources. Though this assessment of the resources of Thrace, or rather lack of them, is perhaps too gloomy, Burstein's theory gains support from the fact of Lysimachus' relative inactivity on the international stage in the first two decades of his reign.[66] Limited funds and a consequent need for care in expenditure need not, however, imply extortionate levels of taxation; as will be seen, it was more often royal extravagance and generosity to friends which was likely to make the king's subjects dig deep into their pockets.[67]

FREEDOM AND AUTONOMY IN THE WEST PONTIC CITIES

If, as far as we can tell, the prosperity of the cities did not greatly suffer, what of their autonomy? Is it true that Lysimachus imposed a harsh government on the Greeks of the West Pontic coast?

Given the lack of other concrete evidence, belief in the cities' loss of internal autonomy must rest heavily on the idea that Lysimachus deprived them of the right to strike their own coinage. Istria's distinctive 'double-head'-type silver coins have been dated to the period from *c.* 410 BC to 310 BC; the termini for Callatis' Heracles types are less easily established (their iconography may reflect either Alexander's coinage or that of Heracleia), but it is believed that the mint ceased to function during Lysimachus' reign. Conversely, the appearance of new types at both Odessus and Callatis has been linked with the recovery of autonomy after Lysimachus' death.[68]

Given the difficulties in dating these series precisely, it could be argued that one of the foundations for establishing such termini may be no more than the assumption that a ruler like Lysimachus would deprive the cities of the right to coin. If, however, one accepts a general picture of decline in the issue of city types in the last two decades of the fourth century, this need not be the result of Lysimachus' policy. Martin has argued that decline in city coinage under Macedonian rule should be ascribed to its failure to compete, commercially, with the widely accepted issues struck by the kings, rather than to royal denial of the right to coin; this will be discussed in greater detail in chapter 5. In this particular context, there are two pieces of evidence which should be noted. First, provision of an alternative source of finance, rather than Lysimachus' policy, may explain a halt in city coinage on the West Pontic coast at this juncture; the period immediately preceding the revolt sees a great influx of coinage from abroad, notably Alexander-type staters minted in the cities of northern Asia Minor. Second, when the cities start to coin again, later in the third century BC, they abandon the traditional city emblems in favour of Alexander or Lysimachus types.[69] The assumption, moreover, that these new types herald a new age of prosperity and freedom after Lysimachus' death is questionable; the occasion for their issue may be sinister rather than celebratory. The discovery of large numbers of these coins in hoards in Geto-Dacian territory, combined with the epigraphic evidence for Getic domination already mentioned, suggests that these issues were struck to pay 'protection money' to Getic or Celtic chieftains.[70]

If fluctuations of city coinage on the West Pontic coast do not constitute firm evidence for loss of autonomy under Lysimachus, what of the inscriptions from the cities? Later in the third century, certainly, democracy, or at least its institutions, was alive and well, reflecting in its constitutional forms fidelity to the metropolis; Callatis' eponymous magistrate is the *basileus* just as at Megara; the *meristai* who distribute Istria's public funds recall Miletus' board of *anataktai* (financial assessors).[71] Comparable inscriptions for the Lysimachean period are scarce; this might suggest a muzzling of the democracy, were it not for the fact that epigraphic evidence for the fifth and earlier fourth centuries is likewise lacking. Segre's suggestion that Lysimachus tolerated a tyranny at Apollonia was effectively quashed by Robert. Installation of a governor at Callatis, not implausible given the city's long and stubborn resistance, might be reflected in the restoration *[epi]states* on an inscription with lettering which fits the early Hellenistic period. The text is, however, extremely fragmentary, and an alternative restoration might be *[pro]states*, a magistrate often found in Dorian cities with a democratic constitution.[72]

There is, then, no secure evidence to support the belief that it was Lysimachus' abolition of democratic government which inspired the revolt in 313 BC. While possibly the presence of his garrisons in itself was felt to be sufficiently intolerable to prompt rebellion, the rising's timing suggests that it must be seen primarily as a response to the propaganda of Antigonus. In 315 BC, at Tyre, this self-styled champion of the Greeks offered 'freedom and autonomy'; his promise of liberation from garrisons and *phoros* must have seemed, in prospect at least, a decided improvement on conditions under Lysimachus.[73] Factional division within the cities may also have played its part. Though the cities' governments may have kept their democratic form, it is likely that they were dominated by Lysimachus' partisans. Those who opposed the latter, either on personal or political grounds, might be inclined to favour revolt, particularly if it was backed, as seems likely, by Antigonus' promises of military and financial support. Within the framework of Antigonus' strategic plan, the cities' allotted task seems to have been to keep Lysimachus busy on the Pontic coast while Antigonus launched an attack, via the Hellespont, upon the heart of his realm in southern Thrace.[74] How well equipped were they to carry out this task?

THE MILITARY RESOURCES OF THE WEST PONTIC CITIES

Though the historical narrative yields no direct information, demographic studies and inscriptions from later in the third century BC give some idea of the West Pontic cities' military resources and organisation. Callatis' population has been estimated at around 3,000; Mesambria, with a similar head count, was able to put 700–800 citizen hoplites into the field. Epigraphic reference to taxiarchs at Istria and Mesambria for the later Hellenistic period suggests that throughout the democratic period the *poleis* relied upon a core of citizen soldiers organised on a tribal basis. Callatis employed the military mess system of *syssitoi*, reflecting the city's Dorian roots. An Istrian decree makes reference to a *toxarchos*; the cultivation of specialised light armed troops which this implies may represent a response to the dangerous expertise of the local tribes in such brands of warfare. Concern for the upkeep of the city's fortifications is reflected in the appointment of wealthy and energetic officials entrusted with construction and maintenance of the walls.[75]

Finance for the revolt and the purchase of mercenaries may have come in part from wealthy citizens, the fourth-century counterparts of financiers like Diogenes and Dionysius from Istria, and Hephaistion from Callatis, honoured in third- and second-century decrees for loans to the *poleis*. The scale of the revolt and the high stakes involved may have prompted emergency measures such as the appointment of a *strategos autokrator*, attested later in the third century BC, and parallel with Olbian resistance to Zopyrion, the arming of freed slaves.[76]

THE REVOLT OF 313 BC

The rebels got off to a good start in the summer of 313 BC, expelling the Macedonian garrisons, evidently not strong or determined enough to resist the citizen militia. Forming an alliance, the cities secured the co-operation of the neighbouring indigenous peoples.[77] Subsequent events, however, suggest a lack of cohesion and any real sense of unity between the component parts of the rebel forces, which may have contributed to their eventual defeat.

Lysimachus reacted swiftly; the speed of his advance, perhaps a legacy of campaigns with Alexander, seems to have caught the cities unaware. At any rate, he was able to imitate Philip II's strategy on his Olynthian campaign, picking off the cities one by one. Nothing suggests that he had to face a united army from the *poleis*. Odessus was besieged, then Istria. Evidently the fourth-century fortifications, which at Odessus, at least, consisted of dry-stone walls, proved ineffective against the Macedonian assault. Istrian resistance may be reflected in the destruction of the city walls, which has been dated to the end of the classical period.[78]

Disorganisation is likewise the keynote of Lysimachus' encounter with the cities' Thracian and Scythian allies. Their failure to arrive in time to provide effective aid to the beleaguered cities enabled Lysimachus to take the offensive. Catching them on the march, he appealed to the self-interest of the Thracian contingent, who changed sides, leaving their allies isolated. Lysimachus followed a crushing defeat of the Scythians with the sustained cavalry pursuit which had been a feature of both Philip's and Alexander's campaigns.[79]

Callatis proved a tougher nut to crack. There is reason to believe that the city's long resistance was made possible by financial aid from Antigonus; the Marasesti coin hoard includes a large number of staters minted in the cities of Asia Minor and the Phoenician coast, dated from the mid-320s BC to *c.* 310 BC. At any rate, Callatis was still under siege as Antigonus' advance forces under Lycus and Pausanias approached the Hellespont, probably in the summer of 312 BC. They aimed to wrest control of Thrace from its satrap; following in their wake, Antigonus would then sweep through from the Hellespont against Cassander's Macedon.[80]

For the rebels, this could have been a turning point. Lysimachus faced the prospect of being marooned on the Pontic coast while the enemy took possession of his territory in southern Thrace. Again he acted fast. The decision to cut his losses at Callatis recalls Philip's withdrawal from Byzantium in 340–39 BC and shows the same astute judgement of priorities. With a holding force left at Callatis to prevent a fresh outbreak of trouble there, the main army marched south. Seuthes threatened to block the Haemus passes against Lysimachus but was defeated before reinforcements could come from Antigonus' general Pausanias. The latter, whose troops were perhaps already unnerved by the speed of Lysimachus' volte-face and his unexpected victory against the great Odrysian army, found himself confronting Lysimachus on the Pontic coast. The exact site is uncertain. Diodorus' account is brief and lacks detail, but Lysimachus' enrolment of some of these troops after Pausanias' death may suggest a good proportion of mercenary troops without a strong allegiance to the Antigonids. The ransoming of the rest swelled Lysimachus' coffers.[81]

These victories enabled Lysimachus to secure the Hellespont in anticipation of Antigonus' arrival. Thwarted in his aim of striking at Macedon from this angle, Antigonus switched tactics. Hoping to gain access to Thrace by its back door, the Propontis, he approached Byzantium with an offer of alliance. The Byzantines refused, complying with Lysimachus' request to refrain from action which would harm him or Cassander.[82] Lysimachus' recent string of victories may well have influenced the Byzantine decision to stay neutral.

Byzantium's refusal to abet Antigonus' schemes represented a diplomatic victory to crown those on the battlefield. Lysimachus' success in quelling the Pontic cities' revolt and repelling Antigonus' assault on Thrace and Macedon represents a major victory for the

41

anti-Antigonid coalition. Only swift reactions and battles won against the odds, however, had prevented an attack on Thrace from the Hellespont. Lysimachus' decision, in 309 BC, to found his capital Lysimacheia on the site of ancient Cardia, placed to command the straits, must constitute in part a measure to prevent such a threat recurring.[83]

Antigonus may have continued to supply cash to Callatis, still holding out as the peace treaty of 311 BC was drawn up. In theory, the clause which guaranteed autonomy to the Greek cities posed a renewed threat to Lysimachus' control of the West Pontic coast. In practice, all its participants, while recognising the potential of that clause as a pretext for future hostilities, offered the cities certain privileges which 'freedom and autonomy' implied, when it was politically and strategically affordable, as a reward for loyalty. Saitta's judgement that this clause of the treaty spelled disaster for Lysimachus surely underestimates the cynicism underlying that document.[84]

For Callatis, the peace meant only a temporary raising of the siege. Lysimachus' troops were again before the gates in 310–9 BC. There seems no compelling reason to construe their reappearance as a response to Ptolemy's 'liberation programme' of that year, rather than a renewal of the original assault once the peace of 311 BC had conveniently receded into the past. By the time Callatis capitulated, a large section of the population had fled, taking refuge with the Bosporan king Eumelus.[85] Victor in a vicious dynastic struggle following the death of Parisades I, Eumelus was anxious to make himself popular. His installation of the Callantian refugees in a new city can be ascribed in part to a conscious policy of euergetism, wholly in keeping with the Spartocid dynasty's history. Hostility to Lysimachus may also have been a factor; Zopyrion's attack on Olbia seems to represent Macedonian encroachment upon Bosporan preserves. Lysimachus' control of the West Pontic cities and consequent proximity to Spartocid territory cannot have been welcomed by Eumelus.

Mass flight from Callatis might suggest the expectation of heavy penalties. Though the exact conditions imposed upon the cities are unknown, Callatis' long resistance and a comparison with the methods of Lysimachus and other Hellenistic kings in Asia Minor suggest that a heavy indemnity may have been demanded. The obligation to provide military services implied by Odessus' provision of ships for Pleistarchus in 302 BC may also represent heavier terms imposed after the revolt.[86]

The assumption, however, that Lysimachus' rule represented the blackest days in the history of the West Pontic cities, after 'centuries of autonomy', is dubious. Rather it seems that the cities' relatively small size and their apparent isolation, except in moments of crisis, always rendered them vulnerable to foreign intervention. There is, for example, reason to believe that Philip II's defeat of King Atheas in 339 BC ended a period of Scythian domination for Callatis. Payment of 'protection money' by Istria, Callatis and Odessus to Getic or Celtic chieftains and of tribute by Mesambria to the Odrysian Sadala has already been mentioned. Istria suffered a tyranny earlier in the fourth century, while inscriptions from the later Hellenistic period show the city oppressed by debt, internal strife and food shortage.[87]

The picture in the Diadoch period, it seems, was not much different. Traditionally, Macedonian 'oppression' in the person of Lysimachus has been represented as the unwelcome alternative to 'freedom' for the West Pontic cities. Evidence for Lysimachus' Getic campaign(s) combined with finds from recent and current excavations in north-eastern Bulgaria, however, suggest that instead the cities found themselves the object of competition between Macedonian and Getic 'protectors'.

LYSIMACHUS AND THE GETAE

Prosperity and change in Thrace was not confined to the south-east; the fourth century BC saw also political and territorial expansion on the part of the Getic tribes north of the Haemus mountains. Already organised into some sort of political structure under dynastic rule by the sixth century BC, excavation of Getic settlements reflects a steady expansion out from the hinterland of Istria and Odessus. Dominated by the Odrysae in the mid-fifth century BC, to whom they paid tax and contributed soldiers, the Getae had profited from Philip II's conquest of the latter and his expulsion of Atheas' Scythians from the Dobroudja. By the second half of the fourth century BC, the Getae occupied sites on both banks of the Danube, between the river's two branches and in the south-west Dobroudja. The literary sources suggest some degree of urbanisation by Alexander's day.[88]

Getic prosperity rested on rich natural resources – agricultural land, pasture, timber and fish – combined with command of the Danubian trade route. Magnificent grave goods from princely tombs at Vratsa, Aghigiol, Peretu and Baiceni reflect both the Getic dynasts' wealth and their role as patrons of the arts. Gold and silver-gilt armour and drinking vessels with distinctive motifs, found on both sides of the

Danube and dated to the mid-fourth century BC, reflect an original artistic style specific to the North Balkans and known to us as Thraco-Getic. Finds from the newly discovered site at Sboryanovo, thought to be that of a great cult centre, support the view that Getic aristocrats, like their Odrysian counterparts, aspired to a lifestyle of some sophistication and were ready to adopt the latest fashions in art and architecture from abroad. They include a gold pectoral dated to the fourth century BC in Thraco-Macedonian style, a dedication to Artemis Phosphorus inscribed in Greek, and two fine vaulted tombs with stone sliding doors, a feature found previously only in Asia Minor.[89]

The Getic response to the Macedonians' arrival in the Dobroudja region had been mixed. Philip II's reputation had evidently preceded him and one dynast at least preferred friendship to enmity; Philip added a Getic princess to his long list of wives. Alexander, however, at the start of his reign had clearly needed to demonstrate that he had inherited his father's ability along with the throne. His crossing of the Danube and capture of a Getic town, perhaps Zimnicea, impelled the other 'independent tribes along the Danube to seek his friendship'.[90]

Like the Odrysae, it is probable that the dynasts of north-eastern Thrace profited from Alexander's absence and the discomfiture of his deputy Zopyrion. Lysimachus' arrival and the firm hold he took upon the West Pontic cities cannot have been welcomed by Getic chiefs who had established trading relations with the cities and perhaps saw themselves as their proper 'protectors'. A natural fear that Lysimachus might go on to expand his operations into the hinterland could not have been allayed by his defeat of their kinsmen in 313 BC. Though on that occasion the Thracian neighbours of the West Pontic cities made a pact with Lysimachus and perhaps remained dependent on him,[91] this need not imply that Getic chiefs further afield likewise abandoned all claims to these Greek cities.

After the events of 313 BC the literary sources fall silent on Lysimachus' actions north of the Haemus until a clash with the Getic chief Dromichaetes in the 290s BC which ended, for Lysimachus, in capture and ignominy. The motives which impelled his crossing of the Danube have been much discussed, but past reconstructions of the events preceding this campaign have now become outmoded. In particular, the reassessment of events in south-eastern Thrace, prompted by the discovery of Seuthopolis, must affect our interpretation of the Getic campaigns. Knowing the difficulties which Lysimachus experienced with Seuthes, it is no longer viable to see his crossing of the Danube and the war against Dromichaetes as the final stage of his 'conquest of Thrace' or 'an extension of Greek dominion' beyond the river. Saitta's theory of Lysimachus' intense activity along the Danube between 305 BC and 302 BC is unsupported by any firm evidence and, as Pippidi pointed out, in attempting to take and hold territory beyond the river, Lysimachus would have made a move which both Philip and Alexander had recognised as counter-productive.[92]

If 'conquest beyond the Danube' is abandoned, Lysimachus' campaign in the 290s BC is best seen as a response to Getic actions which encroached upon his interests. The evidence already mentioned for Getic interest in the West Pontic cities after Lysimachus' death supports the view that control of these *poleis* was the issue at stake.[93] Lysimachus' preoccupation with affairs in Asia after 301 BC may well have encouraged chieftains like Dromichaetes to stretch out a 'protecting' hand towards his Greek subjects.

THE WAR WITH DROMICHAETES

Though the evidence for this episode is so fragmentary that even the date at which Lysimachus first took action against Dromichaetes is disputed, the war in which he fell captive to the Getae is set by several sources between 294 BC and 292 BC. Lysimachus' unwillingness to intervene in the dynastic struggle which gave Demetrius Macedon's throne in 294 BC is explicitly connected with his preoccupation with the Getic war. Lysimachus' capture which brought the war to an end is usually dated to the winter of 292–1 BC; his release is placed in the following spring.[94]

Some scholars see this war as the second stage of Lysimachus' action against the Getae, following a period of conflict early in the 290s BC. The evidence cited is a fragment of Diodorus (XXI.F.11) recording the capture of Lysimachus' son Agathocles by 'Thracians'. His subsequent release is ascribed to their hope of regaining territory taken by Lysimachus and to 'an alliance of almost all the most powerful kings' which diminishes their prospects of victory. Pausanias, however, presents this incident as an alternative version of Lysimachus' capture by Dromichaetes in the campaign of 292 BC, an episode which survives in another fragment of Diodorus.[95]

On one view, this 'alliance' should be identified with the reconciliation of Demetrius with Ptolemy which Seleucus engineered *c.* 297 BC. Alternatively, Niese saw the incident as belonging to the campaign of 292 BC, while Beloch rejected it altogether as unhistorical. If Agathocles' capture is accepted as a separate incident, then a date early in the

290s BC seems more plausible than 292 BC; Niese himself admitted difficulties in identifying such an alliance at that date. There is, however, a considerable degree of duplication in the accounts of Lysimachus' capture and that of his son. In both cases, capture is followed by an unexpected release, explained by Thracian hopes of recovering territory previously lost to Lysimachus. Another repeated motif is the idea of Lysimachus' peril. Pausanias describes Lysimachus escaping from a position of extreme danger but his son being captured; in Diodorus, he is advised to save himself in a context of great danger but nobly stands by his army and friends.[96]

Though Pausanias' account of Lysimachus' activities in Thrace is clearly compressed, this does not in itself justify rejecting his suggestion of two source traditions dealing with the same incident. Likewise, Diodorus' use of a superior source, Hieronymus, does not negate the possibility of the material becoming mangled in transition. Moreover, the fragmented state of Diodorus' book XXI leaves the context in which the two incidents were recorded quite unknown. Hieronymus, clearly not an eyewitness to these events, may have been recording alternative hearsay reports, before deciding which one to accept. Saitta saw a Getic campaign in the early 290s BC as the fulfilment of a scheme conceived by Lysimachus as early as 304 BC, but interrupted by the Asian campaign of 302 BC; on the evidence we have, this seems ill-founded.[97]

The dating of Lysimachus' capture by Dromichaetes may be reasonably secure, but very little is known of the events which preceded it. Though current excavations in north-eastern Bulgaria have raised some hopes of a future solution to the mystery surrounding Dromichaetes, at present he remains a far more shadowy figure than Seuthes III. The fullest source of information about his court and kingdom, Diodorus XXI.F.12, must be treated with caution; sections of the passage are highly anecdotal and it will be seen that the intrusion of conventional literary motifs lessens its value as historical evidence.

Traditionally, Dromichaetes' kingdom has been placed beyond the Danube in the region of the Wallachian plain, based on Lysimachus' march across the 'Getic desert', presumably to attack Dromichaetes in his own realm. In recent years, an ingenious article by Daicovicu has proposed a more precise siting for Dromichaetes' capital Helis, in the Arges Valley approximately 75 kilometres beyond the Danube. This is possible, but the discovery of a great Getic cult centre at Sboryanovo in the region of Razgrad, around 75 kilometres south of the Danube, might suggest that Dromichaetes' centre of operations was rather closer to the river. Though as yet no settlement has emerged to be connected with the cult centre, Lysimachus took considerable forces on this campaign, suggesting that he viewed Dromichaetes as a serious threat. This is perhaps more easily explained if Dromichaetes was just beyond the river and threatening to encroach upon Lysimachus' West Pontic possessions than if the centre of his realm was as far away as the Arges Valley. If this is correct, what was Lysimachus doing marching across the 'Getic desert' if not planning to attack his enemy's kingdom on its other side? One solution might be to suppose a tactical retreat by Dromichaetes of the sort that Lysimachus himself used to fox Antigonus in 302 BC, deliberately leading the enemy away from his own kingdom and into unfamiliar and inhospitable territory.[98]

Though the campaign ended in disaster, the literary sources suggest that initially the gods smiled on Lysimachus; the forts and territory which provided him with his bargaining power in 292 BC are best seen as the fruits of early success in this campaign. Though it has been suggested that Lysimachus followed Alexander's route of 335 BC, crossing the Danube at Zimnicea and capturing that city,[99] this perhaps takes him unnecessarily far west, since his starting point would presumably have been Asia Minor or the Thracian Chersonese, rather than Macedon.

Crossing the Getic desert proved the turning point; the sources agree that miscalculation of the problems posed by supply and terrain lay behind Lysimachus' defeat. Though Polyaenus suggests that the incautious acceptance of a renegade general from Dromichaetes' army contributed to the disaster, the deserter's name, Seuthes, raises some suspicion of muddle and lessens the reliability of this evidence.[100] On this occasion, Lysimachus lost the chance to meet the enemy in battle; even if he had, there is no reason to think that victory was guaranteed. Renowned for their cavalry strength, the Getae bred an élite type of horse equipped to carry a heavily armed warrior. Darius I included a Getic contingent in his Scythian expedition; the mounted archers in Sitalces' Thracian army in 431 BC probably reflect a legacy of Getic conflict with the Scythians; an army of 14,000 men, including 4,000 horse, had faced Alexander across the Danube in 335 BC. Had the Macedonians counted on superior tactical skills, they could be accused of trying to teach their grandmothers to suck eggs; Getic use of the wedge formation to break through the enemy line, a favourite tactic of Alexander, represents another lesson learnt from Scythia.[101]

In the event, the army which finally faced Dromichaetes was clearly at its last gasp. Lysimachus sustained crushing losses: his personal surrender is variously ascribed to nobility or thirst! For Lysimachus' reception by Dromichaetes and his subsequent release we are largely dependent on Diodorus XXI.F.12. While part of this passage probably derives from Hieronymus, its reliability as a whole as evidence for the constitution of Dromichaetes' 'state' and his economic position is questionable. Thus the debate between the Thracian assembly and their king regarding Lysimachus' fate is presumably the basis for the idea that Dromichaetes led a 'military democracy'. This warrior assembly might, however, be analogous to the Macedonian army assembly, whose well-attested role in voting upon major decisions of policy does not alter the essentially autocratic nature of the Macedonian constitution.[102] Here too, in this case at least, Dromichaetes' decision, to preserve the life of his opponent, prevails.

Still less reliable is the story of Dromichaetes' banquet for his royal prisoner, which contrasts Macedonian luxury with Thracian frugality. Daicovicu's identification of the passage as a literary trope renders it invalid as evidence for Getic wealth, or lack of it. It is, moreover, belied by the splendid grave goods and hoarded treasures from Getic settlements which suggest that the aristocracy, at least, did not lag far behind the Macedonian dynasts in conspicuous display both on the parade ground and at the dinner table.[103]

Dromichaetes' motives for releasing Lysimachus are worth taking more seriously. The implied compliment to Demetrius in the reference to a 'more formidable king' who might succeed Lysimachus suggests that this may well derive from Hieronymus. Presumably Dromichaetes realised that a balance of power preserved among the Diadochs would prove less threatening to Getic ambition than the proximity of a ruler like Demetrius, whose combined control of Macedon and Thrace would render him undesirably strong. In Lysimachus the Getae would have a neighbour with strong reasons for gratitude towards them and an obligation to abide by the terms they could demand; Demetrius might privately thank them for doing his dirty work for him but would be unlikely to express his appreciation in concrete terms. For Lysimachus, the price of freedom was a daughter given in marriage to Dromichaetes, who seems also to have taken the initial precaution of holding high-born hostages like Lysimachus' stepson Clearchus. The obligation for Lysimachus to surrender also his possessions 'beyond the Danube' has been the subject of some dispute. Rather than proving Lysimachus' mastery of an enduring empire beyond the Danube, it is more reasonable to suppose that these comprised the gains he had made earlier in the campaign. Pippidi interpreted this phrase as a demand that Lysimachus must abandon the West Pontic cities to Getic control; while not inconsistent with the evidence for Getic influence over the cities later in the third century BC, it is difficult to understand Pausanias' phrase, *ta peran Istrou*, in this sense since he is describing the deal from Lysimachus' standpoint.[104] It is preferable to suppose that the cities came under Getic 'protection' only after Lysimachus' death.

CONCLUSIONS

This survey of Lysimachus' achievement in 'Thrace' cannot, of course, claim to be in any way complete. Apart from new evidence still emerging from both south- and north-eastern Bulgaria which may provoke yet another reassessment of his dealings with the tribes there, nothing at all is known regarding his influence in the western regions of his satrapy.

Both in the Danube area and in the south-eastern hinterland, Lysimachus was obliged to compromise in his dealings with the indigenous tribes. In the early years the cost of military subjection of the Odrysae had proved too high; beyond the Danube, problems of supply and terrain were primarily the cause of his defeat. In these areas his achievement fell short of the sort of conquest envisaged by the panegyrist who was Justin's source; he did, however, enjoy greater success on the West Pontic coast, where both conquest and continued control were more easily achieved. Moreover, the establishment of alliance with the Odrysians and Getae and recognition of their dynasts' independence seem to have resulted in sufficient stability in Thrace to allow Lysimachus the freedom to concentrate his energies more profitably elsewhere.[105]

Finally, on the subject of stability and the reaction of both Greeks and Thracians to the Macedonian presence in Thrace, it must be remembered that the satrapy's position rendered it at all times potentially vulnerable to pressure from the peoples beyond the Danube. For example, it took Philip's strong hand to expel the Scythians, whose movement into the Dobroudja in the late fourth century BC may be explained as the result of pressure upon them from Sarmatian migration. Similarly, it is hard to explain the timing of the Celtic invasion in 279 BC as pure coincidence rather than an exploitation of the period of chaos after Lysimachus' death in 281 BC and

Ptolemy Ceraunus' seizure of his throne.[106] To see Lysimachus' fall as a cause for celebration in Thrace is somewhat naïve; the 'freedom' gained with his demise merely laid Thrace open to anarchy and then to conquerors of a far less temperate nature.[107]

3

THE ACQUISITION OF EMPIRE

Ambition, enmity and alliance

This chapter and the next will follow Lysimachus through the complex political manoeuvrings of an era in which allegiances shift as fast as the protagonists rise and fall. The aim is to examine how his political choices contributed to the acquisition of his great Hellespontine empire, which foreshadowed those of Pergamum and Byzantium and made him, by 285 BC, an object of fear and loathing to his contemporaries.[1] His aims and aspirations will be considered and the extent to which success represented the fruits of a consistent and deliberate 'policy', as opposed to the rewards of successful opportunism. Lysimachus' abilities as warrior and diplomat will also be examined.

Before this discussion can proceed, however, an assumption underlying many modern reconstructions of the Diadoch period must be challenged. In the narrative of ancient and modern historians alike, Hieronymus of Cardia exerts a powerful influence.[2] This is nowhere more apparent than in the belief that after Perdiccas' death, only Antigonus, and perhaps his son Demetrius, dreamed of reuniting Alexander's empire under their own rule. The other Diadochs, it is said, had different and far more modest aims, to be recognised as rulers of a limited territory, comprising only a part of Alexander's realm. Lysimachus, in particular, is often presented as a cautious and relatively unambitious character. Will, for example, remarks vis-à-vis Antigonus' dream of a united Europe and Asia, 'ce que réalisera un instant Lysimaque, sera d'une partie et d'un caractère differents de ce qu'avait rêvé Antigonus'. Struggle between the 'unitarist and particularist tendencies' is seen as a major theme of the period.[3]

A central feature of Hieronymus' narrative is Antigonus' greed for power or *pleonexia*, his desire for *pasa arche* and *ta hola*. The negative element in such a presentation of events by Hieronymus, the

Antigonid protégé, has probably encouraged its uncritical acceptance.[4] Whether this is justified is uncertain; Hieronymus may deplore Antigonus' *pleonexia*, but his portrait of a man in pursuit of a magnificent dream, destroyed by ambition, does make of Antigonus a tragic heroic figure, rather than a pitiable failure. Even if this presentation is accepted as historical, it need not imply so definitive a contrast between Antigonus and his opponents as those who favour the unitarist/particularist view propose. Explicit evidence for the aims of Antigonus' opponents is limited. Ptolemy might possibly be labelled a 'particularist'; he refused guardianship of the kings after Perdiccas' death and his early opposition to the central authority is stressed, though this in itself need not imply limited ambition. Similarly it is clear that for Cassander, in 319 BC, rule over Macedon and Greece, lands he saw as his rightful inheritance from Antipater, was the prize at stake.[5]

It should, however, be noted that the phrase *ta hola*, taken to signify the whole empire when used of Antigonus, also appears with reference to the aims and actions of the other Diadochs. Significantly, in these cases, the phrase is translated in such a way as to avoid any suggestion of the empire as a whole. For example, when Cassander, faced with Antigonus' demand for his unconditional surrender in 302 BC, summons Lysimachus *pros ten ton holon koinopragian*, the term *ton holon* is rendered as 'their highest interests'.[6] Since the idea that all Antigonus' opponents sought only to acquire a limited territory seems to derive more from hindsight than any testimony in the ancient sources, the validity of such a working method, based as it is on a circular argument, is questionable.

Furthermore, the neat dichotomy between the Antigonids and their opponents which is presupposed by the 'unitarist/particularist' view implies that each Successor had from the outset a clear vision of a goal which remained unchanged throughout four decades of warfare in which territories constantly changed hands and new and often dazzling possibilities arose. This is unlikely. Such a view owes too much to hindsight and a tendency to see actors in the ancient world as entirely rational, fixed in their purposes and not susceptible to the lure of unexpected opportunities. There is strong evidence to suggest that the aspirations of Lysimachus and Seleucus, at least, were very much less limited than the 'unitarist/particularist' view supposes.[7] With this in mind, the examination of Lysimachus' political career can begin.

THE EARLY YEARS; 323 BC – 315 BC

If our knowledge of Lysimachus rested solely on Diodorus' book XVIII, he might justly be dismissed as a peripheral figure of minor importance. The satrap of Thrace hardly looms large upon the international stage in these years. Burstein's judgement that he was

> a follower rather than a leader . . . who between 323–302/1 campaigned only against the Thracians and the transdanubian Getes and the rebellious cities of his satrapy . . . while avoiding anything beyond the most perfunctory involvement in the affairs of Macedon and the Aegean

is, however, too harsh. First, his action against the Pontic cities from 313 BC to 312 BC played a vital part in the war fought together with Ptolemy, Cassander and Seleucus against Antigonus from 315 BC to 311 BC. Second, such a judgement lays too much stress on military action alone as a sign of influence, ignoring the importance of Lysimachus' possession of the land linking Asia and Europe.[8] If those who held power in Asia and Macedon came to blows, his support could be invaluable in facilitating troop-movement and communications. Conversely his opposition could represent a major obstacle.

The first years of the Successor period do indeed witness two such conflicts. From 322 BC to 321 BC, the European regent, Antipater, supported by Craterus, Antigonus and Ptolemy, fought against Perdiccas, who had effectively made himself the representative of central authority in Asia. In 319 BC, a struggle arose between Antipater's son Cassander, backed by Antigonus, fast rising to a position as master of Asia, and the new regent in Macedon, Polyperchon. Brief glimpses of Lysimachus during these conflicts do show him taking sides, though his co-operation is largely restricted to grants of access to his strategically important territory, apparently stopping short of military support on a large scale. The outcome of events suggests that on both occasions his choice was sound, contributing to his enhanced prestige and security.

In 323 BC, at Babylon, Lysimachus had received the newly created satrapy of Thrace; how he felt about this assignment must remain unknown. Bengtson's suggestion that his vision of a kingdom bridging the Hellespont prompted a specific request for Thrace seems unlikely. The ugly situation brewing in Thrace in 323 BC, the limited resources available to Lysimachus on his departure, his early experiences there, and his status in 323 BC as a prominent but not leading figure among Alexander's friends suggest rather that Thrace perhaps came second only to Cappadocia on a list of dirty jobs. The encomium which presents Lysimachus as the only man militarily capable of such a challenge may contain an element of defensiveness.[9]

As satrap of Thrace, Lysimachus was officially subordinate to Antipater, the *strategos* of Europe. Potentially such a situation was rife with difficulties. In 323 BC, however, both men were limited in their resources and faced with war in their respective territories; disunity between them could only benefit their opponents. The evidence suggests that, recognising this, they took steps to establish a reasonable working relationship.[10]

Among the Diadochs, marriage alliance has rightly been emphasised as an important source of security and influence. Antipater's choice of Lysimachus as bridegroom for his daughter Nicaea, Perdiccas' repudiated wife, suggests cordial relations between the two and represents a considerable enhancement of Lysimachus' prestige. Another mark of favour comes at Triparadeisus in 321 BC when Antipater appointed Autodicus, Lysimachus' brother, to the post of Bodyguard to the Kings. Plausibly Lysimachus, whose first years in Thrace saw no startling success, also owed his tenure of the satrapy in that year to Antipater's friendship.[11] These signs of a positive relationship suggest that Antipater's scheme to settle several thousand disfranchised Athenians in Thrace was an attempt to relieve Lysimachus' manpower shortage, rather than an unwelcome assertion of his superior status. Likewise Lysimachus' failure to lend the regent aid in the Lamian War need not be construed as sinister; he was short of troops himself and preoccupied with his war against Seuthes.[12]

When Antipater got involved in conflicts outside Europe, the value of Lysimachus' friendship became clear. In 322 BC when Antipater and Craterus marched on Asia for war against Perdiccas, it is probable that a short-cut through Thrace greatly eased the journey. On another occasion, right of free passage through Lysimachus' satrapy may have helped Antipater to extricate himself from a sticky situation. Returning from Triparadeisus to Macedon with the kings in 321 BC, he was faced at Abydus with mutinous, unpaid soldiers. A secret night crossing of the Hellespont enabled him to evade their demands![13]

In supporting Antipater against Perdiccas, Lysimachus found himself on the side of those who claimed to represent the Argead house against a usurper.[14] That this reflects any personal feelings of loyalty to Alexander's heirs, the epileptic Philip and the infant Alexander, is highly doubtful. Despite Lysimachus' public emphasis on his intimacy with Alexander, events after Antipater's death suggest that his allegiance to the latter was determined primarily by the need to be on good terms with a powerful neighbour. With the knowledge that 'all was quiet on the western front', he could concentrate his energies where they were most needed, first against Seuthes in south-eastern Thrace, subsequently on the West Pontic coast.

Antipater died in 319 BC, probably in the autumn. His named successor, Polyperchon, found his governorship of Macedon and Europe contested by Antipater's son Cassander, who, according to some sources, had effectively governed Macedon in the last months of his father's life. The friendship which Lysimachus formed with Cassander is often cited as the exception to a rule of treachery characterising relations between the Diadochs and their followers, but its origin and precise nature are not generally examined.[15]

Mobilising support for a coup against Polyperchon, Cassander held secret negotiations with Ptolemy and 'the other commanders and cities'. Subsequently, he crossed to Asia to enlist aid from a former foe, Antigonus, now only too glad to see Polyperchon kept busy in Europe while he himself arranged affairs in Asia to his own liking. While there is no explicit reference to Lysimachus, Cassander was able to dispatch trusted friends to the Hellespont without arousing suspicion, and subsequently went secretly from Macedon to Asia via the Thracian Chersonese.[16] This makes it almost certain that Lysimachus was among the *hegemones* whom Cassander successfully approached with an offer of alliance.

By the summer or autumn of 318 BC, there is positive evidence for Lysimachus' active co-operation with Cassander and Antigonus against Polyperchon, who now stood as representative of the kings. Cleitus, Polyperchon's admiral, was sent to guard the Hellespont against Cassander's return to Europe. After an initial victory over Antigonus on the Bosphorus, he was forced to flee for his life after the latter made a surprise attack on his camp. He was caught and duly dispatched by Lysimachus' men. Since Cleitus had won over the Propontis cities shortly before the battle, Lysimachus thus combined support for Cassander with defence of his own interests; the potential vulnerability of Thrace, given a strong enemy presence in the Propontis, is reflected in Antigonus' later attempts to bypass the Hellespont and gain entry to Thrace by the back door.[17]

What does Lysimachus' choice of Cassander as an ally and action against Polyperchon say about his own aims? Will suggests that he 'was not averse to restoring the union of Macedon and Thrace to his own advantage'; to accept that Lysimachus had his sights already set on Macedon, however, credits him with taking a very long view. While the sources certainly ascribe lofty aspirations to Antigonus as early as 319 BC, there is little suggestion that Lysimachus had any thought of rule in Macedon before 294 BC. It is surely too complicated to think that Lysimachus, like Antigonus, hoped initially to use Cassander as a pawn, but on perceiving Cassander's capability and independent success, swallowed his disappointment and accepted him as an ally on equal terms. The problem of Lysimachus' stance towards Cassander and Macedon is compounded by the uncertainty as to his exact movements in Thrace, but the new construction put on events there by the discovery of Seuthopolis makes it most unlikely that at this stage he was in a position to think seriously of Macedon. At this point his attention was probably still fixed on Thrace and the Pontic coast; it was therefore in his interest to have a strong and capable ruler of Macedon, who would fill for him the same role as Antipater.[18]

If so, Lysimachus showed himself a better judge of character than Antipater who seems to have doubted Cassander's ability to cope with the regency. That Lysimachus made his choice on the basis of personal observation is possible. Although Cassander had probably taken no part in Alexander's expedition, he was in Babylon in 324 BC. This may have given Lysimachus a chance to remark on the *energia* and *epieikeia* noted by Diodorus. Another possible context for contact is the period when Cassander was acting as his father's proxy in Macedon. Initially, Lysimachus' decision to back Cassander against the central authority may have seemed risky, but the calibre and resources of Cassander's other allies, notably Ptolemy and Antigonus, must have reassured Lysimachus as to the high chances of being on the winning side.[19]

The gamble paid off; by spring 315 BC Cassander had eliminated all opposition, including the powerful figure of Olympias, Alexander's mother and a bitter enemy of Antipater's house. He established himself as uncrowned king of Macedon, a position consolidated by a royal marriage, the burial of his predecessors and the foundation of a royal seat.[20]

The precise terms of Lysimachus' alliance with Cassander remain uncertain. The assumption that they inevitably co-operated and consulted each other's interests perhaps lays too much weight on Diodorus who refers to Cassander's habit of calling on Lysimachus for aid because of 'his proximity and his valour'. It is perhaps more accurate to say that he did this in times of crisis; it is notable that on two occasions at least, in 313 BC and 302 BC, Cassander was prepared to negotiate separately with Antigonus before reverting to this 'habitual practice'.[21] At times when their own interests were not directly threatened, it is quite possible that Lysimachus and Cassander took independent lines.

Thompson saw the provision of coined money as one of the more tangible advantages of Lysimachus' alliance with Cassander. This is possible; Philip and Alexander-types struck at Lysimacheia after 309 BC are the first issues which can be firmly linked with Lysimachus; his own Alexander-Ammon/Nike types do not appear until after 301 BC, struck initially from mints in Asia Minor. The deal with Cassander may even have given Lysimachus use of the Amphipolis mint, close to the border of their respective kingdoms. Price suggests that issues of Alexander-type tetradrachms from that mint marked with a *lambda* may be connected with Lysimachus. Such an arrangement, however, must post-date spring 315 BC, when Cassander first took firm control of Macedon. How did Lysimachus manage for the first eight years in Thrace? Though Antipater may well have provided initial finance, Lysimachus' supply of coined money must have been disrupted in the period between the regent's death in summer/autumn 319 BC and spring 315 BC when Cassander got his hands on Macedon's mints. Though lack of access to his own mint facilities would not have rendered Lysimachus totally incapable of action, as a twentieth-century observer might be tempted to assume, it may help to explain why he failed to launch or take part in any large-scale military operations outside Thrace in this period.[22]

The evidence we have, then, for Lysimachus' relations with his fellow Diadochs in these early years shows him taking care to secure himself on the western front, cultivating good relations first with the powerful regent Antipater and then with his son Cassander. Though the problems posed by Thrace and, perhaps, financial difficulties kept him from active involvement in the first Diadoch wars, the significance of his territory as the door from Europe to Asia meant that his support was sought by the combatants. In the first war he found himself on the side of those who claimed to represent 'the kings', in the second he opposed Polyperchon, the self-styled representative of the Argead house. Loyalty to Alexander's house, then, clearly played no part in his decision-making; both times, however, he chose the winning side.

THE WAR AGAINST ANTIGONUS 315 BC – 311 BC

The very success of the coalition against Polyperchon proved the cause of its collapse. In 318 BC, Polyperchon had found a valuable ally in Eumenes, appointed satrap of Cappadocia in 323 BC but outlawed two years later by Antipater for supporting Perdiccas. Commanding the 'royal army' in Asia for Polyperchon, Eumenes had proved a sharp thorn in Antigonus' side. Finally, however, he was defeated at Gabiene in the winter of 316/5 BC; Eumenes' troops swelled Antigonus' already considerable resources, and left the latter in control of territory stretching from the Tigris to the Aegean. So great an increase in influence cannot have failed to disturb his colleagues. It is unclear whether the coalition members had made any formal agreement regarding division of possible spoils. If so, the aftermath of Gabiene, which saw Antigonus systematically sweep away all potential opposition in the Asian satrapies, must surely have dispelled any lingering hopes that Antigonus' 'allies' would share his profits. Two powerful satraps, Peithon in Media, and Peucestas in Persis, both, significantly, ex-Bodyguards of Alexander, were eliminated.[23]

The next target was Seleucus; originally Perdiccas' man, holding a prestigious cavalry command in 323 BC, he took a leading role in the assassination of his master and was rewarded, at Triparadeisus, with the satrapy of Babylonia. Despite attempts to conciliate Antigonus, Seleucus was forced to flee from Babylon in spring 315 BC. Taking refuge in Egypt, he persuaded first Ptolemy and subsequently Cassander and Lysimachus that Antigonus' aspirations to rule a reunited empire presented a real threat. United action must be taken against him.[24]

The first move took the form of diplomacy; marching towards upper Syria, Antigonus received an ultimatum from his erstwhile allies. They demanded considerable territorial and financial concessions on the grounds that, as colleagues in the war against Eumenes, they were entitled to share the profits of victory. This document has been the subject of much discussion on both juridical and textual grounds.[25] In a work focused on Lysimachus, it is enough to say that the ultimatum aimed not merely to prevent Antigonus from further conquests, but to reduce his territories considerably and seriously restrict any attempt at maritime expansion. Some of the clauses were frankly unreasonable, among them the demand that Hellespontine Phrygia should be 'returned' to Lysimachus. Legally, the latter had not a leg to stand on; certainly, Antigonus had seized the territory from its satrap Arridhaeus in 318 BC, but if it were to be confiscated on grounds of usurpation, it could just as well go to another governor as to Lysimachus. What is important here is whether this demand reflects a readiness for territorial expansion on Lysimachus' part, and whether his decision to join the coalition of 315 BC was inspired primarily by that aim rather than by his obligations to his ally Cassander.[26]

Saitta denies that the claim to Hellespontine Phrygia in any way reflects Lysimachus' real aims in 315 BC, citing his relatively small part in allied operations before 313 BC, his primarily defensive role in that war, and the limited nature of Antigonus' action against him. It is true that the ultimatum should probably be seen more as a challenge to Antigonus, and even a pretext for war,[27] than a settlement which Antigonus might realistically be expected to accept; this does not, however, mean that its terms bear no relation to the genuine aspirations of its authors. It is quite feasible that Lysimachus was in a position in 315 BC to consider expansion into wealthier and less troublesome terrain. The new problems that emerged in 313 BC in Thrace and the West Pontic region are best seen as a response to Antigonus' propaganda and his activities once war broke out. It is probable that by 315 BC Lysimachus had reached some sort of compromise with Seuthes; this and his successful takeover of the West Pontic cities make it quite credible that he should begin to look across the Hellespont to a territory which would consolidate his control of the Straits. Lysimachus' failure to launch immediately an active offensive against Antigonus is not proof that in 315 BC he had no genuine desire for expansion into Asia. The events of 302 BC suggest his manpower resources were not sufficient for such action without support from allies. Furthermore, such a view places too much weight on Lysimachus in isolation, rather than regarding his actions in the context of the coalition's combined operations.

Antigonus, seeking above all to overcome the allied thalassocracy which Diodorus stresses, concentrated his initial efforts on Phoenicia. Subsequently, while besieging Tyre in spring 315 BC he launched a propaganda war against Cassander, denouncing him for his crimes against the Argead house, and getting himself proclaimed guardian (*epimeletes*) to Alexander IV. His simultaneous announcement of Greek autonomy was designed primarily to stir up a reaction in the cities of mainland Greece against the oligarchies supported by Cassander. In the first two years of the war Cassander himself led the operations in mainland Greece, with subordinates commanding his troops in Cappadocia and Caria.[28] It seems probable, therefore, that Lysimachus' 'defensive role' represents part of the allied strategy rather an individual unwillingness for territorial expansion. In winter 314–13 BC Lysimachus proved his effectiveness as an obstacle to Antigonid attack on Macedon, securing the Hellespont against Antigonus.[29] The latter's attempt, early in 313 BC, after victory over Cassander's troops in Caria, to make a separate peace with Macedon, acknowledges the problem posed by Lysimachus, whom he hoped thus to isolate. Simpson assumed that since Lysimachus subsequently collaborated with Cassander against Antigonus he was likewise included (from the start) in the peace negotiations. This is not necessary. The circumstances of 302 BC provide a perfect parallel; initially ready to negotiate separately with Antigonus, Cassander summons Lysimachus only when Antigonus' terms prove extortionate. Antigonus' own letter to Scepsis hints at some mysterious intervention which caused the talks of 313 BC to fail. If Saitta is correct to see Lysimachus as the figure lurking behind these cryptic words, then his success in impressing upon Cassander the full implications of Antigonus' policy of 'divide and rule' marks an important diplomatic victory.[30]

Foiled in his hopes of attacking Thrace directly, Antigonus turned his attention to the West Pontic coast, hoping that the cities' revolt would divert Lysimachus from the Hellespont, enabling him to make a direct assault on Macedon. The brilliant campaign in which Lysimachus averted this danger, and the diplomatic coup which followed it have already been discussed.

THE PEACE OF 311 BC

315 BC to 312 BC were years which Lysimachus might recall with some satisfaction. The rejection of the allies' ultimatum and his own demand for Hellespontine Phrygia probably came as no surprise and should not be seen as in any sense a real setback. Having gained the war they wanted, the allies had no reason to regret enlisting Lysimachus on their side; his military and diplomatic skills had saved not only Thrace, an important prize strategically, but also Macedon from Antigonid attack. This success offset in part Antigonus' victories elsewhere, mainly at Cassander's expense. Antigonus' seizure of Caria early in 313 BC had given him mastery of all the Asian provinces, while his generals had deprived Cassander of important possessions in mainland Greece.[31]

Lysimachus' victory in Thrace, moreover, marked a turning point in the allies' fortunes. The threat of a renewed Antigonid attack on Macedon was averted by events in other theatres of war. In the spring of 312 BC Ptolemy inflicted a great defeat on Demetrius' fleet at Gaza. In Babylonia, too, Antigonus found his hands full as Seleucus launched a campaign to recover his satrapy. Probably both events contributed to Antigonus' willingness to make peace.[32]

The course of hostilities from 315 BC to 311 BC had shown Antigonus the difficulties of fighting a war on several fronts. His attempts and near success, in the course of the peace negotiations, to divide his opponents both reflect his awareness of this and expose the essential artificiality of the coalition, whose members would only unite when their own interests were directly threatened or involved.

Antigonus' letter to Scepsis, dated to 311 BC, suggests that Lysimachus and Cassander were ready in winter 312–11 BC to make a separate peace in Europe, leaving Ptolemy and Seleucus exposed to enemy assault. Ptolemy acted fast to secure his inclusion in the peace. He saved himself, but was forced to abandon Seleucus; it is generally agreed that the latter was not included in the treaty of 311. From *c.* 310 BC to 308 BC war raged between Seleucus and Antigonus, glimpsed only fleetingly in fragments of the Babylonian Chronicle series. The odds against Seleucus should have brought Antigonus a swift victory; instead he was defeated. The brutal impact which his army made upon Babylonia – Chronicle 10 speaks of 'weeping' and ravaging of the land – may well have swelled support for Seleucus' cause. The calculations on which Antigonus had made peace in 311 BC had proved incorrect.[33]

Back in 311 BC, Seleucus' exclusion must, however, represent a concession to Antigonus, as was the clause which made him master of 'all Asia' and the grant of 'freedom and autonomy' to Greek cities in Asia and Europe. Proclaiming the principle at Tyre in 315 BC, Antigonus had used it to some effect against Cassander in Greece and Lysimachus in the West Pontic region. His letter to Scepsis presents Greek freedom as a major factor in his decision to make peace; probably copies of the same document were sent to all the Greek cities under Antigonus' sway.[34]

Nevertheless, to take that letter at face value and see the peace as an Antigonid triumph would be mistaken. Welles's judgement, that Antigonus 'utilised an unfavourable peace as a splendid stroke of propaganda', is surely correct. The treaty of 311 BC represents a compromise for all parties concerned, reflecting the indecisive nature of the war of 315 BC to 311 BC. Though Cassander had to cede any claim to Asian territory, he was granted the title – *Strategos* of Europe – which he clearly felt to be his inheritance, carrying with it the guardianship of Alexander IV. In theory his office was limited, ending with the young king's majority; whether this really posed a serious problem for Cassander and whether a similar limitation was imposed on the other participants in the peace have been much debated. Whatever its juridical implications, in practice this clause spelled death for Alexander's son. His assassination at Cassander's behest in 310 BC brought sighs of relief all round; the last serious threat to the Diadochs' rule of their individual kingdoms had been removed. Given this reaction, it may not be too cynical to see in this clause a tacit agreement as to the elimination of the young king. Antigonus, then, was forced to cede the title of *epimeletes* which he had claimed at Tyre. This, and his acknowledgement of Ptolemy and Lysimachus as masters of Egypt and Thrace respectively, represents a defeat.[35]

THE POSITION OF LYSIMACHUS AFTER THE PEACE

'From now on, each of those who ruled over peoples or cities cherished hopes of kingly power, and held their territory as a spear-won kingdom' (Diodorus XIX.105.4).

Lysimachus' success in the recent war had won him formal recognition as ruler of Thrace, but the allies' action from 315 BC to 311 BC had not put sufficient pressure on Antigonus to compel his surrender of the Asian satrapies demanded in 315 BC. Hellespontine Phrygia remained in Antigonus' hands and Lysimachus' aspirations towards rule in Asia were still unsatisfied.

Another source of trouble, in Saitta's eyes, was the clause in the treaty of 311 BC which granted Greek autonomy; while favouring the Antigonids, whose very promise of liberty would bring them support from the cities of Greece and Asia, it represented a potential menace for Lysimachus whose policy for securing his satrapy directly opposed that of the Antigonids. Saitta concludes: 'le condizioni di Lisimaco nel 311 erano disastrose'. How valid is this view? First, the theory that Lysimachus and the Antigonids were poles apart in their methods of governing the Greek cities is doubtful and will be challenged in a later chapter. Second, such an assessment takes the letter of the treaty of 311 BC far more seriously than any of its participants seemed to do! Lysimachus was not the only ruler who barely paid lip-service to its terms. As will be seen, the autonomy clause represented, above all, a means of winning Greek support for any Diadoch who could afford to employ it, as well as a useful pretext for war against an opponent. None of the Successors, Antigonus included, actually intended to give up any real control of the Greek cities in his territory.[36] Lysimachus was neither more culpable than any of his colleagues in his disregard of the autonomy clause, nor more seriously threatened by it.

FROM 311 BC TO 302 BC

Though Lysimachus' first major entry into the arena of the Diadoch wars had proved a personal success, likely to enhance his standing among his contemporaries, the years following the peace seem to see him retreating once more into the wings. Barely a year after the signing of the treaty, Ptolemy adopted an aggressive stance towards Antigonus, using the latter's own autonomy clause against him in the 'liberation' of Miletus, Cos and perhaps Iasus. His invitation to his former allies to renew co-operative action against Antigonus, however, fell on deaf ears. The refusal of Cassander and Lysimachus to take up arms again has been ascribed to that division of interest between the coalition members in Europe and Asia which had informed the negotiations of 311 BC. Satisfied with the confirmation of their rule in Macedon and Thrace, they had no interest in co-operative action when their own interests were not directly threatened or involved. In Lysimachus' case, a relatively limited involvement in the wars in Greece and Asia in this period has been seen as a withdrawal from international affairs after 'the unhappy experience' of the peace of 311 BC, in order to concentrate on 'internal problems'.[37]

Certainly it is plausible that Cassander's disastrous foray into Asia had decided him for the present to concentrate his energies on Greece and Macedon, where recent developments had raised the prospect of unrest. At home, there might be a hostile reaction to Cassander when news got out of Alexander IV's disappearance; in Greece, the autonomy clause was likely to prompt revolt against the pro-Antipatrid oligarchs who governed many of the cities.[38] Whether Lysimachus had likewise turned his back on Asia is less certain. The significance of his actions in the years immediately following the peace, actions which may explain his refusal to co-operate with Ptolemy in 310 BC, is not purely 'internal'. Rather they constitute a response to the recent threat posed by Antigonus' planned invasion of Thrace.

In 311 BC Lysimachus may have lifted the siege at Callatis, paying lip-service to the autonomy clause; its resumption, the following year, can be seen as punishment for the city's leading role in a revolt which Antigonus had done his best to foment. The year 309 BC saw the foundation of Lysimacheia on the site of ancient Cardia, a position commanding the Straits. This expresses Lysimachus' determination to prevent a repetition of the crisis posed by Antigonus' invasion of Thrace in 313 BC. Nor was the site determined only by considerations of defence; Lysimacheia's prime position as a base for carrying an offensive into Asia is obvious.[39]

In the context of long-term strategic planning, Lysimacheia's foundation date is important. Within the limits of the evidence, it seems to have preceded Antigoneia in the Troad, a conclusion drawn reluctantly by Tscherikower, as damaging to his concept of Lysimachus as a relatively conservative and retiring figure in contrast to the energetic and ambitious Antigonus. He therefore suggested that Antigonus' other three Phrygian foundations, of uncertain date, may have preceded Lysimacheia. To base historical judgement on assessments of 'personality' in this way is surely hazardous, particularly in this case where the evidence is so unbalanced. There is, moreover, no lack of evidence which reflects Lysimachus' ability to act aggressively and decisively when necessary.[40]

Lysimacheia's site, then, supports the view that its founder had not abandoned the vision of rule in Asia which he had cherished in 315 BC. If this is so, how does one explain his limited participation in the Diadoch wars from 308 BC to 302 BC? The answer may lie partly in his limited resources which would make a solo offensive against Antigonus highly risky,[41] combined with the fact that former allies at this time were active in areas where Lysimachus' involvement was unlikely to bring him profit. Moreover, by the time the construction of Lysimacheia was well under way, the 'coalition' of 315 BC could no longer be counted on. The division of interest between its members in Europe and Asia, already manifest in 311 BC, now took the form of open hostilities between two of them.

In 309 BC, Ptolemy, after turning the autonomy slogan against Antigonus in Asia Minor, now thought it might be profitably deployed in Greece against Cassander. Lysimachus' policy in this period seems to have been one of narrow self-interest. This should not be surprising; Cassander had done the same in 313 BC and the historical narrative of the Successor period suggests that such a stance was the rule rather than the exception. The assumption that friendship between Cassander and Lysimachus expressed itself in constant co-operation has already been mentioned. Evidence which suggests otherwise is often dismissed as improbable and elaborate hypotheses are constructed to explain any failure of Lysimachus to show himself at Cassander's side. Diodorus himself, however, makes it clear that joint action was expected only in the greatest crises (*kata tous megistous phobous*).[42]

In 308 BC, certainly, Cassander had little need of help. Two years before, Antigonus' ambitious nephew Polemaeus, leaving his satrapy of Hellespontine Phrygia in the hands of a *philos*, Phoenix, with orders not to obey Antigonus, had defected to Cassander in Greece. In 309 BC Cassander successfully defused the threat posed by Heracles, Alexander's bastard son, whom Polyperchon was championing as rightful king of Macedon. Heracles was eliminated in return for Polyperchon's promotion to *Strategos* of the Peloponnese; in one stroke, Macedon was secured and a potential foe in mainland Greece became an effective instrument. Ptolemy's volte-face and his initial success in Greece – in particular his acquisition of the key cities of Sicyon and Corinth – might have posed a major threat to Cassander; finally, however, Ptolemy's attempt to revive the League of Corinth under his own hegemony failed; in 308 BC he made peace with the ruler of Macedon.[43]

It was not until summer 307 BC that Cassander suffered a major blow. If Plutarch's account is correct, the deal done with Ptolemy, ironically, contributed indirectly to Cassander's loss of Athens, the 'gangway to Greece', which he had held since 317 BC. A fleet sighted off the Attic coast, believed to be Ptolemy's, sailed into the Piraeus unopposed; the discovery that the admiral was Demetrius, implementing stage one of a major 'Greek liberation' programme, came too late. Demetrius of Phalerum, Cassander's governor since 317 BC, departed for Thebes, 'the ancestral constitution' was restored and the Athenians hailed the Antigonids as kings and saviour-gods.[44]

What was Lysimachus' stance at this juncture? He had shown himself unwilling to take action against Antigonus in 310 BC, nor is there any evidence for his co-operation with Ptolemy in Asia Minor or Cassander in Greece. More curiously, there is no sign that he took steps to exploit a golden opportunity, Polemaeus' revolt and Antigonus' consequent loss of Hellespontine Phrygia. Perhaps the timing was unfortunate; Polemaeus' defection came at a time when Lysimachus' priority was probably the securing of the Pontic cities and the construction of his capital. Shortly afterwards, Antigonus sent his son Philip to deal with Phoenix; though no more is heard of these operations, Phoenix' position as commander at Sardis in 302 BC suggests that he capitulated, and was welcomed back into the Antigonid camp.[45]

It has even been suggested that Lysimachus chose to preserve positive relations with Antigonus at the expense of his friendship with Cassander. The evidence is an Athenian inventory traditionally dated to 307–6 BC which includes among the objects listed a crown awarded to [Ly]simachus, generally identified with the ruler of Thrace. Recently, however, Burstein has argued plausibly that 307–6 BC indicates only the 'general period' to which the text belongs, rather than covering each and every item listed, with Lysimachus' crown awarded in the period after 301 BC, probably in 299–8 BC.[46]

One major obstacle to acceptance of a date after 305–4 BC for Lysimachus' crown might seem to be the omission of the title *Basileus*, unthinkable, one might suppose, in a text intended for public display, inscribed in a year which saw him bestow generous benefactions on Athens and when the influence of his *philos* Philippides was at its height; Burstein's suggested parallel – the Bosporan king Spartocus in the same text – is not wholly convincing; his status, as ruler of a wealthy but semi-barbarian kingdom whose dynasts performed benefactions as a means of securing Hellenic approval, is hardly equivalent to that of Lysimachus, whose kingdom in 299–8 BC comprised Thrace and most of Anatolia. There is, however, another inventory, dated firmly to 306–5 BC which refers to money brought by Xenocles of Sphettus 'from Antigonus'; though there is a later reference in the text to the Antigonids as *Basileis*, the title is not at this point appended to his name, despite the text's publication soon after Antigonus' assumption of the royal title and in the very city which apparently was first to hail him king. One can only assume that the compilers of this sort of text, at least, were less concerned for correct protocol than modern commentators would like to believe. This is perhaps particularly true of the early years of the Successor period before the Hellenistic monarchies had become firmly established.[47]

On balance, it seems best to assume that relations between Lysimachus and Cassander remained positive in this period; this premise gains support from the fact that as enemy pressure mounted against Macedon in 303 BC, Demetrius focused his diplomacy in the areas to the west of Cassander's realm. This may well reflect the increased difficulty of an attack from the Hellespont, via Thrace, posed by the new city of Lysimacheia. Certainly the city's defensibility and its importance as a key to the whole of Thrace is stressed at the time of its rebuilding in 196 BC by Antiochus III. Whether continued friendship with Cassander must necessarily imply Lysimachus' active involvement in all his affairs is, however, less certain. Simpson's comment on the alliance of Ptolemy and Seleucus in 311 BC, 'that each should act primarily for himself but with regard to the other man's position',[48] might pertinently be applied to Lysimachus and Cassander in the last decade of the fourth century BC. It is probable that their connection both with each other and with the other members of the coalition was rather looser than is often supposed.

Certainly the course of events in the next couple of years supports the belief that the opposition to Antigonus was far from united. After their unexpected success at Athens in the summer of 307 BC, the Antigonids turned their attention to Ptolemy, who had shown himself dangerously ambitious in recent years. Apart from his attempts to exploit Antigonus' own autonomy slogan to win support in Asia Minor and Greece, he had come close to carrying off a royal prize coveted by all the Diadochs. His plans for marriage to Cleopatra, daughter of Philip and sister of Alexander, were only nipped in the bud by assassination of the bride at Sardis, in 308 BC, on Antigonus' orders.[49] In spring 306 BC the struggle for naval supremacy, a major feature of the first coalition war, was at last resolved with Demetrius' dazzling victory over Ptolemy at Salamis. Ptolemy's retreat to Egypt gave the Antigonids control of Cyprus, a major source of Lagid naval strength. Celebrating victory with the assumption of the kingly title, an act which expressed unequivocally a claim to the succession of Alexander, the Antigonids lost no time in taking action to realise that claim. In late autumn 306 BC they launched a full-scale expedition against Egypt which aimed to crush Ptolemy once and for all.[50]

It is probable that it was only at this point that the coalition members, rejecting Antigonus' claim to Alexander's empire and seeing Ptolemy's projected destruction as foreshadowing their own, decided on concerted action. Clearly the coalition was again in force, in some sense, by spring 305 BC; after Antigonus had failed to breach Egypt's defences and abandoned the campaign, Ptolemy wrote to Seleucus, Lysimachus and Cassander telling them of his success. There is, however, no suggestion that they had sent Ptolemy any military aid. This may reflect a genuine unreadiness and disunity at the time of Antigonus' invasion in autumn 306 BC; the desire to expend military resources only in a field where co-operative action could neatly be combined with pursuit of personal goals may, however, be an underlying factor. Cassander's actions in the following year and Ptolemy's recovery of Coele-Syria in the campaign preceding Ipsus certainly fall into this category.[51]

In the summer of 305 BC, Antigonus renewed his attack on Ptolemy with the siege of Rhodes. Ostensibly neutral but effectively pro-Lagid, the island, a vital link in the trade route between Egypt and Greece, had resisted Antigonus' offers of alliance. The revival of an active coalition is reflected in Rhodes' dispatch of embassies not only to Ptolemy, but also to Lysimachus and Cassander, asking for help. Ptolemy sent substantial military aid as well as money and supplies. Cassander and Lysimachus contented themselves with sending grain. Nevertheless their contribution had its effect, nor was it unrecognised. The cost of the Rhodian siege to the Antigonids, in terms of time and resources, was high; Demetrius' persistence with it is generally regarded as a major mistake. The Rhodians acknowledged the allies' contribution to their city's safety with cult worship for Ptolemy and statues of Cassander and Lysimachus in the *agora*. In the summer of 304 BC, the Antigonids abandoned the siege and made terms; a major factor in inspiring this decision was Cassander's success in Greece in the early phases of what is sometimes called the Four Years War.[52]

The period which saw Antigonus' opponents deal him this double blow also witnessed their own assumption of the title *Basileus*. As regards Lysimachus' policy, this action has been thought to mark a turning point; as *Basileus*, he moves from a stance of withdrawal to active participation in the Diadoch wars. A major obstacle to this idea of a dramatic change of role, however, is Lysimachus' apparent failure to take part in Cassander's Four Years War against Demetrius' troops in Greece. Though Saitta wishes to explain this in terms of an early Danubian campaign against the Getae, there is no secure evidence to support the historicity of the operations he envisages. Such a hypothesis seems over-elaborate and unnecessary.[53]

Instead, the course of events from summer 304 BC to the launch of the Asian campaign in 302 BC suggests that relations between the Diadochs were governed by the same principles in force between 310 BC and 306 BC. Lysimachus could not expect to profit sufficiently from the expenditure of his resources in Greece to justify his participation in the Four Years War. Though the terms of his alliance with Cassander may have obliged Lysimachus to send aid in an emergency, the early stages of the war in Greece saw Cassander in little need of help. Though his first assault on Athens in 306 BC was repulsed by the

Strategos Olympiodorus with Aetolian help, Cassander's ally Ptolemy held the key positions of Sicyon and Corinth and had evidently handed over the latter by 303 BC. Cassander made an alliance with the Boeotians; with their help a second assault on Athens very nearly succeeded; the besieged city was only saved by Demetrius' sudden arrival. Polyperchon also enjoyed conspicuous success, on Cassander's behalf, in the Peloponnese.[54]

In 303 BC, however, events took a turn for the worse, both in mainland Greece and in regions where enemy influence could pose a serious threat to Macedon itself. Demetrius won Sicyon and Corinth, and Cassander's influence in the area of the Isthmus was virtually wiped out. In Epirus, on Macedonia's north-west border, the young king Pyrrhus, hostile to Cassander, made an alliance with Demetrius. The deal was sealed with the Besieger's marriage to Pyrrhus' sister Deidameia. The threat from the west increased when the Spartan general Cleonymus, then master of Corcyra, rejected Cassander's offer of alliance; that he also refused to join forces with the enemy was presumably some comfort.[55] Diodorus explicitly states that Demetrius saw the elimination of Cassander's generals in Greece as a prelude to attacking Macedon itself. Plans for the instrument which would effect this must have already been under way and well publicised in 303 BC; the actual revival of Philip's II's league of Greek states, under Antigonid hegemony, recorded in an inscription from Epidaurus, has been dated to the spring of 302 BC. Before this, however, the 'alarm' aroused in Cassander 'by the increasing power of the Greeks' drove him to send envoys to Antigonus, suing for peace. Only the uncompromising nature of the reply, a demand for Cassander's unconditional surrender, led to the re-formation of the coalition which Justin describes.[56]

Saitta, with his hypothesis of a Danubian campaign which kept Lysimachus out of the action until spring 302 BC, saw Cassander's decision to seek peace with Antigonus as the consequence of Lysimachus' inability to bring him aid. Quite apart from the uncertain historicity of this Danubian campaign, such a judgement relies too heavily on the idea of Lysimachus and Cassander as a team who invariably co-operated regardless of their individual interests. Cassander had exploited the opportunity provided by Demetrius' stubbornness over the Rhodian siege to recover the territory in mainland Greece which he regarded as his dynastic inheritance. Presumably he hoped to gain sufficient ground there to be able to maintain a strong position on Demetrius' return, and the early stages of the campaign seemed to justify his decision. Nor is it likely that he would wish to share the profits. Thus, while the war was going well, he did not need or want help from Lysimachus, who in turn had no strong incentive to intervene in an area which his neighbour clearly regarded as his own preserve. In seeking peace with Antigonus as opposed to immediate action in tandem with Lysimachus, Cassander may simply have thought it preferable to save Macedon, even at the cost of his recent gains in mainland Greece, than to expend further resources in a campaign in which success was far from certain. The organisation of the expedition of 302 BC certainly reinforces the view that Cassander, whose prime concern was Macedon and Greece, wished, if possible, to avoid campaigning personally in Asia. In asking for terms in 303 BC perhaps he hoped that Antigonus, learning from his mistakes in 313 BC, would be ready to make peace on the basis of the status quo. Instead, Antigonus' exorbitant demands recreated the situation of 315 BC and 306 BC; Hieronymus, for one, saw this as a grave error.[57]

The period from 311 BC to 302 BC, then, is one in which Lysimachus seems initially to have concentrated on strengthening his position in Thrace, achieving Callatis' submission and the construction of Lysimacheia. The location of this capital suggests that his ambitions towards rule in Asia were undiminished; his failure to take action towards this end should probably be connected with the danger of facing Antigonus' superior forces without support from his fellow Diadochs. Since potential allies, like Cassander or Ptolemy, had their eyes set on other targets, notably mainland Greece, Lysimachus seemingly preferred to bide his time, conserving his resources, rather than expending effort in areas of the empire which were already 'spoken for'. While Cassander held his own in Greece, there was little incentive for Lysimachus to get involved; Demetrius' successes there in 303 BC and Antigonus' avowed intention to wipe Cassander off history's page gave Lysimachus his long-awaited opportunity. In spring 302 BC, the coalition of 315 BC re-formed to launch an offensive into Asia.

THE CAMPAIGN OF 302 BC

Twenty years after his appointment as satrap of Thrace, the chance had come for Lysimachus to take a leading role. While it is undeniable that the threat of Cassander's elimination by Antigonus brought the danger very close to home, it would be wrong to see Lysimachus' stance now as primarily defensive. While self-interest may have determined his staying aloof from Cassander's earlier operations in Greece, the present crisis offered a powerful incentive for action; Bengtson rightly stresses Lysimachus' determination to extend his kingdom at Antigonus' expense, though his comment that 'Lysimachus had nothing to fear from Antigonus' rather overstates the case.[58]

Diodorus makes it clear that it was with Lysimachus that Cassander initially conferred, before envoys were dispatched to Ptolemy and Seleucus. If Macedon and Thrace were lost, then Egypt or Syria would be the next target for an Antigonid attack; accordingly they agreed with enthusiasm to re-form the coalition.[59] Subsequent events suggest that Ptolemy, at least, hoped to use the campaign primarily to settle some old scores.

The coalition strategy aimed to put sufficient pressure on Antigonus in Asia to force Demetrius out of Greece. Command of the army which would cross the Hellespont fell to Lysimachus. Though Wehrli sees this plan very much as Cassander's brainchild, the major responsibility which it placed on Lysimachus, particularly in the early stages, makes it likely that he also played some part in its formulation. An offensive into Asia Minor appealed to the self-interest of both kings; its success would give Cassander a much-needed breathing space in Greece and remove from Macedon the pressure posed by the revived League of Corinth. In return, Cassander was prepared to grant to Lysimachus the troops whose lack may have deterred him from such an offensive before. For the king of Thrace, the march to Asia in 302 BC carried with it a chance to win the territory there which he had claimed in 315 BC and been denied in 311 BC.[60]

Cassander's readiness to cede command of the Asian army to his neighbour may also have been determined by military considerations. Lysimachus had distinguished himself against heavy odds in 313 BC to 312 BC; it is probable too that he had superior knowledge of campaigning in Asia, gained on the march with Alexander. Cassander himself had not accompanied Alexander and his previous foray into Caria had been conducted by subordinates. Interestingly, it was one of these, Prepelaus, a distinguished diplomat and soldier, who was appointed, with the title of *strategos*, to accompany Lysimachus to Asia.[61]

On reaching Asia Minor, Lysimachus sent this lieutenant south with a force of 6,000 infantry and 1,000 horsemen to win over the cities of Aeolis and Ionia; he himself was to deal with those on the Asian coast of the Straits before marching into Hellespontine

Phrygia. By dividing his forces, Lysimachus clearly aimed to enforce his authority on as wide an area of western Asia Minor as possible before the enemy was alerted to his presence. Alexander had employed a similar method of conquest through the dispatch of relatively small forces to different parts of the country in his campaign of 333 BC.[62]

Both commanders initially enjoyed considerable success. Sweeping along the western coast, Prepelaus, though thwarted at Erythrae and Clazomenae, took Adramyttium and wealthy Ephesus, a major Antigonid naval base, and won over Teos and Colophon. An inscription from Ephesus, honouring Archestratus, Demetrius' *strategos* in Clazomenae, for his loyalty and his 'saving of the corn-ships', has been connected with these operations, but it may be better placed in the context of the *koinos polemos* which the Ionian cities fought against Lysimachus after Ipsus. Meanwhile, Lysimachus himself had not been idle, winning over Lampsacus and Parium and taking Sigeum by force.[63]

Nor did the campaign owe its early success to military skills alone. In an age in which stratagem was elevated to an art and Odysseus was perhaps a more popular role model than Achilles, the use of diplomacy to subvert a rival's officers and troops was a common phenomenon. Marching inland, Prepelaus used his persuasive skills to win over Phoenix, Antigonus' commander at Sardis, the Hellenised Lydian city situated in one of the richest areas of Anatolia and renowned for its grain, wine and gold. The reputedly impregnable acropolis, however, remained in the loyal hands of Philip.[64]

Lysimachus, meanwhile, had failed to take Abydus by siege, but the sour taste was perhaps washed away by his success in laying hands on the royal treasury at Synnada, high among the volcanic mountains of upper Phrygia. Its riches fell to Lysimachus with the help of its commander, the ambitious and flexible Docimus. Lysimachus' war fund, a vital ingredient for success in a period in which mercenary service was at its peak, was further swelled by the capture of 'other royal treasuries'. Not only individual commanders, but cities too, were offered positive inducements to desert the Antigonid cause. Lampsacus and Parium, which voluntarily pledged their allegiance to Lysimachus were rewarded with 'freedom'. Sigeum, which resisted, was punished with the imposition of a garrison.[65]

So far, the invaders had enjoyed the advantage of surprise; when Antigonus, alerted to their presence as he celebrated games at his new capital on the Orontes, unlocked his treasury at Cynda to pay the great army which set off in pursuit, their position became far more dangerous. From the outset, the coalition strategy carried considerable risks for its proponents; even with reinforcements from Cassander, Lysimachus' army was no match, numerically, for that of Antigonus. Accordingly, his strategy during the summer and autumn of 302 BC reflects the knowledge that he must, at all costs, avoid a pitched battle at this stage. As Antigonus advanced, reconquering en route the cities of Lycaonia and upper Phrygia, Lysimachus withdrew northwards into Hellespontine Phrygia.[66]

For Lysimachus, survival, let alone victory, depended on the junction of his forces with those of Seleucus and, presumably, Ptolemy. Justin suggests that a location was named in the negotiations preceding the invasion. If the plan went awry, of course, Lysimachus could find himself isolated, facing Antigonus' great army alone. How much of a gamble was he taking?

To answer this question is not easy, since it depends in part on Seleucus' exact whereabouts at the time when the coalition re-formed. After his victory over Antigonus, probably in 308 BC, Seleucus had waged war against the Mauryan dynast, Chandragupta. This ended, after indecisive fighting, in the famous treaty recorded by Strabo; Seleucus ceded all the lands beyond the Indus in exchange for 500 elephants. Though its terms were clearly common knowledge by 302 BC when Demetrius hailed Seleucus as *elephantarchos*, the treaty can be dated only to the period from 305 BC to 303 BC. It is, however, usually assumed that it was from the borders of India that Seleucus had to march in the late spring/early summer of 302 BC. This implies an awesome journey of over 3,000 kilometres, encompassing difficult terrain and involving major problems of supply and accommodation.[67]

An alternative reconstruction, however, has been proposed, which sees Seleucus already back in Babylon by 302 BC. The danger of Lysimachus' position would therefore be greatly diminished. The evidence cited is a Babylonian astronomical text, interpreted by Kugler as evidence for Antigonus' possession of the city in 302 BC, and a fragment of Arrian's *Indika* which describes Ptolemy sending camel-mounted messengers to Seleucus across the 'Arabian isthmus'. Tarn saw the use of such a route as an emergency measure contingent on Antigonus' possession of the Damascus road; accordingly he dated this incident to 302 BC, suggesting that Antigonus sent troops to take Babylon, hoping in this way to force Seleucus to turn back from his march to meet Lysimachus.[68]

This theory has its attractions, not least in solving the problem of how Cassander and Lysimachus communicated with Seleucus in the months before the launch of the Asian offensive. Nevertheless, certain objections can be raised. First, the context and source of the passage of Arrian are quite uncertain. Second, the dispatch of couriers between Egypt and Syria via the Arabian peninsula and then the Syrian desert is not as outlandish as Tarn assumes. Lastly, Kugler's reading of the text to date Antigonus' possession of Babylon to 302 BC is dubious.[69]

From the strategic standpoint, moreover, it makes sense to think that Antigonus' failure to anticipate a coalition reaction to his aggressive treatment of Cassander stemmed in part from his confidence in Seleucus' apparent inaccessibility. Diodorus makes it clear that Lysimachus' presence in Asia came as a complete surprise; even on the eve of Ipsus, Plutarch's account stresses Antigonus' confidence in the disunity and ineffectiveness of 'the young men's alliance'. Similarly both the delay of at least six months before Seleucus' arrival in Cappadocia and Diodorus' explicit statement that he marched 'from the upper satrapies' support the view that the Indian border was his starting point. Finally, Seleucus' army, though described as 'large' was not remotely of a size to challenge that of Antigonus. This suggests some limitation on numbers imposed by problems of supply, combined perhaps with heavy losses en route, both of which are consistent with the long and arduous journey envisaged by Bengtson.[70] If India, then, was Seleucus' starting point, it must be accepted that in placing himself in the vanguard of the coalition attack, Lysimachus, often presented as a rather cautious character, was prepared to run great risks for a major prize.

The late summer and autumn of 302 BC saw Lysimachus in controlled retreat before the forces of Antigonus. His handling of this stage of the campaign does much to reinforce his reputation as an outstanding general; he displays a cool determination combined with the capacity to act boldly and decisively when necessary, exploiting to the full changing conditions of weather and terrain. After consultation with his *philoi*, Lysimachus' plan of action took the form of a series of entrenched camps, where the army dug itself in and faced investment by the enemy. In this way he engaged Antigonus in time-consuming and unprofitable operations, which utilised resources perhaps better employed elsewhere; Antigonus' preoccupation with Lysimachus in western Anatolia has been thought to explain his failure to defend effectively the routes from Iran against Seleucus' advance.[71]

Such a strategy, however, demanded considerable discipline and loyalty from Lysimachus' troops, involving as it did the prospect of short supplies added to the frustration of inaction. Initially the army camped at an unspecified site in Phrygia, but finally the pressure which Antigonus put on Lysimachus' supply lines compelled a forced march of 400 stades to Dorylaeum, whose rich resources offered a breathing space. The outcome of a series of skirmishes here against Antigonus' men reinforced the wisdom of avoiding a pitched battle. By the time famine again threatened, winter, it seems, was fast approaching; under cover of a dark and stormy night the army slipped out of the camp, a manoeuvre which can probably be identified with one of the stratagems recorded by Frontinus; apparently the troops, after filling this section of the trenches with debris, exited by the back door. Heading towards Bithynia, the army took refuge in the Salonian plain near Heracleia Pontica. The city provided the troops with food and their leader with a new wife.[72]

Lysimachus' marriage to Amastris, Craterus' Susa bride and, in 302 BC, widow of the Heracleian tyrant Dionysius, brought him immediate practical advantages. Heracleia gave him possession of a port which would facilitate communications with Thrace, and command of the route which would bring Seleucus from the east. The marriage may also have had some symbolic importance. Union with a Persian princess, niece to the last Achaemenid Darius III, may have served to reinforce Lysimachus' claim to the territory which Alexander, the last Great King, had 'inherited' from the Achaemenids. Though Memnon's assertion of a love-match between the two may be doubted, Lysimachus clearly took great care to show honour to Amastris, installing her, after Ipsus, as his consort at Sardis.[73]

Lysimachus' success in evading Antigonus in the summer and autumn of 302 BC, and the increased likelihood that he would effect the planned meeting with his allies, worked to Cassander's advantage in Greece. As Antigonus gave up the pursuit to make an early withdrawal into winter quarters, he ordered Demetrius to break off his operations in Thessaly, where he had enjoyed some success against Macedon's king. The Besieger made peace with Cassander and embarked for Asia.[74]

Though this development probably accorded with the coalition plan, it constituted a new threat for Lysimachus. The late autumn and early winter of 302 BC, as he waited in Bithynia for the advent of Seleucus, witnessed a series of reverses which might have proved fatal. First, Demetrius proceeded to recover much of the ground lost in western Asia Minor. An inscription from Ephesus, dated to 302 BC, which honours Demetrius and bestows a crown and citizenship upon his officer Apollonides must be connected with Poliorcetes' recapture of the city. Though Demetrius also regained Parium and Lampsacus, the latter, at least, did not give in without a fight; Polyaenus mentions a military defeat at Lampsacus which preceded the defection of Lysimachus' Autariataean troops, an incident generally dated to 302 BC. Presumably Lysimachus had either sent these Thracian mercenaries to defend the city, or had left them to protect Lampsacus when it went over to him earlier in the year. In this case they must have fled to him at Heracleia following their defeat. An inscription from Lampsacus which honours Nossikas of Thasos for his services to Lampsacene prisoners taken in 'the sea-battle' has also been connected with this incident.[75] If correct, it suggests that Lysimachus' favourable treatment had kept a faction in Lampsacus loyal enough to fight for his cause.

Demetrius then advanced to the Propontis, encamping for the winter at Calchedon. This created danger for Lysimachus in another quarter. His communications with Europe were threatened and only his timely possession of Heracleia gave him a lifeline to Thrace, via the Black Sea. The shrewdness of Demetrius' move is reflected in the fate of the reinforcements which Cassander tried to send his ally at this juncture. Only one-third of the 20,000 troops shipped from Odessus, under the command of Cassander's brother Pleistarchus, reached their destination. Some of the rest were shipwrecked in the stormy winter sea, others fell into Demetrius' hands.[76]

This disaster represented a considerable blow to Lysimachus, whose hopes of boosting his limited manpower were dashed still further by subsequent events. Firstly, Ptolemy had shown himself in no hurry to join Lysimachus, instead spending the autumn in the reconquest of Coele-Syria, a project close to his own heart, but not perhaps vital for the coalition victory. While besieging Sidon, he received false news of his allies' defeat and Antigonus' advance on Syria. He made haste to return to Egypt, though not without securing the newly captured cities with garrisons. Seibert thought that the 'false report' was little more than a pretext, with Ptolemy's failure to unite with his allies at Ipsus reflecting a long-considered intention. This does not seem over cynical.[77]

Second, Lysimachus was faced with large-scale desertions among his own troops. Two thousand Autariataean mercenaries, perhaps originally supplied by Cassander, went over to Antigonus. With them went 800 Lycians and Pamphylians; their recent recruitment from areas which had long been held by Antigonus may help to explain their defection. Demetrius' arrival and his recent triumphs may also have played their part. The defection of the Autariatae, however, may have been caused by Lysimachus' own injudicious action; though the identification of this incident with the massacre of Autariatae described by Polyaenus is problematic, it is likely that the two incidents belong to the same campaign. Both emphasise demands for money as the cause for revolt, and Polyaenus' reference to Lampsacus suggests Demetrius' recapture of the city in autumn 302 BC. If the massacre is accepted as historical, it may represent an attempt by Lysimachus to stamp out incipient unrest with stern measures; in this case, the plan misfired badly. Alternatively, as Saitta suggests, the massacre may follow the revolt, representing punishment for attempted defection.[78]

This incident suggests that by now Lysimachus may have been running short of funds, despite Heracleia's wealth; alternatively the rewards of defection may simply have been too attractive to resist. Polyaenus tells us that the Autariatae had suffered the loss of their baggage (*aposkeue*) at Lampsacus. While Lysimachus seemingly would not or could not make good this loss, Antigonus gave them not only the pay 'which *they said* Lysimachus owed them' but a bonus on top. Such defections by mercenary troops are a common feature of the Diadoch period, reflecting the instability created by almost constant warfare in which great prizes rapidly changed hands. The problem afflicts all of the Successors[79] and the incident need not be seen as proof of either poor generalship or excessive avarice on Lysimachus' part.

Lysimachus' position was beginning to look desperate; presumably the crisis was resolved by the onset of winter which brought campaigning to an end and by news of Seleucus' arrival in Cappadocia. His army is thought to have wintered in the plain of Phanaroia; from there he commanded the route across Armenia which would enable him to join Lysimachus in the Boli plain, just south of Heracleia.[80]

THE BATTLE OF IPSUS

At this point, the detailed narrative of Diodorus breaks off and little is known of the movement of either side before their arrival on the plain of Ipsus in central Phrygia. The precise site of the battle, long-disputed, has been plausibly identified with the modern village of Sipsin, just north of the Byzantine fortress of Afyon-Karahisar. With

Ptolemy absent and Lysimachus' army depleted by the recent disasters, the coalition forces could not be confident of a victory based on superior numbers. In infantry, indeed, Antigonus outstripped them comfortably, in terms of both quantity and possibly quality.[81] There is little reason to think that he had cause to be pessimistic about the battle's outcome. Though the sources stress the appearance of various portents in the hours before the battle, these may originate either in Hieronymean defensiveness, or the later propaganda of Antigonus' opponents, wishing to present themselves as the favourites of the gods.[82]

Against this, the kings of Syria and Thrace could set a slight numerical superiority in cavalry and the 'tank division' represented by Seleucus' elephants, which, according to the sources, outnumbered those of the enemy in a ratio of six to one. Though Tarn was sceptical of these large numbers as unprecedented in a Greek army, lack of precedent does not necessarily make something historically impossible; the dubbing of Seleucus as *elephantarchos* does, moreover, suggest, if not 500, an unusually large elephant corps. Whatever their precise numbers, the Seleucid elephants appear to have played a decisive part in a battle which could be described as lost by Demetrius as much as won by his opponents.[83]

With the loss of Diodorus' narrative, the only detailed source for the battle is Plutarch's *Demetrius*. It is probably the biographer's selectiveness rather than extreme Hieronymean understatement that explains the loss of all detail as to Lysimachus' role at Ipsus. Plutarch focuses on the events that decided the Antigonid defeat; Demetrius' over-impulsive pursuit of the routed enemy cavalry under Seleucus' son Antiochus left the flank of the infantry centre, led by his father, exposed to attack. Seleucus responded quickly to this unexpected turn of events, placing the famous elephants in such a way as to block Demetrius' return. He then harassed the enemy infantry, crowding it by an encircling movement of cavalry. Seemingly he aimed at the defection rather than the destruction of the enemy phalanx; since the Successors' armies contained a high proportion of mercenary soldiers, loyalty, beyond a certain point, was misplaced. His calculations proved correct; a large section of the infantry went over to him, the others fled. Antigonus, standing his ground with a few followers, found himself the object of a determined onslaught and fell. Demetrius with 5,000 followers fled to Ephesus, his hopes set on mainland Greece.[84]

The part taken by Lysimachus at Ipsus must remain obscure, but the recognition that without his masterly campaign of the previous year the battle might never have been fought, came with the division of the spoils. With his eye upon territory in Asia as early as 315 BC, Lysimachus had bided his time and conserved his resources until the time was right; with Antigonus dead and Demetrius a landless fugitive, Lysimachus found himself with the greater part of Anatolia added to his possessions in Thrace.

4

AFTER IPSUS: THE EMPIRE EXTENDED

FROM 301 BC TO 294 BC

'After the battle had been decided in this way, the victorious kings proceeded to carve up the realm which Antigonus and Demetrius had ruled like the carcass of some great slaughtered beast' (Plutarch *Demetrius* 30).

Suitably heroic in its imagery, frustratingly short on detail, Plutarch's account of the division of the spoils after Ipsus is characteristic of the shortcomings of the biographies which are now our major narrative source. Other literary and epigraphic evidence, combined with Plutarch's narrative of subsequent events, has, however, permitted a general reconstruction of the division of Antigonus' realm, although some grey areas still remain.[1]

As architects of the Ipsus victory, it was Lysimachus and Seleucus who received the bulk of Antigonus' Asiatic kingdom. Cassander had preferred to concentrate on Greece and Macedon in 302 BC and was presumably content to see Antigonid influence in the Hellenic peninsula wane following the coalition victory. Though his brother Pleistarchus was given a kingdom in Cilicia, subsequent events seem to place him in the role of Lysimachus' protégé rather than Cassander's representative; this arrangement may represent a reward for his part in the campaign of 302 BC, rather than a response to Cassander's demand for Asian territory.[2]

Ptolemy, however, was surely less than happy to be excluded from the spoils, the result of his failure to join his allies on the field. Coele-Syria, which he had made his first priority in the months before Ipsus, was officially granted to Seleucus, whose new realm, according to Plutarch, stretched from the River Indus to the Syrian coast; the border between his kingdom and that of Lysimachus in Asia was probably the River Halys. Appian gives more detail, naming Seleucus' territories as 'all of Syria from the Euphrates to the coast, Mesopotamia, Media, Persis, Parthia, Bactria, Arabia, Tapyria, Sogdia, Arachosia, Hyrcania and the other peoples as far as the Indus'.[3]

Compared to this vast expanse of land, Lysimachus' prize, 'the whole of Asia Minor north of the Taurus mountains', might seem limited. These lands, however, in theory at least, gave Lysimachus control of both sides of the Hellespont, and represented a compact realm, advantageous in terms of communication and administration. If, moreover, he had any thoughts of reuniting the two halves of Alexander's empire, the centring of his kingdom on the Hellespont, a natural link between his territories in Europe and Asia, left him better placed to do so than Antigonus had ever been. In addition, the lands of the central Anatolian plateau and its western coast were rich in those resources which were vital for success, men and money.[4]

The Ipsus victory had in essence given Lysimachus the realm built up by Antigonus between 323 BC and 318 BC; the potential resources of these lands are indicated in Diodorus' account of Antigonus' career. Adding Eumenes' satrapy (Cappadocia, Paphlagonia 'and the adjacent lands') to his original holdings of Greater Phrygia, Pamphylia and Lycia, Antigonus was able, in 319 BC, to support an army of 60,000 infantry and 10,000 cavalry and expected to be able to mobilise still greater forces 'since Asia could provide pay without end for the mercenaries he might muster'.

In terms of manpower, Lycia and Pamphylia were seemingly a fruitful source of mercenary troops. In 318 BC Antigonus conquered Lydia and Hellespontine Phrygia; shortly before his expulsion, Arridhaeus, satrap of the latter, could afford to employ over 10,000 mercenaries in the army which he took against Cyzicus. The rich treasuries of northern Phrygia have already been mentioned.[5]

Asia Minor's proverbial wealth derived largely from its natural resources; the mountainous Anatolian plateau was a rich source of timber and minerals with fertile valleys and plains formed by great rivers like the Hermus and Cayster and their tributaries cutting through it. Strabo describes the wide stretch of rich land round Sardis as 'the best of all plains'; Sardis itself was already famed as a centre for textiles under Achaemenid rule. The legendary wealth of the Lydian king Croesus was founded on the gold mines of Mt Tmolus – by Strabo's day the supply was exhausted, but the city's function as a major mint for the Seleucids and probably Lysimachus too suggests that the mines were still worked in the early Hellenistic period. The

Troad too was rich in precious metals; gold was mined near Abydus
and Lampsacus, copper in the central region and the mountains north
of Pergamum. The Hermus, Cayster and Maeander valleys produced
abundant olives and figs; the Caicus valley was the chief granary for
Lysimachus' Pergamene successors; Lydia was famous for wine;
northern Phrygia and the Troad produced ship timber, pitch, marble
and grapes.[6]

Apart from Sardis, important urban centres in the hinterland
included Celaenae, an Achaemenid royal residence, later used by
Antigonus as the centre for his administration, Synnada and
Docimeium high in the mountains of central Phrygia, an area famous
for its marble, Colossae in the Lycus valley, described as 'populous and
prosperous' in the fifth century BC, and Tralles on the eastern border
of Caria; these last two cities combined excellent defences with
commercial importance.[7]

That Lysimachus encountered little opposition in the Anatolian
hinterland seems probable. With the dissolution of the Antigonid
land army after Ipsus, capitulation would have been the only sensible
course for the garrisons which remained and found themselves
suddenly isolated. Lysimachus' appearance with his bride Amastris at
Sardis, soon after Ipsus, may suggest that affirming control of the
Anatolian hinterland and attending to its administration was one of
the first tasks at hand. Little is known of his dealings with the
indigenous communities there but it is realistic to suppose that like
Alexander and the Achaemenids before him, he levied tribute from
these cities, many of them industrial centres of some importance.[8]

Nothing is known of his relations at this time with the independent
dynasts of the interior, notably Zipoites in Bithynia and Mithridates
in Pontus. Though the former was later to give him considerable
grief, initially, amicable or at least neutral relations are a possibility;
Zipoites had been humiliated by Antigonus, who wrested from him
the coveted cities of Calchedon and Astacus – Diodorus makes it clear
that the alliance he then contracted with Antigonus was not made by
choice. For Zipoites, any change of rule in Asia Minor was likely to be
an improvement. From Lysimachus' point of view, conciliation of the
Bithynian dynast, for the present, may have seemed advisable until
his position in Anatolia was more secure. Mithridates too had started
his dynastic career under the cloud of Antigonus' jealous hostility. In
the immediate aftermath of Ipsus, moreover, it seems unlikely that
much trouble would come to Lysimachus from this quarter, since
Mithridates II had only just acceded to the throne.[9]

In theory, the settlement after Ipsus gave Lysimachus also the Greek cities on Anatolia's western coast. Rightly described as the most valuable possessions of his new territory, control over them was vital for full exploitation of the resources of the interior. Cities like Ephesus, Miletus and Smyrna not only formed the termini of the trade routes from the hinterland but were themselves major industrial centres. Miletus was famous for textiles, Ephesus for perfumes and other luxury goods; the fame of Artemis' sanctuary there also assured a constant stream of visitors from all over the Greek world who swelled the city's coffers. The *poleis* on the Hellespont's Asian side, Lampsacus, Parium, Sigeum and above all Abydus, had strategic as well as commercial importance; without them Lysimachus' control of the Hellespont and its traffic was a chimera and communications between the European and Asian sections of his realm were threatened.[10]

In practice, however, for Lysimachus, the situation echoed that of 323 BC; the settlement on paper was very much better than the actual state of affairs. Many of the cities on Asia's coast would have to be wrested from Demetrius' control. How then did Lysimachus fare in this task?

Evidence for Lysimachus' acquisition of the Greek cities in the first years after Ipsus is extremely sparse. Logically one might suppose that cities which had welcomed him in 302 BC, only to be recaptured by Demetrius, might be among the first to capitulate; these include Lampsacus and Parium on the Hellespont and Teos and Colophon further down the coast in Ionia. Generally, Hellespont cities and those in the Troad might seem a promising target; their proximity to Thrace rendered them more vulnerable than those further south whose citizens could hope for protection from Demetrius' fleet. There is, however, no literary or epigraphic evidence to confirm these hypotheses. There are of course the coins, identified with Lysimachus by his lion symbol or the legend *Basileus Lysimachos*, which have been attributed by Thompson to different mints in Asia Minor and dated with some degree of precision. For example, coins linked to Abydus and Lampsacus have been dated 301–0 BC – 300–299 BC and 299–8 BC – 297–6 BC respectively. Price, however, is critical of the methods by which the Lysimachus coins have been dated and classified and there are several striking peculiarities in Thompson's picture of the Lysimachus coinage as it stands; for example, despite Sardis' status as a major trade and administrative centre, the bronze Lysimachus coins which Thompson links to that mint are found only rarely.[11] By itself, then, the numismatic evidence cannot support any firm conclusions as to the date at which Lysimachus gained control of these cities in Asia Minor.

Travelling down the coast, the first city where there is evidence for a change of control early in the third century BC is Priene, where civil disturbances culminated in Hiero's tyranny, established probably in 300 BC. Though this coup might be seen as part of the same campaign in which Lysimachus tried and failed to take Ephesus, a connection between Lysimachus and Hiero is far from certain.[12] If the installation of Hiero was Lysimachus' work, then his control of Priene was shortlived. After a rule of three years, probably in 297 BC, the tyrant fell; a decree from Priene honours all those who participated in the recovery of freedom and ordains commemorative celebrations. Also connected with Hiero's departure is a decree restoring honours to a certain Evander of Larissa. Demetrius' friendships with others from that city, Medeius and Oxythemis, are well documented and it is not impossible that Evander is yet another Thessalian *philos* of that king.[13]

Lysimachus may have profited, if only indirectly, from a temporary change of regime at Priene, but the greatest Ionian cities eluded his grasp. Fleeing from Ipsus, Demetrius had found refuge in Ephesus and it was from its harbour that he set sail for Greece. Though the Athenians refused to admit him, they returned to him his fleet. Combined with control of Cyprus and the Phoenician cities of Tyre and Sidon, this assured him the thalassocracy which Poseidon's image on his new coinage aimed to impress upon the world. For the great trading cities on Asia Minor's western coast, Demetrius may well have seemed a more dangerous enemy than Lysimachus. Fear of his wrath, combined presumably with other factors – the presence of his garrisons, the self-interest of politicians whose regimes had received Demetrius' support, feelings of gratitude inspired by Antigonid benefactions – contrived to keep many of the cities loyal to the Antigonid cause. The Ephesian *demos* congratulated Demetrius and his officer Apollonides on their recovery of the city in autumn 302 BC, and Lysimachus' subsequent attempt to subvert Diodorus, the garrison commander, was foiled. A likely context for this incident, known only from Polyaenus, is 301 BC, perhaps following Demetrius' departure for Greece.[14]

Demetrius' continued possession of Clazomenae and Erythrae is probable. Both had successfully resisted Lysimachus in 302 BC and a decree from Ephesus praises Archestratus, Demetrius' *strategos* in Clazomenae, for his part in protecting corn-ships headed for Ephesus.

Dittenberger and Hicks connected this with Prepelaus' attack on Ionia in 302 BC, but a date in the first years of the third century BC is equally possible. The necessity for Ephesus to be supplied by sea suggests a context of prolonged assault upon the Ephesian *chora*, a situation which is echoed in the city's debt law *c.* 297 BC. This takes its impetus from serious damage to Ephesian estates as a result of the *koinos polemos* fought on Demetrius' behalf against Lysimachus. By contrast Prepelaus' occupation of Ephesus lasted only a few months at the most.[15] The connection between prolonged resistance at Erythrae and Lysimachus' possible imposition of *phoros* on the city has already been mentioned. It is likely that the Carian coastal cities too, most importantly Miletus, were still in Antigonid hands, since Lysimachus' operations in spring 302 BC do not appear to have extended this far.[16]

Consequently, while his new vicinity to Seleucus and the great increase in power and status which both now enjoyed might spell trouble for the future, Lysimachus' real enemy was still Demetrius and his first priority the recovery of the *poleis* still in Poliorcetes' control. This tug-of-war was to last for fifteen years and, judging from anecdotes which presumably reflect the propaganda of both courts, the competition for power between the two was further fuelled by strong personal antipathy. The bitter enmity between Demetrius and Lysimachus is repeatedly stressed in the narrative of Plutarch. Demetrius casts aspersions on Lysimachus' virility, Lysimachus sneers at his rival's subjection to an ageing courtesan, Demetrius ripostes with a slur upon the chastity of Lysimachus' wife.[17]

DIPLOMACY IN ATHENS: 301 BC – 299 BC

While Lysimachus' early attempts to wrest Asia Minor's great trading cities from Demetrius may have met with limited success, diplomatic action taken in another quarter certainly bore fruit. Plutarch makes it clear that after Ipsus, Demetrius' hopes of a swift revival of influence rested largely on Athens and the other cities of mainland Greece. If they confirmed their loyalty to him, the odds on his recovery of Antigonus' empire in Asia from Seleucus and Lysimachus would greatly improve. Thus, Lysimachus' new diplomatic prominence in Athens and elsewhere in mainland Greece after 301 BC, a departure characterised by some as 'a new philhellene policy',[18] represents first and foremost not a volte-face in ideology, but a pragmatic move in the context of his struggle against Demetrius.

The first signs of this diplomatic offensive are recorded on an

Athenian inscription honouring Lysimachus' friend Philippides of Cephale and reviewing his political career. Exiled from Athens shortly before Ipsus for his violent opposition to Stratocles and the pro-Demetrian faction, he took refuge with Lysimachus. After the Ipsus victory, Philippides took pains to secure burial for the Athenian dead and ransomed Athenian prisoners at his own expense.[19] If this occurred in the immediate aftermath of the battle, then it is likely that the return of the captives singing the praises of Philippides and his patron Lysimachus contributed to a shift of popular feeling at Athens. This, perhaps combined with a natural tendency to dissociate oneself from the defeated, found expression in denial of entry to Demetrius and the fall of Stratocles and his party. Officially, the Athenians were 'neutral', but a decree dated to 299-8 BC, honouring Poseidippus for a successful embassy to Cassander, supported by a fragmentary entry in the Marmor Parium for 301-0 BC, suggests that they made haste to protect themselves against Demetrius' future assault through alliance with Macedon's king. Subsequent events show that those who dominated political life in this period included Cassander's partisans.[20]

Unwillingness to compete directly with Cassander may have stopped Lysimachus from any comparable intervention in Athenian affairs, but his diplomatic initiative was swiftly followed by generous benefactions. The gifts he sent, perhaps on Philippides' advice, were designed to remind the Athenians of the disasters which the last years of Demetrius' patronage had brought. A gift of 10,000 medimnoi of corn, distributed to all citizens, presented a marked contrast to the poor harvests of 302 BC, when hailstones which destroyed the crops were attributed to divine displeasure at the hubris of Demetrius and his Athenian followers. Still more pointedly, a new mast and sail for the *peplos* ship for the Panathenaia of 298 BC, reminded the Athenians of the festival of 302 BC when the figures of the gods embroidered on the sacred *peplos* had included Antigonus and Demetrius; ominously, the mast had broken during the procession.[21]

Demetrius was swift to retaliate. If Philippides' benefactions after Ipsus were timed as suggested above, then Demetrius' naval raids on the Thracian Chersonese, probably made in 300-299 BC, may represent a reprisal for Lysimachus' diplomatic success at Athens as well as meeting the more practical purpose of building up a new land army. Whether Demetrius was in a position at this time to aim for anything so ambitious as to split Lysimachus' kingdom by seizure of the Hellespont area is uncertain.[22]

Lysimachus' new prominence in international diplomacy, added to his increased territory and resources, did not go unnoticed by his colleagues. In the context of Demetrius' raids of 299 BC, Plutarch notes that 'the other kings made no attempt to help Lysimachus; they considered that he was by no means more reasonable than Demetrius, and that because he possessed more power he was more to be feared'.[23] Such an explanation for Lysimachus' isolation at this point may, however, owe something to hindsight on the part of Hieronymus, probably Plutarch's source. Seleucus, by reason of his proximity to Lysimachus, might already have harboured feelings of hostility towards him, but at this moment the Syrian king's priority was Coele-Syria and his real enemy Ptolemy. The latter, as the campaign of 302 BC had shown, was unlikely to stir himself on another's behalf unless there was the prospect of personal profit. Cassander's failure to lend aid might be seen as evidence for a breach with Lysimachus, inspired by competition for Athenian favours, but it is equally possible to see Lysimachus' euergetism there as part of a co-operative effort aiming to rout Demetrius from mainland Greece. Within the limits of the evidence, subsequent events at Athens suggest that after his benefactions had had their desired effect, Lysimachus refrained from intervention in Athenian affairs until after Cassander's death. Seemingly he was not prepared to risk conflict with Macedon's king to promote the interests of his Athenian *philoi*, Philippides and perhaps Demochares. When stasis broke out in 298/7 BC it was Cassander's partisan Lachares who profited, dominating Athenian affairs, first as *prostates tou demou* and then as tyrant, until spring 294 BC, while Lysimachus' supporters remained in exile.[24]

The failure of his former allies to bring aid to Lysimachus in the face of Demetrius' assault in 300–299 BC can be seen simply as a reversion to the Diadochs' practice for the period before Ipsus. Unless the situation was critical and the very survival of one ruler was threatened by an enemy whose victory would make him unduly powerful, self-interest prevailed and co-operation was not expected. Following his rebuff in mainland Greece, the threat posed by Demetrius must have seemed greatly diminished and Lysimachus might be expected to deal with him on his own. His isolation was not, in any case, to be long-lasting; in the following year new alliances were formed as repercussions of the Ipsus settlement began to make themselves felt.

THE ALLIANCES OF 299 BC

Socii ... in semet ipsos arma vertunt et, cum de praeda non convenirent, iterum in duas factiones diducunt (Justin XV.4.22).

Justin's summary of the new line-up of forces two years after Antigonus' death rightly emphasises discontent over division of the spoils as the catalyst. Ptolemy, unnerved by the prospect of imminent conflict with Seleucus over Coele-Syria, offered Lysimachus alliance. Lysimachus' acceptance was presumably prompted in part by the sense of his inability to deal with Demetrius' fleet, which the recent raids on Thrace had emphasised. Common enemies also made the kings of Egypt and Thrace natural allies; Lysimachus was unlikely to welcome any increase in the power of his neighbour Seleucus, while Ptolemy had long contested maritime supremacy with Demetrius.[25]

For Lysimachus, then, the chief boon of this alliance lay in the hope of Ptolemy's naval support for the recovery of the Greek cities still held by Demetrius. Evidence for Ptolemy's activities in Caria and perhaps Cilicia in the period from 299 BC to 297–6 BC suggests that Lysimachus was not disappointed.[26] Moreover, if Ptolemy decided to challenge Demetrius' control of Cyprus or the Phoenician cities, this would effectively divert the Besieger's energies and resources from the Asian coast, leaving its cities vulnerable to Lysimachus' attack. In return, it is just possible that Lysimachus acknowledged, or at least turned a blind eye to, Ptolemy's seizure of certain points on the coast of Lycia and Pamphylia, which may be dated to the same period as his occupation of Coele-Syria in 302 BC.[27]

The deal was sealed by Lysimachus' marriage to Arsinoe, Ptolemy's eldest daughter by Berenice. To secure kinship with the Ptolemies, Lysimachus was obliged to renounce Amastris and with her, direct claim to Heracleia Pontica. Subsequent events show, however, that Lysimachus had no intention of letting this wealthy and strategically important city out of his hands for long. His care, in the interim, to preserve good relations with Amastris aimed to ensure his continuing influence over the city which she now governed during the minority of her sons. Memnon stresses the friendship between the two courts and Amastris' son Clearchus is found at Lysimachus' side on the Getic campaign of 292 BC.[28]

Faced with this combination of the powers to the west and south of his kingdom, Seleucus held out the hand of friendship to the only possible contender, Demetrius. Emboldened by the prospect of Seleucus' support, Demetrius took the opportunity, en route to Syria, to encroach upon Cilicia, Pleistarchus' kingdom. The immediate purpose of his landing seems to have been money; the wealth stored in the royal treasuries there, notably Cyinda, is well attested. Despite past depletions, Demetrius was able to clean the treasury out of its last 1,200T before going on to Rhosus where the pact was confirmed by Seleucus' marriage to the Besieger's daughter Stratonice.[29]

In the longer term, Cilicia represented a rich source of ship timber, mineral resources and a number of important naval bases. Bengtson suggested that Seleucus, threatened by Pleistarchus' control of the Taurus mountain passes, tacitly approved the conquest of Cilicia which Demetrius completed on his return home. Evidence for good relations between Pleistarchus and Lysimachus supports this belief. Seleucus had ignored Pleistarchus' appeals after Demetrius' first landing in Cilicia and it was left to Lysimachus first to attempt action against Demetrius and then to compensate the dispossessed prince. An anecdote in Plutarch concerning Lysimachus' attempt to raise the siege of Soli is usually placed in this context, and Robert has plausibly suggested that Pleistarchus' later appearance as dynast of Heracleia on Latmos in Caria reflects Lysimachus' grant of the city to him.[30] Lysimachus' action on Pleistarchus' behalf has been dismissed as a token expression of good will for Cassander, who was unwilling or unable to risk conflict with Demetrius for his brother's sake. More probably, Lysimachus acted on his own account; neither the existence of a hostile presence beyond the Taurus,[31] requiring extra vigilance in guarding the passes against possible attack, nor the increased resources which Cilicia would give Demetrius would be welcome to him. The Soli incident may represent just one episode in a campaign fought by Ptolemy and Lysimachus, of which the other details are lost; Burstein sees the presence of Lagid troops at Aspendus *c*. 297 BC as signifying operations against Demetrius in Cilicia.[32] In the face of Seleucus' collusion and Cassander's indifference to Pleistarchus' pleas, these operations did not, however, suffice to keep Cilicia out of Antigonid hands.

For Lysimachus, Seleucus' alliance with Demetrius had another disturbing aspect. The two kings launched a propaganda campaign aimed at the Greeks of Asia Minor. A decree from Ephesus honouring Nicagoras of Rhodes, sent by Seleucus and Demetrius to announce their alliance and their continued goodwill to the Greeks, is clearly only one of a series sent to the coastal cities. In the same period, Seleucus' son Antiochus is active in strengthening the links forged by his father with the Milesian sanctuary at Didyma, although the precise political implications of this are uncertain.[33]

Plutarch follows his account of this alliance with a fleeting reference to a peace treaty between Demetrius and Ptolemy, arbitrated by Seleucus, implying previous hostilities between Egypt and Antigonus' son; Corradi's suggestion that Demetrius had gone on to attack Coele-Syria is attractive. Demetrius' incentive for making peace may be connected with recent Ptolemaic activity in Caria; Burstein argues persuasively for Lagid possession of Miletus between c. 299–8 BC and 295–4 BC when Demetrius' stephanephorate signals his renewed control. This reconstruction supports the suggestion made above that Ptolemy lent Lysimachus naval support for the conquest of the coastal cities. If, however, Burstein is correct in supposing that the return of Miletus to Demetrius was one of the conditions for peace in 297–6 BC, then it seems that, not surprisingly, Ptolemy's anxiety over the possible loss of Coele-Syria outweighed his sense of obligation to Lysimachus.[34]

How did this new development affect Lysimachus? Saitta argues that Seleucus and Ptolemy approved Demetrius' return to Greece in the following year as constituting a blow struck against Lysimachus. This is not persuasive. Of the three rulers in Asia, it was Ptolemy who consistently cherished hopes of rule in mainland Greece, whereas Lysimachus' intervention, even as king of Macedon, was seemingly restricted to combating Antigonid pressure. Such a theory also ignores the fact that not only Seleucus and Ptolemy, but Lysimachus too could hope to profit from Demetrius' departure from Asia. At this point, the conquest of the Greek cities on Asia Minor's western coast was surely his first priority. Moreover, Ptolemy's longstanding dispute with Demetrius over Cyprus and Phoenicia makes it unlikely that he would actively co-operate with him against Lysimachus, who at this stage posed far less of a threat to Egypt's vital interests.[35] The peace of 297 BC need not represent a sinister move directed against Lysimachus, rather it is a temporary halt to hostilities, expressing the desire of all participants to maintain the status quo.

In the event, any unease which Lysimachus might have felt at this combination was soon dispelled by the breakdown of Seleucus' alliance with Poliorcetes. Demetrius' success in Cilicia, followed by his move into Coele-Syria, was too conspicuous for Seleucus to ignore. If there had been any agreement that Seleucus was to receive Cilicia, or at least share the spoils, clearly Demetrius reneged upon it. Alternatively, Seleucus' demand for Cilicia may represent a testing of the water; when Demetrius refused the role of compliant puppet,

Seleucus effectively declared war on him with the outrageous request for Tyre and Sidon, rich in trade revenues and central to Demetrius' supremacy at sea. Seeing that Demetrius' ambition was quite undiminished by the chastening experience of Ipsus, the coalition re-formed, this time aiming to wipe out all traces of the Antigonid presence in Asia.[36]

Alarm at the prospect of facing their united forces, combined with news of Cassander's death in May 297 BC, followed shortly by that of his young heir Philip, convinced Demetrius that mainland Greece held better prospects for success. His departure for Athens, probably in the winter of 296–5 BC, left his cities on Asia's western coast newly vulnerable to Lysimachus' assault.[37]

ATHENS, MACEDON AND ASIA: 295 BC – 294 BC

> Just when the whole course of events seemed to be moving in conjunction to increase his power and sovereignty, the news reached him that Lysimachus had seized the cities in Asia which had belonged to him, and that Ptolemy had captured the whole of Cyprus except for the city of Salamis.
>
> (Plutarch *Demetrius* 35)

As this passage suggests, the period of less than two years from winter 296–5 BC, when Demetrius sailed to Greece, to the autumn of 294 BC which saw him proclaimed king of Macedon, is one of major upheaval. At its end, the split between Europe and Asia seems more strongly marked than at any time since Antipater's regency from 322 BC to 319 BC. Paradoxically, Macedon and mainland Greece, once regarded by the Antipatrids as their rightful inheritance, lay in Demetrius' hands, while Asia, Antigonid for more than twenty years, was divided among Poliorcetes' surviving opponents. Ptolemy's capture of Cyprus and Seleucus' conquest of Cilicia, generally dated to this period,[38] also marked a major blow to Antigonid supremacy at sea.

Demetrius' decision to quit Asia and the rift between him and Seleucus left Lysimachus well placed, at last, to realise fully the kingdom officially assigned to him after Ipsus. Plutarch's account suggests that he had substantially succeeded in this by the summer of 294 BC.[39] Since the biographer's focus is on Demetrius, details of the campaign are almost non-existent, though epigraphic and numismatic material serve to fill some of the gaps.

Lysimachus' control over all twelve cities of the Ionian *koinon* is clearly established by 289–8 BC, when Miletus honours its citizen Hippostratus for his services as *strategos* of the Ionians. A second copy of this decree from Smyrna confirms that city's inclusion in the *koinon* by this date, probably under Lysimachus' auspices; though Smyrna issued coinage under its new name, Eurydiceia, this does not really help to fix a firm date for the city's conquest. A new decree for Hippostratus' successor (or predecessor) is the first evidence we have which confirms Lysimachus' possession of Chios. Ephesus' appearance under its new name, Arsinoeia, in the decree for Hippostratus suggests that the city's refoundation was completed or near completion by 289–8 BC; the coinage issued by Arsinoeia runs for eight or nine years, *c.* 289 BC to 281 BC. Lysimachus' acquisition of Lebedus *c.* 294 BC is presupposed by the resettlement of its citizens at Arsinoeia.[40]

Possibly Lysimachus' task of winning the great Ionian cities was facilitated not only by Demetrius' absence but by the high cost of loyalty to him. Financial hardship among the cities is reflected as early as 299–8 BC with Apollo's stephanephorate at Miletus, while the Ephesian debt law of *c.* 297 BC implies widespread damage to the citizens' property. Though Demetrius held Miletus at the beginning of 295–4 BC, it probably passed to Lysimachus soon after. Lysimachus' possession of other cities on the Carian coast, certainly by 287 BC, is suggested by Plutarch's reference to his 'provinces of Lydia and Caria' as targets for Demetrius in that year. The decree for Hippostratus suggests that Lysimachus' conquest of this stretch of the coast may have extended offshore to the island of Samos, though the first clear testimony for his control there is his arbitration between Samos and Priene *c.* 283–2 BC. The belief that Lysimachus ruled Samos as early as 300 BC rests on the uncertain assumption that the tyrant Duris was his protégé.[41]

In many places, Lysimachus' conquest of the Greek cities was followed by major reconstruction, which seems to have occupied his attention to the exclusion of all else. Although it is probable that following Cassander's death and that of Philip, Lysimachus was careful to reaffirm his links with the Antipatrid dynasty by a marriage alliance, there is no sign of further intervention in Macedon until the crisis of the summer of 294 BC.[42] Nor is there anything to suggest an attempt to step into Cassander's shoes as patron of Lachares, whose domination of Athens now began to look increasingly precarious. Opposed by Olympiodorus, whose faction occupied the Piraeus, the one-time champion of the people took the classic step of establishing a tyranny, probably in spring 295 BC. Although his opponents' hopes had been dashed the previous winter by storms which wrecked Demetrius' fleet as it approached Attica, the breathing-space that this gave Lachares was short. Demetrius, meanwhile, had mustered another fleet and gained control of several cities in the Peloponnese. His second assault proved successful and in the spring of 294 BC Athens capitulated. Since the Besieger, supported by the Piraeus faction, concentrated on depriving Athens of supplies, Lachares' one hope of salvation was aid from Demetrius' enemies; the fact that he was reduced to pillaging Athena's treasures to pay his mercenaries suggests that if any was sent, it was too little and came too late. Though two stratagems in Polyaenus suggest a link between Lysimachus and Lachares, this is attested only for a later date; the fact that Lachares' flight from Athens took him to Boeotia, rather than Lysimachus' court,[43] diminishes the likelihood of any such bond at this point.

For Lysimachus, Ptolemy and Seleucus the first priority in these years was to secure possessions long coveted and closer to home than mainland Greece. A Ptolemaic fleet was sent to combat the Athenian blockade, but its inability to face Demetrius' superior numbers must be explained by Ptolemy's concentration on Cyprus, which Plutarch suggests was still in Demetrius' hands. The only suggestion of active intervention by Lysimachus rests on connecting with these events a Delian decree for the king's Spartan friend Demaratus. Though Dittenberger saw this text as Lysimachus' response to Demetrius' activity in the Peloponnese after Athens' fall, the only basis for this dating is that this is the only known possible context for Lysimachean aid to Sparta. The import of the text is actually the establishment of positive relations between Lysimachus and Delos, and while the Delians are careful to flatter Demaratus by emphasising the benefactions of his Spartan forebears, his nationality may have no direct bearing on the inscription's political context.[44]

Despite literary emphasis on the mildness of Demetrius' settlement at Athens, the product of an apologetic source which, surprisingly, has gained ready acceptance in many modern accounts, epigraphic evidence makes it clear that Demetrius established an oligarchy in the city. In addition he held both the Piraeus and the city in a firm grip, with garrisons installed at Munychia and on the Museion hill.[45]

Demetrius' recovery of Athens did not directly threaten Lysimachus, who may have seen it as the necessary price paid for the completion of his own conquests in Asia. Within a few months, however, developments in Macedon, coinciding with pressure exerted upon his possessions on the Black Sea coast by the Getic tribes,[46] found the king of Thrace with a crisis on his hands.

With the death of the young Philip IV, Cassander's widow Thessalonice became regent; her status as daughter of Philip II seems to have made her rule acceptable to the Macedonians. This arrangement obtained for less than three years, during which time it is likely that Thessalonice sought or welcomed the alliance of both Lysimachus and Ptolemy. The elder of her two young sons, Antipater, married Eurydice, daughter of Lysimachus; Alexander took Lysandra, Ptolemy's daughter, as his bride. That both kings saw in this alliance the basis of a future claim upon Macedon is not improbable.[47]

In the spring or summer of 294 BC, perhaps coinciding with Antipater's majority, the fragile equilibrium achieved in Macedon was shattered. Enraged at his mother's proposals to ignore his status as heir and divide the kingdom between her sons, Antipater committed matricide and seized the whole kingdom. His brother Alexander was quick to call for aid from stronger forces; Demetrius, preoccupied with the Spartan campaign which followed his conquest of Athens, was unable to respond immediately and found himself forestalled by his one-time confederate Pyrrhus, now back on the throne of Epirus. Pyrrhus expelled Antipater from Macedon, installing Alexander as king in return for the western lands which Philip II and Cassander had added to the Macedonian kingdom.[48]

In other circumstances, there is no doubt that Lysimachus would eagerly have seized the opportunity afforded by his relationship with Antipater to add Macedon to his Hellespont realm. Quite apart from its resources in terms of men and money, it is likely that for all the Successors, Macedon, the homeland, had a special lure. On this occasion, however, Antipater's pleas fell on deaf ears. Anxious to restore peace in Macedon with the aim of forestalling Demetrius' arrival, Lysimachus contented himself with reconciling Cassander's sons and instructing Antipater to buy Pyrrhus' departure from Macedon at a price of 300T. Within a few years, Lysimachus and Pyrrhus would come to blows over Macedon; in 294 BC, however, Pyrrhus preferred a deal with the king of Thrace which perhaps acknowledged Epirus' ownership of the lands ceded by Alexander,[49] to having Demetrius as his neighbour in Macedon.

Plutarch makes it clear that Lysimachus' reluctance to commit himself to war in Macedonia at this point was not due to limited ambition, but the result of preoccupations elsewhere. The timing of

Antipater's appeal, in summer 294 BC, suggests that initially the completion of his Asian conquests may have precluded intervention in Macedon. Subsequently, pressure from the Getic tribes in north-eastern Thrace, focused perhaps on the West Pontic cities, required preparations for a full-scale campaign. In autumn 294 BC, Antipater was again expelled from Macedon, this time by Demetrius, who had by now wound up his affairs in the Peloponnese; by this time, Lysimachus was either already on the march against Dromichaetes or perhaps conducting a preliminary campaign to reaffirm control of the West Pontic coast.[50] Antipater had at least escaped with his life; his brother Alexander, embarrassed by the arrival of a now unwanted patron, was murdered on Demetrius' orders at Larissa in Thessaly. Poliorcetes' subsequent enthronement by the Macedonians may be explained in part by the desire for a strong and energetic ruler, after four years of internal struggle which had seen Macedon's importance in the Greek-speaking world decline.[51]

For Lysimachus, the importance of securing the northern sector of his realm against barbarian invasion, whether by arms or diplomacy, was well understood and, at this point, clearly took precedence over Macedonian affairs. It is reasonable to suppose that the demands made on his resources by the Getic campaign, in addition to those required to keep his newly conquered possessions in Ionia, precluded military intervention in Macedon for the present. Accordingly, Lysimachus made peace with Demetrius and acknowledged his great enemy as Macedon's king. Clearly this was only a temporary measure; Lysimachus' intention, once the time was right, to contest Demetrius' claim to Macedon is underlined by his welcome of Lysandra, Alexander's widow, to his court. Soon after he tightened the knot that linked his house to Cassander's by her marriage to his eldest son Agathocles.[52]

The threat posed by Demetrius' new proximity to Thrace soon made itself felt. The news in 292–1 BC of Lysimachus' defeat and capture by the Getic chief Dromichaetes sent Demetrius racing to Thrace in an attempt to capture the heart of his enemy's realm.[53] Like his father, twenty years before, he failed, but this time, Lysimachus' salvation rested not on his own military expertise, but on the centre of resistance which had formed against Demetrius in central and western Greece, a movement which, however, Lysimachus' diplomacy may have helped to foster.

CENTRAL GREECE 293 BC – 290 BC

Following his success at Athens and in the Peloponnese, it was logical that Demetrius, now king of Macedon and Thessaly, should take steps to complete his conquest of Greece by securing control of Boeotia, the territory which linked his possessions in the north and south.[54]

Though supporters of the Antigonids from 304 BC to 302 BC, with Thebes perhaps the recipient of lavish Antigonid benefactions in that period, soon after Ipsus the Boeotians were in a position to make some kind of claim to independence. An alliance with the Aetolians, dated by Flacelière to between 300 BC and 298 BC, greatly strengthened their chances. Renowned for a military prowess which had long made them prized as mercenaries, the Aetolians had a history of resistance to Macedonian rule. Recently their resources and prestige had been greatly enhanced by the acquisition of Delphi; apart from its wealth and the political influence conferred by control of its oracle, Delphi also commanded the route from Phocis to Aetolia.[55]

While the powers of central Greece at the end of the fourth century BC may initially have perceived Cassander as a greater threat than Demetrius, the danger that this would throw them into the Besieger's arms seems to have been averted. Cassander's euergetism at Thebes suggests a realisation that diplomacy and benefaction were better weapons than military operations whose effect would merely be alienating. These presumably aimed also to offset the negative impression made by his recapture of Elateia.[56]

Lysimachus too seems to have been active in wooing the Boeotians, with communications perhaps established even before Ipsus. Diogenes Laertius mentions embassies led by Menedemus of Eretria to Lysimachus and Ptolemy. Their precise purpose is unknown, but they may represent a sequel to the philosopher's unsuccessful plea in 304 BC, asking Demetrius to return Oropus (given by the Antigonids to Athens) to the Boeotians. Demetrius' accusation that Menedemus was plotting with Ptolemy against him lends support to the idea of a Boeotian appeal for help to the opponents of Antigonus. Lysimachus' name has also been convincingly restored on the inscription recording contributions to the rebuilding of Thebes; Holleaux cites the parallel of his benefactions at Athens in 299 BC and a similar motive, the sustainment of hostility to Demetrius in mainland Greece.[57]

By itself, such diplomacy might not have been enough to provoke the active hostility to Demetrius which was already apparent by spring 294 BC, when Lachares sought refuge in Boeotia. However,

Demetrius' successive conquests of Attica, the Peloponnese, Macedon and Thessaly posed a very real threat of encirclement to the Boeotians and Aetolians. This fear is surely the key to the determined resistance to him mounted in central Greece from late 294 BC to 291–0 BC.[58]

Finally, Boeotian resistance failed, but the demands made on Demetrius' energy and resources by the war in central Greece were a vital factor in determining Lysimachus' survival. Demetrius' first attack on the Boeotians at the end of 294 BC may have taken them by surprise, but the revolt of the following year saw them reinforced by Cleonymus of Sparta and probably by the Aetolians. Polyaenus suggests that Lachares had taken a leading role in this rising; with Demetrius' victory and Hieronymus of Cardia's installation as governor of Thebes, Lachares fled to Lysimachus. This is not, however, proof of a prior association between them, nor need it imply Lysimachus' instigation of the revolt. Lachares' decision to seek refuge at Lysimacheia may simply have been determined by Lysimachus' well-publicised hatred for Demetrius.[59] The second rising, in 292 BC, in which Pyrrhus actively co-operated with the Aetolians to aid Boeotia, effectively foiled Demetrius' hopes of taking Thrace.[60] If, as seems likely, Lysimachus needed a breathing-space to recover from the damages wrought on his manpower and prestige by the Getic campaign, then Boeotia's stubborn resistance, which kept Demetrius busy until the end of 291–0 BC, provided it.

Nor did Boeotia's submission mark the end of Demetrius' troubles in central Greece; Aetolian hostility continued to express itself forcibly, striking at his possessions and prestige. The Athenian hymn of 291 BC which hails Demetrius as the only true god also appeals for help against the Aetolians who menace Greece like the legendary sphinx. Demetrius' celebration of the Pythia at Athens the following year has been seen as a symbolic prelude to the war launched against the Aetolian usurpers of Delphi, who again received the support of Pyrrhus. According to Plutarch, the latter's prowess prompted the Macedonians to compare him with Alexander and his dramatic victory in Aetolia against Demetrius' general Pantauchus may well have contributed to a growing discontent which finally ensured Demetrius' fall in Macedon in 287 BC. In 289 BC, however, Pyrrhus' invasion of Macedon, the sequel to his victory, proved premature; Demetrius expelled him from Macedonia but decided to make peace with the Epirote rather than continue the war.[61] This suggests that he found these attacks from the west a serious and unwelcome diversion from what was now his major task in hand, the recovery of Asia Minor.

In the winter of 289–8 BC the shipyards of Macedon and mainland Greece were the scene of furious activity as Demetrius gave orders for the construction of a massive fleet. The mints at Pella and Amphipolis worked overtime to issue the coinage required to pay for this and the tens of thousands of soldiers mobilised for a great campaign whereby Demetrius aimed to recover the Asiatic empire of Antigonus.[62]

THE LAST ROUND WITH DEMETRIUS: MACEDON, ATHENS AND ASIA 289 BC – 285 BC

Following his return from the Danube, little is heard of Lysimachus. Though possibly he responded at this time to signs of incipient unrest among the Ionian cities with a new administrative system,[63] apparently he was happy to leave any actual fighting to others. Some scholars date his conquest of Heracleia to 289–8 BC, based on Diodorus' reference to the seventeen-year rule of Clearchus and Oxathres, Amastris' sons by the tyrant Dionysius who died in 306–5 BC. However, Justin and, more importantly, Memnon, place Lysimachus' recovery of Heracleia after his conquest of Macedon. Saitta dismissed this as an error of chronology due to the use of a common and unreliable source, Theopompus, but though the latter may be Memnon's authority for the career of the elder Clearchus, tyrant of Heracleia from c. 364 BC to 352 BC, it is probable that for the downfall of Clearchus, Amastris' son, Memnon drew on Nymphis, contemporary with these events and unlikely to be mistaken on a factual detail such as Lysimachus' status at the time of the takeover. This supports the placing of these events in the year 284 BC.[64]

The threat to Lysimachus posed by Demetrius' preparations for the Asian campaign, however, called for decisive action. Though Plutarch's figures for Demetrius' projected forces are generally seen as exaggerated, Lévêque points out that since the coalition of 302 BC re-formed in consequence, the distortion is probably not excessive. The allied plan, implemented the following spring, aimed to prevent Demetrius completing or launching his Asian armada by a concerted attack on his possessions in Macedon and mainland Greece, thus forcing him to divert his resources onto several fronts.[65]

Pyrrhus, in Plutarch's account, bombarded by letters from Lysimachus, Ptolemy and Seleucus, reneged on his recent peace with the

Besieger to join the enemy. That he neglected to mention this to Demetrius seems certain; the two-pronged attack which he and Lysimachus launched against Macedon seems to have owed its success largely to Demetrius' concentration of his forces on the eastern front. Here he enjoyed some success against Lysimachus, who was defeated near Amphipolis, but meanwhile Pyrrhus, advancing from the west, reached Beroia without encountering serious resistance. Presumably Demetrius' confidence in his 'ally' Pyrrhus led him to neglect Macedon's defence on the western front.[66]

According to Plutarch, the news of Pyrrhus' capture of Beroia proved decisive; Macedonian discontent with Demetrius, perhaps exacerbated more by the financial demands which his planned campaign had made on the people than by the autocratic behaviour which Plutarch stresses, came to a head. By the time Demetrius turned south to deal with Pyrrhus, many of his men had deserted to Lysimachus; those who did accompany him to Beroia defected to Pyrrhus before a battle could be fought. Clearly propaganda played some part in this bloodless victory; Lysimachus was careful to remind the Macedonians of his companionship with Alexander, while Pyrrhus exploited a fancied resemblance to the Conqueror. Epirote propaganda later ascribed this strategy to the advice of Alexander himself, appearing to Pyrrhus in a dream! Attractive terms offered to defectors were another powerful inducement. Demetrius made his escape, while Pyrrhus was proclaimed king of Macedon.[67]

With Demetrius' flight, the two victors found themselves rivals for the throne. The campaign itself had shown that Pyrrhus, like his mentor Ptolemy, had an eye for the main chance. Instead of advancing from Beroia to join Lysimachus, at this point hard pressed, he had halted there to consolidate his possession of western Macedonia; Lévêque's suggestion, that he was not averse to seeing Lysimachus and Demetrius wear each other out, is astute. Faced with Lysimachus' demand for a share of the spoils, however, Pyrrhus was forced to comply. Whether his patron Ptolemy would have been ready, at any time, to risk a breach with Lysimachus for Pyrrhus' sake is unclear; certainly he would not do it now, when his energies were concentrated on mainland Greece, still a strong card in Demetrius' hand. The fiction of amity between the two rulers of a now divided Macedon was sustained for the present.[68]

For Lysimachus, this campaign, probably relatively inexpensive in terms of manpower, certainly economical in terms of time and therefore money, had brought not only the satisfaction of seeing his great enemy deposed, but also the eastern sector of Macedon. This included not only Cassandreia, but also Amphipolis and its gold mines. This city, whose capture had seemingly eluded him in the campaign's early stages, was taken by stratagem after Demetrius' flight. As Polyaenus tells it, the bribe promised to the garrison commander Andragathus in exchange for the city was not forthcoming and Andragathus himself came to a nasty end.[69]

Now ruler of half of Macedonia, Lysimachus lost no time in disposing of a rival claimant, his son-in-law Antipater. Though originally Lysimachus may have seen Antipater as a passport to Macedon, it is significant that during the invasion he laid claim to it in his own right, as Alexander's friend, rather than as patron to Cassander's son. This presumably reflects a swift decline in prestige of the Antipatrid house. Antipater, now an embarrassment rather than an asset, received short shrift when he dared to protest at the loss of his kingdom. Justin places his death, at Lysimachus' hands, immediately after the king's acquisition of eastern Macedonia.[70]

ATHENS AND CENTRAL GREECE 287 BC

The allies' success in Macedon had repercussions elsewhere. Though Ptolemy had sent a fleet to mainland Greece to rebel-rouse at the time when Lysimachus invaded Macedon, it is probably best to see the news of Demetrius' fall there as the catalyst that sparked off revolt in Athens. This climaxed in Olympiodorus' capture of the Museion hill and the expulsion of Demetrius' garrison. Since the city is described as free, democratic and autonomous when Phaedrus of Sphettus ended his year of office as *strategos* of the hoplites, Habicht has convincingly argued that the city of Athens was free by late spring 287 BC.[71]

Demetrius' first response was to besiege the city, but finally he was persuaded to make peace. Though Plutarch stresses the intervention of the philosopher Crates and the threat of Pyrrhus' arrival as the motivating factors, the Athenian decree for Kallias of Sphettus reveals the biographer's account as misleading and guilty of significant omissions. It is Ptolemy, through his agent Sostratus, who negotiates a peace with Demetrius; the Athenians participate essentially as his protégés.[72]

Under the terms of the peace, Demetrius was persuaded to abandon his claim upon the city of Athens; in return he kept the Piraeus, which the Athenians had failed disastrously to capture earlier in the year, with the liberating force massacred. The importance which recovery of the Piraeus assumed, both for Athens and the kings opposed to Demetrius, is reflected in a flurry of diplomatic activity during 286–5 BC. Lysimachus is conspicuous among the benefactors who are thanked for sending corn and money; the decree honouring his *philos* Philippides shows that the specific aim of this euergetism was to maintain the city's independence and to recover the Piraeus and other forts still in Antigonid hands. The recent identification of Lysimachus' friend Bithys with the honorand of the Athenian inscription *IG* II^2 808 suggests that the king may have also supplied Athens with military aid.[73]

The years following Athens' liberation see Lysimachus' partisans at last prominent in the city's affairs. Philippides returned home in 286–5 BC; in 284–3 BC, as *agonothetes*, he inaugurated a new festival of Demeter and Kore, to commemorate the recovery of Eleusis from the Antigonids. Closely involved in this last success was Demochares, another returned exile who quickly assumed a leading position; in 286–5 BC he headed the financial board of administration. His leadership of an embassy to Lysimachus, which bore fruit in the form of gifts totalling 130T, has been thought to suggest a previous association with the king. In this period the Athenians may also have recovered Sunium and Rhamnus, while Elateia, a key point for entry from the north into central Greece, was liberated by another 'friend' of Lysimachus, the Athenian Xanthippus.[74]

The ultimate success of the 'Piraeus recovery scheme' is, however, less certain. As late as 282–1 BC, a decree praising Euthius, *archon* for 283–2 BC, promises further honours in the event that 'the city and the Piraeus are reunited', suggesting a certain confidence at this time that the mercenary garrison could be bought off. Apparently this confidence was misplaced. If, as Gauthier suggests, the continuing faith of the garrison soldiers in the Antigonid cause was an important factor, then possibly the news of the death of Lysimachus, an obdurate foe of the Antigonids, at Corupedium in February 281 BC, may have caused a last-minute change of heart.[75]

Following his account of Demetrius' peace with Athens, Plutarch tells us that the Besieger mobilised his remaining troops and set sail for Asia, aiming to recover from Lysimachus 'the satrapies of Lydia and Caria'. In this light, the peace which Demetrius made, first with Ptolemy and then with Pyrrhus, has sinister implications. Pyrrhus' agreement to a peace that would speed Demetrius on his way to a campaign in Asia at Lysimachus' expense is not surprising. Ptolemy's abandonment of co-operation against Demetrius, even if only temporary, was potentially more disturbing. Though it is probable that Lysimachus had been building up his naval strength, the speed with which Demetrius reached Asia, via the Cyclades, some of which were already in Ptolemaic hands, and the ease with which he recovered the west-coast cities suggests that for Lysimachus loss of Lagid support was a serious blow.[76] For Demetrius, clearly, the chance to isolate Lysimachus was the major factor which inspired his peace with Egypt; his acknowledgement of Ptolemy's possession of the Cyclades has been suggested as a plausible *quid pro quo*. At Miletus Demetrius celebrated his long-delayed marriage to the princess Ptolemais, but this need not mean his formal alliance with Ptolemy. It is her mother Eurydice's relationship with Demetrius' late wife Phila, rather than her marriage to Ptolemy, that Plutarch stresses; since by now Berenice had replaced her at the king's side, the marriage may even represent Eurydice's own initiative.[77]

On the other hand, Shear's suggestion that Lysimachus was protected by his inclusion in a common peace, negotiated at a summit conference in Athens attended by all the kings or their representatives, is unconvincing. The argument that Demetrius aimed, in making peace with Ptolemy and Pyrrhus, to reduce the number of his enemies, enabling him to focus on Lysimachus' possessions in Asia is compelling. Since Lysimachus' participation in a peace treaty is improbable, it is better to see his Perinthian envoy, Artemidorus, honoured by the Athenian *demos* in 286-5 BC, as working in connection with the Piraeus recovery scheme, rather than representing the king in negotiations for a common peace.[78]

DEMETRIUS LEAVES THE FIELD – 286/5 BC

'Demetrius set himself to win over the cities of Ionia. Many joined him of their own accord, while others were compelled to submit' (Plutarch *Demetrius* 47).

Though Plutarch's account of the early stages of Demetrius' campaign is characteristically vague, the traces of his progress that survive in inscriptions and the stratagem handbooks support this picture of a mixed reaction to his arrival. Lysimachus' later imposition of a heavy indemnity on Miletus confirms the city's inclusion among those which welcomed Demetrius with enthusiasm. Ephesus also fell into Demetrius' hands, but the assumption that this was a voluntary defection is undermined by Polyaenus' description of Demetrius' general Ainetus ravaging the city's *chora* as though on enemy territory. Subsequently Ephesus was recaptured by Lysimachus' officer Lycus, apparently by an elaborate stratagem involving the subversion of pirates previously in Demetrius' service.[79] Priene, likewise, found itself the object of Demetrius' attentions; our evidence comes from a series of beautifully inscribed stones from the *anta* of the temple of Athena Polias. The neighbouring Magnesians, who had presumably defected to Demetrius, joined forces with Priene's own indigenous Pedieis to ravage the city's *chora* and kill many of its citizens. Aid came also from an anonymous force of 'soldiers', plausibly identified as Demetrius' troops. Forces sent by Lysimachus under the general So[sthenes], however, successfully repelled the attack; subsequently Priene voted Lysimachus cult honours for his contribution to its safety, while he commended the Prienean *demos* for their loyalty.[80]

Following his conquests on the Ionian coast, Demetrius marched inland to Sardis, where the defection of some of Lysimachus' officers gave him possession of the city. That his operations extended as far north as the Hellespont seems unlikely, and it is probably best to put the capture of Sestos, described by Polyaenus with reference to Lachares' adventures, in another context, perhaps Demetrius' march on the Hellespont in 292–1 BC. Demetrius' success, was, however, shortlived; it is probable that Sardis, like the rebel cities on the coast, was recaptured soon after by Lysimachus' son Agathocles, who had been put in charge of this campaign. This decision to delegate, whatever its later repercussions, proved sound in military terms. The suggestion that Agathocles blocked Demetrius' path to the coast, cutting him off from his greatest asset, his fleet, is plausible.[81] Otherwise, Demetrius' decision to strike inland through Armenia to the upper satrapies, planning to pursue some sort of guerrilla warfare from there, is inexplicable. At the start of his campaign his infantry numbered only 11,000; though defections from Lysimachus may have swelled these forces, a number of troops must also have been left behind to guard the recaptured coastal cities. At any rate, it is clear that numerically he was in no position to risk facing the 'strong force' with Agathocles; the decision to fight on land in the interior must therefore represent necessity rather than choice, something which is supported by his troops' reluctance to follow him. Finally famine, disease and natural disaster, which greatly depleted his forces, forced Demetrius to abandon this plan and turn south, with Agathocles in hot pursuit. On reaching Cilicia he threw himself on Seleucus' mercy.[82]

Initially sympathetic, Seleucus promised support. Though his subsequent volte-face is conveniently ascribed to the influence of his friend Patrocles, this may reflect the apologia of a pro-Seleucid source. More cynically, Seleucus' initial pose of friendliness may be explained as a time-winning device while he mobilised the large army with which he then confronted Demetrius. The latter, thus forced to abandon his conciliatory stance, and to treat Seleucus' land as enemy territory, enjoyed a brief revival of his fortunes, but finally pursued by Seleucus into Cyrrhestica and deserted by his remaining troops, he surrendered.[83]

For Lysimachus, the welcome news of Demetrius' captivity was soured somewhat by the clear hostility of Seleucus, who had refused his offers of help at the time of Demetrius' last stand. Lysimachus' attempt to buy Demetrius' death was angrily rejected. While Demetrius lived, there was the danger that Seleucus might use him as a weapon against Lysimachus in Asia, or even as a pretext for an attack on Macedon. In the event, Seleucus' fear that Demetrius might prove a double-edged sword apparently prevailed, while Poliorcetes himself seems swiftly to have abandoned any hopes of his release. It is therefore plausible that it was the news of Demetrius' capture which told Lysimachus that now was the right time to assert his claim to Pyrrhus' kingdom, This now included Thessaly – Lysimachus himself had persuaded Pyrrhus to break his recent peace with Demetrius and invade this rich territory.[84]

Despite these outward signs of amity, both rulers of Macedon, it seems, took preliminary steps to fortify themselves, diplomatically, for the oncoming conflict. Phoenicides' comedy *The Flute-Players*, produced in 284 BC, mentions a 'secret treaty' recently made between Pyrrhus and Demetrius' son, Antigonus Gonatas. On the other side, Lysimachus' friendship with Pyrrhus' one-time allies, the Aetolians, reflected in inscriptions and the naming of Aetolian cities after Lysimachus and his wife, may pre-date Pyrrhus' expulsion from Macedon.[85] In Egypt, Ptolemy II had just acceded to the throne against a background of dynastic struggle; concerned above all to establish himself securely, he would not risk war with Lysimachus for Pyrrhus' sake. Despite Lysimachus' reception of Ptolemy Ceraunus, Ptolemy II's displaced rival, Egypt reaffirmed her ties with Thrace; Ptolemy II's marriage to Lysimachus' daughter Arsinoe sealed the deal.[86]

Pyrrhus was left isolated. Plutarch's account suggests that he felt himself unable to confront Lysimachus' forces in the field, retreating to Edessa where he holed himself up. Such behaviour by the 'new

Alexander', and in particular his abandonment of Pella without a fight, is not easy to explain; Hammond's recent suggestion that Plutarch's account has omitted a military confrontation which preceded Pyrrhus' retreat to Edessa is attractive. Disappointed in Pyrrhus and perhaps longing for the reuniting of their country under a strong ruler, the Macedonians swiftly succumbed to the propaganda of Lysimachus, Alexander's companion in arms. In the spring of 285 BC, starved of supplies and deserted by his Macedonian followers, Pyrrhus retreated to Epirus. As Pausanias tells it, Lysimachus followed up his victory by invading Epirus and desecrating the royal tombs, but the historicity of this episode is generally doubted.[87]

Rather, 284 BC sees Lysimachus rounding out his kingdom to its fullest extent, with the seizure of Heracleia Pontica and the annexation of Paeonia on Macedon's north-west border. In both cases, stratagem, diplomacy and a timely exploitation of weakness caused by dynastic struggle were the keys to success. Lysimachus' desire to renew a personal control of Heracleia should probably be connected with the threat posed to the city by an aggressive neighbour, Zipoites of Bithynia. Lysimachus' war with the latter had proved his one distinct failure in the first half of the 280s BC. Rather than lose the link between the Black Sea and his possessions in northern Phrygia and the shipbuilding centre which alliance with Heracleia gave him, Lysimachus was prepared to seize the city himself.[88]

The apparently suspicious death of his ex-wife Amastris provided a suitable pretext. Capitalising on his past friendship with her sons Clearchus and Oxathres, Lysimachus' skill at dissembling, accorded grudging admiration by Memnon, gained him entry to Heracleia. He then accused his stepsons of matricide and had them executed. Memnon suggests that Clearchus and Oxathres had not shared the popularity enjoyed by their father Dionysius. Shrewdly, Lysimachus exploited this; his restoration of Heracleian democracy won him a brief period of popularity.[89]

In Paeonia, it is probable that dynastic struggle followed King Audoleon's death in 284 BC. Audoleon's participation in the Athenian 'Piraeus recovery scheme' suggests friendly relations with Lysimachus; this is supported by the fact that his heir Ariston, expelled from Paeonia, turned to the king of Thrace for aid. As Cassander's sons had found in 294 BC, such a course was perilous; Polyaenus suggests that no sooner had the young king been enthroned than the forces which had aided his restoration were turned against him, forcing him to flee. This may, however, be due to the compression which the stratagem format tends to impose, and Merker's suggestion that Ariston was deposed only when he proved insufficiently compliant is attractive.[90]

The addition of Macedon, Thessaly, Heracleia and Paeonia to his possessions in Thrace and Anatolia significantly advanced Lysimachus' position both in terms of resources and prestige. In Athens and elsewhere in mainland Greece he enjoyed an influence secured by diplomacy rather than military aggression. Wisely, he seems to have recognised that overt attempts at conquest would simply make him the enemy in the place of Antigonus Gonatas, whose continued grip on key points such as Corinth, Chalcis and the Piraeus aroused deep hostility.[91]

Whether Lysimachus had inherited from Antigonus, along with his kingdom, a vision of Alexander's empire united under his own rule, must remain an open question. Certainly in 284 BC, he had come closer to achieving this than any of his contemporaries, and his consistent care to promote himself as Alexander's companion and heir may suggest that his ambitions were less limited than is often supposed.[92] Among his former friends, Lysimachus could not avoid the odium that comes with conspicuous success, and his enjoyment of this vast empire was to be shortlived. The dynastic struggle which split his court in two and which gave Seleucus his golden opportunity to reach for a kingdom which fell little short of *ta hola* will be examined in the final chapter. Since, however, it is a commonplace in many modern histories of the Successor period that a major factor contributing to Lysimachus' fall from grace was his harsh government of his subjects, the next chapter will attempt an assessment of this problem.

5

GOVERNOR OF THE GREEKS

'It is neither descent nor legitimacy which gives monarchies to men, but the ability to command an army and to govern a state wisely, as was the case with the Successors of Alexander' (*basileia* – Suda Lexicon).

Lysimachus' possession of this first quality deemed essential for successful kingship has been amply demonstrated in the last three chapters, which examined his rise from satrap of Thrace to ruler of a vast and powerful kingdom. The swiftness of his fall from these dizzy heights, ending in defeat at Seleucus' hands and death on the field at Corupedium in February 281 BC, is commonly ascribed to a failure to fulfil the second requirement for *basileia*.

Lysimachus is often characterised as a 'harsh' ruler, unpopular with his Greek subjects on whom he imposed oppressive taxation. 'Proverbially avaricious', he piled up the revenues thus extorted in the famous treasuries which earned him the title *gazophylax*, and which have been seen as exceptional for the period. Other practices cited to uphold the view that it was his unphilhellene behaviour which brought him down are his foundation of new cities by synoecism, which 'destroyed' existing cities and forced their inhabitants to leave their ancestral homes and shrines; his garrisoning of the *poleis*; his suppression of city coinages; his support of tyrannies and oligarchic governments. Frequently his regime is contrasted with that of the 'liberal' Antigonids which preceded it; they saw the Greeks as 'allies', Lysimachus treated them as 'subjects', incorporating them directly into his kingdom, under the administration of a *strategos*.[1]

Despite past attempts to redress the balance, this view continues to dominate the most recent research, although the evidence is scant and sometimes uncertain. Before examining the material, mostly from Asia Minor, which bears on Lysimachus' relations with the Greek cities within his kingdom, it is worth identifying some of the problems raised by such a task, which are perhaps too often overlooked.[2]

First, to make judgements on Lysimachus' methods of government in isolation from those of his predecessors, and still more importantly his contemporaries, is not constructive. Shipley, for example, cites, somewhat emotively, with reference to synoecism, 'the cruel side-effects of Lysimachus' "progress" ', concluding that 'he was unlikely to endear himself to the Ionians by a wholesale disregard for institutions and traditions.' Undeniably, deep feelings were attached to the ancestral city and its temples, but synoecism can only be cited as symptomatic of unusually harsh government, and decisive, therefore, in effecting Lysimachus' downfall if the practice were unique to him or his innovation. Quite apart from the synoecisms of Alexander and the Carian dynast Mausolus earlier in the fourth century BC, letters from the 'philhellene' Antigonus to the city of Teos propose a similar scheme, affecting cities in the same region which later 'suffered' Lysimachus' synoecisms and plainly no more popular.[3]

Second, the evidence for Lysimachus' dealings with the Greeks, both literary and epigraphic, tends to give information on the status of individual cities at random and unrelated moments in time. To infer from such evidence an empire-wide policy, applied throughout the reign, seems injudicious. The theory of 'oppressive taxation', for instance, rests largely on two inscriptions from Miletus, both of which are open to reinterpretation.[4] Such generalisation satisfies the desire to see a neat administrative system in force in the Diadoch kingdoms, but pays too little heed to the instability of this period and the fierce rivalry among the Successors to attract and maintain Greek support. In such a context, success must rest largely on the ability to be flexible, and to apply the method – be it conciliation or deterrence – most likely to work in the particular circumstances. A city's past history, rivalry of political factions within it, its initial response to the king's approach, its strategic and economic importance, are all factors which might influence its treatment by the monarch.[5]

Thirdly there is 'the snowball effect': the belief that Lysimachus' government was harsh has induced scholars to read signs of oppression into evidence which may be quite neutral. An inscription from Thasos, where the word *eleutherothentos* was restored and interpreted as a sign of liberation from Lysimachus, is a classic example. Pointing out that the formula *demou eleutherothentos* is quite unparalleled, Robert suggested, more plausibly, *Eleu[ther]ionos*, the name of the Ionian month, representing part of the dating formula in the preamble to the decree.[6]

Then there is the Hellenocentric approach of sources which concentrate, when they deal with problems of administration and government at all, almost exclusively on the Greek cities. This has had its own effect on modern historiography which tends to see oppressive taxation of the Greeks as the only possible explanation for Lysimachus' evident wealth and reputation as a financier. Other royal resources are largely ignored; Burstein has rightly emphasised the importance of booty and the acquisition of mines as an explanation for Lysimachus' estimated reserves of at least 20,000T. Similarly, revenues deriving from royal land, in terms of cash-crops, cash payments from concessionaires and taxes paid by the *laoi* who worked it, should not be overlooked. The slight evidence we possess suggests that Lysimachus took steps to maximise such revenues and it may have been in this area, rather than in the more politically sensitive sphere of the Greek cities, that he really cracked the whip.[7]

Finally, the view that the cities' mass defection to Seleucus in 282–1 BC expresses simply a reaction against long-term oppression is questionable. This problem will be discussed in chapter 7. Certainly before the dynastic crisis of 283–2 BC, it has been seen that the cities were divided in response to successive 'liberators'; some welcomed Lysimachus in 302 BC and were duly rewarded; some defected to Demetrius in 286–5 BC, but others remained loyal.

Generally, then, the foundations on which the common view of Lysimachus as oppressor *par excellence* rest are not entirely firm. Passing from such broad questions of method and approach, it is time to set Lysimachus' government of the Greeks in Asia in its historical context. A brief look at the cities' relations with the rulers preceding him, the Lydian and Achaemenid kings, Alexander and the Antigonids, shows 'freedom and autonomy' to be a major theme; indeed Lysimachus' tug-of-war with the Antigonids for possession of the Greek cities has been thought to embody a struggle for the survival of the principle of Greek autonomy itself. What then did 'freedom and autonomy' actually mean to the Diadochs' Greek subjects in Asia?

FREEDOM AND AUTONOMY

As Wehrli points out, the slogan's form and meaning change several times from its first appearance during the Persian Wars. Prominent both in the literary sources and decrees issued by cities and kings, 'freedom and autonomy' is presented as the ideal to which the Greek cities of the Hellenistic kingdoms aspired. By modern commentators it is commonly defined as embracing the broadest powers of action, in terms of internal government and foreign policy. Simpson defines 'autonomy' as 'the absolute freedom and independence of a city both in its internal government and in its relations with outside powers'; Martin, more cautiously, discussing 'sovereignty' in relation to coinage, sees it as 'the ability to exercise the power to establish and to fulfil some goals in the political, economic, social and other areas of government'.[8]

The ancient evidence, however, suggests that such definitions represent an ideal, rather than the real experience of the Greeks in Asia in the Successor period, for whom 'freedom and autonomy' essentially designated the grant of certain privileges. Jones's definition of the term as 'the enjoyment of one's own ancestral constitution, the absence of a garrison and immunity from tribute' is more realistic than those quoted above. Indeed, in practice, even those who define 'freedom and autonomy' in ideal terms accept this more limited conception in looking for the presence or absence of such conditions as a means of assessing the character of a monarch's rule.[9]

For the citizens and statesmen of the early Hellenistic *poleis*, this interpretation of 'freedom and autonomy' may have represented the debasement of an earlier ideal. Nevertheless the privileges thus conferred were clearly highly prized. This is borne out by the cities' practice of selectively publishing decisions which favoured them, in order to secure their continuation under future kings; the recently identified 'archive' at Priene is a classic example. The kings could, however, revoke or reduce these privileges if political expediency so demanded; by the late third century BC at least, there is no apparent sense of contradiction in naming as 'autonomous' a city which paid tribute or dated its decrees by the regnal year.[10]

Such anomalies raise further questions. Did the Greeks perhaps value a grant of autonomy primarily as a mark of respect, a formal recognition of what was due to their *poleis*? Saitta, for example, admits that conditions for the cities under Lysimachus differed little from those during Antigonid rule; where Lysimachus sinned was in his disregard for Greek sensibilities, an unwillingness to mask the reality of his rule with the formal assurances of 'freedom' granted by his 'philhellene' predecessors. This, however, assumes an extraordinary naïvety on the part of the Greeks, if the repetition of empty assurances of autonomy sufficed to blind them to the measures undermining it. From a twentieth-century standpoint such an explanation is not implausible; governmental exploitation of the population's short memory, political indifference or essential optimism, a phenomenon which might be called, in Orwellian terms, 'the chocolate ration syndrome', is a familiar occurrence. It is less certain whether such an explanation is applicable to the fourth-century BC Greek *polis*, with its relatively small number of citizens and a tradition of widespread active involvement in public life which is alien to the modern nation-state. A look at the history of the Greek cities in Asia may suggest rather that their statesmen had grown used to accommodating themselves to a succession of rulers whose superior power must be acknowledged and whose very real benefactions should be received with gratitude, while accepting that the ideal of 'Greek autonomy' in its fullest sense could no longer be achieved.[11]

THE GREEK CITIES BEFORE ALEXANDER

For the *poleis* on Asia Minor's western coast, 'liberation' was a familiar concept, touted by a bewildering variety of 'protectors' during the fifth and fourth centuries BC. Promised in the context of imperial expansion, 'Greek freedom' was almost invariably abandoned or betrayed by 'the liberators' in exchange for some more tangible prize. For instance, 392 BC saw Sparta hand over the Greeks of Asia to the Great King; in return, with the King's Peace of 386 BC, he recognised mainland Greece and the islands as independent. Apart from the period of the Pentecontaetia as 'allies' of the Athenians, who themselves organised the cities into tribute-paying districts on the lines of the former Persian satrapies, the Greeks of Asia Minor formed an integral part of the empire ruled, successively, by the Mermnad, Achaemenid and Argead kings; unsurprisingly, Appian says, 'The Ionians and Aeolians are accustomed to obedience, even to barbarian kings.'[12]

Under the Lydian and Persian kings, the cities were included in the empire's regular administrative system, paying the *phoros* which symbolised their subject status, and supplying contingents for the royal army and navy in time of war. As regards internal affairs, the Ionians asked the Persian conqueror Cyrus for the same conditions as had obtained under Croesus; some see this as reflecting a considerable degree of local autonomy; others dismiss it as Lydian propaganda. While the cities lost the right to make war amongst themselves after the failure of the Ionian revolt in the 490s BC, the seeming paradox of

King Artaxerxes' statement in 395 BC, that 'the Greeks might have their autonomy as long as they continued to pay the ancient dues', supports the view that the Persian kings were not interested in intervention in the cities' internal affairs for its own sake.[13]

In terms of economic prosperity, however, 'subjection' and the peace that accompanied it may have been preferable to the times when the cities found themselves the object of yet another 'liberation campaign'. Plutarch, Diodorus, the pseudo-Aristotelian *Oeconomica* and the stratagem handbooks show the cities as frequently vulnerable to the depredations of Athenian and Spartan 'protectors'.[14] Often they came under the control of tyrants and oligarchs, whose rule was promoted or tolerated by the Great King and his satraps as long as it suited their interests. In the mid-fourth century BC the Hecatomnid dynast Mausolus expanded his 'empire' to include Greek *poleis* in Caria and further afield. If the *Oeconomica* is to be trusted, he surpassed even the *gazophylax* Lysimachus in money-making schemes, though the effect of his famed rapacity is difficult to gauge. Ambitious temple-building programmes at Miletus, Ephesus and perhaps Priene in this period have been cited as proof of 'prosperity' among the 'Greeks of Asia Minor', but this need not mean that the population as a whole was flourishing, merely that some sections of it enjoyed considerable wealth.[15]

For citizens of *poleis* whose prosperity relied heavily on trade, it is probable, then, that neither 'liberation' nor 'subjection' had quite the same connotations as the orators, pamphleteers and politicians would have us believe. It is likely, too, that this historical experience had to some extent shaped both the expectations of the Greeks themselves – archives attest an awareness of past conditions and privileges going back several centuries[16] – and informed the attitude of their new rulers.

For the latter, however, probably still more important was the precedent set by Alexander, the Greeks' most recent 'liberator'. Lysimachus and Antigonus both stressed their right to rule as Alexander's heirs and had practised or observed the art of government in Asia Minor under his regime. Nor was Alexander himself operating in a vacuum; recent analysis, based on non-Greek evidence, has undermined the traditional view that Alexander and his Successors imposed a Graeco-Macedonian system of administration upon a 'barbarian' world perceived as culturally inferior.[17] Alexander's debt to his Achaemenid predecessors must be acknowledged.

THE GREEK CITIES OF ASIA MINOR UNDER ALEXANDER

Though historians may strive for 'objectivity', their perceptions are, of necessity, coloured by the preoccupations of their own time. This is nowhere made more clear than in the way opinion has shifted as regards 'Alexander, champion of Greek freedom'. The general assumption, at the beginning of this century, that Alexander, whose dynasty claimed Hellenic descent, must therefore have treated his fellow Hellenes as 'free allies', perhaps owed more to a background of British and German colonial imperialism and strong nationalistic feelings than to the ancient evidence. This rose-tinted vision was challenged by Bikermann and Ehrenberg, writing in the 1930s as Europe witnessed the rise of a new nation of conquerors. Their view, that Alexander's attitude towards the Greeks of Asia was defined primarily by his position as heir to the Achaemenids and master of the Asian *chora*, is still generally held today.[18]

Certainly Alexander's earliest administration in Asia Minor shows no divergence from the existing system; his nominee, Calas, simply replaces the Persian Arsites as satrap of Hellespontine Phrygia, with authority over Greeks and non-Greeks alike. Only later does Alexander take up the 'liberator's' sword, using the 'autonomy slogan' to win Greek support; this action represents an intelligent and flexible response to circumstances, rather than the ideological mainspring or justification for his invasion of the Persian empire.[19]

As regards grants of 'freedom and autonomy', Alexander's stance is grounded in pragmatism, not idealism. At its fullest extent, *eleutheria kai autonomia* entailed democratic government, in place of the oligarchs or tyrants lately favoured by Persia; the cities enjoyed their own laws, were exempt from the *phoros* previously paid to the Great King, free from garrisons and from direct control by the satrap or royal financial officials. A grant of 'freedom and autonomy' did not, however, acknowledge the Greeks' unquestioned right to such conditions; they were privileges, accorded by the king's favour, revocable at any time and varying from city to city. There is no question of a uniform grant of this status to all Greek *poleis*. Above all, there is a clear connection between the city's response to Alexander and the conditions subsequently imposed. Tyre and Gaza resisted and were destroyed; cities like those of Ionia and Aeolis which offered submission were granted 'freedom and autonomy'.[20]

Moreover, though loyal cities might be rewarded in this way,

Alexander's potential rights over his Greek subjects remained the same as those of his Achaemenid predecessors. Though royal favour exempted some cities from payment of taxes to the crown, sometimes called *phoros*, sometimes the more innocuous *syntaxeis*, Alexander did not relinquish the right to levy such taxes. Chios, for one, was obliged to supply ships at her own expense. Some cities were garrisoned, others were placed under the direct supervision of the satrap. The king could grant city revenues as gifts to his *philoi*; Eresus was allowed to judge the fate of its expelled tyrants, but only by virtue of Alexander's *diagraphe*; new laws at Chios had to be submitted to him for approval; at Ephesus, Rhodes, Methymna and Imbros, Alexander's official, Philoxenus, puts citizens on trial and decrees their punishment.[21]

Towards the end of Alexander's reign, Philoxenus reappears as 'commander of Ionia/the seashore'. Though this has been interpreted as a further limit placed on the Greeks' already precarious freedom, the appointment may rather represent a security measure taken in response to Ionian unrest during Alexander's long absence in India. Revolt, disloyalty and official misconduct is attested in other parts of the empire, notably Egypt and the upper satrapies, at this time. The appointment may even have a Persian precedent; after the unsuccessful Satraps' Revolt, Orontes had hopes of being appointed 'overseer of the Aegean shore'.[22] If this is correct, then Philoxenus' appointment follows the expected pattern of treatment as related to conduct.

To sum up: as a weapon to win Greek support in the first years of his Asian campaign, 'freedom and autonomy' had served Alexander well, and there was no reason to cease granting such privileges when he could afford to. After Gaugamela, however, Alexander was undisputed master of the *poleis*. Like his Achaemenid predecessors he saw them as subjects; this is reflected in the fact, rightly stressed by Badian, that Perdiccas' division of the empire among its new satraps in 323 BC at Babylon makes no special provision for the Greek cities. No more is heard of Greek 'freedom and autonomy' until 315 BC, when Antigonus assumes the role of 'liberator'.[23]

Before the evidence for Antigonid philhellenism is examined, it is worth considering the effect of Alexander's death on conditions for Asia Minor's *poleis*. The fierce rivalry among the Diadochs that marked the next four decades created a situation closer to that of Alexander's early years in Asia than the last years of his reign. The same link between city behaviour and royal treatment might therefore be expected, and indeed the Successor period sees attractive inducements offered for defection from a rival; loyalty is rewarded; monarchs strive to show themselves as benefactors of the Greeks. Cities which resist, or defect and are recaptured are likely to be sanctioned.

ANTIGONUS – CHAMPION OF THE GREEKS?

Invoked first and foremost as a weapon in the war with Cassander, who kept control of mainland Greece with garrisons and the support of oligarchies, Antigonus' proclamation of 'freedom and autonomy' naturally emphasised democratic government, freedom from garrisons and from *phoros*. Carried over into Asia Minor in the period from 314 BC to 312 BC to win Caria from its satrap Asander, on the enemy side and described as 'strong with a considerable number of cities *subject* to him', the success of the autonomy slogan is mirrored in the epigraphic record.[24]

Miletus' stephanephorate list marks 312 BC as the year which saw the city 'free and autonomous' by the grant of Antigonus, with 'democracy . . . restored'. A letter from Antiochus I (?) to Erythrae acknowledges its claim to be 'autonomous and exempt from tribute' as 'under Alexander and Antigonus'. A list of subscribers for a wall-building project at Colophon, perhaps initiated under Antigonus' auspices, refers to 'King Alexander's grant of freedom to the *demos*', praising Antigonus' strenuous efforts to protect the *doxa* of his ancestors. The Prieneans also proclaim themselves *autonomoi* on a series of decrees, but these may date to the period of Alexander's 'liberation' campaign rather than that of Antigonus' government. Subsequently, Antigonus' concern for Greek freedom is used to justify his acceptance of the Peace of 311 BC; Demetrius conquers Athens in 307 BC and most of mainland Greece from 304 BC to 302 BC as 'liberator'; his treaty with Cassander in 302 BC included the provision that the Greeks of both Europe and Asia should be free, autonomous and exempt from garrisons.[25]

Though his opponents, notably Ptolemy, likewise proclaimed themselves liberators, it was Antigonus who really made the autonomy slogan his own. His consummate skill as a propagandist is reflected not only in the positive response of the Greeks to his promise of 'liberation', but also by the conviction of many modern scholars that he, alone among the Successors, was a 'genuine Philhellene'. They cite his designation of the cities as his 'allies' as reflecting a genuine independence; his carefully phrased letters to them, 'advising and recommending' rather than 'ordering', is proof of Antigonus' tact and sensitivity to Greek feeling. Often a contrast is drawn with the brutally direct approach of Lysimachus, his successor in Asia Minor.[26]

Redressing the balance, Wehrli makes the following points: it is unwise to read into the word *symmachos* all the modern connotations of 'ally' (a member of an equal and voluntary partnership). In Greek it may mean simply 'companion in arms'; precedents such as Athens' Delian League, where 'ally' is a euphemism used of those who are effectively subject to the ruling power, are important. The view that Antigonus promoted Greek freedom from some longstanding ideological conviction is false; earlier he had co-operated with the 'unphilhellene' Cassander and only the need for Greek support against the allied coalition inspired his volte-face.[27]

More important, however, in the context of this study, than Antigonus' ideological sincerity is the extent to which his grants of autonomy, proudly proclaimed by the cities, actually represented an advance on the 'precarious autonomy' of Alexander's day. Did Lysimachus' style of government really constitute a retrograde step? Wehrli has shown that, as with Alexander, 'freedom and autonomy' did not preclude financial obligations, garrisoning and intervention in the city's internal affairs if Antigonus deemed it necessary.

Thus, while Antigonus' 'allies' were officially *aphorologetai* (exempt from paying tribute or tax), he himself cites their heavy 'expenses' (*dapanemata*) as a reason for making peace in 311 BC. Evidence for financial hardship at Ephesus and Miletus in the first years of the third century BC has already been discussed. The case of Miletus suggests that privileges like exemption from *phoros* could be withdrawn subsequent to 'liberation'; the 'harsh and oppressive taxes and duties' imposed on Miletus by 'certain of the kings', later lifted by Ptolemy I, may have been not Lysimachus' work, as is often supposed, but that of the Antigonids.[28]

Exemption from garrisons featured prominently in Antigonus' 'autonomy package'. It is, however, generally accepted that all the Diadochs applied a double standard on this issue, attacking a rival's garrisoning policy for propaganda purposes, but quite determined to retain their own garrison forces.[29] Indeed, in a period of constant warfare, wholesale removal of garrisons was quite unrealistic, especially from cities which had strategic importance or which housed a royal treasury or mint. True, Antigonus did leave some cities in the

Peloponnese ungarrisoned, among them Chalcis, that famous 'Fetter of Greece'. Often cited as proof of his sincerity, the value of this action in terms of real 'freedom' was negligible, since he took care to station troops at the Euripus instead. In Asia Minor Antigonus drove Asander's garrison out of Miletus in 313 BC, but the installation of his own troops is attested for cities in Cilicia, at Ephesus, Sardis and Iasus.[30]

If garrisons were a necessary evil, what of the cities' freedom to conduct foreign and domestic policy under Antigonid rule? Foreign policy, in the sense of an independent initiative to another ruler, was likely to be frowned upon, but surely the philhellene Antigonus would permit these 'autonomous' cities to conduct their internal affairs without royal interference. Not so. While self-interest ensured that his promise of democracy, widely regarded as inseparable from 'autonomy' for the citizens of the early Hellenistic *poleis*, was largely fulfilled, complete independence in running the city's financial and judicial affairs was not assured. Though carefully phrased to play down his role as master, Antigonus' letters to Teos about his planned synoecism with Lebedus reflect serious interference in city affairs. The new city's laws must be submitted for Antigonus' approval and authors of unsuitable legislation risk punishment at his hands. In the realm of finance, Antigonus tries initially to refuse the citizens of Teos and Lebedus their request for a loan to buy grain, hoping to impose on them purchase of his own surpluses; finally this scheme is abandoned, but the export of corn by both citizens and the inhabitants of the *chora* is still subject to his regulation. Though this synoecism seemingly did not come off, the foundation of Antigoneia in the Troad which compelled the mutually hostile peoples of Cebren and Scepsis to rub shoulders suggests that Antigonus' famous sensitivity to Greek feelings was rather more prominent on paper (or stone!) than in practice.[31]

Wehrli has certainly taken off the rose-tinted spectacles through which Antigonus has been seen in the past. If Antigonus is not the 'genuine philhellene' of tradition, what of Demetrius, the cities' alternative to Lysimachus after 301 BC? The evidence, albeit limited and in Athens' case at least perhaps distorted by partisan sources, reveals an equal, if not greater, tendency to make financial demands upon some Greek *poleis* and to restrict their internal autonomy. Our only detailed evidence for *phoros* exacted from a Greek city in the Diadoch period is the story that the philosopher Menedemus persuaded Demetrius to reduce Eretrian tribute from 200T to 150T, still a staggering amount.[32] Plutarch mentions an extraordinary levy of 250T upon the Athenians, who were also subjected to oligarchic government between 294 BC and 287 BC, while Arcesine on Amorgos in Caria and the Nesiote League had to take out loans from Apollo to pay 'contributions' to Demetrius.[33]

'Genuine freedom and autonomy' under the Antigonids, then, is a myth, the product of successful dynastic propaganda, combined with modern preconceptions as to the meaning of certain terms in Greek. It remains to examine the evidence for Lysimachus' government of the Greeks, aiming to establish whether freedom of action in day-to-day city life was actually diminished under his rule.

THE GREEK CITIES UNDER LYSIMACHUS

The assumption that Lysimachus' regime in Asia Minor was marked by loss of autonomy across the board, with garrisons, *phoros*, suppression of city coinage and non-democratic government, must take its origin from the belief that his government of the Greek cities in Thrace copied that of the Antipatrids in mainland Greece. The validity of this has already been questioned.[34] Furthermore, even if there were firm evidence for harsh government of the West Pontic *poleis*, it should not be assumed that Lysimachus automatically used the same methods in Asia Minor, where he faced the continual threat of competition from Demetrius. The success of Antigonus' 'liberation' campaign against Cassander's oligarchies in Greece might also have served as an object lesson.[35]

Certainly the campaign of 302 BC suggests Lysimachus was aware of the need to woo the cities. Imitating the policy implemented so successfully by his own brother on Alexander's behalf in 334 BC and used by Antigonus to win Caria two decades later, he offered continued 'freedom' to cities like Lampsacus and Parium which defected to him. Those which resisted, like Sigeum, Erythrae and Clazomenae were punished. Sigeum was garrisoned; Erythrae probably lost its tax-exempt status.[36] At Ephesus, however, fears regarding military security seemingly vied with the desire to conciliate so wealthy and powerful a city. Despite its resistance, Ephesus was left 'free'; Lysimachus' general Prepelaus acknowledged the Artemis temple's tax-exempt status and freedom from military billeting; possibly the city was also given greater control over the sanctuary revenues. As a vital naval base for Demetrius, however, Ephesus could not be left ungarrisoned and its fleet was destroyed.[37]

On entering Asia Minor, then, Lysimachus recognised the value of a flexible policy which rewarded the compliant and punished the disobedient. Nor was he unsuccessful; Simpson's view that 'Lysimachus' experience was mostly unfavourable', with Lampsacus and Parium isolated cases, is too gloomy, ignoring Prepelaus' success in 'winning over' Teos, Colophon and the Hellenised Lydian city of Sardis and Lysimachus' acquisition of Hellespontine Phrygia by the same method. The evidence we have for Demetrius' recovery of the cities later in the year does not suggest a complete push-over, with Ephesus, for instance, 'forced' to return to its former status.[38]

Certainly events in 302 BC do not seem to justify the view that Lysimachus, disgusted by the ineffectiveness of his 'liberation' campaign, resolved henceforth upon a repressive regime which denied the cities any freedoms at all. It remains to test this hypothesis by a detailed examination of the available evidence for Lysimachus' intervention in city affairs, in the constitutional, financial, judicial and religious spheres.

TYRANTS AND OLIGARCHS

Despite the evidence which shows that Lysimachus had no objection to the continuance of democratic government in cities which submitted to him, the belief that his arrival in Asia Minor was marked by the widespread installation of tyrants and oligarchs in the *poleis* persists. Shipley, for example, claims that 'a characteristic peculiar to Lysimachus among the Diadochs was a tendency to support tyrants'.[39]

Logically, of course, Lysimachus' role as successor to and rival of the pro-democratic Antigonids might make him a potential supporter of non-democratic government. Strife between rival factions, who then call in opposed external powers, is a dominant motif in the history of the Greek cities in both Europe and Asia in the sixth, fifth and fourth centuries BC.[40] There is, however, nothing to justify the idea that Lysimachus had some sort of ideological predilection for non-democratic government; it would be wrong to assume that any tyrant whose rule might fall in the early third century is invariably his protégé or automatically to date inscriptions which refer to tyrants to his reign. Lysimachus did support and co-operate with the Clearchid tyrants at Heracleia Pontica, but so had Antigonus before him. Subsequent events there show that pragmatism rather than ideology informed Lysimachus' approach in these matters; when the waning popularity of the last Clearchid tyrants gave him the opportunity for a takeover, he was happy to co-operate with the democrats at Heracleia. What mattered was support; its political coloration was largely irrelevant. It is true that in the last years of Lysimachus' reign Heracleia again came under one-man rule, with Heracleides of Cyme appointed as *epistates*, the one attested example of such an official in Lysimachus' kingdom. Questions of military security may, however, have prompted this appointment; Heracleia and its environs were subject to heavy pressure from the ambitious Bithynian dynast Zipoites in this period.[41]

The case of Heracleia, then, suggests that there was little incentive for a ruler like Antigonus or Lysimachus to remove a tyrant, if like Dionysius, he combined loyalty with a rule that was seemingly neither oppressive nor unpopular.[42] In practical terms, however, to promote this type of government actively might have been unproductive if there was an alternative. Tyrants, with the large mercenary forces they invariably require, are expensive to maintain. Tyranny, moreover, is often accompanied by political instability and divisiveness; in a period as volatile as that of the Diadochs, this might too easily be exploited by an opponent. Also, there is evidence that city politicians in Asia Minor, eager to preserve their personal influence, were as ready to be flexible in the face of a new conqueror as their Athenian counterparts. The Ephesian Philaenetus, proposer of the decree for Nicagoras of Rhodes, ambassador for Seleucus and Demetrius *c.* 299 BC, is a good example. His continued prominence in public life under Lysimachus' rule is suggested by his proposal of honours for Melanthius of Theangela, a royal official appointed to guard the fortress of Phygela, one of the cities incorporated into Lysimachus' new foundation of Ephesus.[43]

Where the democrats were ready to co-operate, there was no incentive to change the constitution for its own sake, nor is there any reason to think that cities which had welcomed Lysimachus and been left 'free' suffered any such change subsequently. Insofar as constitutional realities can be inferred from inscriptions, admittedly a problematic affair, the continuance of democratic forms under Lysimachus is attested for Samothrace, Samos, Priene, Miletus and Ephesus.[44]

Despite this evidence for Lysimachus' readiness to co-operate with regimes of all political colours, so long as loyalty was assured, the traditional view persists. Shipley, for instance, sees the Samian tyranny of both Duris and his father Kaios as Lysimachus' work. Citing the king's 'support' for tyrannies at Ilium, Nisyros and Priene, he concludes that 'there is an *a priori* likelihood that it was Lysimachus' takeover that entailed this new regime'.[45] What then is the evidence for Lysimachus' link with the tyrants in these cities?

Our knowledge of tyranny at Ilium rests on a strongly worded law prescribing severe penalties for anyone attempting to support or uphold an oligarchic or tyrannical regime. Grammatically, the text is curious; its main body, with conditional clauses, suggests a preventive measure against future or potential dangers; the final section, marked by imperatives, looks like legislation drafted in the light of experience. Consequently its meaning is disputed; some see the law inspired by Ilian determination to avoid the unhappy experience of tyranny suffered by neighbouring states; others see the 'vague' section as a blueprint drafted by exiled democrats and published on their return to power.[46]

On stylistic grounds the text has been dated to the early third century BC; Dittenberger noted the lettering's similarity to that of the Aristodicides dossier, issued under Antiochus I. Though loss of the first lines precludes a certain dating, Bruckner's date of 281 BC has received general credence. For him, the decree follows the expulsion of a tyrant supported by Lysimachus. Nothing in the text links the tyranny to Lysimachus, but the belief that he was *persona non grata* at Ilium has lent the theory some weight. Three pieces of evidence are cited in support of Lysimachus' 'unpopularity'; cult honours for Seleucus at Ilium *c.* 281 BC; Sigeum's shortlived bid to break away from the synoecism with Ilium, which Lysimachus had engineered; Ilian destruction of the city walls built by Lysimachus by the time of the Galatian invasion of 278 BC.[47]

Against this, it could be argued that the cult for Seleucus represents no more than a politic response to a conqueror who had shown himself prepared to brook no resistance, while archaeological finds and Livy's testimony contradict Strabo's source Hegesianax regarding the destruction of the city walls. Though the synoecism was possibly unpopular with the smaller cities whose identity was lost, the fact that the Ilians punished Sigeum for defecting suggests that they did not share this feeling.[48] Lysimachus' early relations with Ilium were positive, expressed in conspicuous benefactions; evidence for a change of stance which might find expression in the establishment of a clearly unpopular tyranny is lacking.

Its early editors saw the Ilian anti-tyranny law as arising from a period of 'great upheaval'; Bellinger has identified this period as the aftermath of Seleucus I's sudden death in autumn 281 BC. This gains support from Ilium's decree for Seleucus' heir, Antiochus I, which shows him preoccupied on his accession with revolt in the Seleucis and unable to attend to Troad affairs for some time. Both events at Priene early in the third century BC, and the upheavals in the Ionian cities with the Macedonian invasion of 336 BC suggest that periods of transition between rulers or instability when the central government faces other threats, are likely breeding grounds for tyranny. Though Haussoulier objects to this interpretation, arguing that Antiochus is praised for maintaining democracy rather than restoring it, this is not conclusive. The Ilian opposition may itself have succeeded in expelling the tyrant before the king arrived upon the scene, just as Hiero's opponents at Priene managed to dislodge him.[49]

Our second case of 'Lysimachean tyranny' rests on a fragmentary inscription from Nisyros, dated only to 'the third century'. It imposes heavy fines on anyone attempting a burial or placing a grave monument in certain circumstances; the precise details of these are lost. Its identification as an anti-tyranny law rests on its similarity to clauses in the Ilian decree ordering the obliteration of the names of offenders against democracy from all public records or monuments. Uncertain as regards date, context and meaning, the Nisyros stone is a flimsy piece of 'proof' for Lysimachus' support for tyrants.[50]

At Priene, Pausanias tells us, one of the citizens, Hiero, established a tyranny which was clearly unpopular. Four inscriptions supplement our knowledge of this shortlived regime: *I.Priene* 37 describes the struggle by Prienean exiles based at the Karion fort to overthrow the tyrant and sets the date for Hiero's rule in the period *c.* 300 BC to 297 BC; another text records Ephesus' loan of arms to exiles from Priene, who are probably to be identified with those at *to Karion*; a third decree concerns the establishment of a festival celebrating the 'recovery of freedom and autonomy' after Hiero's fall; the fourth provides for the reinscription of honours to Evander of Larissa, clearly an enemy of Hiero's regime whose privileges had been cancelled during the tyranny.[51]

The supposition that Lysimachus either tolerated or actively supported Hiero[52] may stem partly from the belief in his anti-democratic tendencies, but its main basis is the evidence that Demetrius supported Hiero's opponents. Ainetus, the phrourarch at Ephesus working with the Karion exiles, has been identified as a Demetrian officer; Evander of Larissa may be a *philos* of the Besieger; a decree for King Demetrius is cited among the documents issued during the period of exile at the Karion fort.[53] Demetrius' loss of

Priene, presumably in the uncertain period following Ipsus, does not, however, inevitably mean Lysimachus' gain. Possibly Hiero was an independent operator,[54] perhaps an old enemy of Demetrius' supporters at Priene who exploited their loss of credibility in 301 BC to seize power for himself. Demetrius, eager to regain Priene, was a natural 'protector' for the dispossessed and disgruntled democrats.

Shipley, however, actually claims that Lysimachus responded positively to a plea for help from Hiero; the evidence which might seem to suggest this is a reference to 'the decrees for King Demetrius and King Lysimachus' in *I.Priene* 37, but this is not the evidence cited. Instead the argument is based on the recapture of Ephesus from Ainetus by Lysimachus' officer Lycus and the fact that Priene was 'Lysimachean . . . soon after' this episode. This is not conclusive. First, the clash between Lycus and Ainetus quite possibly belongs not to this period, but to the campaign of 286–5 BC. Second, the precise date at which Lysimachus gained Ephesus and Priene is uncertain but the year 294 BC, suggested by Plutarch's account, is generally accepted.[55] By this time Hiero was long gone.

What then of the 'decree . . . for King Lysimachus'? Must we assume that it was issued by Hiero's faction? If the tyrant was an 'independent', then his opponents might naturally appeal to all likely candidates for aid, as Cassander's son, Alexander, had called on both Pyrrhus and Demetrius in 294 BC. It is notable too that the decree for Lysimachus is mentioned in the same breath as four others: one for Demetrius, two appeals to Rhodes (one 'concerning the expulsion of the tyrant's party', the other requesting a loan of money) and one 'concerning the gift of weapons'; in other words it appears in a list of documents which all seem to come from the exiled party in the Karion fort, containing pleas for help. Accordingly, it seems reasonable to assume that the exiles applied to both kings, as well as to powerful neighbouring *poleis*, for aid. Demetrius responded; Lysimachus seemingly did not, perhaps because he was preoccupied with affairs elsewhere,[56] or because Demetrius simply beat him to it. The evidence for Hiero's regime, then, supplies no positive proof of a link with Lysimachus.

If there is no secure connection between Lysimachus and the tyrannies at Ilium, Nisyros and Priene, the assumption that, *a priori*, the Samian tyrants are his creatures, is questionable. Although the precise dates and duration of the tyranny at Samos are far from certain, it seems likely that, as at Heracleia, the regime was tolerated first by the Antigonids and then by Lysimachus. Our knowledge that

Duris combined the writing of histories, whose fragments suggest the ancient world's answer to tabloid journalism, with the role of tyrant in his native Samos comes from Athenaeus. After a period studying in Athens, probably in the last years of the fourth century BC, Duris returned to Samos; c. 300 BC he issued coins, but probably in the capacity of mint magistrate rather than tyrant. It is likely, therefore, that his rule begins some time after that date. If he was installed by Lysimachus, then the start of his tyranny should probably be postponed to c. 295–4 BC.[57]

Alternatively, like Hiero, Duris may have exploited the uncertain situation after Ipsus to seize power; it is possible too that he inherited the tyranny, either directly or after an interim period, from his father Kaios. This raises the question of Antigonid toleration of tyranny at Samos. We know from Pausanias that Kaios was victor in the boys' boxing at Olympia during the period of Samian exile from 365 BC to 322 BC; combined with the appearance of his son Lysagoras as proposer of a decree c. 300 BC, this sets his birth date in the period from c. 385 BC to c. 350 BC. Pausanias' text, now damaged, may also have named Kaios as tyrant.[58] Though the Diadoch period is notable for protagonists who are remarkably long in the tooth, Shipley's vision of the aged tyrant, installed by Lysimachus c. 296 BC, is less satisfactory than Kebric's reconstruction which sees Kaios, in the prime of life, still remembered for his Olympic victory, come to power when the Samians returned home in 322 BC.[59]

If correct, then the Antigonids must have tolerated Kaios' rule as they had that of Dionysius at Heracleia. Though the tyranny has left no mark on the epigraphic record for the period from 322 BC to 300 BC, this is not a valid objection; the same is true for the *stelai* dated to Lysimachus' reign.[60] Signs of Lysimachean oppression can be seen, it might be claimed, in the diminished number of popular decrees from Samos after 300 BC.[61] It should, however, be said that many of the forty-eight decrees assigned to the Diadoch period are grants of proxeny and citizenship rendered anonymous by loss of the opening lines. While Habicht is inclined to ascribe the majority of these to Antigonus' reign, it seems impossible to draw any certain conclusions as to their date. Of those which can definitely be assigned to the Antigonid era, several arise from a special context, the Samians' return from exile and their desire to show gratitude to their benefactors in those dark days; another five concern honours voted for Antigonid officials and possibly some of the anonymous texts may do the same. The highly visible presence of Antigonus' officers which is implied by these decrees is compatible with other evidence for fairly close royal supervision of Samos; there was a garrison, an 'officer placed in charge by the king', and possibly military and financial obligations to help with the Antigonid war effort.[62] The subsequent fall-off of decrees may reflect not so much a muzzling of the democracy as a more *laissez-faire* attitude on Lysimachus' part. At Samos, then, as at Heracleia, it is likely that Lysimachus tolerated a regime, already in power under his predecessors, which was autocratic, but not obviously oppressive.[63]

Passing from tyrants to oligarchs, and from Samos to the mainland opposite, it remains to discuss the claims that Lysimachus installed oligarchies at Ephesus and Erythrae. Describing Lysimachus' refoundation of Ephesus, Strabo makes reference to a *gerousia* which was 'enrolled' (*katagraphomene*) and to the *epikletoi* 'who administered the city's affairs'. These bodies appear again in two inscriptions which are generally dated to periods of Lysimachus' control and cited as evidence for his establishment of an oligarchic government in his new city.[64]

The known history of Lysimachus' relations with Ephesus suggests two possible contexts in which an oligarchy might have been installed. In 302 BC, as we have seen, Ephesus was left 'free'; this implies some privileges, but whether they were enough to offset the penalties also imposed or whether they included the right to democratic government is unclear. Though Demetrius recovered the city a few months later, Diodorus' comment that Ephesus was 'forced' to return to its 'former status' suggests that the city was divided into factions, one of which gave Lysimachus its support;[65] plausibly his partisans included the city's property owners who had suffered considerable financial damage in the war fought on Demetrius' behalf in the years after Ipsus.[66] The picture is complicated, however, by evidence which suggests that at least some of those in power under Demetrius bent with the winds of change and welcomed Lysimachus in exchange for continued prominence in public life. Philaenetus has already been mentioned; another possible candidate is Echeanax, a mint magistrate under Lysimachus; identified with the son of the tyrannicide Diodorus, his family background would seem to make him a likely democrat. Such changes of allegiance need not, however, involve a change of constitution. In a period when constant shifts of power demand that city politicians must be, above all, flexible, the difficulties of labelling them firmly as 'oligarchs' or 'democrats' are notorious.[67] One context, then, for installation of an oligarchy is

Lysimachus' rewarding of these supporters on recovery of Ephesus in 294 BC.

Alternatively, an oligarchy might represent royal reprisals for the popular resistance offered to the city's refoundation; Strabo tells us that only Lysimachus' flooding of the old city induced the citizens to move![68] Such action would be consistent with a policy which mixed rewards and penalties in response to city behaviour. Unfortunately, the epigraphic evidence for those supposedly oligarchic bodies, the *gerousia* and *epikletoi*, is inconsistent with this hypothesis. The city decree honouring Euphronius for his services as go-between with Prepelaus, usually dated to 302 BC, shows that these bodies already existed at the time of Lysimachus' first contact with Ephesus. While it could be argued that existing institutions only now received the extended powers which Strabo's account seems to imply, the activities of the *gerousia* and *epikletoi* in this period, seemingly limited to temple affairs, suggest otherwise. The belief that the *gerousia* is in fact an institution attached to the temple, rather than a body governing the city,[69] is supported by two pieces of evidence. First, the *gerousia* must submit its decision to the *boule* and *demos* for ratification. Second, it is nowhere to be seen in either the decree which honours Athenis of Cyzicus for his support for a wall-building project which should probably be linked to Lysimachus' refoundation, or a more recently published proxeny decree for two Milesian benefactors, which may also date to his reign, since one of the honorands, Phanodicus, appears again, standing security for Miletus' loan from the Cnidians in 283/2 BC.[70]

How then is Strabo's suggestion that the *gerousia* and *epikletoi* played a central role in city affairs to be explained? While Oliver suggests an allusion to the unofficial but powerful influence which the members of these bodies exerted on the direction of city policy by virtue of their prestige and their association with the king, Van Berchem's less sinister explanation is perhaps to be preferred – the discrepancy arises from a sloppiness in Strabo's writing method![71]

In conclusion, while the history of his relations with Ephesus makes it quite plausible that Lysimachus might have installed an oligarchy there, the existence of the *gerousia* and *epikletoi*, contrary to the traditional belief, does not in itself prove that democracy was overthrown.

Another possible candidate for oligarchy during Lysimachus' reign is Erythrae. Again, the city's recent history is not incompatible with the imposition of such a regime. Erythrae had successfully resisted

Prepelaus in 302 BC and may well have remained in Demetrius' possession until 294 BC. Lysimachus' name is notable by its absence in a letter from Antiochus I(?) confirming the privileges of autonomy and exemption from *phoros* which had obtained under his predecessors. Welles ascribed the omission to Seleucid enmity; while obliteration of a rival's name or image from public records or monuments is a well-known political tactic, both in the ancient world and today, it is just as likely that Lysimachus would punish prolonged resistance by revoking former privileges.[72]

Did Lysimachus' displeasure with Erythrae express itself also in support of the oligarchs known to us from a decree concerning a statue of the tyrannicide Philites? Robbed of his heroic and revolutionary aspect by the oligarchs, who simply removed his sword, Philites' rehabilitation is planned under the auspices of a restored democracy. Sadly, the text cannot be precisely dated; Heisserer's insistence on the *stele* as commemorative, being inscribed some time between 275 BC and 200 BC, seems unnecessary; the stylistic features which he points to as a 'striking contrast' to lettering of the late fourth and early third century BC do not in fact seem to preclude inscription in the latter half of the Diadoch period. His proposed context for the tyranny, however, the period immediately after Ipsus, is plausible.[73] The impression given of an unstable period with power shifting rapidly between Erythrae's opposing factions, suits the uncertain years after Ipsus better than a period when the city was under the firm control of a ruler like Lysimachus who had the financial and military means to keep the oligarchs in power, if he so wished.

To sum up: there is no firm evidence to link Lysimachus with the tyrants at Ilium, Nisyros and Priene; more probably, their reigns belong to the periods of turmoil which followed the great battles between the Diadochs, first Ipsus, then Corupedium. At Heracleia Pontica and Samos, Lysimachus tolerated the rule of tyrants, but this represents a continuation of Antigonid practice rather than a complete change of policy. In the two cases of oligarchy discussed, it is quite plausible that Lysimachus might have imposed such a regime in response to resistance, but the evidence traditionally cited in support of this belief is not conclusive.

TREASURIES AND TAXATION – LYSIMACHUS THE FINANCIER

Central to the view of Lysimachus as the king who stood with his foot planted heavily upon the necks of the Greeks is the belief that he imposed a system of crushing taxation upon the *poleis* of his realm. Apart from the evidence from Erythrae, discussed above, Lysimachus is generally identified with the figure lurking mysteriously behind a veiled reference to 'certain kings' who imposed 'harsh duties and taxes' at Miletus; this gains support from another decree which sees Miletus, in debt to Lysimachus, taking out a loan from Cnidus to meet the second instalment. The other evidence is anecdotal; Lysimachus is dubbed *Gazophylax* by Demetrius' friends; recovering from one of Lysimachus' nastier practical jokes, a cheeky parasite returns the shock by asking for a talent; Lysimachus' court is unsophisticated, peopled by slavish oafs; he tries, unsuccessfully, to impose a salt-tax in the Troad; Plutarch suggests that his mercenaries were paid well below the going rate.[74]

Andreades' study of Lysimachus' financial administration combines this material with evidence relating to Lysimachus' establishment of several treasuries, something which he seems to see as unique among the Diadochs. The reserves which these imply, and Lysimachus' abundant issues of high-quality coinage, lead Andreades to conclude that he stood alone among the Successors as a genuine financier. Those who paid the price for this financial acumen were of course the Greek cities, since the ability to accumulate such reserves in the face of heavy expenses must imply high taxation of his subjects.[75]

This image of Lysimachus the miser has strongly influenced interpretation of the evidence for his rule in Asia Minor. For example, Tarn's belief in Lysimachus' avarice leads him to present the king's quite respectable benefaction of 130T to Athens *c.* 286–5 BC as a handful of small change. Likewise, evidence which suggests that the Ephesians were expected to pay for the new walls built as part of Lysimachus' refoundation has been cited as an illustration of his miserly habits. This ignores other evidence which shows that Lysimachus was by no means alone in expecting *polis* citizens to contribute to public works launched under royal auspices. A subscription list from Colophon, generally dated to the period of Antigonus' rule and perhaps instigated by him, shows hundreds of citizens and foreign benefactors advancing money for the construction of new city walls. Funds for the eventual repayment of these creditors come not from the king but from the city revenues. A similar project at Erythrae, also citizen-funded, may also fall under Antigonus' auspices.[76]

In recent years Burstein has done much to correct this view of Lysimachus as a monster of avarice, pointing out that the only explicit description of Lysimachus' government as harsh comes from the none too impartial lips of Seleucus' *kolakes* (flatterers). He has also reassessed the Milesian evidence. Following Seibert, who doubted whether Ptolemy I could actually have made an alliance with a city under Lysimachus' control, let alone dictate financial terms for it, Burstein agrees that Ptolemy must have been master of Miletus at the time. The possible dates for Miletus' alliance with Ptolemy are 314 BC, 308 BC or a date in the early 290s BC. Since Lysimachus was in Thrace until 302 BC and his operations in that year seemingly did not extend to Caria, he cannot be identified with the author of the fiscal oppression which preceded Ptolemy's arrival. Like the imposition of *phoros* on Erythrae, Miletus' payments to Lysimachus in the late 280s BC may represent a punitive measure in response to resistance; Burstein suggests an indemnity following defection to Demetrius in 286–5 BC. The epigraphic evidence, then, is not proof of a uniform system of oppressive taxation exacted empire-wide throughout the reign.[77]

What of the anecdotes? The most famous, the *Gazophylax* story, will be discussed in detail in the following chapter, since its value seems to lie more in what it reveals of contemporary ideas about kingship than in what it tells us about Lysimachus' fiscal policy. Burstein, indeed, makes the point that this nickname, bestowed on Lysimachus in 302 BC, cannot stand as evidence for oppressive taxation of his subjects in Asia after 301 BC. He cites other sources of wealth, notably war-booty and lands rich in precious metals, to account for Lysimachus' ability both to meet his expenses and to build up his famous reserves.[78]

More, however, can be said about the anecdotes. The uncertain value of this type of evidence has already been discussed in the first chapter. Of those pertaining to Lysimachean avarice, the source in three instances is Phylarchus, whose stance seems to be one of general hostility to monarchs. The possibility that he drew on Duris, hardly a byword for accurate and unbiased reporting, as a source for the Diadoch period has already been raised. The other source quoted, which labels Lysimachus as 'very mean', is one Aristodemus; the most likely candidate is Aristodemus of Nysa, Strabo's mentor; the little that survives of his work shows a penchant for the romantic, dramatic and moralising style of history, but no certain conclusions can be drawn as to a political stance that might bias his work one way or the other.[79]

These stories are cited as proof of an exceptional meanness which drove Lysimachus to adopt a style of government in direct contrast to that of his Antigonid predecessors. To treat these anecdotes as pieces of evidence isolated from their literary context is, however, misconceived. Such stories are not confined to Lysimachus – Plutarch and Athenaeus tell similar tales of his contemporaries. Though Antigonus the One-Eyed may chide his 'parasite' Aristodemus for criticising his open-handedness, his grandson Gonatas attracts two versions of the story which might be called 'The Parasite's Request'. One petitioner, Bion, succeeds by persistence, but the other is not so lucky; Plutarch adds that Gonatas 'was the most adroit and plausible of kings at brushing such importunities aside'. The fact that in both cases, as in the Bithys story, the sum involved is a talent seems to underline the conventional nature of these tales. Likewise, Lysimachus' plan to impose a salt-tax in the Troad is paralleled by a similarly unsuccessful attempt by 'the generals of Antigonus' to tax the healing waters of the River Aedepsus. As for the story in Plutarch's *Laconica*, the reluctance or inability of kings and generals to pay their mercenary troops in full or on time is a well-worn theme in literary texts covering the fourth and third centuries BC.[80]

So much for the anecdotes. Burstein also makes the point that Lysimachus' concern to increase the cities' prosperity and his readiness to spend money in benefactions is well attested. Andreades, anticipating this argument, wished to dismiss it on the grounds that this generosity was politically motivated. This is naïve, to say the least; surely the euergetism of Lysimachus' fellow rulers was likewise inspired, at least in part, by thought of the political capital that might accrue? On the positive side, there is also the story that Lysimachus offered to give anything he owned to the Athenian Philippides, usually ignored in this context.[81]

Taken as a whole, the evidence suggests that though Lysimachus may have lacked the extravagant generosity of Alexander or Antigonus, he was not pathologically mean in the sense that reluctance to let a drachm slip from his fingers inspired policies that left the cities impoverished and finally proved politically disastrous. Certainly he was keenly aware, as all the Diadochs had to be, of the value of money as a political asset, but this manifests itself in expenditure as much as in accumulation. The infamous offer of 2,000T for Demetrius' life at once comes to mind; similarly, he is ready to offer Pyrrhus a hefty bribe to leave Macedon in 294 BC.[82] Nor, finally, need a king's relative carefulness with funds inevitably imply excessive taxation of his subjects. The tales of Demetrius' exploits in Athens, though requiring a certain caution, since a likely source is Duris or his brother Lynceus, suggest rather that it was royal generosity or extravagance which might empty Joe Public's pockets. There is, moreover, no such explicit evidence for Lysimachus' heavy taxation of the Greeks as we have for Demetrius. Apart from the story of the Athenians subsidising Lamia's beauty treatments, perhaps less outlandish than it sounds, there is the information, supplied by Hieronymus, that in Boeotia in the late 290s BC 'he levied large sums of money from the people'. The high 'tribute' demanded of the Eretrians has already been mentioned.[83]

Finally, Andreades' belief that Lysimachus' establishment and maintenance of several treasuries within his kingdom was somehow exceptional for the period must be challenged.[84] It is not sufficient to say that Lysimachus is the only Diadoch whose *gazophylakia* are explicitly mentioned; after 301 BC, there is little sight of Ptolemy or Seleucus in action within their own kingdoms, as the Antigonid-centred sources focus on Demetrius and his opponents, Pyrrhus and Lysimachus. Also, the early years of the Successor period show first Perdiccas and Eumenes, then Antigonus, clearly utilising the Achaemenid treasury system which Alexander had inherited. The continuity of the system is implied by the very use of the Persian-derived words *gazophylakion* and *gazophylax* by Alexander and the Diadochs. Diodorus tells of treasuries at Cyinda, Susa and Ecbatana, another somewhere in Media; in 302 BC Lysimachus took 'royal treasuries' at Synnada and other places in Hellespontine Phrygia, previously in Antigonus' hands. Since later Seleucid history reveals the same system of a number of treasuries in operation, it is hard to credit that Seleucus I did not inherit and continue to use the treasuries which he took from Antigonus between 312 BC and 308 BC and from Lysimachus in 281 BC. The sheer size of the Seleucid empire, even after Ipsus, seems to demand such a set-up.[85] If Lysimachus' possession of multiple treasuries is not exceptional, then it is not evidence for exceptional avarice.

Another feature of Lysimachus' administration which is seen as a denial of Greek autonomy is his installation of royal mints in the *poleis* of his kingdom. Though the most precise details of Thompson's analysis, which sees Lysimachean mints operating in at least fifteen cities in Asia Minor and the islands off its western coast, cannot be confidently accepted,[86] Lysimachus' use of some Greek city workshops to strike his royal coinage is not in doubt. Equally, the king's establishment of his own mint inside the city walls, with the presence of his officials as a constant reminder of royal control, undeniably represented interference in the cities' internal affairs. Since the aim of this chapter is, however, to determine whether Lysimachus' methods of government represented a new and unparalleled degree of oppression, his practice here must be compared with that of his predecessors and contemporaries. Again, the evidence suggests that this was in no sense an innovation. Alexander had likewise established mints in the Greek cities of Ionia; Demetrius, Lysimachus' great rival for the favours of the Ionians, coined at Miletus and at Ephesus. After Lysimachus, Ionian and Aeolian cities such as Cyme, Phocaea and Myrina housed Seleucid mints issuing the royal silver coinage.[87]

Closely connected with this issue is the question of sovereignty and coinage. Those who see his royal mints in Greek cities as an intolerable infringement of autonomy presumably believe that this practice must entail Lysimachus' suppression of the civic coinage issued by the cities under Achaemenid rule. It might be said that the precedent had been set by Philip II and Alexander; royal monopoly of the right to coin and the compulsory abolition of city coinage, in pursuit of a system of uniform monetary circulation, has been seen as a hallmark of the Macedonian conquerors, expressing their sovereignty over the conquered peoples.[88]

What, then, is the evidence for the issue of civic coinage under Lysimachus' rule? Cities which continue to strike coins displaying the city emblems and legends include Ephesus, Smyrna, Priene, Scepsis, Samothrace and Cyme, while Alexandria, Troas and Ilium produce their first civic issues under his auspices. Colophon's issues dwindle, but this presumably results from the transfer of part of its population to New Ephesus, rather than a suppression order.[89] These issues are, however, invariably restricted to bronze and small denomination silver. Coins bearing the city symbols, whose importance as an expression of civic pride is often emphasised,[90] were effectively limited to small change, circulating only within the immediate environs of the city.

To see this as a sign of Lysimachus' brutal determination to impress his mastery upon the Greeks, in contrast to his more tactful predecessors, would, however, be mistaken. Coinage at Ephesus, for instance, with the production of the city's Attic octobols alongside the royal issues, follows exactly the same pattern under Lysimachus as it had in Demetrius' reign. Silver coinage issued by Ionian cities, like Ephesus, Magnesia, Miletus and Priene under early Seleucid rule is likewise restricted to small change denominations.[91] The limiting of city coinage to local circulation, then, is not a reflection of Lysimachus' unusually harsh rule, but a general phenomenon which begins with Alexander and continues into the Diadoch period and beyond.

This might seem to confirm the idea of a 'Macedonian policy' which denied the Greek cities the sovereignty which finds expression in the right to issue an internationally circulating coinage. A recent study by Martin has, however, seriously questioned the idea that civic coinage in the ancient world functions primarily as a symbol of sovereignty. On this point, one might add that 'the right to coin' does not appear among the traditional privileges of autonomy requested by cities, granted by kings and published on stone. Martin's reassessment of the Thessalian hoard evidence, usually taken as the classic illustration of Philip II's suppression of city coinage, has effectively undermined the whole idea of a Macedonian precedent for the actions of the Hellenistic kings. As regards Alexander's supposed 'policy' of suppressing city coinage, Martin has shown that under his rule there is often no correlation between the continuance of city coinage and other conditions imposed. The classic case is Rhodes, which resisted Alexander and received the usual sort of penalties (a garrison and a compulsory change of constitution), but continued none the less to strike civic issues. This is hardly compatible with the idea that the presence or absence of city coinage reflects, respectively, a royal grant or denial of autonomy.[92]

Martin argues that the function of coinage in the late Classical and early Hellenistic periods was primarily economic, not political, with Macedonian royal policy on coining determined largely by practical motives; thus Alexander's first aim was to produce a coinage for quick and easy distribution to his troops stationed in Asia Minor, an area of crucial strategic importance. Its high quality, assuring its acceptability in markets throughout the empire, contributed indirectly to the decline of the cities' own issues. With royal demand pushing metal sources up in price, issue of civic coinage was viable only for the wealthiest *poleis*. At the same time, the competition such issues faced from the royal coinage cast doubt on the economic wisdom of such a practice.[93]

Martin admits the possibility of a change of stance under the Successors. The idea that anxiety about the legitimacy of their rule would prompt an explicit statement of sovereignty through the suppression of city coinage is, however, hardly compatible with other evidence which shows the Diadochs competing to woo the cities with benefactions and the concern displayed, particularly by the Antigonids, to mask the naked truth of royal domination.[94] In Lysimachus' case, it is highly likely that economic, rather than political, factors played their part in determining the pattern of city coinage. The widespread acceptability of his royal issues is reflected both by the prominence of 'Lysimachi' in hoards throughout the Hellenistic world and by the issue of posthumous Lysimachus types by Greek cities like Byzantium and Calchedon for more than half a century after his death. An attempt by these cities c. 235 BC to produce a civic issue proved unsuccessful; the reversion to 'Lysimachi' c. 220 BC suggests that this 'royal coinage' proved a far more attractive proposition commercially than the civic issues.[95]

To sum up. While the presence of his mint officials in the cities may have been an unwelcome reminder of royal control, Lysimachus' practice was not innovatory; both those who ruled before and after him in Asia Minor did the same. Similarly, the effective limitation of city coinage to local issues is paralleled under Alexander and the Seleucids, and there is reason to believe that this results from economic competition from the royal issues rather than deliberate suppression as a statement of royal sovereignty.

KINGS, CITIES AND TEMPLES

Once one leaves the council chamber and the counting-house for the temples of the gods, the sparse nature of the evidence relating to Lysimachus makes it futile to try to draw any conclusions as to a 'general policy'. All that can be done is to set the available evidence in the context of the general picture that emerges from contemporary evidence for other kingdoms.

Lysimachus' display of royal *eusebeia* and the question of royal cult, issues which relate to the concept of kingship in the Diadoch period, will be dealt with in the next chapter. Here, where the subject is government, it remains to discuss the issues of royal interference in temple administration and the temples' freedom to cultivate relationships with other rulers. Since a king's decisions regarding temples are often cited as evidence for the nature of his rule over cities and their enjoyment of autonomy or otherwise, it is worth discussing briefly the relationship between the temple and the city in whose *chora* it stood.

In one sense, temples on city land can be seen as separate entities, able to receive privileges which do not automatically extend also to the city. Thus, temples receive sacred and inviolable status (*asulia*) from monarchs of Asia as far back as Croesus, but city *asulia* is first attested only in the mid-third century BC, with most examples postdating 200 BC. Alexander's decision that Ephesian *phoros* should in future benefit Artemis rather than the royal purse might appear to favour the temple at the city's expense.[96]

Some degree of identification between city and sanctuary is, however, expressed in numerous decrees of the *demos* praising a benefactor for *eunoia* towards *ton ieron kai ten polin* and by the prominence of the *neopoiai* (temple officials) who liaise between the sacred and secular spheres. In addition, the major role which a sanctuary could have in the city's economic life, as treasury, banking centre and tourist attraction, must have bestowed upon its authorities a certain political clout.[97]

Given the wealth of sanctuaries like Ephesus' Artemision and Lysimachus' reputation as the Great Financier, the accusation that he tried to siphon off the gods' revenues for himself is not surprising. The evidence cited is that relating to the Ephesian *gerousia*, already discussed. Though Oliver clears Lysimachus of installing an oligarchy at Ephesus, his interpretation of the *gerousia*'s function is still somewhat sinister. Aiming to take control of the Artemision's funds from the priesthood which traditionally administered them, Lysimachus ostensibly transferred them to the citizens of Ephesus, as represented by the *gerousia*. Since, however, this body was to be 'advised and restrained' by the *epikletoi*, whom Oliver sees as royal appointees, Artemis' wealth would effectively be brought more closely into royal control, admittedly not for immediate appropriation, but as 'a reserve in case of necessity'.[98]

How plausible is this? The traditional view that Hellenistic kings regularly deprived sanctuaries of their land and resources has long been questioned. Though there is some appropriation of sacred funds or treasures by rulers or cities, such action could easily attract accusations of sacrilege, and it is usually a last resort for those with their backs against the wall.[99] Would Lysimachus, generally concerned to display *eusebeia*, and with other resources available to him, have thought it worth alienating the feelings of the Ephesians and his other Greek subjects to secure funds against some future and quite hypothetical crisis? Though one might see a parallel in the Attalid 'practice', mentioned by Rostovtzeff, of appointing trusted courtiers as *neokoroi* (temple wardens) in temples 'like those at Sardis, Ephesus and Magnesia' in place of their indigenous priests, a closer look shows this theory to be based on one example, the appointment of Timarchus, formerly court treasurer at Pergamum, as *neokoros* at Sardis. The context of this appointment is unknown and the possibility that it was prompted by special circumstances, such as misconduct by the temple officials, cannot be ruled out. By itself, it does not justify the assumption of a widespread 'policy' applied to other sanctuaries in Asia Minor. Similarly, even if it were accepted that Lysimachus' action at Ephesus was financially motivated, there is no evidence to suggest that he took similar action elsewhere. At Didyma, the obvious parallel, it is clear that Lysimachus allowed the Milesians to administer the shrine and its resources without interference.[100]

The major sanctuaries' economic importance and the close ties that often existed between temple and city make it tempting to see royal patronage of temples as primarily political in intent. Sumptuous dedications and privileges granted to the temple are thought to reflect an attempt to win the city's loyalty. Certainly there is a political element; an inscription recording the first Seleucids' grant of *asulia*, *iketeia* and exemption from taxes to the Plutonium near Nysa, if correctly restored, serves also as a blatant manifesto of Seleucid philhellenism. In the case of Miletus, however, a purely political interpretation of relations between the Didyma temple and the Seleucid kings has led to some curious conclusions regarding Lysimachus' stance towards the city.[101]

The Milesian decrees from the first years of the third century BC, honouring Seleucus' queen, Apama, and their son Antiochus for aid for the temple's construction can be discounted from this discussion, since at this date Miletus was not in Lysimachus' hands. Seleucus I's lavish dedication to the Saviour Gods at Didyma, has, however, caused some problems; securely dated by the stephanephorate list to 288–7 BC, it post-dates by one year a decree passed by Miletus and its fellow members of the Ionian *koinon* praising Hippostratus, Lysimachus' *strategos* 'of the Ionian cities'. For some commentators, these texts reflect Miletus' ability to pursue a more or less independent foreign policy, thus casting a whole new light upon Lysimachus![102]

Though it has been seen that Lysimachus did allow individual cities a fair degree of internal autonomy, it is less certain whether Seleucid dedications at Didyma in 288–7 BC are proof of Miletus' freedom to conduct an independent foreign policy. Those who see the dedication as politically motivated construe it as a Seleucid attempt to keep Miletus loyal to the anti-Demetrian 'alliance'. This, however, assumes that Seleucus and Lysimachus were still firm friends, perhaps a doubtful proposition by this date. Nor does the rather brusque tone of the inscription accord with its supposed context. Lastly, those who propose a political motive for the dedication must admit that, seen in this light, the enterprise failed dismally – Miletus received Demetrius with open arms the following year.[103]

Burstein's solution, which sees the dedication rather as a religious thank-offering for some achievement or for the aversion of some crisis, whose details are lost to us, has a certain appeal. Such an explanation may also shed light on the much-disputed meaning of Seleucus' wish in ll.11–12, that the Milesians should pour libations in connection with his 'health and good fortune'. Welles thought that libations were to be poured 'on behalf of' Seleucus' health and good fortune; Orth saw Seleucid health and good fortune as resultant on this sacrifice to the Saviour Gods. Alternatively, the genitive absolute could be seen as causal, meaning that the Milesians are to pour libations 'since' or 'because we [Seleucus] are in good health', alluding to the king's survival and triumph over some kind of threat.[104] Quite apart from the traditional connection between dedications and victory, emphasised by Garlan, the city custom of congratulating the monarch on his success and safety in the aftermath of crisis is well attested – obvious examples are the decrees from Priene and Ilium for Lysimachus and Antiochus I respectively.[105] Seleucid patronage of Didyma, then, need not be seen exclusively in terms of the dynasty's political relations with Miletus; nor is this royal patronage of a 'foreign' sanctuary unparalleled. Ptolemy II, for example, dedicated his Propylaeon at Samothrace when the city was under Lysimachus' control; the Asclepion on Cos maintained relations with the Ptolemies long after they had lost control of the island; Philetaerus made two dedications to Apollo's temple near Aegae when Aeolis was under Seleucid rule.[106]

The sum of the evidence suggests that, despite the political influence which temple authorities might wield, the early Hellenistic kings made no attempt to restrict access to sanctuaries within their kingdoms. Concerned themselves to display *eusebeia* to the gods, it may be presumed that they respected also the rights of their fellow rulers and their subjects to do the same. Protected by their 'sacred and inviolable' status, their long tradition of attracting worshippers from all over the known world and the genuine religious feeling which attached to them, the sanctuaries remained, in some sense, truly 'international' institutions.[107]

LAW AND JUSTICE

Eusebeia may have prompted the kings to a certain tolerance regarding the religious freedom of their subjects, but when it comes to man-made law, the literary tradition paints a dramatic picture of monarchic disregard for city *nomos*. Seleucus speaks of 'the law which is common to all, that what the king ordains is always right'; Antigonus tells a sophist, 'You are a fool to speak to me of justice, when you see me sacking other peoples' cities.' Though this may represent more a conventional picture of the autocrat than verbatim reporting, it is true that the Successors, like Alexander before them, represented the ultimate source of law for the cities. While epigraphic evidence suggests that the kings were not quite so prone to flaunt these powers as the literary tradition would have it – royal ordinances (*prostagmata*), for example, are enshrined in the city laws by means of popular decree, at the tactful request, rather than the order, of the king – the fact remains that their powers of intervention in this sphere were very wide; nor did they hesitate to use them when necessary.[108]

Antigonus' actions at Teos have already been discussed. Though a king might have some grounds for regarding a city created by synoecism as 'his own' new foundation and therefore a special case, its individual citizens, of course, came from Greek *poleis* with a long tradition of drafting their own legislation and governing by it. The Eresus dossier, dealing with repeated appeals by exiled tyrants to the crown for restoration, suggests that in theory the king had the power to overturn city legislation though in this case both Alexander and his Successors instructed the suppliants to abide by the *polis* decision. The king might establish a royal tribunal in a Greek city – Antigonus' *dikasterion* at Cyme in Aeolis is an early example, with the appearance of a Seleucid *dikastes Basilikon* in the same region perhaps suggesting some continuity in the system. At another Seleucid *dikasterion* in Caria, one of the king's friends acts as chief judge, implying close royal supervision of such courts, under Seleucid rule at least.[109] There is no reference to any such tribunal set up by

Lysimachus, but the continuance of this system from the Antigonids to the Seleucids makes it likely that he too would have used it.

Though lack of detailed evidence makes it impossible to assess the extent to which these tribunals impinged upon the citizens' freedom, it is clear that the king or his officials were ready to intervene in cases where the action of a city or its individual citizens constituted a major threat to the kingdom's security or stability. Alexander's 'commander of Ionia', Philoxenus, is active on several occasions in punishing men from the Greek *poleis* convicted of treason; clearly citizen status gave them no protection from the summary execution of justice by the ruler or his officials. Similarly, a city engaged in a prolonged and bitter dispute with a neighbour or some other body might have a settlement imposed upon it by the king: Alexander pronounces upon the ownership of land in Macedonia disputed by Philippi and the neighbouring Thracian tribes; Antiochus II settles Aegae's border dispute with Myrina, defining the limits of the city *chora*; a dispute between Teos and the Dionysian guild of *technitai* is resolved by the decision of Eumenes II. It has been suggested that Lysimachus too, albeit more beneficently, took a 'unilateral decision' to change the limits of Priene's *chora*, with a gift of royal land and *laoi* to work it. Since the evidence for this 'gift' is problematic, and this interpretation hinges on certain assumptions regarding the status of the indigenous peoples in the Hellenistic kingdoms, the question will be discussed in the final section of this chapter.[110]

Evidence for Lysimachus' intervention in the cities' judicial affairs is restricted to three or four episodes; of these, two concern territorial disputes, an area in which kings seem regularly to have intervened if the dispute had escalated into war or threatened to do so. At Samothrace, he restores to the citizens the 'sacred *chora*' on the mainland opposite the island, and is responsible for judging and punishing those who had wrongly taken the land. The fragmentary decree which records his settlement of affairs at Priene following the Magnesian attack of 286–5 BC may likewise include provision for punishment of the Pedieis who joined the Magnesians. Lysimachus' personal action here may be explained by the serious nature of their crime which entailed military co-operation with the king's enemies. By contrast, though he intervenes in a similar fashion to 'save' the Samothracians from *asebeis* attacking the sanctuary of the Great Gods, the punishment of these wrongdoers is left to the citizens.[111] He arbitrates (*c.* 283–2 BC) in the longstanding dispute between Samos and Priene over the Batinetis area and the Karion fort. Despite hints that his health was failing and the attempted gamesmanship of the Prieneans, his judgement is generally regarded as notable for its exemplary impartiality. On this occasion, royal intervention was clearly prompted by request of the *poleis* themselves and Burstein has rightly emphasised the significance of the whole episode as reflecting the considerable degree of internal autonomy allowed to some cities.[112]

In these cases, Lysimachus acts as judge and arbiter himself rather than delegating the task to officials. There is no reason to think that such personal involvement was unpopular. Indeed, if the main value of anecdotes lies in their reflection of contemporary attitudes, then the story, told of more than one king, where royal reluctance to deal with petitions personally earns an invitation to abdicate, suggests the contrary.[113] It cannot, of course, be assumed from these few examples that Lysimachus invariably dealt with such matters himself; as will be seen, Lysimachus' *'strategos* of the Ionians' may well have had powers to intervene in the judicial sphere.

SATRAP AND *STRATEGOS* – ROYAL OFFICIALS AND THE GREEK CITIES

On the evidence that survives, then, there is little basis for the belief that on Lysimachus' accession Greek cities throughout Asia Minor suffered a significant diminution of their constitutional, economic, religious or judicial freedoms. Those reluctant, however, to jettison the idea of a dramatic contrast, in ideology if not in actual practice, between Lysimachus and the Antigonids, point to his 'direct incorporation of the cities into his kingdom', with the appointment of a *strategos epi ton poleon ton Ionon*. This is contrasted with the 'alliance' which bound the cities to the Antigonids. It has already been shown that the Antigonid *summachia* fell far short of what we would understand by the term 'alliance'.[114] It remains to discuss what the presence of Lysimachus' *strategos* implied for conditions of city life and the extent to which this appointment represents an innovation.

It is generally accepted, following Bengtson's lengthy analysis of the *strategos'* changing role under Alexander and the Diadochs, that in Asia Minor, by Antigonus' time, the title of this erstwhile military officer had come instead to designate the governor of the administrative regions which kept the Achaemenid title of satrapy. The *strategos* combined military with civil powers and might have considerable funds at his disposal. Bengtson identified three Antigonid *strategoi* in Asia Minor. As early as 310 BC Polemaeus governed Hellespontine Phrygia, a satrapy which may later have been combined with Greater Phrygia under Docimus' government, while Phoenix held the post in Lydia.[115]

The system continued under the Seleucid, Ptolemaic and Attalid kings, attested by inscriptions which supply the kind of information that the literary references to the Antigonid *strategoi* omit. In Asia Minor, the Hellespont and Thrace, from the 280s BC, at least, the *strategos'* authority extended to the Greek cities lying within the satrapy; his intervention might take various forms and is often beneficent in effect. Meleager, Antiochus I's *strategos* of the Hellespontine satrapy, acts as go-between for the king and Ilium regarding a grant of royal land made to Aristodicides of Assos and to be attached to the Ilian *chora*; on another occasion, he 'recommends' the royal doctor Metrodorus as a suitable candidate for Ilian honours. Hippomedon, the Ptolemaic governor 'of the Hellespont and Thrace' in the second half of the third century BC, supplies Samothrace with troops, munitions and money when its territory on the mainland near Maroneia is attacked and settles citizen cleruchs on the *peraea* (land, owned by Samothrace, on the Thracian coast) at their request. The citizens do, however, need his permission to import tax-free grain. Corrhagus, governing the same region for the Attalids, acts as intermediary with the king to secure the restoration of a city's laws, ancestral constitution and sacred precincts. It is interesting to note that this request for acknowledgement of the city's autonomy and the intervention of the *strategos* are not felt to be mutually exclusive. An inscription from early second-century BC Ephesus shows a certain Demetrius installed as *strategos* for the surrounding region; there was a Seleucid *strategos* of Cappadocia before 281 BC, another in Cilicia, and a Ptolemaic official with this title governing Caria early in the third century and perhaps before.[116]

The *strategos*, then, turns up in every area of western Asia ruled by the early Hellenistic monarchs, from Cappadocia to Cilicia. His potential powers as regards the Greek cities are considerable, embracing the extent and settlement of the city *chora*, citizenship grants, questions of importation and food supply, even the city's status. However, as Bikermann points out, the *strategos'* ability to act as go-between for city and king and to confer privileges that might be thought royalty's prerogative, does not imply denial of the city's right to deal directly with the king.[117]

How then does Lysimachus' *strategos* of the Ionians fit into this framework? Until recently, only one incumbent of the post was known to us, the Milesian Hippostratus, *philos* of the king and recipient in 289–8 BC of conspicuous honours awarded by the cities of the Ionian *koinon*. Now, another *strategos*, Hippodamus, also from Miletus, has stepped out of the shadows, courtesy of a recently published inscription from Chios.[118]

The formula which expresses the appointment of these men, *epi ton poleon ton Ionon katastatheis*, has suggested a position analogous to that of the regional *strategoi* described above. In consequence, Hippostratus has been seen as the harbinger of a new era for the *poleis*, now placed under close and constant supervision.[119] If, however, the precise title of officials under Alexander and the early Hellenistic kings has any significance, then Lysimachus' *strategoi*, with their authority limited to the 'cities of the Ionians', differ somewhat from the officials appointed to govern geographical regions like 'Caria' or 'the Hellespont', terms which presumably embrace both Greek cities and indigenous communities. The position of Hippostratus and his colleague recalls rather past instances, under the Achaemenids and then Alexander, when 'Ionia' or 'those on the coast' were treated as a separate administrative region, under a 'supervisor'; the title given to Alexander's officer, Philoxenus, by Plutarch is *o ton epi thalattes strategos*. Lysimachus' *strategoi*, then, are hardly unprecedented, but some see the return of such officers as a rude shock after Antigonid rule when 'alliance' meant freedom from official inclusion in the satrapal system and presumably from direct control by the king's regional governors.[120]

Whether Lysimachus' *strategoi* actually represent such a divergence from Antigonid practice is doubtful. The decree for Hippostratus makes it clear that 'the Ionian cities' designates the Ionian *koinon*; Bengtson therefore inferred Lysimachus' appointment of *strategoi* also over the other Greek city leagues, such as those of Aeolis and Ilium. This is questionable; Bengtson's own discussion of Antigonus' administration in Asia Minor warns against looking for an organisation structured down to the last detail; similar caution is required when dealing with Lysimachus' equally ephemeral kingdom. Moreover, study of the successive dynasties, Assyrian, Lydian, Persian and Macedonian, which ruled in Asia, suggests that in the administrative sphere kings were ready to be flexible, adopting methods that had succeeded for their predecessors, rather than imposing a uniform system right across the realm. In Caria, certainly, traditionally a land of dynasts, inscriptions from Heracleia on Latmos, Tralles, Euromus and Hyllarima dated by the rule of Pleistarchus, Lysimachus' old associate, suggest that here, like Alexander before him, Lysimachus preferred to administer the satrapy by time-honoured methods.[121]

A network of *strategoi* across Lysimachus' kingdom may be doubted, but the precedent for a *koinon*-based system of administration, headed by a royal official, actually lies, as Bengtson recognised, with Antigonus, who is generally credited with founding the Islanders' League. The system in force under the Ptolemies, with a royally appointed Nesiarch controlling the League council's agenda, with powers to intervene in the members' judicial and financial affairs, is thought to go back to Antigonus' rule. Antigonus' predilection for using city leagues as a channel for control is also reflected in his revived Hellenic League of 302 BC; here again the king's *philoi* play a prominent role in directing League activities.[122]

Antigonus, then, had no ideological objection to imposing his will upon the cities of mainland Greece and the Cyclades through the medium of royal appointees standing at the head of *koina*. Since these are regions where the citizens' claim to 'freedom and autonomy' might be thought stronger, historically, than that of their Ionian kinsmen, it is possible, therefore, that Antigonus adopted a similar system in Asia Minor; in this case, Lysimachus' *strategoi* of the Ionians would represent not a dramatic contrast with Antigonus' methods but actually a continuation of them. No firm conclusions, however, can as yet be drawn regarding Antigonus' system of administration in Asia Minor. In the period between Alexander's death and Antigonus' takeover of the satrapies there (from 319 BC to 314 BC), Diodorus' account suggests that the Ionian *poleis* were assigned to satrapies on a regional basis: in 319 BC Arrhidaeus clearly regarded Cyzicus as part of his satrapy of Hellespontine Phrygia; later, Miletus and other Carian cities are described as 'subject' to the satrap Asander.[123] Under Antigonus, the satrapies of Lydia, Hellespontine Phrygia and Greater Phrygia were governed by *strategoi* whose authority seemingly extended to the Greek or Hellenised cities of the hinterland, like Sardis and Synnada. The position of the coastal *poleis*, however, remains unclear. Antigonus' probable responsibility for refounding the Ionian League, and his practice elsewhere, both seem to support the hypothesis that the cities were governed through a *koinon*-based system. There is, however, no direct evidence for an Antigonid '*strategos* of the Ionians'; those officers with the title, like Archestratus at Clazomenae or Hipparchus of Cyrene, honoured at Samos, seem to play a purely military role.

This may simply be due, however, to the chance survival of evidence; our knowledge of Hippostratus, after all, rests on one inscription. Evidence for Ionian cities dealing directly with the Antigonid kings does not rule out a *strategos*; inscriptions from Lysimachus' reign show that Hippostratus' presence did not prevent *koinon* members like Samos or Priene from approaching the king directly.[124]

In conclusion, Lysimachus' appointment of a *strategos* 'over the Ionian cities', if not actually a continuation of Antigonus' practice in Asia Minor, is not a method to which Antigonus was a stranger. The decrees which honour Lysimachus' *strategoi* unfortunately tell us little about the nature or limits of their authority; the decree for Hippodamus is fragmentary and heavily restored; the services for which Hippostratus is praised are obscured in conventional formulas, but the honours he receives, *ateleia* (exemption from taxation) throughout the *koinon* cities and a bronze cavalry statue, suggest benefactions of some magnitude. On an analogy with both the Ptolemaic officials of the Nesiote League and Alexander's officer Philoxenus, it is probable that Lysimachus' *strategoi* had powers, potentially, to intervene in the cities' financial and judicial affairs. However, as Burstein argues, the *koinon*'s ability to make these grants of *ateleia* suggests that in normal circumstances the League enjoyed a degree of internal autonomy consistent with that already noted for some individual cities.[125]

Bengtson cited the relatively moderate tone of the decree for Hippostratus as proof of sincere gratitude towards the *strategos*.[126] While this interpretation is not incompatible with the evidence for Lysimachus' benefactions and his readiness to allow cities which stayed loyal a fair degree of autonomy, the tone of the decree should not be given too much weight. Its moderation may be explained in part by its relatively early date; as time passed and their dynasties became more firmly established, the Macedonian rulers might naturally grow used to, and indeed expect, extravagant compliments, while the cities in turn grew more adept at providing them. Also, the emergence of the decree for Hippodamus, seemingly couched in almost identical terms, makes it more likely that such praise represents convention rather than a sincere tribute to an individual.

The context in which Lysimachus first appointed his *strategos* of the Ionians is uncertain, nor is it clear whether the office continued until the end of his reign. Bengtson saw Lysimachus install a network of *strategoi* over the *koina* in response to the military threat posed by Demetrius' fleet, to replace a single *strategos* whose authority had embraced both Aeolis and Ionia. He suggests that Prepelaus was appointed in 302 BC as the first incumbent of that post. This seems unjustified. Though Prepelaus' title is *strategos* with specific responsibility for 'the Ionian and Aeolian cities', his task is primarily that of conquest and his administrative powers, as Bengtson himself noted, stem from his military office. His position is closest to that of Alcimachus in 334 BC, who has exactly the same title. There is no evidence that either man, after taking the administrative measures required by conquest, remained in the area with supervisory powers over the cities.[127] Bengtson's identification of So[sthenes], the general active in saving Priene from attack by the Magnesians and Pedieis *c.* 286–5 BC, as a possible successor to Hippostratus is also questionable. Lysimachus' letter to Priene after the crisis refers to his orders to 'obey the general So[sthenes]'; Bengtson saw this as a reference to So[sthenes]' recent appointment as *strategos* of the *koinon*, announced to Priene and the other cities by royal letter. Quite apart from the fact of Hippodamus' emergence as a possible successor to Hippostratus, one could argue that So[sthenes]' role is purely military, and that it is in his capacity as the king's trouble-shooter, sent to deal with a specific crisis, that the citizens are told to co-operate with him. He is given no title in the inscription, as one might expect if he were indeed the important *strategos* of the Ionians, particularly in a letter where Lysimachus does not hesitate to impress upon the Prieneans the correct protocol.[128]

If the *strategia* of the Ionians is not definitely a permanent fixture throughout Lysimachus' reign in Asia Minor, what is the likely context for its establishment? There are two possibilities: if 'the cities of the Ionians' denotes the full membership of the *koinon* as the emphasis on that body in the decrees for the *strategoi* suggests, then the *strategia* is unlikely to pre-date 294 BC when Lysimachus finally got his hands on the League's more important members like Ephesus and Miletus. The decree for Hippostratus, which emphasises his continued *arete* and *eunoia*, suggests that his appointment pre-dates the stone's inscription in 289–8 BC by some time; Hippodamus' period of office was therefore brief, or perhaps more plausibly, he was Hippostratus' successor.[129]

Alternatively, the *strategia* may represent Lysimachus' response to specific circumstances. Past events suggest that the application of a special administrative system to the Ionian cities – the appointment of 'supervisors' like Philoxenus and perhaps Orontes – had been prompted by revolt in the cities or fear of it. If the same is true of

Lysimachus' *strategia*, then a possible context for its establishment might be *c.* 290 BC, a time when Trogus hints at trouble among the Ionian cities. Though Geyer doubted the historicity of this 'revolt', events in the late 290s BC make such a development quite plausible; Lysimachus had been heavily defeated by the Getae and only events in central Greece had saved Thrace from Demetrius; perhaps the latter tried also to capitalise on Lysimachus' loss of resources and prestige to recover his Asian possessions.[130]

To sum up: as officials whose titles proclaim authority over the 'Ionian cities', rather than a satrapy of 'Ionia', Lysimachus' *strategoi* seem more akin to the officials heading the Hellenic or Nesiote leagues than the later regional governors to whom they are traditionally compared. As such, they represent no contrast to Antigonus' administrative system. There is no evidence to support the view that such officials were appointed throughout Lysimachus' Asian kingdom or that this *strategia* remained in force for the whole of his reign. Rather these Ionian *strategoi* may represent a special security measure to protect an area of high commercial and strategic value which had recently been under threat; if so, this follows a precedent set by Alexander and perhaps by the Achaemenids too.

LYSIMACHUS AND THE *LAOI*

So far, the focus has been almost exclusively on Lysimachus' government of his Greek subjects, an emphasis which in part reflects the nature of the literary sources. Where these touch on questions of administration at all, it is on relations between king and city that they concentrate. Direct information on the Diadochs' government of the indigenous peoples of their realms is scarce. Accordingly, it is perhaps not surprising that many modern commentators follow their ancient predecessors' lead in seeing the government of the early Hellenistic kingdoms almost exclusively in terms of the *poleis*. It is assumed, for instance, that Lysimachus' evident wealth must imply crippling levels of taxation for his Greek subjects.

To see the economy of the Hellenistic kingdoms solely in terms of the royal administration and the Greek cities is to look at a jigsaw with a piece missing. As heirs to Alexander and the Achaemenid kings, the Diadochs found themselves masters of vast tracts of royal land, in extent comprising the greatest part of their kingdoms. This land represented rich sources of minerals, timber, livestock and agricultural produce; it was worked by its indigenous peoples (*laoi*), who had paid taxes, in money, kind and labour, to the successive dynasties ruling Asia. The value of such workers in terms of royal revenue is reflected in Cyrus' order to his troops not to massacre their prisoners of war since 'a peopled land is a prize of great wealth'; the Persepolis Fortification tablets reflect Achaemenid concern to maintain their numbers; Briant describes the *laoi* as the 'major productive force' in the economy of Achaemenid and Hellenistic Asia. In terms of the Hellenistic kingdoms' economic structure, the *laoi* form a link in a chain of transactions involving also the *poleis* and the king and his officials. Their labour provides raw materials for goods manufactured and exported by cities like Ephesus and Miletus, which in turn may serve as a market for the surplus produce grown on royal land. Bikermann describes the revenues accruing to the Seleucid kings from royal land as 'enormous', and it is the ownership of this land which makes possible royal benefactions to the Greek cities in the form of grain and money.[131]

What then did the royal land and *laoi* mean to Lysimachus in terms of revenues and what obligations characterised the relationship between him and his non-Greek subjects? Only two pieces of evidence relate directly to Lysimachus; the uprising of the Pedieis living in the environs of Priene, *c.* 286 BC, and an anecdote in Plutarch where a disgruntled peasant in Greater Phrygia sighs for the good old days of Antigonus' rule, suggesting that under Lysimachus and perhaps his Seleucid successors, the *laoi* were subject to increasingly heavy burdens. Two factors, however, permit some inferences to be drawn from the practice of his near contemporaries. First, the surviving evidence for conditions for the indigenous peoples of Asia Minor suggests a certain continuity. Second, it is increasingly recognised that the Macedonian conquerors, far from imposing wholesale a 'superior' Greek administrative system upon their Asian kingdoms, were ready and willing to learn from their predecessors. The system which the Achaemenids inherited from their predecessors for administration of the royal lands and government of the *laoi* was essentially still in force at the end of the Seleucid era and later.[132] Acknowledging the disparate forms of community which made up their empire (cities, villages, nomadic tribes, military colonies), the rulers of Asia maintained these traditional units for purposes of administration and taxation. The Hellenistic kings extend royal *eusebeia* to indigenous sanctuaries as well as to the temples of the Olympians and govern through liaison with local élites, including them in the administrative hierarchy.[133]

The precise extent of Lysimachus' *basilike chora* in Asia is unknown, but evidence for the gift or sale of royal land by his Seleucid and Attalid successors indicates some of the areas it comprised. In the Troad, Antiochus I grants, in total, 2,000 hectares of land to Aristodicides, who can choose to attach it to the territory of either Ilium or Scepsis. This implies the existence of royal land on the borders of both Gergis and Scepsis, with more between Ilium and Gergis since Aristodicides also receives the fortress of Petra, sited by Cook in the area of the Scamander gorge. Seleucid sales of land to Pitane and Antiochus I's grants of land in the territory of Zeleia suggested to Rostovtzeff that a large part of the fertile coastline of Aeolis and the Troad belonged to the kings. In Hellespontine Phrygia, Philetaerus exempts the Cyzicenes from duty paid on goods taken through his territory, presupposing royal land on the borders of that city. Plutarch's grumbling peasant anecdote suggests the cultivation of extensive royal lands in Greater Phrygia, a hypothesis supported by its largely village-based structure and the relative scarcity of Greek cities. In Ionia, Antigonus reassures the citizens of Teos as to his ownership of corn-rich lands, presumably not far away, whose inhabitants were clearly obliged to pay him *phoros*. Finally, it is possible that the documents which record some kind of settlement made by Lysimachus for the indigenous Pedieis at Priene reflect his possession of royal land nearby in the fertile Maeander valley.[134]

As a source of ready cash, the king might 'sell' a portion of royal land to friends, relations or petitioners; Antiochus I received 350T for the land sold to Pitane. Alternatively he might 'give' land to a faithful follower or a loyal city.[135] In some cases at least, when the buyer or recipient died, the land reverted to the king and could be resold. The king was careful to keep track of lands which temporarily passed to a concessionaire; Antiochus II's sale of land to his ex-wife Laodice shows that all sales contracts were registered in an archive, in this case at Sardis.[136]

Even while temporarily 'alienated' by gift or sale, the land continued to be a source of profit to the king. The long-held view of Asia Minor under Persian and Macedonian rule as essentially 'feudal', with land divided into 'estates' centred on fortified dwellings, whose holders had complete and undisputed ownership both of this land and the workers 'attached' to it as 'serfs', was first questioned by Bikermann. In recent years his views have been taken up and developed by Briant, who argues plausibly for a system whereby what was 'sold' or 'given' was not the land itself, or its workers, but its revenues. For purposes of taxation, which they continued to pay to the king, not the concessionaire, the *laoi* were 'attached' to the villages of their birth, but this did not prevent them from living elsewhere. Neither 'slaves' nor 'serfs', they remained personally free with their own property and houses, and a considerable degree of local autonomy, although the demands of royal taxation and obligatory service to the king might in practice render them dependent upon him.[137]

Some insight into the precise nature of these burdens is provided by the mid-third(?)-century inscription from Sardis dealing with the estate of the concessionaire Mnesimachus. The *phoros* which the king levies on the villages on Mnesimachus' 'estate' is paid partly in money and partly in kind; the *laoi* must also provide certain services (*leitourgia*) to the king. Briant suggests this took the form of labour on road-building and other public works.[138] A more recently published inscription from Aegae in Aeolis, which seems to deal with an indigenous community, also gives detailed information on the kind of taxes and services involved. The first surviving lines mention a tithe (*dekaten*), perhaps to be paid as a 'gift' to the king; in addition the people must contribute one-eighth of the produce from their fruit trees and one-fiftieth of their sheep and goats; exemption from tax on this livestock's offspring is clearly a privilege. The products of bee-keeping and the hunt are also taxed; the king receives one-eighth of the yield from the hives and one leg from each boar and deer. There is also a reference to *leitourgia* 'for the army', though whether this entails military service, the provision of military supplies or billeting is unclear.[139]

The identity of the king who issued this decree is uncertain; Malay dates the stone to the early third century BC on stylistic grounds, suggesting Antiochus I as the author because of his 'long reign'. Though the term *Basilikon*, attested elsewhere in Seleucid texts, might suggest that dynasty, the Attalids also use it. While not directly attested for Lysimachus, there is no evidence that he used another term. The assumption that so elaborate a taxation system implies a reign of long duration is questionable, given the continuity in administrative methods discussed above. Even if it were accepted, is Antiochus' twenty-year rule much more likely than that of Lysimachus, whose hold on Aeolis lasted, on the most conservative estimate, around thirteen years? The text's lettering perhaps favours a late fourth- or very early third-century date over one in the second quarter of the third, as does the stoichedon style of the first section.[140] Though no certain attribution can be made, on epigraphic grounds there seems

149

no good reason to exclude Lysimachus, or even Antigonus, from authorship.

The *laoi*, then, were a steady source of profit to the king; in return, he secured their protection in times of warfare or other emergency – Aristodicides is obliged to receive the *basilikoi laoi* at Petra under such circumstances. The text from Aegae may likewise illustrate royal concern to protect or redress wrongs done to the indigenous peoples and their property; the king or his officer restores a recently dispossessed community to their land and property. A clause which seems to provide for the supply of agricultural equipment at royal expense may suggest a context of devastation by a hostile army. Protection of a similar kind might also be offered by a city to *laoi* working its *chora*; a Prienean decree honouring the *neokoros* Megabyzus grants him right of abode in Priene's territory, but prohibits his encroachment upon the property of the indigenous Pedieis.[141]

Though generally a rich source of royal profit, the indigenous peoples could, on occasion, prove something of a liability. The crisis at Priene *c.* 286 BC suggests that discontent among the non-Greek peoples might be harnessed by a king's opponents to cause him trouble. Following a violent attack upon citizens and *chora* by the Pedieis, acting in concert with the Magnesians and perhaps Demetrius, a fragmentary decree records a royal settlement, most probably issued by Lysimachus. Though the first half of the text is severely damaged, its provisions seemingly concern the status and living conditions of the Pedieis; the second half concerns the punishment of those who participated in the violence.[142]

Traditionally the text has been interpreted thus: the clauses which seem to concern the right of the Pedieis to dwell (*paroikein*) in the villages (*kata komas*), with reference also to a time limit (?) of 'thirty days', were thought to describe an upgrading of their status from that of serfs attached to the king's land (*basilikoi laoi*), to a position of 'greater freedom' as dependants of the Greek city. The term *paroikein* has presumably prompted an analogy with the Spartan *perioikoi*, who enjoyed rather better conditions than the helots. Some scholars see Lysimachus 'giving' Priene, then suffering a labour shortage, only the *laoi*. Others assume that the movement of *laoi* from king to city must imply also a gift of royal land to Priene; this settlement therefore entails a 'unilateral decision' by Lysimachus 'to define in detail the terms of Priene's relationship with its new subjects'. Both Welles and Burstein see this 'promotion' of the Pedieis as preceding the ructions of 286–5 BC; the latter explained Magnesia's part in the attack as inspired by thwarted desire for the land 'given' to Priene. This is a plausible motive for Magnesia, but it is harder to understand why the Pedieis' *improved* status should make them take violent action.[143] Accordingly it is best to follow Hiller and Sherwin-White in seeing the clauses which concern the Pedieis' habitat as prompted by the troubles rather than preceding them. If the right to *paroikein* does represent an upgrading of status, then it must refer only to those Pedieis not involved in the attack; certainly a clear distinction seems to be made between the Pedieis who are the recipients of this settlement and those responsible for the pillaging of Priene, by the preposition *de* in l.11.[144]

It is, however, questionable whether an improvement in the Pedieis' status is actually the point at issue. Both this and the idea of the Pedieis' 'transfer' to Priene along with a slice of royal land rest heavily upon the outmoded belief that the *laoi* were serfs, 'attached to the land' and 'subject' to its successive owners. *Paroikein* can mean simply 'to dwell', and Sherwin-White sees a definition of the Pedieis' proper place of abode (the *komai*) after their unlawful incursion onto Priene's territory as the main aim of Lysimachus' pronouncement. This was made in terms already defined by Alexander who had explicitly stated his ownership of the *komai* and consequent responsibility for their indigenous inhabitants; the relevant section of his edict was accordingly now published by the Prieneans as a preface to the decrees which record the crisis of 286–5 BC.[145] If then the Pedieis who attacked Priene were *basilikoi laoi*, either working royal land outside Prienean territory or, as Welles supposed, detailed by the king to solve a labour shortage at Priene, then Lysimachus' settlement does not constitute interference into Priene's relations with 'her subjects'.[146] As Alexander's heir and master of the royal land, the Pedieis remain his responsibility and it is only proper for him to take steps to prevent the repetition of such an incident and to punish the transgressors.

If the rising of the Pedieis at Priene is not the result of a specific decision of Lysimachus, as was previously thought, it is perhaps best ascribed to poverty and generally unsatisfactory, perhaps worsening, conditions, something hinted at in Plutarch's Phrygian peasant anecdote, mentioned above. Possibly Lysimachus' efforts to maximise the exploitation of Anatolia's agricultural resources led to harder conditions for the *laoi*. The situation was probably exacerbated by the constant warfare which characterises the Successor period. The villagers might see their fields ravaged by armies passing through, their carts and baggage animals requisitioned, or, perhaps still worse, find themselves unwilling hosts to hungry soldiers billeted on them for a long stay. Despite these drains on their resources the taxman would still be making the same demands.[147]

CONCLUSIONS

The extant evidence for Lysimachus' government of his kingdom suggests that his methods did not differ greatly from those of his predecessors or contemporaries. Nor is there any suggestion that those who followed him as rulers of Asia Minor regarded him as an awful object lesson, avoiding such practices like the plague. As regards the Greek cities, consciousness of their strategic and economic value, in the context of fierce competition from his fellow Diadochs, seems to have dictated a policy fuelled by pragmatism rather than ideology, which mixed incentives and deterrents in response to particular circumstances. In the long term, several cities greatly benefited from his policy of synoecism which brought increased stability and prosperity; in more than one case, posterity had good reason to thank him, as the following chapter will show. The indigenous peoples, governed along traditional lines which may have lacked flexibility in the context of the war-torn age, and demanding less consideration in terms of their value as a political force, may have fared less well.

6

KINGSHIP, CULT AND COURT

So far we have followed Lysimachus' rise from governor of a somewhat insalubrious satrapy to ruler of a large and powerful kingdom, and examined his methods of government. Though topics such as benefaction and city-building have been touched upon in passing, the focus has been largely on his military and diplomatic skills and his deployment of monetary and manpower resources in the pursuit and acquisition of power. Traditionally, the study of such methods has often been thought to encompass all that is really central to an understanding of political action.

While, however, the conquerors and rulers of great kingdoms may be able to maintain power through money and military force alone – at least for a time – the processes whereby power changes hands, throughout history and in diverse societies, suggest that this approach is rarely seen as profitable. Instead the power-holders seek ways to persuade those whom they rule 'to acquiesce in a polity where the distribution of power is manifestly unequal and unjust'.[1] Frequently this is achieved in part through ceremonies and rituals which surround the person of the ruler (or ruling group), setting him apart from the mass of his subjects. The importance of such rituals and the media by which the ruler presents himself to his subjects – paintings, sculpture, public inscriptions, costume, construction of temples and cities and other benefactions – are increasingly acknowledged by historians and anthropologists alike as integral to the successful exercise of power and 'central to the structure and working of any society'. Similarly there is a growing recognition that the response to this presentation, reflected most obviously in the honours paid to royalty, says much about the way his subjects view the world they live in and how they accommodate themselves to dramatic changes in it.[2]

IDEAS ON KINGSHIP

For the Successors, who transformed themselves from governors of a limited territory, with their authority sanctioned by a central power, into monarchs of independent kingdoms, it was perhaps more than usually important to convey a convincing image of kingship. The fierce competition between Lysimachus and his colleagues to win territories, wealth, and support from courtiers, troops and subjects gave the whole business an extra edge. As claimants to power from outside the Argead dynasty, operating in a context of political instability, the kingly image which the new rulers strove to promote predictably lays its emphasis on tradition.[3] Inspiration came from several sources.

Kingship is a favourite topic for political theorists like Aristotle and Isocrates. While the impact of such theory on events in the Greek-speaking world of the mid-fourth century BC has been over-estimated in some quarters, and it would be naïve to imagine Lysimachus and his colleagues with their copies of Aristotle and Isocrates ever at hand, these writers do draw a useful portrait of the ideal monarch from within the context of the Greek city-state. To define early Hellenistic kingship wholly in terms of the Greek writings on it would, however, be misleading. The reinterpretation and full evaluation of non-Greek evidence from the Near East, unblinkered by what might be called the 'colonial approach', has shown that ideas of kingship, both for Alexander and his successors in Asia, were strongly influenced by the practices of their Achaemenid predecessors.[4]

Contemporary ideas of kingship can be found also in the work of theorists attached to the Diadochs' courts, like Hecataeus of Abdera, Euhemerus of Cardia and possibly Berossus in Babylon.[5] These form a slightly different category. Their beliefs on kingship, though often projected back into a mythical past, may serve to justify their patron's actions after the event rather than representing the inspiration for them.

This chapter aims to examine, in the context of these contemporary and traditional ideas of kingship, Lysimachus' achievement of royal status and the way he chose to present himself to his subjects. Since the Successors operated in an atmosphere of intense competition, Lysimachus' royal propaganda, his benefactions, the cults established for him, his court and the cities which he founded cannot be considered in isolation but must be compared with what is known of the practices of his rivals.

THE ROAD TO KINGSHIP

Alexander's premature death in 323 BC left his empire with no heirs save the epileptic Philip Arridhaeus and the infant Alexander IV. Perdiccas' redistribution of satrapies at Babylon therefore effectively placed its government in the hands of Alexander's erstwhile *philoi*. Loyalty to the new regent and good luck in being 'on the spot' may both have played a part in determining these appointments. To entrust the empire in an interregnum to talented and energetic men who had occupied a privileged position at court was not itself untoward. Lysimachus and his colleagues might even be seen as filling the role of the 'stake-holders' who traditionally 'stand in' in the period between one ruler's death and his heir's accession. Unlike many of these 'stand-ins', however, their powers were far from being negligible. While it would be wrong to see the formation of the Hellenistic kingdoms as predestined, given the situation in 323 BC, an interregnum always renders the 'state' highly vulnerable to change[6] and this promised to be a long one. Also, the early signs of personal ambition displayed by Perdiccas may have aroused suspicion regarding his integrity as representative of the Argead heirs. Both factors would increase the likelihood of competition for power among the 'stake-holders' themselves.

Though Hieronymus' stress on the aspirations of these men to *kingly* power from the first days after Alexander's death may owe too much to hindsight, it is significant that, as the new satraps jockeyed for position, two themes emerge which remain central to the Diadochs' later claims to royalty. These are an insistence on themselves as Alexander's heirs and an emphasis on ability, primarily in the sphere of war. Military victory's importance as a means of achieving and maintaining royal power has been rightly emphasised by Austin. Victory brings wealth and personal support; these in turn increase the prospect of further military success.[7]

Thus Leonnatus, with blood ties to the Argead house, styled his hair like Alexander and dressed with royal extravagance. Where ties of blood were lacking, bonds of matrimony could be forged. Perdiccas, with Alexander's Royal Seal already in his hands, was ready to risk Antipater's wrath, repudiating his daughter Nicaea when the prospect of marriage to Alexander's sister Cleopatra beckoned. Cassander followed victory over Olympias in 316 BC with marriage to Alexander's half-sister Thessalonice.[8]

Ability and its rewards, wealth and support, are likewise stressed. Cassander, 'fair' and 'energetic' (*epieikes* and *energos*), wins the support of the mainland Greek cities from Polyperchon who acted in a lazy and stupid fashion (*argos kai aphronos*). Ptolemy cultivates the goodwill of the Egyptians: Egypt's wealth buys him soldiers and a devoted circle of *philoi*; by 321 BC he holds Egypt as 'spear-won' land.[9]

Long before his formal assumption of kingship in 306 BC, Antigonus was hailed as king by the Persians. Plutarch tells us that Seleucus too, by 306 BC, 'had already assumed royal prerogatives when he gave audience to the barbarians'.[10] Little is said regarding Lysimachus' kingly aspirations, but this is probably the result of his preoccupation with Thracian affairs in the first years after 323 BC, which excluded him both from an active part in the early Diadoch wars and from a major role in this section of Hieronymus' narrative. It cannot, therefore, be assumed that at this stage kingship held no allure for him. Diodorus tells us that, like his fellow Diadochs, he sued for Cleopatra's hand, while his demand for Hellespontine Phrygia in 315 BC plausibly represents a challenge to Antigonus' claim to be Alexander's successor in Asia. He took pains to publicise his intimacy with Alexander and his success is mirrored in Demetrius' later perception of him as a more formidable rival than Pyrrhus for Macedon's throne, because he was 'known to many through Alexander'.[11]

BASILEUS LYSIMACHUS

The timing and context of the Diadochs' assumption of the title *Basileus* underlines the importance of victory and the support which follows in its wake. Though Cassander's murder of Alexander IV in 310 BC obviously smoothed their path, clearly it was Demetrius' victory over Ptolemy at Salamis in 306 BC which prompted the Antigonids to adopt the kingly title. Antigonus' *philoi* take a prominent role in acknowledging his claim to royal status; we are also told that he was acclaimed as king by *to plethos*. If it is correct to see this term as designating the army, then the tripartite foundation of the monarchy, later acknowledged in the epigraphic formula, 'King, Friends and Army', is already in force.[12]

Antigonus' opponents were not slow to respond; the following year Ptolemy's *philoi* conferred the title *Basileus* upon him. A Babylonian king list names Seleucus as king in 305–4 BC; probably by summer 304

BC Lysimachus and Cassander had followed suit. As both kingship ritual and history make clear, possession and use of royal regalia is closely linked with claims to legitimacy in rule.[13] Though the Diadochs may have long been kings in all but name, their adoption of the title *Basileus* and wearing of the diadem is no mere formality, but marks a moment of supreme importance.

For the Diadochs, *Basileus* had the significance which Alexander gave it. Connoting barbarism in Classical Greece, the word was seldom used in official documentation and then usually qualified by an ethnic which defines the national quality of the monarch's sovereignty. Alexander's use of it as a pre-name without the article is rightly seen as signifying his claim to the Achaemenid heritage, but the idea that *Basileus Alexandros* also expressed the idea of a monarchy that was above all personal is less compelling. The strong evidence for continuity in royal ideology and kingship practices deliberately fostered by the successive dynasties who ruled in Asia,[14] suggests rather that it was the traditional aspect of his kingship which Alexander wished to emphasise.

Closely associated with assumption of the royal title was the wearing of the diadem. Originally part of the Great King's adornment, it becomes the archetypal symbol of royalty with Alexander. Worn as his official royal headdress, it is thought to express to the indigenous peoples of the empire his status as heir to the Achaemenids. Its potency as a symbol of royalty is reflected in anecdotes attached to both Seleucus and Lysimachus; a temporary wearing of Alexander's diadem is a portent of future kingship.[15]

Scholars discussing the meaning of title and diadem for the Successors generally make two main points. Both express a claim to Alexander's Asiatic territories, but while the Antigonids are claiming *ta hola*, the other Diadochs wish only for acknowledgement as independent rulers in a section of the empire and their claim is only to part of the Asian territory.[16] Since, however, the validity of the contrast traditionally drawn between Antigonid aims and those of their opponents is doubtful, so the idea of the 'different meanings' of title and diadem is also open to criticism. The famous anecdote in Plutarch's *Demetrius* where Poliorcetes' *philoi* toast his rivals, using titles which express his rejection of their claim to *Basileia* certainly supports this view of Antigonid ambition. The literary evidence, however, also makes it clear that their opponents' assumption of title and diadem expresses above all a reaction to the Antigonid claim to *ta hola* and a rejection of it, as does their consistent use, subsequently, of

the title in official documentation. No statement is made to support
the idea of a more limited territorial objective.

The belief that both title and diadem express a claim to Alexander's
Asian empire has also caused problems in Lysimachus' case. It is clear
he had assumed both long before the Ipsus victory gave him
Antigonus' Anatolian possessions. Though it has been suggested
either that Thrace was seen as part of the Asian empire in the period
between 331 BC and 305–4 BC or that Lysimachus' title is validated by
his claim to land in Asia in 315 BC and active pursuit of it from 305 BC
to 301 BC[18], such solutions are unnecessary. First, since Alexander had
conquered an empire comprising much of the known world, it is
questionable whether his Successors still saw this inheritance in terms
of the strict division between Europe and Asia which modern
historians insist on. Second, the concept of a perfectly harmonised
pattern underlying the Diadochs' assumption of kingship should be
jettisoned. If, instead, their action is seen as inspired by two factors,
the need to stand firm against a rival and the timely show of that
support from friends and army which was essential for *basileia*, then
the so-called difficulties are resolved.

THE VERY IMAGE OF A KING: PROPAGANDA AND SELF-PRESENTATION

In declaring themselves *basileis* the Successors took upon themselves
certain obligations in relation to their subjects and placed themselves
in a new position as regards the gods. Though royal ideology and
kingship ritual may vary considerably in their particulars in different
societies at different times, certain themes recur consistently. The
king is the protector of his people: he must be victorious in war; he
builds walled cities as a place of refuge for his subjects. The king
stands as guarantor of order against chaos; he uses his great wealth
both to stave off disaster by propitiatory gifts to the gods and to
relieve his people's distress when faced with irresistible forces such as
famine, disease, earthquake or enemy devastation.[19] The king has a
special relationship with the gods. Often the chosen favourite of a
god, he accedes to the throne by divine will and his victories are the
proof of divine favour.[20]

Closely connected to the idea of the king as a symbol of stability and
continuity is the concept of an inherited claim to rule. The Cypriot
prince Nicocles, for whom Isocrates wrote a treatise outlining the
advantages of monarchy, justified his position saying: 'Teucer ori-

ginally founded the city . . . later after it had been lost it was recovered by my father Evagoras . . . this is to show that I hold my office by natural right.' A ruler unable to claim blood ties with his predecessor presents himself as his natural heir on the basis of victory, ability, success and the other kingly qualities which themselves reflect divine approval. Nabonidus, reaching the neo-Babylonian throne as victor in a bloody dynastic struggle, declared himself 'the real executor of the wills of Nebuchadnezzar and Neriglissar, my royal predecessors!' The failure of the latter's heirs to keep the throne (or their lives) proved divine disfavour; Nabonidus' victory reflected the purpose of the gods.[21]

The line taken by the Diadochs was essentially the same. Promoting their victories and their own heroic qualities, they strove to present themselves as rightful heirs to the kings who had preceded them. Lysimachus and his colleagues emphasised their ties with Alexander, who himself had claimed his 'inheritance' from the Achaemenid kings.

HEIRS TO ALEXANDER

Of the Diadochs, only Ptolemy was bold enough to claim actual blood-ties with the Argead house. One story circulating at his court presented him as Philip II's illegitimate son; the other, which apparently gained official acceptance, promoted the Argead ancestry of his mother Arsinoe. The idea that the Seleucid court spawned a legend linking Seleucus' wife Apama to Alexander is less compelling. Apama's importance seems rather to have lain in her Iranian aristocratic background which helped to make the Seleucid dynasty acceptable to its Persian subjects.[22] Since Philip and Alexander had taken pride in descent from Heracles, the Diadochs also strove to establish links with the Argead house through this shared ancestry. Theocritus' panegyric for Ptolemy II presents Ptolemy I and Alexander on equal terms, as descendants of 'the strong Heraclid'. The later Antigonids, certainly, emphasised descent from Heracles; the identification may go back to the earliest days of the dynasty.[23]

Lysimachus' approach was rather different. Rather than attempting to claim blood-ties with the house of Alexander, he attracted or, more probably, promoted a literary tradition which stressed his intimacy with Alexander in a friendship based on equal ability. The success of this presentation was enhanced by the fact that for most of his career Lysimachus faced opponents who could not claim such a tie. Antigonus belonged to an older generation and had never been part of the élite circle. Too young to have served with Alexander, Demetrius tried to obliterate the memory of the conqueror by emphasis on his own dazzling personality and achievements. Pyrrhus, Demetrius' contemporary, did promote himself as a new Alexander; significantly this won him Macedonian support against Demetrius, but was not effective against Alexander's comrade-in-arms, Lysimachus. Even Seleucus, Lysimachus' last great enemy, though his contemporary, only reached prominence at court at the very end of Alexander's reign and after; the scarcity of literary anecdotes which stress an intimacy with Alexander suggest this was a line which perhaps he felt he could not convincingly pursue.[24]

The 'lion-killer' legend, prominent in Lysimachus' royal propaganda, has already been discussed. Apart from stressing intimacy with Alexander, this episode features other 'royal themes'. Superhuman strength and courage, despite Isocrates' emphasis on the less macho heroic qualities, seems to have retained its allure as a justification of royal status. Then there is the motif of the hunt, an activity with specifically royal connotations. The visual motif of royal hero versus beast as symbolising the king's role as guardian of order against chaos has already been mentioned.[25]

This episode's importance for Lysimachus is underlined by the prominence of the lion motif elsewhere in his royal imagery. The lion-*protome*, facing right or left, appears regularly on his coinage from the earliest Philip II types minted at Lysimacheia, serving also as the reverse type for some of Lysimachus' later bronze issues. Baldus's theory, based on the *protome* format, that the lion symbol known from coins represents Lysimachus' personal seal-device, is plausible. The idea of the lion as Lysimachus' dynastic symbol gains support from its appearance on the coins issued by his son Ptolemy at Telmessus in the mid-third century BC. Recently Baldus has argued that the lion was the seal-device used by Alexander for his European correspondence; if correct, then the lion links Lysimachus to Alexander with a double knot. Finally, Lysimachus' massive flagship, named *Leontophoros*, suggests that, as a lion-slayer, Lysimachus saw himself as lion-like. Alexander, of course, had done the same.[26]

Obviously the lion-slayer motif also recalls Heracles, founder of the Argead dynasty. The discovery of a monumental marble head at Ephesus wearing a diadem bound with olive leaves (Heracles' symbol) and resembling the unbearded portraits of that hero produced by Scopas and his circle has prompted the suggestion that Lysimachus pursued this image in another medium. For the authors, who date the head closely to 285–4 BC, the year when Lysimachus' power reached its height, this pose as Heracles symbolises his readiness to reach out and recover the whole empire of Alexander.[27]

The general identification of the head as an early Hellenistic ruler portrait is acceptable and Lysimachus' role as founder of new Ephesus makes him a likely candidate. The methods used to justify a 'secure identification' with Lysimachus and a precise dating to 285–4 BC are, however, far from sound. The stylistic arguments, for instance, rely heavily on the belief that Lysimachus placed his own portrait on certain of his coins. This is almost certainly wrong. Nor does the statue's lined brow necessarily represent a 'realistic' feature, favouring an identification with the aged king; a regular feature of Alexander's portraits, the lined brow may be intended, in the physiognomic language of the age, to convey not weariness, but courage.[28]

All that can be said is that possibly Lysimachus pursued, in the medium of monumental sculpture, the identification with Heracles suggested by the lion-slayer image promoted in the literary tradition and on his seal and coinage. Anything more than that is pure speculation.

FAVOURITES OF THE GODS

Divine patronage is an enduring and central theme of kingship. Following a longstanding tradition, the Diadochs used portents and prophecies to present their victories as sanctioned by the gods and their rule as the inevitable expression of divine will. Images of their divine patrons appear on their coinage; inscriptions echo the idea of divine ancestry; temple-building and dedications express thanks for past favours or hope of future help.

In return for his prophecy of Seleucus' kingship, perhaps as early as 312 BC, the Seleucids built Apollo a sanctuary at Daphne and commissioned the magnificent Didyma temple. Seleucid coins from the reign of Antiochus I show Apollo, in prophet guise, on the reverse; later Seleucid inscriptions regularly describe him as the founder of their house. The coin types of Ptolemy and Demetrius are likewise thought to express a claim to divine patronage. Ptolemy's eagle and thunderbolt links the dynasty to Zeus. Poseidon, seated, standing, striding or fighting on Demetrius' coins, is a natural 'ancestor' for the Besieger, victor at Salamis and largely dependent on sea-power for the maintenance of his rule. Some statues and coin portraits of Demetrius show him with bull horns, Poseidon's attribute.[29]

Though the issue of such coin portraits, showing the ruler complete with divine attributes, may represent a development from Alexander's Heracles coinage, which merged the hero's features with those of the young king, the practice was by no means universal. Only Demetrius and Ptolemy issued these personal portraits in their lifetime. Like Alexander himself, Seleucus probably left it to his followers and descendants to strike a posthumous portrait. There is no evidence that Antigonus or Cassander struck personal portrait coins, while their ephemeral power precluded a posthumous issue. The same is true of Lysimachus.[30]

Traditionally these portrait coins have been thought to express pretensions to divinity, with fear of hubris explaining a reluctance to issue them. Quite why Ptolemy and Demetrius should have been less concerned about offending the gods than their fellows is left unclear! Smith, more plausibly, sees personal portraits as simply one of several ways to express an assertion of legitimate independent rule. This view is certainly supported by the choice of themes favoured on the Diadochs' royal coinage; the images – divine patrons, victory or the portrait of a predecessor (Alexander) – are all well-established motifs in justifying claims to kingship.[31]

Discussion of the themes depicted on royal coinage also raises the thorny question as to how far Lysimachus and his fellow Diadochs intended their coinage to function as 'propaganda'. The main recipients of the Successors' silver coinage and therefore its 'target audience' were probably mercenary soldiers. Since competition for Greek and Macedonian manpower was intense and defection, sometimes by whole armies, frequent, 'programmatic' coin types might represent a useful method of attracting and maintaining mercenary support. Recent scholarship has certainly laid great emphasis on the propaganda function of the Successors' coinage.[32]

If one accepts that coin types may have a 'programmatic' element, and that periods of upheaval and 'civil war' are perhaps especially likely to spawn such coinage, the question still remains as to the effectiveness of such 'propaganda'. In his study of the public response to coin types in the ancient world, with particular reference to the Roman imperial period, Crawford concluded that coins probably were examined – if only for forgery! Some common types were well enough known to attract nicknames, Darics, cistophoroi, etc. The recipient's first concern, however, was the coin's acceptability in financial transactions and the main element of the coin type which attracted attention was therefore that which said on whose authority it was struck.[33] The type, then, is significant largely through its association with a coinage of high quality and reputation.

The relevance of such factors in assessing Lysimachus' coinage is considerable. What stands out is the consistency of the imagery depicted. Like Cassander and Antigonus, before 301 BC he retained Alexander's own types. This need not reflect mere conservatism or a desire not to offend Cassander. A focus on Alexander, who likewise features strongly in Lysimachus' literary propaganda, could have the same meaning as it is thought to have for Antigonus, an assertion of himself as Alexander's heir. The story, already noted, of Alexander sanctioning Lysimachus' future royalty by binding his diadem round his wounded friend's head sounds the same note.[34]

After the Ipsus victory, a new Alexander portrait adorns the obverse of the gold and silver types issued by Lysimachus until the end of his reign and then posthumously by the independent cities of northern Asia Minor. Showing Alexander in the guise of Zeus Ammon, and described as 'the finest portrait head on any Greek coin', it successfully conveys those qualities which Alexander himself promoted in his own portraiture and which his successors tried to emulate in both life and art. Pollitt suggests that Lysimachus may even have commissioned this portrait from Alexander's favourite gem-carver, Pyrgoteles.[35]

Hadley saw the deified Alexander as an image chosen to promote Lysimachus' recent victory at Ipsus, more blatantly advertised on the reverse, where Athena holds a tiny Nike crowning the initial letter of the king's name. Alexander's image is intended to recall Demetrius' dream, of Alexander abandoning the Antigonid cause because their watchword does not include his name. Though this has a certain scholarly appeal, if the coin type was meant to function as propaganda it surely presupposes an unusually perceptive audience. Similarly Seltman's criticism of the reverse as tasteless and guilty of a 'cheap allegorical effect' may be valid aesthetically, but if the coins were to succeed as propaganda, then only so obvious a 'message' was likely to get through.[36]

If this Alexander portrait does reflect Lysimachus' personal choice, then it may be enough to say that in place of an Olympian patron, he chose Alexander, in the guise of Zeus Ammon, as the god who sanctioned his rule. This is not unparalleled; the coin issued by Seleucus I, depicting a male head with the attributes of Dionysus, probably represents Alexander rather than the king himself.[37] The prominence given to this image by Lysimachus stands out in comparison to the diversity of types issued by his rivals. This might be explained in propaganda terms, aiming to reinforce Lysimachus' image as Alexander's heir. Alternatively the unchanging types may be connected with the swift popularity of 'Lysimachi' on the market. If the consumer associated certain types with reliability then the incentive to replace a familiar and popular design would not be strong.

The significance of the seated Athena on the reverse is less clear. Price sees it as combining some fidelity to the traditional Alexander types with a celebration of Ipsus. Might it represent a compliment to Athens? Lysimachus was active as a benefactor there soon after Ipsus and enjoyed a close friendship with the poet Philippides, but it is unlikely that Athens formed a major part of his plans at the time when his new coinage was conceived. If Athena's presence has any further significance it may lie in Lysimachus' acquisition after Ipsus of the Troad cities comprising the Ilian *koinon*, a federation centred on the worship of Athena Ilias. A bid for its goodwill with the placing of Athena on his coinage is not implausible; Strabo records Lysimachus' active attempts to play the benefactor at Ilium, hoping presumably both to eclipse the memory of Antigonid benefactions and to promote himself as Alexander's heir by fulfilment of the Conqueror's promises. His refoundation of Antigoneia as Alexandria Troas marks a similar instance of two birds killed with a single stone.[38]

On Lysimachus' gold and silver coinage, Alexander stands alone. It is generally accepted that Lysimachus issued no personal portrait; past attempts to identify certain 'Lysimachi' as bearing portraits of the king are unconvincing. The condition of the examples cited by Richter and Brendel is poor;[39] the 'head of Lysimachus' may simply be an inferior version of the standard Alexander Ammon portrait further distorted by damage. The possibility of a posthumous deified portrait is seriously diminished by Lysimachus' failure to establish a dynasty with an interest in issuing it. Moreover, given the abundance of Lysimachean coinage which has survived, one might expect the existence of a personal portrait issue to be reflected by a considerably larger sample than the few dubious examples proposed.

While Lysimachus passed up the chance to proclaim the royal qualities which the personal portrait coin afforded later Hellenistic kings, his presence manifested itself in other, more conspicuous ways.

Apart from decrees recording his benefactions and dedications promoting his *eusebeia*, his statue adorned the *agorai* of several cities.
Apart from the Ephesian statue already mentioned, Pausanias and
Diodorus note the presence of monumental portraits of Lysimachus at
Athens and Rhodes. A decree from Priene *c.* 286–5 BC tells us that cult
honours for the king included a bronze statue; an inscribed base from
the city, restored with Lysimachus' name, may belong to this
agalma.[40]

What is the significance of such statues? Smith makes several
important points: public statuary in the ancient world 'occupied an
immeasurably higher position in the scheme of things than today';
largely a phenomenon of the Hellenistic age, the number of royal
portrait statues mirror the rise and fall of the Macedonian monarchies; the value of royal portraiture in all media lies not so much in
providing information on the king's actual appearance, but in what it
reveals of contemporary perceptions of *basileia*. As the highest
honour offered by the Greek *polis*, and offered only rarely,[41] the
monumental portrait statue gives particular acknowledgement, in the
Hellenistic age, to an aspect of kingship which is universal and
eternal, the idea of the king as the giver of gifts, provider of all vital
resources.[42]

SAVIOURS AND BENEFACTORS

It was kings who discovered the necessities of life and this is the
reason for the bestowal of kingship in early times not on the
sons of former rulers, but on those who conferred the greatest
and most numerous benefits upon the people.

(Euhemerus of Cardia)

As friend to King Cassander, the man responsible for murdering the
Argead dynasty's last legitimate heir, Euhemerus' motives for
emphasising benefaction over the rights of inheritance may not be
entirely disinterested! This does not, however, diminish his statement's validity; the idea of euergetism as absolutely central to
kingship long pre-dates the Diadoch period. Evidence from the
Persian and neo-Babylonian empires has already been cited; in
Homeric Greece, it is 'becoming' for those 'marked out as kings . . .
with power' to offer generous gifts to a guest. For Aristotle,
benefaction distinguishes the good king from the tyrant; it is the
proper outlet for the great wealth that is characteristic of kings and is
rewarded with great honour. Alexander, famed for his generosity,

would not count a man his friend who refused his gifts. Hecataeus of Abdera says that unless a king is generous in sharing his riches, he is a good steward, not a good king.[43]

For the Diadochs, benefaction took the form of gifts of grain and money, the construction of sacred and secular public buildings and costly dedications in sanctuaries. Often the aim was immediate or short-term political advantage, to win and keep support at a rival's expense. The grain and gold which Ptolemy, Lysimachus and Cassander heaped on Rhodes in 305–4 BC kept an important naval power out of Demetrius' hands; gifts from Lysimachus and Ptolemy to Athens in the 280s BC likewise aimed to break the Antigonid hold on the city. Grants of exemption from taxes and other such concessions might also serve as a means of attack on a rival; often, and not always truthfully, the benefactor contrasts his own generosity with his predecessors' oppressive behaviour.[44]

The significance of benefaction, however, goes beyond short-term profit. By acting to relieve distress caused by famine, earthquake or enemy devastation, by honouring the gods to ensure divine favour for themselves and their people, the Successors mirrored the action of those who had successfully ruled before them. In this way they reinforced the idea of themselves as the latest in a long line of kings who stood for prosperity and order. Thus tangible proofs of the king's *eunoia* and *eusebeia* were proffered not only to cities and shrines directly under the king's control but to both Greek and non-Greek recipients throughout the Hellenistic world. Euergetism often goes hand in hand with the acquisition of new territory. Though in crude terms this might be seen simply as a bribe, it also reflects the new ruler's concern to show himself truly royal, aware of his kingly obligations. Both Cassander's rebuilding of Thebes shortly after his takeover of Macedon in 316 BC and Lysimachus' benefactions at Ilium seem to fall into this category. The former, we are told, was inspired to this good deed by hopes of 'undying glory'. These were not unjustified; though sometimes the visible reminder of a ruler's euergetism is destroyed when he loses power, in many cases cult worship persists and statues still stand long after the benefactor's death.[45]

Royal *eunoia* need not always take the form of gifts; apart from his role as provider, the king is also the protector and saviour of his people. This aspect of kingship is reflected in Homeric epithets, with Hector and Achilles both described as 'shepherd of the people'. The almost incessant warfare of the Successor period gave particular emphasis to this role. While the Babylonian Chronicles, for example, show that the Diadochs could and did wreak havoc on their enemies' land, inflicting severe hardship on the subject population through destruction of crops and property, they were also in a position to perform dramatic acts of *soteria* saving their subjects from harassment by enemy troops or the pirates who posed a notorious threat in this period. The king might also lend aid in the event of internal unrest within the city.[46]

THE REWARDS OF BENEFACTION

Though the payment of such attentions by foreign kings to the leading cities of the Greeks was nothing new, the Hellenistic kings' enormous power and wealth enabled them to perform benefactions on an unprecedented scale. Though in part inspired by political self-interest, benefaction undoubtedly served to relieve genuine and extreme distress, particularly in times of siege and famine. The Hellenistic kings were thus able to alter dramatically the quality of their subjects' lives. The scale of their euergetism in turn affected the type of honours accorded them and the very vocabulary of city decrees. To designate the Hellenistic kings *euergeteis* and grant them citizenship, hitherto the rewards for foreign benefactors, seemed insufficient. Instead they were voted the sort of honours previously reserved for citizen benefactors, such as crowns and statues, objects which themselves varied according to the recipient's position on the 'honours scale'. The material used for a statue, the use of gilding, an equestrian design, the base height and the statue's site all told their own story. Kings generally received statues of the most lavish sort. By the end of the fourth century BC the greatest royal benefactions were being rewarded with honours which 'equalled those of the gods'.[47]

Lysimachus' benefactions are well documented; gifts of grain and money to Rhodes in 305–4 BC won him a statue in the city's *agora*. The Athenian decree honouring his *philos* Philippides records a sizeable gift of grain, probably sent soon after Ipsus. Further cash and food subsidies followed in the 280s BC as Athens strove to recover the fortresses still in Antigonid hands; new epigraphic evidence suggests that Lysimachus also sent military aid. Athenian honours for the king included a crown and a statue in the *agora*. Lysimachus' new temple, games and city walls at Ilium displayed his kingly *eusebeia*, honouring both Athena and Alexander whose promises he thus fulfilled. The city and sanctuary at Samothrace received his military protection against a band of *asebeis*, probably pirates, bent on pillage and arson; his queen dedicated the magnificent Arsinoeion there; Samothrace also owed the restoration of its sacred *peraea* to Lysimachus. At Priene, too, he was able to act as *soter*, sending troops to repel an attack by the indigenous Pedieis, the Magnesians and perhaps Demetrius' troops. The citizens' loyalty to the king on this occasion may have won them further favours; the suggestion that the envoys who carried Priene's thanks and offer of cult honours to Lysimachus also delivered a successful request for some improvement in the city's status is attractive. A decree from Delos honouring Lysimachus' *philos* Demaratus suggests some patronage of the sanctuary there; Lysimachus may also have contributed to Cassander's project for the restoration of Thebes.[48]

On the basis of the surviving evidence, both the scale of Lysimachus' benefactions and the honours he is decreed are on a par with those proffered by and to his fellow Diadochs. At Rhodes, his benefactions are overshadowed by those of Ptolemy, but this is explicable given Ptolemy's longstanding patronage of the city. Lysimachus' gift does, moreover, compare favourably with that of Cassander. His financial subsidies to Athens in the 280s BC likewise outweigh Ptolemy's contribution. Like his fellow Diadochs, he is rewarded with the *megistai timai* which the *poleis* had previously reserved for their greatest citizen benefactors and for the gods. A gold crown worth 1,000 staters at Priene and the cult honours offered there and at Samothrace rival those granted to the Antigonids at Athens, Ptolemy at Rhodes and Seleucus at Ilium.[49]

Since benefaction was an essential part of kingship, it should not be surprising that Lysimachus should thus strive to demonstrate his fitness for the throne. The evidence for his euergetism does, however, conflict with the reputation for avarice which has, until recently, been accepted uncritically by most modern commentators. A key piece of evidence is the *Gazophylax* anecdote, already mentioned. Hauben's detailed analysis aims to clarify the significance of the mocking titles applied to Demetrius' enemies. Though the story's central point is clearly Demetrius' rejection of his rivals' right to kingly status, Hauben's attempt to discern some coherent pattern in the names chosen is not altogether successful. Though Ptolemy and Agathocles are dubbed 'admiral' and 'island-dweller' with reference to recent military disasters, the point of calling Seleucus 'elephant-keeper' is harder to fathom – the value of this elephant-cavalry was proved only too clearly the following year at Ipsus. It may, however, be a jibe at

Seleucus' abandonment of Indian territory in return for a few elephants.[50]

If, then, it is accepted that Demetrius chose these titles to pinpoint some aspect of his rivals' history or circumstances which was potentially a source of embarrassment or shame, the same must be true of that applied to Lysimachus – *gazophylax*, usually assumed to refer to the king's great wealth and unwillingness to part with even a fraction of it. Hauben, who seems slightly at a loss on reaching Lysimachus, concurs. Remarking only that the king 'seems to have had little or no sense of humour', and ignoring Plutarch who clearly sees the insult's thrust as sexual rather than financial, he concludes that what Demetrius' cronies were really attacking was Lysimachus' 'proverbial meanness'.[51]

Circularity, however, mars this argument, since apart from this same anecdote, the evidence for Lysimachean avarice is a handful of other stories whose sources are similarly far from impartial. Given the context – Demetrius' insistence on an Antigonid monopoly of kingliness – it may be better to look at the term *gazophylax* in connection with Hecataeus' remark that 'unless a king share his riches generously, he is a good steward, not a good king.' In early Hellenistic thought, then, the financial official and the king are seen as directly opposed; concern to conserve financial resources, something which may have been imposed on Lysimachus in the first half of his reign by the relatively limited resources of his satrapy, was not kingly.[52] Rather than alluding to Lysimachus' great wealth, Demetrius may rather be attacking his inability, at this stage in his career, to bestow largess in a suitably royal fashion. Certainly there is no reason to see in such a title, without supporting evidence, historical proof of lifelong Lysimachean avarice, any more than one takes seriously the idea of Seleucus as an elephant-keeper. The evidence for Lysimachus' benefactions is certainly not consistent with such an idea.

HONOURED LIKE THE GODS

> The Egyptians perform proskynesis to their kings and honour them as gods, in the belief that they have not obtained supreme power without the help of divine providence and that such as have the will and ability to confer the greatest benefits share in the divine nature.
>
> (Hecataeus of Abdera)

It might be tempting to dismiss this statement, penned by a Ptolemaic court historian, merely as an ingenious piece of anachronising, aiming to justify the godlike honours paid to Hecataeus' patron. The theme is repeated in Euhemerus' *Sacred History*, a Utopian work set in the land of Panchaea, which presents Zeus and his forebears as originally kings on earth, deified for their benefactions. Like Euhemerus' patron Cassander, Uranus is *epieikes*, while Zeus is a conqueror and traveller, circling the earth five times before dividing his *imperia* among his friends and kinsmen; he wins undying remembrance and glory, and is honoured like a god by many nations.[53]

Though the parallels between Euhemerus' gods and Alexander and his Successors are obvious, these ideas cannot be dismissed merely as early Hellenistic apologia. The ruler's divinity is a consistent theme in diverse societies at all periods of history; the nineteenth-century king of Nepal saw himself as an embodiment of the god Vishnu; in Japan, that part of the enthronement ceremony (*Daijosai*) which is believed to effect the emperor's transformation into a living god, is still performed. There is, moreover, a longstanding connection between an individual's ability to perform great services and a perception of that person as worthy of the kind of tributes which men pay to the gods. From Homer onwards, the phrase 'he is a god to me' denotes one who has done the speaker a great service. Odysseus thanks Nausicaa for saving his life, saying he will pray to her 'as to a goddess'. The same idea underlies the institution of the Greek city hero-cults, which honour city-founders, tyrannicides and benefactors. Heroes like Heracles and Dionysus are deified, after death, by virtue of their *arete* and achievements.[54]

Though the link between these hero-cults and the early Hellenistic ruler cults is undeniable, it would be wrong to see the 'godlike' honours decreed to the kings simply as 'bigger and better presents', merely a quantitative upgrading of the tributes traditionally paid to citizen benefactors. This interpretation denies ruler cult its significance as an acknowledgement of immortal and universal power, expressed in the offer of *isotheoi timai* made during the life-time of the king.[55]

In the later Hellenistic period, ruler worship also finds expression in dynastic cult established by the king, but this comes only with Ptolemy II's inauguration of a festival to honour his father, aiming presumably to ease the succession by encouraging loyalty to the dynasty. There is no sign of any such institution established by the first generation of Alexander's successors, whose cults, like those for Alexander, represent the initiative of the cities themselves.[56]

Crowns and statues have already been mentioned; other cult honours for the Hellenistic kings include altars, sacrifices and an annual festival held on the ruler's birthday or the anniversary of his benefaction, the renaming of a month or a tribe after him or members of his family; these last honours had also been paid to the cities' founder heroes.[57]

What then inspired the Greek cities to pay these particular tributes to Alexander and his Successors? From a twentieth-century standpoint it is easy to be cynical, seeing them merely as marks of empty flattery, inspired by fear or political self-interest. Fundamental to this stance is the argument that the citizens of the Greek *poleis* could not possibly have believed that the kings were gods, but the idea that belief is integral to religion is a Christian preconception. Recent scholarship has rightly urged the need to shed such assumptions when considering Greek religion in general and cult worship in particular. Greek religious practice lays its emphasis rather on acknowledgement of the gods through payment of the honours which are their due. The relationship between worshipper and god is one of mutual obligation, established by prayer and sacrifice on one side, aid and protection on the other. For the ancient Greeks, living in a world where life was cheap and 'the threat of chaos never far away', religious practice represented a 'system of responses to those agents of experience which threatened to overturn the sense of an intelligible order'.[58]

This reassessment does much to illuminate the payment of godlike honours to Alexander and the Hellenistic kings who, like the gods, were immensely powerful and potentially unpredictable. They had the same ability to effect great changes in the lives of their subjects, to wreak destruction, or to protect and save. The instability of the Diadoch period, the nigh incessant competition for possession of the *poleis* meant the close impingement of the kings upon the lives of their Greek subjects in a way that was probably new. Greek religious practice had always been flexible, ready to acknowledge new powers in the world with appropriate honours; accordingly the cities' response to the appearance of these new and potentially menacing forces was to bring their relations with them into a well-established and intelligible framework.[59]

The context in which cult honours are decreed certainly underlines the idea of reciprocal obligation. In return for action which ensures survival or brings safety or prosperity, the king expects loyalty and support. The honours voted by the city can be seen as a pledge of that support; they also serve to acknowledge his godlike powers. The titles which cities give to kings reinforce the link between a specific action and cult honours. Demetrius' landing in Attica in 307 BC was celebrated with an altar on the very spot to *theos kataibates*; Samothrace set up an altar to Lysimachus as *kallistos euergetes* for his action against the impious pirates. Cult honours offered to a king in his capacity as city-founder again puts emphasis on his powers of action – the city owes its very being to him.[60]

If Greek religion is not a belief-based system, then the idea that ruler cult was, by definition, sacrilegious, implying a decline in traditional worship,[61] can be abandoned. Royal cult flourished alongside those of the established gods; nor did it preclude the kings' own expression of *eusebeia*. Apart from Demetrius' supposed antics at Athens, there is little emphasis in the literary sources on royal cult as sacrilegious. Even there, it is the outrageous toadying of the Athenians and actions which would have been regarded as unthinkable at any period – such as parties in the Parthenon – which are criticised rather than cult honours as such. The sources for this material are, in any case, hardly irreproachable.[62]

Nor does the extant evidence suggest that ruler cult was generally unpopular or resented by the inhabitants of the *poleis*. While some orators and politicians express cynicism over the vote of cult honours, it need not follow that this attitude was common even among the educated classes. For the man in the street, the king's immense wealth and fabled exploits may well have given him an aura of the superhuman, particularly on those occasions when he appeared, literally like a *deus ex machina*, to avert a crisis. Demetrius' unexpected appearance off the Attic coast in 307 BC before a startled crowd which initially mistook his fleet for Ptolemy's is a fine example. Lysimachus' aversion of the pirate menace at Samothrace is another.[63] Evidence for private prayer and sacrifice to the ruler, reflected in inscriptions and the finds of small-scale, relatively cheap images from domestic shrines, argues against a general perception of ruler cult as simply the city politicians' latest game. In addition, the sacrifices, festivals and processions which regularly form a part of cult honours offered the prospect of spectacle and holiday, a welcome opportunity to eat, drink and be merry. The huge popularity of such occasions is reflected in Aristotle's advice to aspiring oligarchs to offer 'splendid sacrifices' – and thereby splendid feasting – as the way to the people's hearts![64]

The abandonment of a Christianising view of Greek religion has yet another consequence. If cult honours acknowledge the ruler's extraordinary powers of action rather than his innate divinity, then his acceptance of such tributes signifies his recognition of the obligations that go with 'godlike' powers, not a belief in his own divine nature. Though literary anecdotes may describe acts of royal hubris, their value is diminished by the hostility of their sources and the impact of a later Roman moralising tradition. The Successors' apparent failure to promote their own worship or, often, to adopt officially the divine titles bestowed by the cities, together with the individual and specific context in which cult honours are decreed, tend to give these tales the lie.[65]

Only one story of this sort survives about Lysimachus. His boast to a Byzantine embassy that he is touching heaven with his spear meets with the riposte that they had better make tracks before a hole appears in the sky! There are too many stories of 'clever replies' to kings for confidence in this anecdote as historical. As evidence for divine pretensions it is of little value. The doubts surrounding Lysimachus' pose for a statue as Heracles have already been aired; he avoided the opportunity afforded by coin-portraits to identify himself with some god and the known cults established to him all seem to represent a city's response to a specific benefaction along the usual lines. At Priene and Samothrace he was honoured for the acts of *soteria* mentioned above. Though the Samothracians hailed him as *kallistos euergetes*, nothing suggests that he adopted this or any other cult title in an official sense. At Ephesus he was honoured as founder (*ktistes*); a silver statue dedicated in the theatre by a certain Gaius Vibius Salutaris in AD 104 is thought to reflect the revival of his worship as the city's second founder. Demetrius' acceptance of similar honours as the second founder of Sicyon provides a useful parallel. The motive for cult honours paid to Lysimachus at Cassandreia is less clear; two inscriptions from the city – a decree honouring the Aetolian Androbolus and the new land-grant inscription for Limnaeus – are dated by the eponymous priesthood of Lysimachus. Evidence for a similar priesthood of Cassander suggested to some scholars that Lysimachus had 'inherited' the founder cult of his predecessor. Hatzopoulos' suggestion, however, that these honours may have been prompted by some benefaction, perhaps the extension of the city's territory, is attractive.[66]

In number, Lysimachus' cults may seem limited in comparison with the plethora established for his rivals. Habicht lists nine known cults for Seleucus I, three of them shared with Antiochus I, five for Ptolemy I, at least ten for the first Antigonids.[67] This need not be a comment on the quality of his kingship; it can be explained in part by his failure to hand on his kingdom to an heir with an interest in promoting his worship. One can compare Ptolemy II's active promotion of the Nesiote League festival for Ptolemy Soter, the continued use of Soter's portrait on Lagid coinage and the titles *Soteres* and *Theoi Soteres* to describe him and his queen Berenice on coins and dedications. Similarly, at least two of the cults for Seleucus I, at Nysa and Apollonia in Caria, were established posthumously.[68]

It is possible too that there were other cults for which the evidence is destroyed or not yet forthcoming. Lysimacheia, as the king's first foundation and European capital, is a strong contender. Its foundation date, in 309 BC, before Lysimachus assumed the kingly title, is no obstacle – Scepsis had voted cult honours to Antigonus two years earlier in 311 BC. Appian's description of Lysimachus' burial there in a temple bearing his name may lend support to this theory. It cannot be safely assumed, as the existing evidence might seem to suggest, that Lysimachus only attracted cult-worship in the latter part of his reign.[69]

FOUNDER OF CITIES

Though city foundations are often considered primarily in terms of economic and military motives, the act of foundation also gives visible expression to the enduring concepts of the king as protector, provider and favourite of the gods. This is reflected in the vote of cult honours to city founders and by kingly emphasis on such projects as personal initiatives which express the superior wisdom bestowed on them by the gods. Stories of favourable omens which precede the building project abound. The idea of city-building as a specifically royal activity is underlined by Herodotus; the walls of Ecbatana start to rise the moment that the Mede Deioces is 'firmly on the throne'; when the building is complete, he introduces 'for the first time the ceremonial of royalty'.[70]

For the Diadochs, the Argead example could only reinforce this message; Philip II had marked his gain of Mt Pangaeus' gold, crucial for Macedon's rise, by founding Philippi; Alexander's first youthful victory against the Maedi was crowned with the creation of Alexandroupolis; legend later ascribed over seventy city foundations to him. Once accepted without demur, it is now recognised that Alexander's still considerable achievement had become exaggerated by Plutarch's day.[71]

The Successors followed suit. Cassandreia was founded as early as

316 BC, the year of Olympias' death and Alexander IV's imprisonment. Though the first formal proclamation of kingship among the
Diadochs came only in 306 BC, the peace treaty of 311 BC, which
recognised the sovereignty of Alexander's Successors in their own
realms, had effectively passed the death sentence on Alexander IV.
Significantly, the following years see a capital city built in every
'satrapy': Lysimacheia, Antigoneia in the Troad, Seleuceia-on-Tigris
and Ptolemais(?).[72] The names of these and others that followed them
reflect the importance of royal foundations as lasting monuments to
kingly achievement and visible expressions of 'dynastic glory'. For
example, four of the known Seleucid foundations from the Diadoch
period are named for the king himself, three for his wife Apama; his
son Antiochus and his wife Stratonice get one apiece.[73]

Lysimachus too proclaimed his kingship with cities named for
himself and members of his family; apart from his capital on the site
of Cardia, there were Lysimacheias in Aetolia and near Atarneus.
Nicaea commemorates his marriage to Antipater's daughter; Ephesus,
refounded c. 294 BC, is renamed for his queen, Arsinoe, who is also
honoured with an Aetolian Arsinoeia. New Smyrna issues coinage in
the name of Eurydiceia, Lysimachus' daughter. Coins from Agathopolis, a city in Mysia, suggest an eponymous foundation by Lysimachus' ill-fated heir.[74]

Apart from glorifying the dynasty, foundation or renaming of cities
could express *eusebeia* for a royal predecessor or strike a blow at an
opponent's prestige. Strabo cites Lysimachus' Alexandria Troas as
illustrating the concern of his Successors to express *eusebeia* for
Alexander. Conveniently, this act served also to obliterate a memorial
to the kingship of Antigonus, the city's original founder. The
significance of Lysimachus' building programme at Ilium in this
context has already been discussed.[75]

The legend surrounding Smyrna's foundation may likewise illustrate the importance of city-building as an expression of continuity
and succession to Alexander. Alexander, it seems, dreamed of a visit
from the Nemeseis who told him to found a new city on Mt Claros.
The Claros oracle approved the move and the people co-operated
joyfully. This idea of Alexander as Smyrna's founder conflicts with all
the other evidence which makes Antigonus initiate the scheme and
Lysimachus complete it. Generally considered unhistorical, this
legend has been explained as a local invention.[76] Alternatively, it may
originate with Antigonus or Lysimachus, who aimed in this way to
present their work as a fulfilment of Alexander's plan. Other evidence

shows that both men took pains to present themselves as Alexander's heir and the case of Ilium provides a useful parallel.

Many of the Diadochs' new cities were created through synoecism and were often initially unpopular. In consequence, while strategic or economic factors may have been primary in inspiring the reversal of a defeated enemy's project, it also allowed the victor to assert himself as the city's new founder, with the power, as such, to determine its extent and status. Lysimachus' decision to allow the inhabitants of Scepsis to leave Alexandria Troas is a good example of this practice. The victor might also pose as founder of the reinstated city; Cebren, absorbed into Alexandria Troas and subsequently 'liberated' by Antiochus I after Lysimachus' death, becomes another Antiocheia.[77]

If 'undying glory' was a strong motivating factor in founding cities, then Lysimachus perhaps fared better than some of his contemporaries. Though he failed to establish a lasting dynasty and his empire was divided among his enemies, several of his cities still stood as a monument to his achievement a century after his death. The idea that this was due to his opponents' relative indifference to his memory, by contrast to the bitter hatred and fear engendered by Antigonus, is not compelling. The literary sources certainly stress the strong negative feelings which Lysimachus' success inspired among his rivals, while Seleucid inscriptions from the campaign of 282–1 BC and the years after may reflect a deliberate programme to blacken his reputation.[78]

It may be better to ascribe the survival of Lysimachus' cities to their judicious siting, on both military and commercial grounds, and to the excellent workmanship which Tscherikower also comments on. The resiting of Ephesus brought the city the prosperity which gave it a leading position among the cities of Asia Minor; the name Arsinoeia did not persist, but the debt owed to Lysimachus was recognised by the revival of his cult in the imperial period. New Smyrna, an Antigonid project completed by Lysimachus, likewise achieved power and prosperity. Nicaea in Bithynia has been described as one of the best examples of the new Hellenistic building style. Lysimachus' Seleucid successors acknowledged the strategic value of Lysimacheia in Thrace with a treaty signed by Antiochus I (?) promising to protect the city's 'democracy and autonomy' and the city's reconstruction in 196 BC by Antiochus III, ambitious 'to rebuild a city of such renown'. Livy's reference to the city's 'recent' destruction by Thracians, combined with coin finds which suggest the continuation of issues from Lysimacheia from 280 BC to 220 BC, give the city a considerably longer life than Appian suggests.[79]

While Tscherikower ascribes the durability of Lysimachus' cities to the employment of architects and engineers of considerable skill, literary descriptions of other royal building projects suggest that much of the donkey work was done by the troops – another area in which the army made an essential contribution to the maintenance of kingly power. Evidence for kings' personal involvement in the construction of their cities[80] makes it likely that Lysimachus too was on hand to supervise some of these foundations, ensuring that they would stand as suitably imposing memorials to his kingship.

It is possible too that Lysimachus planned another, more personal monument to his achievement. Sited 16 kilometres from Ephesus and one of a series of funerary monuments in southern Asia Minor which look to the Halicarnassus Mausoleum for inspiration, the Belevi mausoleum, never completed, was planned on a grand scale. Certain features like the deep square relief-carved ceiling coffers recall both the Mausoleum and Priene's temple of Athena Polias, both designed by the architect Pytheos; possibly the later Belevi tomb was the work of an artist of his school. Though the mausoleum cannot be precisely dated, its vaulted grave chamber and the couch-shaped sarcophagus found there are characteristic of early Hellenistic Macedonian tombs. Most scholars agree on a broad period spanning the last decades of the fourth century BC and the first decades of the third, with two or three distinct phases of construction. Plausibly the later work, which shows a strong Persian influence, was conducted under Seleucid auspices and the tomb's eventual occupant may well have been Antiochus II who died at Ephesus in 246 BC. The tomb's original commissioner remains unknown, but Lysimachus, with a well-documented interest in Ephesus, is a strong contender. His resiting of the city made provision for its future power and prosperity; it is likely, too, that Ephesus served as one of his royal seats in Asia. He was, moreover, Ephesus' second founder and the recipient of cult honours there; in this context, it may be more than coincidence that the Belevi mausoleum was built near the site of an archaic shrine to a local hero, Pixodarus. The history of the building work, breaking off after an initial phase of construction, is also consistent with events in the Diadoch wars; this interruption may plausibly be connected with Seleucus' invasion of Asia Minor and takeover of Ephesus in 281 BC.[81]

COURT AND COURTIERS

Monarchic rulers appoint large numbers of men as their eyes, ears, hands and feet. For such people as are friendly to themselves and their rule, they make sharers in it. If they are not friends, they will not act according to the monarch's intentions.

(Aristotle *Politics* 1,287b 25)

The wealth of material devoted to the king's friends in the homilies of the political theorists reflects the vital part they played in the conduct of his rule. Among the sayings which emphasise the need for loyal and virtuous friends to advise the king and to refrain from harmful flattery, this quotation from Aristotle is particularly choice. It combines several important themes – the dynamic and versatile role of royal *philoi* in the kingdom's government; the exchange of substantial power and responsibility for loyalty and support; the idea of a special intimacy between king and friends; the expectation that in the final analysis these 'advisers' will pursue the king's interests unquestioningly – with a greater realism than the lofty sentiments of Isocrates.[82]

To see the *philoi* of the Hellenistic kings as the direct successors of the Argead kings' *hetairoi* is probably correct; the concept of a group of 'friends' who surround the prince from boyhood onwards does seem peculiarly Macedonian. Royal reliance upon a group of trusted companions as advisers and agents in war, diplomacy and government, does, however, find parallels in Achaemenid history. On his tomb, Darius I is shown flanked by his weapon-bearers; the Behistun inscription shows that one of these, Gobryas, was among those who helped Darius gain the throne. The other, Aspathines, turns up in Herodotus as Darius' confidant, wounded while supporting him during the conspiracy of the Magi. In terms of their function men like these have much in common with Seleucus' friend Patrocles or Lysimachus' Philippides. It is significant that Themistocles, after winning Artaxerxes' favour, is honoured with the title 'Friend of the King'.[83]

Clearly in the early Hellenistic period, *philoi* were a *sine qua non* for any self-respecting king; this is reflected in Hecataeus' attachment of a band of Companions to his legendary Egyptian king Sesoosis. The new satraps of 323 BC, themselves Alexander's erstwhile friends, who had dazzled their fellows with golden bridles and silver-studded boots, lost no time in attracting to themselves a similar following of ambitious men. Aiming for the regency in 319 BC, Cassander forms a faction of his *philoi* prior to approaching Ptolemy and others with a view to alliance. In the same year Antigonus summons his friends to a council and appoints the most outstanding among them as satraps and *strategoi*.[84]

The *philoi* of the Diadochs are, in modern parlance, true 'Renaissance men', serving as generals, admirals, ambassadors, garrison commanders, councillors and treasurers. They govern as *epistateis* or *epimeletai* in the cities or as *strategoi* over an administrative district. Lysimachus' friend Philippides was an accomplished and prolific comic poet. As friend to Eumenes and then the Antigonids, the career of the historian Hieronymus of Cardia spanned ambassadorial duties, a spell as councillor to the young Demetrius in 312 BC, a commercial expedition to explore bitumen resources in the Nabataean desert and appointment as governor of Thebes.[85] Rightly regarded as one of the vital resources for which the Successors had to compete, *philoi* expected substantial rewards in return for their multifarious talents; benefits bestowed on friends, Isocrates says, are an acceptable area for magnificent display by a monarch. From the king himself came gifts of land, money, goods of high value and entertainment at court; a new inscription from Cassandreia records Lysimachus' gift of 2,480 *plethra* of land to a certain Limnaeus and reveals the existence of an estate nearby belonging to his *philos* Bithys.[86] Royal *philoi* could also expect conspicuous honours in the cities where their diplomacy had secured royal benefaction. The Athenians hymned Demetrius' friends as stars around his sun; Epicurus addressed Mithres, Lysimachus' finance minister, as Healer and Lord. Honorary decrees record edited highlights from the careers of men like Philippides or Kallias of Sphettus, friend and admiral of Ptolemy I, emphasising their patriotism. Crowns, statues and various privileges and exemptions enjoyed in the relevant city constitute a more tangible proof of gratitude.[87]

In ideal terms, sacred ties of loyalty bound king and friends. Lysimachus' obligations to his *philoi*, we are told, prevented his evading capture by the Getae. Such loyalty was not unique, but often the ambitions of these *philoi*, combined with the volatile character of the Diadoch period, encouraged opportunism. Instances of betrayal in the face of a better offer are legion. Notable among such 'flexible friends' is Docimus. Leaving Perdiccas for Antigonus and Antigonus for Lysimachus, he seems to have prospered, founding a city, Docimeion, and issuing his own coinage.[88]

Recent scholarship has laid much stress on the *philoi* of the new kingdoms as a ruling class of an entirely new kind, chosen above all for merit and reflecting a greater ethnic and social mix than had been seen at either the Achaemenid or the Macedonian courts. Though the sources do emphasise ability as an important criterion for advancement under the Diadochs, there is no reason to see this as a great innovation. For example, the Lydian Croesus, defeated by Cyrus, then appears as a valued adviser at the Persian victor's side. Greek exiles are prominent at the Achaemenid court, advising the Great King and receiving handsome presents. The Persian Artabazus and his sons were rewarded for their loyalty to the last Achaemenid king with privileged positions at Alexander's court. So much for the ethnic mix.[89] As regards the social background of the kings' friends, the position is complicated by the Greek literary penchant for presenting the intimates of kings as the scum of the earth, the lowest of the low. Though Herman puts much emphasis on this very point when discussing the contrast between the literary and epigraphic depiction of royal *philoi*, rather curiously, he is still ready to accept the idea of 'propertyless nonentities' as cronies of the Diadochs. Certainly one cannot see this literary convention as inspired by a new egalitarianism at the Successors' courts; Theopompus' presentation of Philip II's friends as a bunch of ruffians has already been mentioned.[90]

Equally, there is little evidence that the claims of kinship, noble blood or political prominence had really ceased to exert their traditional pull. The kinsmen of the Diadochs are prominent in the historical narrative. Apart from Demetrius, among Antigonus' generals are his son Philip and his nephews Polemaeus and Dioscurides. Cassander's brother Pleistarchus co-operates with Lysimachus in 302 BC and is rewarded with a kingdom in Cilicia. Lysimachus' son Agathocles routs Demetrius out of Asia Minor in 286–5 BC; his stepson Clearchus is with him on the Getic expedition in 292–1 BC; Lysimachus' dedication of a statue of his sister-in-law Adaea at Oropus suggests the continued prominence of her husband Autodicus at the Thracian court.[91]

Similarly the emphasis which Isocrates put on the desirability of Greek courtiers still holds good. A high proportion of the early Hellenistic rulers' friends are men from the Greek cities both within and outside their kingdoms. Antigonid courtiers include men from Athens, Miletus, Ephesus, Samos, Chios and Larissa, while Demetrius' sneer at the shortage of Greeks at Lysimachus' court represents a slur upon his kingship.[92]

Whether this image of Lysimachus as a backwoods king, presiding over a second-rate court filled with courtiers of slavish origin, is anything more than the product of hostile propaganda is doubtful. Certainly he was ready to appoint men of non-Greek origin to the highest positions; Plutarch describes Mithres, his minister of finance, as 'Syrian', but the name suggests rather Iranian origin. Such an appointment is, however, less controversial than is supposed by the traditional view, which sees the Macedonian rulers imposing a 'superior' Greek culture and administrative system upon Asia.[93] Of the *philoi* sneered at by Demetrius, the name Bithys may suggest Thracian origin; Paris, known only from this anecdote, is perhaps Phrygian. No firm conclusions can be drawn about their social status; the dichotomy between the literary portrayal of royal *philoi* as servile flatterers and early Hellenistic city decrees which imply a more equal informal relationship has already been mentioned.[94]

Lysimachus' 'parasite' Bithys provides a striking example of this phenomenon; literature presents him only as a jester and recipient of wooden scorpions! Though attempts have been made to elevate him to a more dignified position, identifying him with Bithys, son of Cleon, honoured with Athenian citizenship, the link, until very recently, remained uncertain. Without a precise date for the decree, Demetrius II's general Bithys seemed as likely a candidate. The new land-grant inscription from Cassandreia, mentioned above, greatly increases the odds in favour of Lysimachus' 'parasite'; one portion of the land granted to Limnaeus borders upon the estate of 'Bithys *son of Cleon*'. The juggler of wooden scorpions is thus transformed into a landowner and a military man – the phrase *eis tagma* in the Athenian decree suggests that Bithys was honoured at Athens in connection with military aid supplied by Lysimachus *c.* 285–4 BC.[95]

Of the known courtiers in Lysimachus' service, non-Greeks are, moreover, outnumbered by a group of Hellenes whose pedigrees easily put them on a par with the *philoi* of his rivals. The best known is Philippides of Cephale, with whom Lysimachus seemingly enjoyed a genuinely warm and intimate friendship. Bitterly opposed to Stratocles, Demetrius' favourite, Philippides probably spent the years of his voluntary exile from 301 BC to 286 BC at Lysimachus' court where he used his influence to secure generous gifts for Athens. As was expected of a good *philos*, he was probably at Lysimachus' side for the victory at Ipsus.[96]

Another illustrious Athenian, Demochares, led two successful embassies to Lysimachus to raise funds for the Piraeus recovery scheme *c.* 286–5 BC. He too may have spent some part of his exile at Lysimachus' court. A text from Delos records the presence of a

Spartan, Demaratus, at Lysimachus' court. The royal rank suggested by his patronymic, son of Gorgion, has prompted the argument that he is unlikely to be an established courtier of the king. This is not sound; in offering friendship to exiled Spartan royalty, Lysimachus would merely have been following in the footsteps of an Achaemenid predecessor. Inscriptions from Athens and Ephesus identify two or perhaps three brothers from Perinthus engaged in diplomacy on Lysimachus' behalf. Two men from Miletus, Hippostratus and Hippodamus, serve in turn as *strategoi* of the Ionians.[97] Their common home town and patronymic may suggest yet another pair of brothers among the agents of the Hellenistic kings.[98] Moving from Ionia to central Greece, Xanthippus of Elateia, like Docimus, is a another 'friend' noted for his flexibility. In 301 BC he had worked with the Athenian Olympiodorus to save Elateia for Demetrius against Lysimachus' ally Cassander; in 285 BC it is as 'King Lysimachus' friend' that he expels Demetrius' garrison from his home town and liberates Phocis.[99]

CONCLUSIONS

In almost every area of kingship, then, Lysimachus holds his own against the competition. In the realm of propaganda, he takes his own line, promoting himself as hero, warrior king and intimate friend and successor to Alexander. He advances his interests in the Greek cities and promotes himself as protector and provider through generous benefactions which are reciprocated with conspicuous honours. His choice of *philoi* reflects both an awareness of the prestige conferred by illustrious associates and the same readiness as his Argead and Achaemenid predecessors to reward talented individuals of diverse ethnic origins. Though his kingdom proved ephemeral, his cities and his coinage, by dint of their excellence, remained as a memorial to his achievement.

Despite his well-attested concern to meet kingship's obligations, there was one maxim which Lysimachus was finally unable to observe: 'If kings are to rule well, they must try to preserve harmony . . . also in their own household.' The dynastic struggle which lost him his heir, the support of friends and army, his kingdom and his life will be discussed in the next chapter. The circumstances of his death, aged between 70 and 80 years old, fighting at the forefront of his troops, do, however, conform to the image of the king as warrior first and foremost. Isocrates advises: 'If the king is forced to risk his life, it is

better to die honourably than live in dishonour.' If Lysimachus failed
to achieve the continuation of his dynasty, the ultimate aim of royal
power, at least his death, unlike that of his great enemy Demetrius,
was thoroughly in keeping with what was expected of a king.[100]

7

SCHEMING WOMEN AND SENILE DECAY?

The last days of Lysimachus

> Around the same time there was an earthquake in the region of
> the Hellespont and Thracian Chersonese. In particular the city
> of Lysimacheia, founded twenty-two years previously by King
> Lysimachus was destroyed. As well as representing a terrible
> disaster for this troubled region, this was a portent which
> signalled ruin for Lysimachus, his house and his kingdom.
>
> (Justin XVII.1.1–4)

Justin's account, which sees clouds of doom already massing over
Lysimachus' head in 287 BC, portended by the earthquake which shook
his Thracian capital, is, strictly speaking, inaccurate. That year and
those which followed saw his fortunes reach their greatest height,
with Demetrius' final eclipse followed by major conquests in Europe.
Lysimachus' meeting with Seleucus, and with death, at Corupedium
came only in 281 BC. If the earthquake represented, as Justin has it, a
portentum, then divine retribution clearly took its time.

This presentation of Lysimachus' last years can of course be
explained by hindsight, combined with a tradition of history concerned to present its protagonists primarily as moral exempla. For
Justin, or his source Trogus, events at the end of Lysimachus' reign
cast him in the classic role of tyrant, a foul fiend finally brought to
justice by the anger of the gods. This is not an isolated case of literary
stereotyping. As will be shown, all accounts of the dynastic struggle
which preceded the Corupedium campaign are highly coloured by
literary *topoi*. In consequence, it is doubtful whether a search for the
'best source', the approach generally taken in analysing these events,
is actually appropriate.[1]

While Justin's motives for ante-dating the start of Lysimachus'
downfall to 287 BC may be suspect, his choice of that year as a crucial

turning-point is not unjustified, since the profitable years which followed brought also certain developments, both at his court and within his rivals' kingdoms, which contributed significantly to the final disaster.

First, the Asian campaign of 286–5 BC brings under the spotlight the king's heir Agathocles, hitherto an almost unseen figure. His success in routing Demetrius seems to have brought him prominence and popularity among Lysimachus' Greek subjects in Asia Minor.[2] Presumably Lysimachus' supporters there saw Agathocles as a guarantor of their continuing influence after his father's death. Victory also brought him the support of a strong group of *philoi*, an essential asset for successful kingship. Predictably, when the claim of his young half-brother Ptolemy posed a threat to Agathocles' prospects, these men rallied round him, splitting Lysimachus' court into factions. This seriously damaged the kingdom's strength. Second, Lysimachus' very success aroused the resentment of his former ally Seleucus. For the latter, Agathocles' death and the appeal for help from his supporters served as a welcome pretext for war upon his dangerously powerful neighbour.[3]

Egypt's stance towards Lysimachus is less clear, but reasons for envy and mistrust can be found. As heirs to Antigonid thalassocracy, secured through possession of a large part of Demetrius' fleet, the key cities of Tyre and Sidon and control of the Nesiote League, the Ptolemies cannot have welcomed signs that Lysimachus was actively extending his naval resources. Though in 302 BC Lysimachus' pitiful shortage of ships had obliged him to commandeer those of the West Pontic cities, by the end of his reign he clearly possessed a fleet of some size. Though it is unclear whether the islands and coastal cities of Asia Minor were obliged to provide him with ships, as some had done for Alexander, his conquest of Macedon in 285 BC brought him Pella's shipyards where Demetrius had prepared his great armada of 287 BC. Heracleia Pontica's part in augmenting Lysimachus' fleet emerges from the account of its victory, under his successor Ptolemy Ceraunus, over Antigonus Gonatas. The Heracleian contingent included 'fives' and 'sixes', not to mention the massive flagship *Leontophoros*, with eight banks of oars, supposedly capable of carrying 12,000 marines![4] Whether this build-up of naval power came only with Lysimachus' takeover of Heracleia is unclear; possibly his continued friendship with the city after his divorce from Amastris *c.* 299 BC enabled him to use Heracleia as a naval base and shipyard from 301 BC onwards.

Around the same time as his acquisition of Heracleia, Lysimachus may also have made moves to extend his influence in the Aegean area. A decree from Delos, centre of the Ptolemaic-controlled Nesiote League, honours Lysimachus' agent Demaratus, and exchanges assurances of *eunoia* with the king. Whether this should be seen as a sinister move is uncertain. Another potential bone of contention was mainland Greece, traditionally an area for Ptolemaic 'liberation'. Lysimachus had increased his diplomatic influence considerably there since Athens' release from Demetrius in 287 BC. Finally, some time after 287 BC, Lysimachus had welcomed to his court Ptolemy Ceraunus, dispossessed son of Ptolemy I, potential rival to his new heir, and clearly ambitious to recover his throne. Anxious for a quiet life on his accession in 285 BC, Ptolemy II's marriage to Lysimachus' daughter Arsinoe (I) suggests he thought it prudent to renew his alliance with Thrace,[5] but there is no sign that this bore fruit in anything so concrete as military support against Seleucus in 282–1 BC.

THE DYNASTIC STRUGGLE

Evidence for events at Lysimachus' court in the late 280s BC is mainly literary. Amidst diverse and often contradictory accounts, this much seems clear. The last years of Lysimachus' reign see his court split into two factions. One supported the claim of his official heir Agathocles, presumed to be his son by Nicaea. Probably in his late thirties by this time, Agathocles is presented as an accomplished soldier and a popular figure, seemingly an ideal successor. Against him, Arsinoe, Lysimachus' current wife, sought to secure the throne for her eldest son Ptolemy. The precise chronology of events is uncertain, but Agathocles' great command of 286–5 BC suggests he was then still in his father's favour. The start of growing tension must come after that year, reaching a climax with Agathocles' death c.283–2BC; both its precise date and the circumstances remain unclear. Memnon sees Agathocles escape a poison plot, only to be imprisoned by Lysimachus' order on a trumped-up treason charge. Justin actually does ascribe his death to poison. Strabo's brief notice, however, that Lysimachus 'beset by domestic troubles, was compelled to kill his son', may suggest a genuine conspiracy.[6]

Most accounts give Arsinoe a major role in Agathocles' death, though in some she is the plot's chief instigator, in others the all-too-willing accomplice of her husband. The portrayal of Lysimachus varies accordingly; to some he is a frail old man, putty in the hands of his scheming wife, to others the classic tyrant, outraging by his act the norms of paternal/filial affection and of humanity itself. On Justin's account, the murder was followed by a purge of Agathocles' supporters; those who survived, including his widow Lysandra, her brothers and her children, fled to Seleucus who was only too happy to take up the avenger's sword.[7]

The best known of the defectors is Philetaerus, Lysimachus' governor of Pergamum; apparently at odds with Arsinoe, he put himself, the nigh-impregnable fortress and its treasure of 9,000T at the service of Seleucus. The presence of Alexander, another of Lysimachus' sons, among the refugees suggests that the dynastic struggle split the court in two, involving even those members of the royal house who did not stand to gain or lose the major prize. Possibly his brother Autodicus and his family were among those who stayed loyal to Lysimachus; the statue of Lysimachus' sister-in-law Adaea, which the king dedicated at the Amphiaraon at Oropus, in recognition of her *arete* and *eunoia*, may plausibly be dated to the last years of his life, perhaps erected in the course of a diplomatic mission which took Ptolemy, Arsinoe's young son, to Boeotia.[8]

Generally, modern analysis of these events is based on following, from among the confused and conflicting literary accounts, the source deemed to be 'the best'. Though Corradi, for one, noted 'the legendary and romantic character' of the sources for this period of Lysimachus' life, and there is some general recognition that it is nigh impossible to discover 'the truth' when dealing with topics like dynastic murder and intrigue, these factors have made little impact on the method by which these events are examined. Though reaching him by diverse routes, most scholars plump for Memnon, who draws on Nymphis, a Heracleote historian of the third century BC. Tarn, for instance, is clearly impressed by Nymphis' 'objectivity' – despite Heracleia's later friendship with Ptolemy Ceraunus, Memnon's account does not hesitate to name him as Agathocles' murderer.[9] Longega's monograph on Arsinoe II includes a lengthy analysis of the different traditions and their possible sources; Memnon/Nymphis seems to represent the least of three evils, steering a middle course between an 'apologetic tradition' seeking to exculpate Lysimachus entirely, and a 'hostile' one which makes him primarily responsible for the crime. The former, embodied in Strabo and in one of the *logoi* cited by Pausanias, is thought to derive from Lysimachus' protégé, Duris; the latter, reflected in the account of Justin/Trogus, is ascribed to Hieronymus. Though avowedly more sceptical of Nymphis' objectivity than previous scholars, she cites his relative restraint in dealing with the matricide of Clearchus and Oxathres, given his 'well-known hatred' for the Clearchid dynasty. She admits that Nymphis' exile from Heracleia, which she dates to the period of Arsinoe's government, may have led him to place undue emphasis on the queen's part in Agathocles' murder, but concludes, none the less, that Memnon's is 'the version least far from the truth'. This account has Lysimachus fabricating a charge of conspiracy against his son and ordering his death, but at the same time he is presented as a man enfeebled by old age and strongly influenced by the persuasive skills of his determined and ambitious wife.[10]

Several objections can be made to this view and indeed to the wisdom of attempting to isolate one tradition as encapsulating 'the truth'. First, the long-held belief in Nymphis' 'absolute objectivity', established by Jacoby, must be challenged. The validity of the examples cited above is questionable. Second, it is doubtful whether Nymphis, a leading statesman at Heracleia at the time of its friendship for Ceraunus, did actually accuse him of Agathocles' murder. Heinen has plausibly argued that the Ptolemy named in Nymphis' text was actually Arsinoe's son. As for Nymphis' supposed restraint regarding Amastris' death at her sons' hands, the deed is characterised, using strong negative vocabulary, as an *ekthesmon de kai miarotaton ergon* conceived by a *mechanei deinei kai kakourgiai.*[11]

More generally, to speak of 'Nymphis' well-known hatred' for the Clearchids is too simplistic. Certainly his exiled status – probably the consequence of his descent from those expelled by the first tyrant Clearchus, rather than the action of Arsinoe's government, as Longega supposes – makes a position of hostility probable. It cannot, however, be inferred purely on the basis of his writings, which present a curiously uneven picture; while the treatment of the first tyrants Clearchus and Satyrus is vituperative, to say the least, their successors, Timotheus and Dionysius, are praised to the skies. It is hard to avoid Burstein's conclusion that Nymphis 'was an original authority' only for 'his own time', presumably the period after Dionysius' death c. 305 BC; for the preceding years, it seems, he made a somewhat uncritical use of partisan sources. If then, the glowing account of Timotheus' reign, for instance, does not represent the exile Nymphis' own interpretation, the foundations for belief in his objectivity crumble. Burstein rightly stresses also the distorting effect of Nymphis' position as an important Heracleote politician in the period after Lysimachus' death . As leader of the restored exiles, he would naturally be keen to emphasise Heracleia's harmony and happiness in this period, and tempted to blacken the preceding regime by contrast.[12] If doubt, then, is cast upon the superiority of Memnon's account, then the viability of a search for 'the truth' via 'the best source' is also in doubt.

Longega's grounds for rejecting the alternative traditions may also be questioned; the idea of Duris and Hieronymus as the source, respectively, of positive and negative traditions on Lysimachus has already been criticised.[13] Such an analysis, moreover, pays too little heed to the impact of literary convention upon our sources. This is likely to be strong, since these authors are all writing several centuries after the event and their subject is dynastic struggle, which is, and is perceived as, a classic feature of autocratic rule. Conventional motifs may serve as a handy padding device for an author whose source is slight or unsatisfactory; they may represent an epitomator's attempt at creativity; they may be invoked in the service of that moralising tendency which seems particularly to afflict Roman authors faced with that famous bugbear, the tyrant.

For example, it is the moral condemnation of Justin's account which has the effect of making Lysimachus the instigator of the crime, with Arsinoe merely his *ministra*. This need not reflect the hostility of a contemporary Greek source, like Hieronymus. Justin, an author with a strong moralising tendency and well known for 'improving' on his original, may have added it himself. A comparison of Justin's account with the brief summary of his source, Pompeius Trogus, supports this: it is Arsinoe's part in the murder that Trogus stresses. Other proponents of the theory that Arsinoe masterminded the conspiracy are the chronicler Porphyry (third century AD), and Pausanias. This tradition may derive in part from Duris, but it should be noted that Memnon/Nymphis and Trogus, drawing on sources which, on Longega's view, had no reason to favour Lysimachus, likewise emphasise the influence of his wife. This makes it less likely that the aim of this tradition is apologia. It is, moreover, questionable whether a reputation as a hen-pecked husband and a senile old fool is more enviable than that of an out-and-out villain. This presentation of events may rather be explained by the influence of what might be called the *cherchez la femme* school of history, both on Duris himself and the Roman writers using him.[14]

Pausanias' account, moreover, is rich in conventional literary motifs. His narrative opens with some philosophical musing on the theme of Love the Great Destroyer, most famously expressed in the second chorus of Euripides' *Hippolytus*; he then goes on to quote diverse sources, without committing himself to belief in any of them. Of the alternative explanations offered for Arsinoe's hatred of her stepson, fear that his accession would mean her children's death is the more convincing. The idea that Agathocles had spurned his step-mother's sexual advances fits too neatly into a classic tragic frame-work – again the obvious reference is to Phaedra and Hippolytus – to be entirely credible.[15] Both the presentation of Arsinoe herself and her relations with Agathocles and Lysimachus also conform to long-established literary stereotypes. 'Good at getting her own way', Memnon's Arsinoe, in the period before Agathocles' death, bludgeons her reluctant husband with repeated demands for the rich city of Heracleia. Finally, Lysimachus, 'whom old age was already making vulnerable', gives in. The historicity of this incident is generally accepted without comment and cited as proof of Arsinoe's overriding influence over her husband.[16]

It is, however, hard to see how Nymphis might guarantee accuracy here. Unless one assumes that Arsinoe's request represented an item of public business to be debated by king and council, only an eye-witness source from the innermost court circle could be in a position to relay such information. Even then the story is likely to have been tainted by gossip and rumour. Moreover, Memnon's account seems to imply that Arsinoe owed her success to womanly wiles, suggesting a demand made in a less than public context! The suspicion remains that this portrayal of Lysimachus as the archetypal old fool, helpless in the hands of a young and reputedly beautiful woman, represents a conventional motif, used to fill the gap where accurate information failed our sources. This argument is supported by the contrast between this Lysimachus and the man depicted by Nymphis himself at the time of his recent takeover of Heracleia. Far from a man enfeebled by old age, the emphasis there is on the king's subtlety; he is a master of the art of stratagem, renowned for his skill as a dissembler.[17]

The scheming woman, the power behind the throne, is, moreover, a familiar figure in ancient historiography. From Ctesias' Semiramis, through Herodotus, Tacitus and Suetonius, reaching a climax with the monstrous female creations of Procopius' *Secret History*, she wields influence through beauty and sexual charms. The action which she initiates, or more usually persuades her male partner to take, is, however, almost invariably destructive. Ambitious and determined, she stops at nothing to achieve her ends and inflicts savage punish-ment on her enemies. She is a witch, an adulteress, a murderess and an unnatural mother. Most of these characteristics are attached, by one source or another, to Arsinoe.[18]

Analysing this stereotype, with reference to the Byzantine period, Fisher concluded that its origins lie in an assumption of women's mental and moral frailty, male fear of female sexuality and its potential force, the belief that independent action and achievement of power by women is improper and offensive. It is hard to acquit any of the authors listed above on this count. Semiramis, for example, portrayed initially as dangerously attractive but nevertheless possessed of good qualities, becomes a kind of Gorgon the minute she ascends the throne. Addicted to luxury and afraid that marriage will mean loss of power, she has her wicked way with the handsomest of her soldiers and then has them executed![19]

As regards the Persian empire, at least, recent research has questioned its traditional presentation as a kingdom ruled 'from the unwholesome atmosphere of the harem', where 'queens decided and kings complied'. If Duris is indeed the source for the tradition which emphasises Arsinoe's part in Agathocles' death, then it is worth remembering that Duris was strongly influenced by Herodotus, and therefore by a tradition of historiography in which kings' wives and mistresses are prominent.[20]

Finally, Arsinoe's relationship to Agathocles at once casts her in another classic role. The wicked stepmother is an archetype of evil in European myth and literature. Ovid, describing the birth of crime in the Iron Age, includes among his gallery of rogues 'ruthless step-mothers mixing brews of deadly aconite'; Tacitus' famous portrait of the Empress Livia lays great emphasis on her role as stepmother to Augustus' ill-fated heirs. The very use of the word *noverca* in the Latin tradition of Justin/Trogus immediately associates Arsinoe with poison and intrigue.[21]

KING AND HEIR-APPARENT

If, then, the literary evidence is unlikely to yield the 'historical truth' about the end of Lysimachus' reign, can these events be approached from a different angle? One possible method is to look at the evidence independent of the literary tradition, and to take a new perspective on these events, with a focus on the relationship between power holders and their successors and the problems that arise with the transition of autocratic power. Though this cannot guarantee to bring us any closer to 'what actually happened' at the Thracian court in the late 280s BC, it may, however, cast fresh light on an episode which must seem curious in the context of what we know of Lysimachus' aims and his previous career.

Neither the fact of a succession struggle, with a culling of potential claimants, nor the idea that Lysimachus committed murder within his own family are in themselves surprising. Plutarch stresses the Antigonids' remarkable restraint in keeping their hands relatively clean of the blood of their nearest and dearest, since

> the chronicles of almost all the other dynasties are full of examples of men who murdered their sons, their mothers or their wives, while the murder of brothers had come to be regarded almost as axiomatic, as a recognised precaution to be taken by all rulers to ensure their safety.

Clearly not squeamish about such matters, Lysimachus had already removed his son-in-law and two stepsons, to his own considerable profit. Antipater had represented an awkward obstacle to his claim to Macedon; the death of Clearchus and Oxathres won him control of wealthy Heracleia.[22] By contrast, the murder of Agathocles proved disastrous for Lysimachus, both politically and personally.

A king's first priority, if concerned for the future of his realm and his own reputation in posterity, is the choice of an able successor. The removal of Agathocles seems a deliberate breach of this rule. Ptolemy I, of course, had set a precedent for deposing a first-born son in favour of a younger candidate, with Ceraunus, son of his marriage to Eurydice, ousted in favour of Berenice's son Ptolemy. The latter was, however, adult at the time of his accession, and though Ceraunus' 'mad dog' image may be in part the product of a hostile source tradition, his subsequent career hardly reassures us of his fitness to rule. Furthermore, Ptolemy I took steps to ensure a smooth transition of rule by abdicating the throne in favour of his heir two years before his death.[23]

Lysimachus' position was rather different. Though possibly unable to predict the massive loss of support after Agathocles' death which laid his kingdom open to Seleucus' attack, his own recent experience should have warned him against removing a mature, militarily able and popular heir in favour of an adolescent with younger brothers, who might start his reign under his mother's regency. Both Demetrius and Lysimachus himself had exploited the inherent weakness of such a set-up to gain, respectively, Macedon and Heracleia Pontica.[24]

It is possible, of course, that our sources have given Agathocles what might be called 'the Germanicus treatment'. Such a white-washing might represent Seleucid propaganda, designed to reinforce Nicator's pose as Agathocles' avenger in 282–1 BC. Alternatively, and more plausibly, it might be the work of a source whose aim of blackening Lysimachus owed nothing to Seleucid patronage; it is hard to see why any of the most likely sources, Hieronymus, Duris or Nymphis, should be pro-Seleucid.[25] If Agathocles' portrait was gilded in order to tarnish that of Lysimachus, then Hieronymus, the Antigonids' protégé, is the most likely candidate. There is, however, little that hints at encomia in the literary references to Agathocles; Justin, whose source is thought to be Hieronymus,[26] says merely that Agathocles was Lysimachus' 'best and oldest son' and refers to his successful warfare on his father's behalf. The description of Agatho-cles as a 'young man', mourned by many, may well be Justin's own addition, aiming to create an atmosphere of pathos; similar effects can be seen in the truly purple passages which recount Ptolemy Ceraunus' later murder of Arsinoe's sons. The tone here bears little resemblance to the generally rather spare, restrained style of Hieronymus which seems to be reflected in Plutarch's account of Agathocles' Asian campaign of 286–5 BC.[27] Indeed Hieronymus, or his patron Gonatas, would have found themselves on the horns of a dilemma had they wished to attack Lysimachus by glorifying Agathocles, since this would highlight the latter's triumph over Demetrius. On these grounds it seems reasonable to conclude that the ability which the sources ascribe to Agathocles must be taken seriously.

What then impelled Lysimachus to commit what looks like an act of political suicide? The literary tradition, which emphasises the influence of his wife, has been shown to be not entirely trustworthy. Admittedly, from the *cui bono* point of view, Arsinoe had the most to gain from Agathocles' death. Quite apart from her ambitions for herself, or for her sons,[28] Agathocles' accession would probably present a serious threat to her life and theirs. That she worked to create tension between the king and his heir is probable, but whether she wielded sufficient influence to be held ultimately responsible for his death is less certain.

Just how much power did Arsinoe have? Longega, among others, credits her with great influence at Lysimachus' court from the first days of her marriage, and sees her as the guiding force behind Lysimachus' 'new philhellenism' in the years after Ipsus. The basis for this theory consists of two inscriptions and selected literary and numismatic evidence which has prompted the belief that Arsinoe 'owned' several important cities within Lysimachus' kingdom.[29]

The relevant inscriptions are Delos' decree for Demaratus, dated by Longega to 295–4 BC, where Arsinoe appears with Lysimachus as the focus of Delian *eunoia*, and a later decree from Siphnos, where Queen Arsinoe III, wife of Ptolemy Philopator, is likewise assured of Siphnian *eunoia*; the context is thought to be the aftermath of the battle of Raphia, where Arsinoe III was active in exhorting Ptolemy's troops to victory. Seeing the two texts as parallel and distinct from the majority of inscriptions where both king and queen of Egypt appear in a cultic context, Longega infers that Arsinoe II's inclusion in the Delian decree must likewise reflect an active political role, namely in Lysimachus' Aegean diplomacy.[30]

Several objections can be made. First, the dating of the Delos text is far from sure and so therefore is its value as a sign of Arsinoe's early influence. Second, if a queen's inclusion in decrees reflects her political influence, as this argument implies, then Arsinoe's absence from other comparable inscriptions, from Priene, Samothrace and Samos, dated to the second half of the 280s BC, suggests that her power was actually less than the literary sources imply. Third, to infer a new policy of 'philhellenism', inspired by Arsinoe, on the basis of one inscription is unwise; there is, in any case, evidence for Lysimachus' euergetism before Ipsus and it is more likely that his increased resources after that victory were what prompted, or enabled, him to play the benefactor on a greater scale, rather than his wife's influence.[31]

What then of 'Arsinoe's cities', namely Ephesus, Cassandreia and Heracleia Pontica? Neither Ephesus' renaming as Arsinoeia nor Arsinoe's 'portrait' (if indeed it is) on the city coinage is proof of her direct control. Smyrna, renamed Eurydiceia, also issued coinage with an obverse of a veiled woman in similar style; there is no suggestion that Lysimachus' daughter Eurydice ever 'owned' Smyrna. Arsinoe's presence at Ephesus after Corupedium does not prove that the city was hers; it only shows that until rumours of Seleucus' victory were confirmed, Ephesus adhered to Lysimachus' cause. Similarly, Arsinoe's control of Cassandreia after Lysimachus' death need not imply prior ownership, but only her ability to pay for mercenary troops and the existence of a faction there who supported her son Ptolemy's claim against Seleucus. Of Arsinoe's supposed possessions, then, only Heracleia Pontica and perhaps its dependencies can be accepted with certainty. Even here, it is possible that Lysimachus' 'gift' did not entail

Arsinoe's full ownership of the city, to govern as she liked, but constituted instead a gift of the city's revenues, as the Achaemenid kings had designated the revenues of certain cities 'for the queen's girdle' or 'the queen's shoes'.[32]

The evidence, then, gives little support to the view that Arsinoe's influence was great enough either to inspire an over-cautious husband to make a major change in foreign policy – if indeed there was one – or to induce him to commit an act, like the murder of his heir, for which he had no personal will or incentive. Possibly the idea of Arsinoe as highly powerful in Thrace stems in part from the knowledge of her later conspicuous position as Ptolemy II's queen in Egypt. Insofar as royal devotion finds expression in public honours, nothing suggests that Lysimachus' feeling for Arsinoe was comparable to that displayed by Ptolemy II, both during her life-time and posthumously.[33]

If, then, Lysimachus was not so in thrall to Arsinoe as knowingly to allow her to issue the execution order for his son, the possibility remains that by this time, as Memnon and Pausanias imply, the king had lost his mental grip. Though any attempt to evaluate a historical figure's sanity is of course fraught with difficulties, some evidence exists which belies this suggestion of senility. Memnon's portrayal of Lysimachus the Schemer shortly before Agathocles' death has already been mentioned. Then there is Lysimachus' letter to Samos, discussing his recent arbitration in a dispute with Priene over the Batinetis land. Clearly the case was highly complicated, involving claims, counter-claims, citation of historical documents going back to the sixth century BC and some serious misrepresentation on Priene's part. Evidently the citizens hoped to pull the wool over Lysimachus' eyes. Despite this and the temptation to favour Priene, whose *demos* had accorded him conspicuous honours in the past, Lysimachus' decision, awarding the land to Samos, seems to have been correct and just. Though this letter might be explained as the work of aides, Welles's comment on its tone is significant: 'although it is perhaps too much to suppose that Lysimachus himself dictated these lines . . . certainly nothing in the royal letters is more markedly personal.'[34] Senility, then, does not seem to be the key which unlocks the mystery of Agathocles' death.

If Lysimachus was neither senile nor helplessly infatuated with his wife, the possibility remains that he knowingly and deliberately eliminated his heir. If so, how is it to be explained? The literary sources focus on the rivalry between Agathocles and Arsinoe, saying little about the nature of his relationship with Lysimachus, despite the fact that the tensions which can arise between ruler and heir-apparent are notorious. The former is unwilling to relinquish power; the latter is impatient to step into his father's shoes. This phenomenon, of course, is not restricted to the ancient world but occurs in all societies where a system of dynastic rule carries with it the danger of a succession crisis.[35]

The little that is known of Agathocles' career and position in the last years of his life suggests that these factors may be relevant. In the prime of life in the 280s BC, Agathocles enjoyed conspicuous military success on Lysimachus' behalf and reaped the expected rewards of victory, notably the support of *philoi* who included leading men in his father's army. Politicians in Asia Minor's Greek cities may also have flocked to his side, but this is more problematic, since it is unclear how far Agathocles' death served as a pretext for revolt among those opposed to Lysimachus for other, more personal, reasons, such as longstanding political enmity for fellow citizens who had flourished under his rule.

Whether Agathocles received comparable recognition from Lysimachus for these services is doubtful. Though his Asian command of 286-5 BC has been thought by some to signify an important governorship, there is no literary or epigraphic evidence to support this. There is, for instance, no suggestion that Lysimachus' *strategoi* of the Ionians, Hippostratus and Hippodamus, reported to Agathocles; they are described simply as 'friends of King Lysimachus'. Similarly, Priene's decree for Lysimachus, generally dated *c.* 285 BC, praises only the king, giving thanks for his safety and that of his army. The *strategos* So[sthenes] is mentioned, but not Agathocles, despite the fact that So[sthenes] was probably serving under his supreme command. As Bengtson argued, Agathocles' command of the campaign of 286-5 BC can be explained purely in military terms, given Lysimachus' preoccupations in Europe.[36]

Agathocles' absence from the official documentation of the 280s BC contrasts strikingly both with contemporary Seleucid texts and inscriptions recording Antigonid actions in the period before Ipsus. Demetrius is crowned king at the same time as his father and enjoys cult worship alongside him in many of the cities. Seleucus had given the eastern section of his kingdom to his son Antiochus as early as 294 BC, as well as his own wife Stratonice. Both father and son issue the letter which grants privileges to the Plutonium at Nysa in 281 BC. Babylonian texts give Antiochus the title of 'Crown Prince' and show a regnal dating by Seleucus and Antiochus from 292 BC. Ptolemy I's abdication to Philadelphus in 285 BC has already been mentioned.[37] Lysimachus' apparent failure to follow suit in publicly relinquishing a share of power to his eldest son, thus acknowledging him as a partner in his rule, could hardly fail to arouse feelings of frustration and resentment.

The question then arises whether Agathocles finally expressed these feelings in openly subversive action. The evidence, unfortunately, is ambiguous. It seems that Agathocles founded a city, named after himself, probably in Mysia, during his father's life-time. This need not be seen as sinister, although similar action by Alexander before the death of Philip II has aroused some controversy. One might argue that if a mere *strategos* like Docimus, Antigonus' governor in Phrygia, was permitted an eponymous foundation, surely such action would be unexceptionable in a prince. On the other hand, the date of Docimus' foundation and his relations with Antigonus at the time are unknown. What is unquestionable is Docimus' flexibility and ambition. His city-building may represent one aspect of a subversive stance which later found expression in defection to Lysimachus.[38]

Our knowledge of Agathopolis comes from coins carrying the city's name and a head on the obverse thought to be a portrait of Agathocles. This of course is not unprecedented; under Achaemenid rule, even the empire's satraps had issued silver portrait coins. The debate over the 'royal monopoly' on the minting of gold coinage is not an issue here, since so far the coins from Agathopolis are restricted to bronze. More disturbing, perhaps, is the fact that the young man depicted on their obverse appears to be wearing the diadem, the symbol of royalty worn only by kings. If it could be securely identified as that of Agathocles, the 'portrait' might be interpreted as a sign of dangerous ambition, particularly since Lysimachus himself avoided striking a personal portrait coin.[39] There is, or has been, however, a tendency among scholars to be over-enthusiastic in identifying heads on early Hellenistic coins as founder portraits, and the head may simply be that of a deity or hero.

Frustrated in the face of Lysimachus' reluctance to relinquish power, Agathocles may also have come to fear that he would be supplanted by the young Ptolemy. Did he have any real grounds for suspicion on this count? An inscription from Thebes, recording Ptolemy's dedication of a statue of Arsinoe on Lysimachus' behalf, is the only evidence which might suggest Ptolemy's increased prominence at court in the late 280s BC.[40] Seen as part of Lysimachus' diplomatic activity in mainland Greece, the text is generally dated *c*. 284 BC to 281 BC, since Ptolemy, child of a marriage *c*. 299 BC, must have been at least adolescent when he was entrusted with such a task. Though there are some epigraphic peculiarities about the text, notably the broken cross bar of alpha, usually thought to characterise lettering of the late third century BC and after, it is probably best to accept this date, and see the lettering as an exception to the usual 'rule'.[41] As regards Agathocles, what matters is whether Ptolemy's Boeotian trip precedes or follows his half-brother's death. The prominence which the stone gives to Arsinoe and her son might reflect the dangerous rise of their faction before Agathocles' death; alternatively it may reflect Ptolemy's new importance afterwards as heir apparent. This cannot be clearly ascertained. In conclusion, while this inscription raises the possibility that Agathocles was being supplanted by Ptolemy before his death, it cannot stand as firm evidence that this was so.

Whatever Ptolemy's position, the evidence discussed above permits the supposition that Lysimachus' great error lay in a reluctance to recognise the claims of the coming generation which spelled out his own mortality. Possibly this expressed itself in a failure publicly to acknowledge Agathocles' achievements in such a way as to leave the prince confident of his imminent accession. Since Agathocles was mature and militarily able, with a strong body of support, frustrated in his ambitions for rule, and perhaps afraid that his long-awaited kingdom would be snatched from him, it is not impossible that he tried forcibly to anticipate his inheritance. The charge of treachery, predictably presented by the sources as trumped up, may have had some substance, as implied by Strabo's comment that Lysimachus was compelled to kill his son.[42]

This reconstruction is, of course, speculative, but it does serve in some measure to explain why Lysimachus, by all accounts a fairly cool customer, with one blow put at risk not only the kingdom he had spent forty years in building, but also his chance, as founder of a successful dynasty, to achieve the immortality that comes with lasting renown.

Following this examination of the mysterious happenings at Lysimachus' court in the last years of his reign and the tensions which may have provoked them, it is time now to look at the impact of these events upon the world outside.

THE CORUPEDIUM CAMPAIGN; SELEUCUS AND THE CITIES

> Lysimachus, however, was justly hated by his subjects because of his son's murder, and Seleucus, learning of these events and considering that it would be easy to deprive him of his power, since the cities were revolting from him, joined battle against him.
>
> (Memnon *FGrH* 434 F.5.7)

Memnon's very cursory account of events preceding the last great battle of the Diadochs presents Seleucus' decision to take up arms against his neighbour as the direct consequence of Agathocles' death. A key factor, seemingly, was a wave of feeling against Lysimachus among his Greek subjects, originating, so Memnon implies, in moral outrage at Agathocles' murder. Justin lays stress rather on pressure from the surviving members of Agathocles' faction, including leading men from Lysimachus' army, as inspiring Seleucus to make a move which jealousy and ambition were already prompting. Pausanias supports this, though his emphasis is on the part played by Agathocles' widow Lysandra.[43]

At first sight, there is little that seems contentious in these accounts. To try and isolate one motive for Seleucus' invasion of Asia Minor in 282–1 BC as primary would be futile; plausibly all these factors played their part. The suggestion that widespread revolt among the *poleis* was prompted by disgust at the king's unnatural murder of his son is, however, questionable, as is the assumption that the cities defected on a large scale before Seleucus' victory at Corupedium.[44] Such a belief implies a uniformity of opinion both within each individual city and among the cities of Asia Minor as a whole which is belied by a study of their history at almost any period. Rather, what emerges as an enduring feature is an essential pragmatism, a readiness to be flexible and, in the context of struggle between opposing 'super powers', to back the likely winner.[45] Tied in with this, of course, is the fact that one cannot regard any one city as a united body, representing one particular opinion or following one policy; instead the *polis* is composed of different groups which pursue their own interests, and whose fortunes wax and wane along with those of their royal patrons and protectors.

Agathocles may have had his supporters in the cities, but it is hardly credible that his personal popularity was sufficient in itself to spark off a united movement of revolt across the kingdom. Modern scholarship favours the idea that Lysimachus' Greek subjects defected in reaction against his unusually harsh rule, but this is a generalisation which has already been questioned in an earlier chapter. What the fragmentary evidence for the period suggests is rather a crisis of confidence in the enduring power of Lysimachus' dynasty. It is likely that news of Agathocles' death travelled through Asia Minor in the following months, carried perhaps by fugitives en route to Seleucus' court. Probably these exiles had guest-friends in the Greek cities who facilitated their journey.[46]

For the politicians who had prospered under Lysimachus' rule, Agathocles may well have stood as the guarantor of continued influence. With his disappearance, and the likely prospect, on Lysimachus' death, of a succession struggle between the three minor heirs, their futures suddenly looked very much less bright. There may also have been a change of perception regarding Lysimachus. Forty years after Alexander's death, the struggle for the spoils of empire was far from over and the Diadoch wars had seen remarkable shifts of fortune among the protagonists in which public opinion had frequently played a crucial part. Accordingly, the importance for a king of maintaining an aura of invincibility and strength cannot be over-estimated. It has already been shown that the adherence and continued support of *philoi* were vital for the achievement and maintenance of kingship. Lysimachus' loss of 'friends', first to Agathocles' faction and then to Seleucus, is stressed by the sources and must have represented a serious loss of credibility.[47] Plausibly, then, this period began to see the rise of those statesmen who, for personal or professional reasons, had opposed Lysimachus' protégés; naturally they would turn to Seleucus for support. The process can be observed at Ephesus, where the existence of a pro-Seleucid faction is attested for the period immediately after Corupedium. The degree to which such factions succeeded in actually seizing control and persuading the *demos* to defect at this particular time is, however, uncertain. At Ephesus, *hoi Seleukizontes* clearly lacked sufficient clout to take over the city until their confidence was boosted by news of Seleucus' victory and his troops' imminent arrival.[48]

Apart from Pergamum, handed over by Philetaerus, formally at least, some time between the summers of 283 BC and 282 BC, there is no clear evidence for city defections from Lysimachus before his defeat at Corupedium. Ephesus has already been mentioned; Priene's loss of autonomy at the beginning of Antiochus I's reign may suggest resistance to Seleucus. Miletus' longstanding friendship with the

Seleucid house, its defection to Demetrius in 286 BC and Lysimachus' consequent imposition of financial penalties make it a likely candidate for revolt. In 283–2 BC, however, its *demos* is still concerned to meet its financial obligations to Lysimachus. This hardly suggests a context of impending revolution. If Burstein is correct to see a royal stephanephorate as reflecting a recent change of control, then seemingly the city was not in Seleucid hands until 281–0 BC, since Antiochus holds the stephanephorate for the following year. Samos and Priene, likewise, still look to Lysimachus as their overlord in 283–2 BC, requesting arbitration on the Batinetis affair.[49] It is, of course, still possible that these important cities did defect some time between summer 283 BC and summer 282 BC, if the decrees belong to the first months of the magistrate's year of office. Their issue at the end of that period cannot, however, be ruled out.

THE ROAD TO CORUPEDIUM

A more likely context for Greek defection might be the period of Seleucus' advance into Asia Minor, with the presence of his troops proving more persuasive than mere indignation at the news of Agathocles' death. The date of Seleucus' arrival in Asia Minor is unclear. A fragment of the Babylonian Chronicle which mentions the launch of a military campaign involving Greeks, dated to the month Sivan, Year 30 of the Seleucid era (June/July 282 BC), suggests that Seleucus had mustered his troops and marched in the month of Sivan, reaching Asia Minor in the late summer of 282 BC. The decisive battle, however, took place only in February 281 BC, an unorthodox season which suggested to Heinen a surprise attack, with Seleucus crossing the Taurus only in winter 282–1 BC.[50] At first sight these pieces of evidence seem irreconcilable; a look at the Babylonian text, however, shows that only the left-hand side survives, with a lacuna between the dating formula (Year 30 S.E., month of Sivan) and the description of Seleucus' mobilisation and departure. Possibly then the campaign's launch belongs to a later month[51] and Seleucus' attack did catch Lysimachus off guard. Alternatively his failure to forestall Seleucus may be explained by difficulties in raising a strong enough army to meet the Syrian king. Though the numbers at Corupedium are unknown, the defection of army commanders mentioned by Justin, combined perhaps with Macedon's enduring manpower shortage, suggests that Lysimachus' military strength was seriously impaired.[52]

It is, however, possible that Lysimachus had taken some measures in the interim to strengthen his hold on his possessions in Asia. The presence of his fleet, or a section of it, at Ephesus after Corupedium might suggest that advance forces were sent by ship to lend some muscle to his supporters in the key coastal cities. Such an action might also make sense of Pausanias' remark – nonsensical in the light of the main army movements – that Lysimachus crossed over into Asia first.[53]

Whatever the reason for Lysimachus' delay, Seleucus reached Sardis before the enemy confronted him. Though the Babylonian Chronicle suggests that victory at Corupedium emboldened Seleucus to lay claim to Lysimachus' whole kingdom,[54] his precise goal at the time of launching his invasion remains unclear. It is futile to spend time discussing Lysimachus' 'motivation' for the war. Since the initiative clearly lay with Seleucus, he had little choice but to fight if he wished to save his Asian possessions.

Seleucus' route into Asia Minor also remains uncertain. The one possible landmark is Cotiaeion in northern Phrygia, taken by Lysimachus' son Alexander by a double stratagem. His defection to Seleucus makes the campaign of 282–1 BC a likely context for this episode, leading Heinen to suggest that one section of the army took the royal road from Ankyra to Sardis while another went south via the Cilician gates to western Asia Minor.[55] This seems preferable to Corradi's theory that Seleucus took the route which had led him to Ipsus twenty years before, via Cappadocia, which relies heavily on the assumption that Seleucus could count on 'the sympathy of the Bithynians and cities like Heracleia'. If these peoples were pro-Seleucid in summer 282 BC, then their sympathy was shortlived; Seleucus faced determined opposition in these very quarters after his victory. If Seleucus' army had marched through these lands in 282–1 BC, then it is likely that its presence aroused fear as much as joyful expectation of freedom. Seleucus may have emphasised his role as liberator of the Greeks, a time-honoured practice, but these events in northern Asia Minor scarcely reflect an expectation that his rule would be very different from or much preferable to that of Lysimachus.[56]

If the cities of northern Asia Minor gave Seleucus the thumbs down after Corupedium, how was he received by Lysimachus' Greek subjects before his victory, as he marched towards the coast? Though the evidence is limited, it does not support the view that he was welcomed everywhere with open arms. In the hinterland, both Cotiaeion and Sardis fell by stratagem, the latter only after an unsuccessful siege. It is probable that many of the cities on the coast preferred to adopt their usual tactic of 'watch and wait', particularly given the likely proximity of Lysimachus' still considerable fleet and Seleucus' apparent weakness as regards naval forces.[57] The possibility remains that defection on a grand scale took place only after Seleucus' victory.

This in turn casts a different light upon the mushrooming of Seleucid cults among the *poleis* on Asia Minor's western coast in the early third century BC. Traditionally, these are thought to reflect a 'wave of enthusiasm' for Seleucus the Liberator; Habicht likened the reaction to that which met Alexander in 333 BC. The comparison is certainly instructive, but it can yield a rather less optimistic conclusion. Arrian's narrative shows that the initial Ionian response to Alexander was uncertain, establishes a close connection between the Granicus victory and the first voluntary submissions, and demonstrates that Alexander was not afraid to take severe reprisals in the event of resistance. That it was Seleucus' victory which similarly prompted a swift change of stance in the coastal cities is probable. In most cases the cults cannot be precisely dated, but the uncertainty regarding mass defection before Corupedium makes it likely that those whose origin is set in Seleucus' life-time post-date the battle.[58] At Ilium, moreover, a date in Seleucus' reign rests solely on linking the city's anti-tyranny law with Lysimachus' regime, something which is far from certain. Colophon might have been more likely to welcome Seleucus, since its resistance to Lysimachus *c*. 294 BC may have led to penalties of the sort imposed on Miletus and Erythrae, but acceptance of a Seleucid cult there in 281 BC also implies Colophon's continuing political existence at that date, refuting the belief that Lysimachus, in typically oppressive fashion, 'destroyed' the city. Doubts about Priene's positive reception of Seleucus in 281 BC have already been raised.[59]

There remains Lemnos, seemingly the most clear-cut example of thanks for Seleucid liberation from Lysimachus, whose harsh treatment of its inhabitants is explicitly stated. Phylarchus tells us that Seleucus received cult honours and libations poured to him as *Soter*. The credentials of this statement's source – Seleucus' 'flatterers' on Lemnos – are, however, dubious. Furthermore, the context of Lemnos' 'liberation' by Seleucus may make it a special case. Performed on the eve of his invasion of Lysimachus' European kingdom, its primary significance is not as an act of benefaction to the oppressed Lemnians, but as a political deal with another power, Athens. Seleucus' return of two Lemnian cities, Hephaistion and Myrina, to Athens would presumably guarantee him continued access to Lemnos, sited off the

Thracian Chersonese and therefore of particular strategic importance at this juncture. His hopes of naval support from Athens have already been mentioned.[60]

The case of Lemnos and the extravagant honours voted to the Seleucid kings by supporters eager to retain the royal favour raises another important issue. Lysimachus' demise and the collapse of his dynasty makes it likely that our evidence on events in Asia Minor in this period will be one-sided. Some material, like the manifesto of philhellenism contained in an inscription from Nysa, recording Seleucid benefactions to the Plutonium temple in the period after Corupedium, clearly represents royal propaganda. Seleucus' role as one in a long line of conquerors acceding to a new kingdom in Asia may also account for some distortion in the presentation of events. Emphasis on a new ruler's beneficence and, by contrast, denigration of his predecessor's regime are familiar features of royal propaganda from both the Achaemenid empire and those preceding it.[61]

Similarly the 'official' nature of the city decrees which comprise most of our evidence must be taken into account. Quite apart from the fact that these were probably published at the behest of politicians who had come to power through Seleucus' favour, the context in which the *demos* votes to inscribe certain decisions on stone must also be considered. It is in the city's interest to emphasise royal benefactions and positive relations between king and city. In the present this secures the royal patron's goodwill. Still more important, it sets a precedent for the city's future treatment at kingly hands. Undercutting the benevolence emphasised by this official documentation is the literary account of Seleucus' response to Heracleia's bid for independence, rightly emphasised by Mehl. For cities which lacked Heracleia's strength and capacity for resistance, cult honours for Corupedium's victor may represent not so much a comment on Lysimachus' rule as an acknowledgement of Seleucus' very real power to do them, as he chose, either good or harm.[62]

In conclusion, the evidence for events in the period after Agathocles' death suggests that Lysimachus' loss of support at home led to a shift of feeling in the cities which favoured the rise of Seleucus' supporters. There is, however, little evidence to support a belief in mass defection before the battle of Corupedium. Victory turned the tide of city feeling in Seleucus' favour. Even then, events in northern Asia Minor, combined with the propagandist and selective nature of the evidence, warn against a too-ready acceptance of the traditional view that the cities' reaction to Seleucus was one of sincere gratitude towards a saviour.

THE LAST BATTLE

Ultimum hoc certamen conmilitonum Alexandri fuit (Justin XVII.1.9).

For Justin, the battle of Corupedium, where the armies of Seleucus and Lysimachus met in February 281 BC, is significant mainly as an illustration of the lengths to which ambition drives men. He draws a contrast between the combatants' advanced age and the youthful keenness of their aspirations towards ever greater empire. With a glorious over-simplification which would have had any self-respecting Ptolemy turning in his grave, Justin reduces the Hellenistic world to a stage occupied by two men – *quippe cum orbem terrarum duo soli tenerent* – each striving for domination of the whole. This, and the emphasis on Lysimachus and Seleucus as Alexander's companions, recalls Hieronymus' presentation of events from 323 BC to 301 BC as the story of a struggle to reunite Alexander's empire under one man's rule.[63]

While allowances must be made for Justin's over-developed sense of drama, which leads him to see the battle purely as a great tragic set-piece, this presentation of the issues at stake should not be rejected out of hand. The enormous increase in Lysimachus' power in the 280s BC had caused his fellow rulers considerable unease as to what his next step might be; similarly, Seleucus' actions in Asia Minor after Corupedium lend support to the belief that he may have aspired to *ta hola*. He was determined to secure acknowledgement of his sovereignty in all quarters, and despite signs of reluctance among his troops pressed ahead with the invasion of Europe and his claim to Macedon. His successors' later claim to a historic right to Lysimachus' whole kingdom presumably reflects the tenor of Seleucid propaganda in 281 BC.[64]

Unfortunately for the modern historian, Justin's preoccupation with Corupedium as a moral example leads him to omit any details regarding the actual battle! We are told nothing of numbers, terrain, arrangement of troops, or of the tactics which brought Seleucus victory, only that Lysimachus died in action – *moriens non instrenue*. Memnon adds only the information that the king fell at the hands of a Heracleote, Malacon, presumably an exile or a mercenary. Non-literary evidence has secured the dating and site of the battle. A

Babylonian king-list dating Seleucus' death 'in the land of the Khani' to the period between 25 August and 24 September 281 BC and Justin's reference to a lapse of seven months between Seleucus' victory and his assassination suggests that Corupedium was fought in February 281 BC. It seems best to accept the precise information of this Babylonian text against another from Uruk whose dating by Seleucus' reign suggests that news of his death had not reached Babylon in December 281 BC. Dating by the regnal years of a king who may have died even several years before is not unknown and seems particularly to occur in periods of transition and dynastic instability.[65] An epitaph for a Bithynian officer, Menas, killed in battle at *Korou Pedion*, by the waters of the River Phrygios, together with Polyaenus' account of resistance at Sardis before the battle, have established its site as the well-used plain to the west of Sardis. As yet, further evidence which might add to our knowledge of the battle is slight and too uncertain by its nature to yield any firm conclusions. Whether, for instance, Bithynians and/or elephants made a significant contribution to Seleucus' victory remains uncertain![66]

The last evidence concerning Lysimachus, like the events of his final years, smacks strongly of legend and literary convention. The tale of the faithful hound which guarded his body on the field and then hurled itself on to his pyre clearly became proverbial among Roman writers. It recalls, among others, the story of Xanthippus' dog, equally famous for fidelity. On a grimmer note, Pausanias tells us that the hatred of his daughter-in-law Lysandra pursued him after death; like Polynices, or the Argive warriors in Euripides' *Supplices*, Lysimachus was in danger of being denied burial. Seleucus' sense of propriety, combined with the entreaties of Lysimachus' son Alexander, prevailed against Lysandra's desire for vengeance. If Lysimachus had dreamed of burial in a hero's tomb at Ephesus, then it was not to be. Instead his body began the journey back to Thrace for burial near Lysimacheia, perhaps along the same road which had taken him to his satrapy, at the start of his great adventure over forty years before.[67]

APPENDIX I

Lysimachus and the problem of Prienean autonomy

The first years of Seleucid rule show Priene to have lost the autonomous status granted by Alexander, and emphatically stated at the head of city decrees in the following years.[1] The evidence of Sextus Empiricus suggests that autonomy was restored at some point during the reign of Antiochus I, apparently at the request of a citizen high in the king's favour.[2] There is no suggestion that autonomy was restored at the time of Antiochus' accession. Logically this might suggest that Priene lost its autonomy at Seleucid hands,[3] perhaps as a consequence of failing to greet Seleucus I with sufficient enthusiasm in 282–1 BC. This would not be inconsistent with the evidence for positive relations with Lysimachus in 286–5 BC, when Priene votes the king cult honours in return for his protection and is praised by him for its loyalty. It is possible that on this occasion he also granted the city certain important privileges.[4] The fact that the *demos* published these communications in an archive recording decisions favourable to Priene[5] argues against the dismissal of this evidence as mere empty formulas, concealing a relationship based on hypocrisy and fear. Burstein, moreover, has argued convincingly for the actual enjoyment by Priene of a considerable degree of local autonomy in the decade preceding these decrees.[6] Formally, however, he believes that the city was deprived of autonomous status during this period, on Lysimachus' order. The context proposed for this loss of autonomy, the probable resistance of the pro-Demetrian government to Lysimachus in 294 BC, is plausible,[7] but it is doubtful whether this state of affairs continued throughout Lysimachus' reign into the early years of Seleucid rule as is often assumed.

Quite apart from the likelihood that his pose of 'liberator' would have impelled Antiochus on his accession to reverse any such decision of Lysimachus, there is the evidence of Lysimachus' letter to Priene.

Thanking the citizens for the honours voted to him and for their loyalty in 286 BC, the king appears to be acknowledging, at the point where the text breaks off, some sort of request on the part of the Prieneans. Sherwin-White follows Welles in supposing that the citizens asked for some kind of privileges in return for their recently demonstrated fidelity.[8] Going one step further, she suggests from the juxtaposition of the Lysimachus decrees with the 'Alexander edict', *inscribed* at the same time, that what was asked for and granted may even have been a return to the status conferred by Alexander.[9] If correct, then Prienean gratitude may have been sufficient to keep the city loyal in 282–1 BC, despite the fact that in the interim the citizens' attempt to pull a fast one on Lysimachus with an unjust claim to Samian land had misfired.[10] Orth sees this incident as the end of the honeymoon period, with defection to Seleucus the following year, reflected in Priene's erection of statues to Nicator and his son some time in the 270s BC.[11] It is, however, equally possible that the city remained loyal to Lysimachus in 282–1 BC, was deprived of autonomy by Seleucus I as a result, and erected statues of the Seleucid kings to express gratitude at Antiochus' subsequent reversal of the decision.

NOTES

1 THE ROAD TO BABYLON

1 Q.C. X.5.8; Arr. *Anab*. VII.26.3–4, 6 for the Bodyguard at Alexander's death bed.

2 Plut. *Demet*. 52, Athen. VI.63 = *FGrH* 76 F. 13.

3 See F. W. Walbank, 'Sources for the period', in A. E. Astin *et al*. (eds) *Cambridge Ancient History*, 2nd edn, vol. VII, Cambridge, Cambridge University Press, 1984, pp. 1–10.

4 Just. XV.3.1, Paus. I.9.4; Arr. *Anab*. VI.28.4, *Ind*. 18.3; Porph. *FHG* III F.4.4; Athen. VI. 259–60= *FGrH* 115 F.81; e.g. Athen. VI.55 = Theopomp. *FGrH* 115 F.209, Demet. *De Eloc*. 27 = *FGrH* 115 225c; for fuller discussion of this phenomenon, see Ch. 6.

5 Arr. *Ind*. 18.3, *Anab*. VI.28.4; I. L. Merker, 'Lysimachus – Macedonian or Thessalian', *Chiron*, 1979, vol. 9, pp. 31–5 – for full discussion, see H. S. Lund, 'Bridging the Hellespont: the Successor Lysimachus – a study in early Hellenistic kingship', University of London Ph.D. thesis, Senate House Library, 1992, Appendix I.

6 J. Hornblower, *Hieronymus of Cardia*, Oxford, Oxford University Press, 1981, pp. 156–9, 197, sees this presentation of Eumenes as the product of apologia; Plut. *Pyrrh*. 12; *Demet*. 11.

7 See Lund, op. cit., Appendix I, for the problems surrounding Lysimachus' birth date; for Alcimachus, see Arr. *Anab*. I.18.1, Hypereides F.77; A. B. Bosworth, *A Historical Commentary on Arrian's* History of Alexander, Oxford, Clarendon Press, 1980, p. 134, M. N. Tod, *Greek Historical Inscriptions*, vol. II, Oxford, Clarendon Press, 1948, p. 180.

8 *Syll*³ 373; Arr. *Succ. FGrH* 156 F.1.37; R. M. Errington, 'From Babylon to Triparadeisos', *JHS*, 1970, vol. 90, pp. 61–71, for the Triparadeisus settlement; Q.C. VIII.2.35–9, Just. XV.3.12; App. *Syr*. 64.

9 See R. M. Errington, 'Bias in Ptolemy's history of Alexander', *CQ*, 1969, vol. 18, pp. 233–42; redressing the balance somewhat, J. Roisman, 'Ptolemy and his rivals in his history of Alexander', *CQ*, 1984, vol. 33, pp. 373–85.

10 Arr. *Anab*. VI.28.4; on the *somatophylakes*, see W. W. Tarn, *Alexander the Great*, vol. II, Cambridge, Cambridge University Press, 1948, pp. 138–41, W. Heckel, 'The *somatophylakes* of Alexander the Great: some

thoughts', *Historia*, 1978, vol. 29, p. 228; Porph. *FHG* III F.3.4; App. *Syr.* 64; Tarn, 1948, op. cit., pp. 138, 141.

11 Arr. *Succ. FGrH* 156 F.1.; Q.C. VIII.2.35–9; though Tarn, 1948, op. cit., p. 139, saw these commands as a late emergency development, Hephaistion held his as early as 330 BC (Arr. *Anab.* III.27.4); Arr. *Anab.* V.24.1.

12 Arr. *Anab.* VI.28.4; Heckel, 1978, op. cit., p. 228; e.g. Peucestas is promoted for saving Alexander's life (Arr. *Anab.* VI.10.2, 28.4.); Errington, 1969, op. cit., p. 233; Roisman, op. cit., p. 383.

13 Errington, 1969, op. cit., p. 233, A. B. Bosworth, 'Arrian and the Alexander Vulgate', in *Alexandre le Grand: image et réalité*, Geneva, Fondation Hardt, 1975, pp. 14–16; Arr. *Anab.* VII.4.4–7; Arr. *Anab.* VII.4.4. Chares (Athen. XII.538b–539a), the other most likely source, clashes with Arrian on the bridegroom numbers, which suggests that Arrian used Aristobulus throughout.

14 Arr. *Anab.* V.13.1 – Errington, 1969, op. cit., p. 236, on Ptolemy and Perdiccas; Arr. *Anab.* V.24.5.

15 L. Pearson, *The Lost Histories of Alexander the Great*, New York, New York Philological Association, 1960, pp. 217–24, 240–2; J. Hornblower, op. cit., p. 50; P. A. Brunt (transl.), *Arrian*, vol. II, 1983, Cambridge, Mass., and London, Loeb, p. 55.

16 Nearch. *FGrH* 133 F.10d, Ps.–Callisth. III 31.8, Metz epitome §98; see W. Heckel, *The Last Days and Testament of Alexander the Great*, Stuttgart, *Historia* Einzelschriften 56, 1988, pp. 5, 10, 34, 72–3, for a new interpretation of this pamphlet's aim.

17 Q.C. VIII.1.46; Arr. *Anab.* IV.8.1–9.4; Arr. *Anab.* IV.8.7 (Errington's suggestion (1969, op. cit., p. 238)) that Ptolemy omitted his own name from a disgraceful affair, but then could not allow the names of his rivals to be prominent (in a disgraceful affair!) does not convince); see T. S. Brown, 'Callisthenes and Alexander', *A. J. Phil*, 1949, vol. 70, pp. 237, 240; assuming that the story was fabricated at the time, rather than after Alexander's death.

18 Q.C. VIII.1.13–17; Pliny *N.H.* VIII.54, Seneca *De Ira* III.17.2, *De Clementia* 1.25.1, Paus. I.9.5; Just. XV.3.7–8, Plut. *Demet.* 27.3, Lucian *Dial. Mort.* 14.4, Val. Max. IX.3. ext. 1; Just. XV.3.7–8, Pomp. Trog. *Prol.* XV. fr. 108b – the central section, at least, of XV.3. copies Trogus exactly.

19 Athen. XIV.616; for other 'cruelty' stories, see Athen. XIV. 620–1, Seneca *De Ira* III.11.4, 14.1, 16.3, 18.1–3.

20 Plut. *Demet.* 27.3; see Ch. 6.

21 Paus. I.9, Just. XV.3.7–8, Val. Max. IX.3. ext. 1; N. G. L. Hammond, *Three Historians of Alexander the Great*, Cambridge, Cambridge University Press, 1983, pp. 63, 77–8 for *ira* as a Cleitarchan feature and Cleitarchus' sensationalism, p. 109 on Justin's sources; Q.C. VIII.1.17.

22 Just. XV.3.1; Arr. *Succ. FGrH* 156 F.1.2, Diod. XX.100.1; see Ch. 7 for the collapse of Lysimachus' dynasty.

23 Paus. I.9.5; Q.C. VIII.1.11–19, included also by Diodorus in the contents list for Bk XVII; see Ch. 6 for Lysimachus' public stance towards Alexander.

24 Plut. *Alex.* 40.4, Ael. *V.H.* XII.39, I. Moretti, *Iscrizioni storiche ellenistiche*, vol. II, Florence, La Nuova Italia Editrice, 1975, no. 73; Istanbul

Archaeological Museum, Cat. No. 68, J. J. Pollitt, *Art in the Hellenistic World*, Cambridge, Cambridge University Press, 1986 p. 38.

25 Just. XV.3.1; P. Goukowsky, *Essai sur les origines du mythe d' Alexandre*, vol. I , Nancy, Nancy University, 1978, App. xxi; see e.g. Plato *Repub*. VI. 484, 487; Isoc. *Ad Nic*. 10–13.

26 Goukowsky, op. cit., App. xxi; Hammond, op. cit., p. 147, likewise sees Onesicritus as a likely source for stories, in Curtius, 'included to please Lysimachus'; Onesic. *FGrH* 134 F.17a = Strabo XV.1.63–5; Plut. *Alex*. 46.

27 Arr. *Anab*. VII.3.4, Diog. Laert. VI.97, Pliny *N.H*. XXV.35; Diog. Laert. II.115, V.37, 97, VII.24.

28 Plut. *Alex*. 69; Onesic. *FGrH* 134 F.17a, 18; Brunt, op. cit., p. 492; the Nisaean horse motif might suggest Duris – R. Schubert, *Die Quellen zur Geschichte der Diadochenzeit*, Leipzig, Theodor Weicher, 1914, p. 86, saw it as a sign of his debt to Herodotus.

29 Athen. XIII.610 = *FHG* IV 358, Plut. *Alex*. 55; e.g. Athen. XII.542, XIII.578.

30 Though Pearson, op. cit., p. 57, doubts that Chares is the source, the story seems to continue directly from that of Hephaistion's clash with Callisthenes for which Chares is cited; Plut. *Alex*. 40, Agatharcides of Cnidus *FGrH* 86 F.1, H. Berve, *Das Alexanderreich auf prosopographischer Grundlage*, vol. I, Munich, C. H. Beck, 1926, p. 241; Plut. *Alex*. 5, 24, 46.

31 Memn. *FGrH* 434 F.5.3; see also Ch. 7.

32 Memn. *FGrH* 434 F.4.9, F.5.3; Just. XVI.2.4, Porph. *FHG* III F.3.3; Polyaen. IV.12.3, IV.12.2; Seneca *De Ira* 3.17; Polyaen. IV.12.1; Plut. *Demet*. 51; Diod. XXI. F.20; for Agathocles, see Ch. 7.

33 For Nymphis, see Ch. 7; compare the actions of Demetrius in 294 BC, and Seleucus in 281 BC (see Chs 4 and 7); Memn. *FGrH* 434 F.5.3; Porph. *FHG* III 688 F.3.3, Just. XVI.2.4; Diod. XXI.F.7, see also Ch. 4.

34 Plut. *Demet*. 36, *Pyrrh*. 7; Just. XVI.2.4, Porph. *FHG* III F.3.3; Diod. XX.20, 28; Polyaen. V.19 – for Docimus and Philetaerus, see Chs 3, 6 and 7; Diod. XX.113.3; J. Hornblower, op. cit., pp. 74–5, sees Hieronymus as Polyaenus' source in Bk IV, but he himself cites a use of multiple sources and the divergence from Diodorus' account may suggest another source here.

35 Seneca *De Ira* 3.17, see also R. Saller, 'Anecdotes as historical evidence for the Principate', *Greece and Rome*, 1980, vol. 27 (2nd series), pp. 69–82; see above, also Cic. *Tusc. Disp*. I.4.3, Plut. *Mor*. 634F.

36 Plut. *Alex*. 46; Plut. *Demet*. 25, 27, Plut. *Demet*. 12, Athen. VI.246 = Aristodemus *FHG* III 310; Athen. VI.246, Plut. *Demet*. 25, Phylarch. *FGrH* 81 F.31.

37 Plut. *Mor*. 457B, 458F (Antigonus): 177D, 177F (Philip II); Plut. *Demet*. 25, Athen. XIV.6114e, XII.577–8.

38 Plut. *Mor*. 458B–C; E. Manni, *Plutarchi: Vita Demetri Poliorcetis*, Florence, La Nuova Italia Editrice, 1953, pp. xii–xiii, R. Kebric, *In the Shadow of Macedon:* Duris of Samos, Wiesbaden, *Historia* Einzelschriften 29, 1977, pp. 5–6, 10, 55; e.g. Athen. III 100E, 101E–F, IV,128A–B.

39 Kebric, op. cit., p. 57; when memory of Cassander's rule over Athens would have been sufficiently fresh for the circulation of stories at the time of Duris' and Lynceus' stay there.

40 Paus. 1. 9.7 = Hieron. *FHG* II F.9; G. Saitta, 'Lisimaco di Tracia', *Kokalos*, 1955, vol. 1, pp. 128–9, G. Longega, *Arsinoe II*, Rome, L'erma di Bretschneider, 1968, pp. 44–54, G. Shipley, *A History of Samos 800–188 B.C.*, Oxford, Clarendon Press, 1987, p. 180. This whole topic is discussed more fully in Lund, op. cit., 1992, pp. 31–47.

41 J. Hornblower, op. cit., p. 72, Appendix I, p. 246.

42 J. Hornblower, op. cit., pp. 35–6, A. K. Grayson, *Assyrian and Babylonian Chronicles*, Locust Valley, NY, J. J. Augustin, 1975, Chron. 10 Rev. ll. 3–43. Left edge ll. 1–2.

43 Manni, op. cit., pp. vi–ix; e.g. Plut. *Demet*. 17 – opening praise of Demetrius suggests Hieronymus, but the following tale of Aristodemus, the 'arch-flatterer', suggests Duris; J. Hornblower, op. cit., pp. 229–32; e.g. Plut. *Demet*. 52, *Pyrrh*. 7.

44 Hieronymus' contribution to the accounts of Justin/Trogus and Polyaenus among others (J. Hornblower, op. cit., pp. 65–7, 74–5) cannot be clearly enough discerned to make them useful for this purpose.

45 Diod. XX.29.1, see also Ch. 6; J. Hornblower, op. cit., p. 56, suggests a Rhodian source (Zeno?) who possibly drew ultimately on Hieronymus; Diod. XVIII.14.2, see also Ch. 2; Diod. XXI.F.12; Plut. *Demet*. 48; Diod. XX.29.1, Paus. 1.9.7; Diod. XX.111.3; Diod. XIX.78.2 for Hieronymus' stress on the sincerity of the Antigonid liberation programme.

46 Diod. XIX.73.3–10, 77.7, Diod. XX.107.2, 4–5, 108.1–3; Diod. XX.106.2, Diod. XXI.F.12.1 – use of another source seems unlikely – Hieronymus' Antigonid patrons are prominent in the Cassander episode and his coverage of the Dromichaetes episode is suggested by the reference to his Theban governorship which precedes it (Plut. *Demet*. 39); Plut. *Demet*. 20.

47 Saitta, op. cit., pp. 128–9, Longega, op. cit., pp. 44–54, Shipley, op. cit., p. 180; Plut. *Demet*. 44, Paus. 1.10.2, Saitta, op. cit., pp. 128–9.

48 This question is discussed more fully in Lund, op. cit., pp. 39–47.

49 See Ch. 5.

50 Duris *FGrH* 76 F.1, Schubert, op. cit., pp. 68, 76, Kebric, op. cit., pp. 15, 33–4, 57–8, 21, J. Hornblower, op. cit., p. 70; Shipley, op. cit., p. 180, Plut. *Demet*. 25, Duris *FGrH* 76 F.55 = Pliny *N.H.* VIII. 143, Ael. *V.H.* VI.25; Arr. *Anab*. VI. 19. 4–6, Q.C. VI. 5.18, Plut. *Them*. 10; Athen. VI.261 = Plut. *Demet*. 25 = Phylarch. *FGrH* 81 F. 31; Manni, op. cit., p. xii, Kebric, op. cit., p. 10; Phylarch. *FGrH* 81 F.12, F.29, see also Ch. 5; Plut. *Demet*. 18 – the comparison with tragic actors suggests Duris as a source, Plut. *Demet*. 41, *Pyrrh*. 8.

51 See Ch. 5; Diod. XVIII.8. 3–7, Kebric, op. cit., pp. 4–5, C. Habicht, 'Samische Volks beschlusse der hellenistischen Zeit', *Ath. Mitt.*, 1957, vol. 72, pp. 154–274 nos 3, 13, 20; Diod. XVIII.18.9, 56.4.7 – compare Seleucus' restoration of Lemnos to Athens in 281 BC (see Ch. 7).

52 For *logoi*, see I.9.6 and 1. 10.3; e.g. Pausanias drags Cassander from his grave to plead for help in 294 BC, while Agathocles' marriage to Lysandra pre-dates the death of her previous husband by six years! (Paus. 1.9.7, compare 1.10.1, Plut. *Demet*. 36); see *FGrH* 703, K. Ziegler, 'Proxenos', in G. Wissowa (ed.) *PW*, vol. XXXIII, Stuttgart, J. B. Metzlerscher, 1957, col. 1033; J. Hornblower, op. cit., pp. 72, 184 n. 12, 195; Polyaen. IV.12.2;

Paus. 1.10.2 suggests that this victory allowed Demetrius' troops to take the offensive, pursuing Lysimachus into Thrace.

53 The most important inscriptions relating to Lysimachus are reproduced in Lund, op. cit., Appendix V.

2 THRACE AND PONTUS

1 For the encomium in Justin's account, see Ch. 1; there is no evidence that Lysimachus held any administrative post under Alexander.

2 N. G. L. Hammond and G. T. Griffith, *A History of Macedonia*, vol. II, Oxford, Clarendon Press, 1979, pp. 259, 364, 559; V. Velkov, 'The Thracian city of Cabyle', in A. G. Poulter (ed.) *Ancient Bulgaria*, vol. I, Nottingham, University of Nottingham, 1983, p. 233, for colonies at Philippopolis, Cabyle and Beroe; H. Bengtson, *Die Strategie in der Hellenistischen Zeit*, 1937, Munich, C. H. Beck, p. 42; Diod. XVI.71.2, Hammond and Griffith, op. cit., p. 431.

3 Plut. *Alex.* 9, Arr. *Anab.* I.1–5, Z. H. Archibald, 'The Greeks in Thrace *c.* 500–270 BC', Oxford University D.Phil. thesis, Bodleian Library, 1984, p. 509; Satyrus, FHG, vol. III, p. 161 (Cothelas), Diod. XVI.71.2, Just. IX.2.1 (Odessus); J. R. Hamilton, *Alexander the Great*, London, Hutchinson & Co., 1973, pp. 46–7.

4 J. G. P. Best, *Thracian Peltasts and Their Influence on Greek Warfare*, Groningen, Wolters-Noordhoff, 1969, passim; Arr. *Anab.* I.5.2, Hammond and Griffith, op. cit., p. 43; Frontinus II.11.3; Bengtson, op. cit., pp. 39–40, Arr. *Anab.* 1.25.2.

5 For Memnon, see Diod. XVII.62.5, H. Berve, *Das Alexanderreich auf prosopographischer Grundlage*, vol. II, Munich, C. H. Beck, 1926, no. 449, K. J. Beloch, *Griechische Geschichte*, vol. III, Leipzig, Walter de Gruyter & Co., 1904, p. 648; for Zopyrion, Just. XII.2.16, Macrob. *Sat.* I.11.33, Q.C. X.1.43, Beloch, op. cit., vol. IV², p. 44, for the dating to 325 BC.

6 Suggested by G. Saitta, 'Lisimaco di Tracia', *Kokalos*, 1955, vol. 1, p. 62; Diod. XVIII.8–11, 13, 15; for Thrace as a land-link, see e.g. Arr. *Succ.* FGrH 156 F.ll.45 and Ch. 3.

7 Just. XIII.5, Diod. XVIII.3.2, Q.C. X.10.4, Paus. I.9.5, Porph. *FHG* III F.3.1.

8 Paus. I.9.5, Arr. *Succ.* FGrH 156 F.I.7; S. M. Burstein, 'Lysimachus and the Greek cities: the early years', *Ancient World*, 1986b, vol. 14, p. 21.

9 Notably Saitta, op. cit., p. 65, who assumes the revolt of a subject when Seuthes 'goes over to Antigonus' (Diod. XIX.73.8); Seuthes might equally have been neutral or an 'ally'.

10 For Sboryanovo, see below; M. Cicikova, 'The Thracian city of Seuthopolis', in Poulter, op. cit., p. 300.

11 M. N. Tod, *Greek Historical Inscriptions*, vol. II, Oxford, Clarendon Press, 1948, no. 193 p. 268; Diod. XVII.63.1 – Agis' uprising in Sparta forced Antipater to come to terms with Memnon; Z. H. Archibald, forthcoming; Q.C. X.1.44.

12 R. Vulpe, 'La succession des rois odryses', in R. Vulpe (ed.) *Studia*

Thracologica, Bucharest, Editura Academiei Republicii Socialiste Romania, 1976, p. 10; Polyaen. VII.32.

13 Bengtson, op. cit., p. 43; Z. H. Archibald, 'Greek imports – some aspects
of the Hellenistic impact on Thrace', in Poulter, op. cit., p. 307; D. P.
Dimitrov and M. Cicikova, *The Thracian City of Seuthopolis*, Oxford,
B.A.R. Supplement Series no. 38, 1978, pp. 6, 9, R. F. Hoddinott, *The
Thracians*, London, Thames & Hudson, 1981, p. 124, Archibald, 1984, op.
cit., p. 512.

14 Diod. XVIII.14.2; suggested by Archibald, 1984. op. cit., p. 511.

15 Thuc. II.97, A. Fol in A. Fol and I. Mazarov, *Thrace and the Thracians*,
London, 1977, pp. 144, 151.

16 Hoddinott, 1981, op. cit., p. 105. Silver *phialai* inscribed with Cotys'
name and Thracian place names, found in Getic and Triballian territory,
may plausibly represent Cotys' tribute from these settlements,
subsequently given as guest-gifts to Getic and Triballian chiefs; for new
examples from the Rogozen hoard, see A. Fol *et al.*, *The New Thracian
Treasure from Rogozen*, London, British Museum, 1986, p. 25, G.
Mihailov, 'Il tesoro di Rogozen: le iscrizioni', *Epigraphica*, 1988, vol. 50,
pp. 9–40.

17 For the lack of a literary tradition, I. Mazarov, in Fol and Mazarov, op.
cit., p. 17, P. Alexandrescu, 'Le groupe de trésors thraces du nord du
Balkans', *Dacia*, 1983, vol. 27, p. 63; Xen. *Anab.* VII.2.31.

18 Mazarov, op. cit., p. 51; Thuc. II.98.3–4, Strabo VII.47 (15,000 cavalry,
200,000 infantry); Diod. XVIII.14.2 – by 5:1 in infantry, 4:1 in cavalry;
Archibald, 1984, op. cit., p. 18, Hom. *Il.* X.436, 474, 519, D. P. Dimitrov
and K. Dimitrov, 'Le monnayage de Seuthes III selon les données de
Seuthopolis', in R. Vulpe (ed.) *Actes du IIe Congres International de
Thracologie*, vol. II, Bucharest, Editura Academiei Republicii Socialiste
Romania, 1980, pp. 166–9, M. Domaradzki, 'Presence celte en Thrace au
début de l'époque hellénistique', in Vulpe, 1980, op. cit., vol. I, p. 460,
Archibald, forthcoming; *IGBR*, vol. III. no. 1731 l.18, Mazarov, op. cit., p.
20, Dimitrov and Cicikova, op. cit., p. 45.

19 Dimitrov and Cicikova, op. cit., pp. 7, 10, Hoddinott, 1981, op. cit., p.
124; 20,000 infantry (Diod. XVIII.14.2) compares favourably with
Athens' hoplite forces in 431 BC (c. 16,000, Thuc. II.31), though Diodorus'
figure may include light-armed troops too.

20 Arr. *Succ. FGrH* 156 F.I.7, Archibald, 1984, op. cit., p. 511, M.
Domaradzki, 'Les données numismatiques et les études de la culture
thrace du Second Age du Fer', *Numizmatika*, 1987, vol. 21, no. 4, p. 9;
IGBR 1731 ll.5,11,15,29, Velkov, op. cit., p. 233; see Map 1.

21 Archibald, 1984, op. cit., pp. 404–12, N. Sekunda, 'The rhomphaia: a
Thracian weapon of the Hellenistic period', in Poulter, op. cit., pp. 275–
88; Best, op. cit., passim.

22 Arr. *Succ. FGrH* 156 F.1.10 describes Lysimachus as going to war
'rashly'; Diod. XVIII.14.1–4; the site suggested by Saitta, op. cit., p. 63.

23 Diod. XVIII.14.5, Saitta, op. cit., p. 65.

24 Dimitrov and Dimitrov, op. cit., pp. 165, 168; Diod. XVIII.14.1,
XIX.73.8.

25 Archibald, 1984, op. cit., pp. 304, 311, 318 and forthcoming; R. F.

Hoddinott, *Bulgaria in Antiquity*, London and Tonbridge, Ernest Bean Ltd, 1975, p. 90.
26 Dimitrov and Cicikova, op. cit., pp. 7–12, 22, Cicikova, op. cit., p. 298; Archibald, 1984, op. cit., p. 51 and forthcoming, Domaradzki, 1980, op. cit., p. 460.
27 i.e. on the West Pontic coast, see pp. 33–5.
28 For the Thracian warrior-élite, see Mazarov, op. cit., pp. 18–20, 24; A. D. Alexandrescu, 'Tombes de chevaux et pièces du harnais dans le nécropole Gète de Zimnicea', *Dacia*, 1983, vol. 27, pp. 62–6, Archibald, 1984, op. cit., pp. 404–13.
29 Diod. XVIII.50.5, see also Ch. 3; Saitta, op. cit., pp. 109–10; for Antigonus' support, see pp. 41–2; Diod. XIX.73.8 seems to imply an alliance by or during 313 BC.
30 Hoddinott, 1975, op. cit., p. 96; Diod. XIX.73.5; see p. 41.
31 Diod. XIX.73.8, Diod. XIX.73.1, A. Balkanska, 'Tirisis-Tirisa-Akra: Die Thrakisch und romisch-byzantinische stadt am Kap Kaliakra (Scythia Minor)', *Klio*, 1980, vol. 62, pp. 28–39, Strabo VII.6.1.
32 Dimitrov and Dimitrov, op. cit., pp. 167–8; *IGBR* no. 1731.
33 Diod. XIX.73.9. For Lysimachus' demand for Hellespontine Phrygia in 315 BC (Diod. XIX.61.2–3,73.1), see Ch. 3.
34 Saitta, op. cit., p. 72, Paus. I.10.5, App. *Syr.* 64, though Polyaenus (VI.12) calls him son of Amastris; Diod. XXI.F.11, Paus. I.9.7, Memn. *FGrH* 434 F.5.1, Plut. *Demet.* 47–8.
35 *IGBR* no. 1731 ll.2,7,17, 36, Hoddinott, 1975, op. cit., p. 96; G. Mihailov, *Inscriptiones Graecae in Bulgaria Repertae*, vol. III.2, Sofia, Academia Litterarum Bulgarica, 1964, pp. 147–8; Burstein, 1986b, op. cit., p.24 n. 33; Berenice's sons are to lead the miscreant Epimenes out of the temple of the Great Gods and hand him over to Spartocus (*IGBR* no. 1731 ll.16–18).
36 Lysimachus may have wed a Persian bride at Susa in 324 BC (Arr. *Anab.* VII.4.4–6), but this does not help much; nothing is known of the duration of this marriage or of possible offspring.
37 If Berenice was Nicaea's daughter, one must assume an initially 'formal' marriage to Seuthes at the age of 6 or 7; if her child-bearing years started around age 12 (*c.* 306 BC), then there is just time for her to have borne four sons by the end of the fourth century BC.
38 *IGBR* no. 1731 ll.2, 8–10; Porph. *FHG* III 688 F.3.3, Memn. *FGrH* 434 F.5.3; see also Ch. 4; for a transcript of the full Greek text of *IGBR* no. 1731, as yet unpublished, see H. S. Lund, 'Bridging the Hellespont: the Successor Lysimachus – a study in early Hellenistic kingship', University of London Ph.D. thesis, Senate House Library, 1992, Appendix II.
39 Mihailov, 1964, op. cit., p. 148, followed by Burstein, 1986b, op. cit., p. 23; Hoddinott, 1975, op. cit., p. 96.
40 L. Ognenova-Marinova, 'Quis autem erat Epimenes?', *Klio*, 1980, vol. 62, pp. 47–8, argued that *epimenes* represents a function assumed by Spartocus and *ta huparchonta* denotes not property, but power or authority.
41 Velkov, op. cit., p. 233; Y. Youroukova, *Coins of the Ancient Thracians*, Oxford, B.A.R. Supplement Series no. 4, 1976, pp. 22, 27, Th. Gerasimov,

'Rare coins of Thrace', *Num. Chron.*, 1957, vol. 17 (series 6), pp. 3–5; Archibald, 1984, op. cit., pp. 513–14.

42 H. Bengtson, 'Neues zur Geschichte des Hellenismus in Thrakien und in der Dobrudscha', *Historia*, 1962, vol. 11, p. 20.

43 See Ch. 5; Dimitrov and Cicikova, op. cit., p. 42, suggest that Seuthes' coinage had a propaganda function.

44 *IGBR* no. 1731 l.2 calls him simply Seuthes; proposed by Mazarov, op. cit., pp. 37–58, D. Popov, 'L'institution royale dans la maison dynastique des Odryses', in Vulpe, 1980, op. cit., pp. 341–2. This issue is discussed more fully in Lund, op. cit., pp. 64–5.

45 *IGBR* no. 1731 l.9, *IGBR*, vol. I, no. 43, see Lund, op. cit., pp. 76–7, for fuller discussion; *IGBR*, vol. III.I, no. 1114.

46 For the Celts, see Domaradzki, 1980, op. cit., pp. 465–6, Archibald, 1984, op. cit., p. 515; Dimitrov and Cicikova, op. cit., p. 58; Cicikova, op. cit., p. 299.

47 Diod. XIX.73.1.

48 Hammond and Griffith, op. cit., p. 557; see p. 33 (Odessus), Just. IX.2.1. (Apollonia), D. M. Pippidi, *I Greci nel Basso Danubio*, Milan, Il Saggiatore, 1971, p. 91 (Istria); *IG* IV² 68, G. Cawkwell, *Philip of Macedon*, London, Faber & Faber, 1978, pp. 170–1.

49 Just. XII.2.16, Pippidi, 1971, op. cit., p. 91, Saitta, op. cit., p. 142; Just. XII.2.16, Macrob. *Sat.* I.11.33.

50 Saitta, op. cit., p. 145; Diod. XIX.51.1, 52.5–6.

51 Pippidi, 1971, op. cit., p. 80, Hammond and Griffith, op. cit., p. 561, I. Stoian, 'Echos de la lutte des classes à Istros', in I. Stoian, *Etudes Histriennes*, Brussels, Latomus, 1972, pp.57–60.

52 Saitta, op. cit., p. 65; Pippidi, 1971, op. cit., p. 180, D. St Marin, 'Il foedus Romano con Callatis', *Epigraphica*, 1948, vol. 10, p. 128, Ch. Danoff, 'Zur Geschichte des westpontische *koinon*', *Klio*, 1938, vol. 31, pp. 438–9; *IGBR*, vol. I, nos. 13, 307.2.

53 Pippidi, 1971, op. cit., p. 93, Diod. XIX.73, see p. 40.

54 Diod. XIX.73.1, see pp. 33–4 for a possible parallel in Asia Minor in 319 BC; Burstein, 1986b, op. cit., p. 24; Diod. XIX.73.6, see p. 41.

55 Diod. XX.112.2–3; D. M. Pippidi and Em. Popescu, 'Les relations d'Istros et d'Apollonia du Pont à l'époque hellénistique', *Dacia*, 1959, vol. 3, p. 242, Pippidi, 1971, op. cit., p. 87, pl. 28; P. Mackendrick, *The Dacian Stones Speak*, Chapel Hill and London, University of North Carolina Press, 1975, pp. 40, 42.

56 A. Stefan, 'Graffite callatien du IVᵉ av. N.E.', in D. M. Pippidi and Em. Popescu (eds) *Epigraphica. Travaux dediés au VIIᵉ Congrès d'Epigraphie grecque et latine*, Bucharest, Editura Academiei Republicii Socialist Romãnia, 1977, pp. 25–32, E. Condurachi and C. Daicovicu, *The Ancient Civilisation of Roumania*, London, Barrie & Jenkins, 1971, p. 79.

57 Mackendrick, op. cit., p. 40, 32, D. Nicolov, 'Caractéristique economique et démographique des colonies grecques du littoral de la Mer Noire', in A. Fol, (ed.), *Thracia Pontica I*, Sofia, L'Academie Bulgare de Sciences, 1982, p. 103; A. Ariescu, 'Mitteilung uber ein bisher unveroffentliches Helle-nistischen dekret aus den Beständen des Archäologischen regio-nalmuseums der Dobrudschens', *Studii Clasice*, 1963, vol. 5, p. 318; D. M.

Pippidi, *Contributii la Istoria Veche Romanei*, Bucharest, Editura Stiintifica, 1967, p. 554; J. G. F. Hind, 'Istrian faces and the river Danube. The type of the silver coins of Istria', *Num. Chron.*, 1970, vol. 10 (series 7), p. 15; see also M. Finley, 'The Black Sea and Danubian regions and the slave trade in antiquity', *Klio*, 1962, vol. 40, pp. 51–60.

58 Hoddinott, 1975, op. cit., p. 52, Pippidi, 1971, op. cit., p. 77.

59 See Ch. 5; compare, for instance, Athenian prosperity in the Lycurgan period when the city was firmly in Macedon's grip (W. S. Ferguson, *Hellenistic Athens*, New York, Macmillan & Co., 1911, p. 10).

60 Odessus, see p. 35; Pippidi, 1967, op. cit., pp. 549, 554–6.

61 See Ch. 5; demand for *phoros* was, in any case, hardly unparalleled among Lysimachus' contemporaries.

62 Pippidi, 1971, op. cit., p. 78, Memn. *FGrH* 434 F.13; *I.Priene* 16 = *RC* no. 8, see also Ch. 5; *I.Priene* 1 and 3, S. M. Burstein, *Outpost of Hellenism: The Emergence of Heracleia on the Black Sea*, Berkeley and Los Angeles, University of California Publications, 1976, pp. 6–11, 15, 28–30.

63 Hoddinott, 1975, op. cit., p. 48, E. Barladeanu Zavatin, 'Terracotta statuettes from a tomb discovered in Callatis', *Pontica*, 1985, vol. 18, p. 98, Mackendrick, op. cit., p. 37; C. Preda, 'Archaeological discoveries in the Greek cemetery of Callatis-Mangalia', *Dacia*, 1961, vol. 5, p. 303, G. H. Poenaru Bordea, 'Le trésor de Marasesti', *Dacia*, 1974, vol. 18, p. 120. Unless extremely *nouveau riche*, their ability to pay such sums suggests considerable individual wealth also during the Lysimachean period.

64 Exemplified by Stoian, op. cit., pp. 58, 61.

65 Plut. *Demet.* 25 = Athen. XIV.614–15; Athen. VI.246, Phylarch. *FGrH* 81.F.65; H. Hauben, 'A royal toast in 302 BC', *Ancient Society*, 1974, vol. 5, pp. 108–13 for 302 BC as the context for the anecdote, see also Chs 5 and 6.

66 S. M. Burstein, 'Lysimachus and the Greek cities of Asia: the case of Miletus', *Ancient World*, 1980, vol. 3, pp. 74–9, S. M. Burstein, 'Lysimachus the Gazophylax – a modern scholarly myth?', in W. Heckel and R. Sullivan (eds) *Ancient Coins of the Graeco-Roman World*, Waterloo, Ont., Wilfred Laurier University Press, 1984, pp. 57–68, Burstein, 1986b, op. cit., p. 24; see Xen. *Hell.* III.2.10 for the rich natural resources of the Thracian Chersonese.

67 For Martin's thesis, see Ch. 5.

68 Hind, op. cit., p. 13, P. Alexandrescu, 'Ataias', *Studii Clasice*, 1967, vol. 9, p. 88; Poenaru Bordea, 1974, op. cit., pp. 116–20.

69 Poenaru Bordea, 1974, op. cit., pp. 111–14; Hind, op. cit., p. 13 (Istria), M. J. Price, *Coins of Alexander the Great*, London, British Museum, forthcoming (Callatis), Poenaru Bordea, 1974, op. cit., pp. 116–18 (Odessus).

70 Price, forthcoming, op. cit., sees the switch from gold to silver for the payments as a sign that Callatis was beginning to 'scrape the barrel'.

71 Pippidi, 1971, op. cit., pp. 82–4.

72 *IGBR*, vol. I, no. 387, M. Segre, 'Decreto di Apollonio sul Ponto', *Athenaeum*, 1934, vol. 12, p. 7, L. Robert, *Villes d'Asie Mineure*, 2nd edn, Paris, De Boccard, 1962, p. 55; G. H. Poenaru Bordea, 'Note epigrafice',

in C. Daicovicu (ed.) *Noi Monumente epigrafice din Scythia Minor*, Constanta, 1964, p. 130, no. 15.
73 Saitta, op. cit., p. 113, Beloch, 1925, op. cit., pp. 101–2, for the chronology; Diod. XIX.61.3–4, *RC* 1 ll.55–6, no. 15. ll.22–3; see also Ch. 5.
74 Diod. XIX.73.6–8, Saitta, op. cit., p. 110.
75 Nicolov, op. cit., p. 104, Pippidi, 1971, op. cit., p. 552; *IGBR* vol. I, no. 325; Stefan, op. cit., pp. 25–32; D. M. Pippidi, 'Note sur l'organisation militaire d'Istros à l'époque hellénistique', *Klio*, 1963, vol. 41, p. 164, Pippidi, 1971, op. cit., pp. 87, 89; Poenaru Bordea, 1974, op. cit., p. 120; Pippidi, 1967, op. cit., p. 549.
76 Pippidi, 1963, op. cit., p. 163; Pippidi, 1971, op. cit., p. 88; Macrob. *Sat.* I.XI.33.
77 Diod. XIX.73.1.
78 Diod. XIX.73.3 – the verb *hormesen* can imply a rapid march; for Philip, see Cawkwell, op. cit., p. 85; Hoddinott, 1975, op. cit., p. 50; Pippidi, 1971, op. cit., p. 256.
79 Diod. XIX.73.5; e.g. Arr. *Anab.* II.11.6–7; Hammond and Griffith, op. cit., p. 672.
80 Poenaru Bordea, 1974, op. cit., p. 112; Diod. XIX.73.6, Saitta, op. cit., pp. 113–14.
81 Saitta, op. cit., p. 69; Cawkwell, op. cit., p. 140; Diod. XIX.73.8–10.
82 Diod. XIX.77.7.
83 Diod. XX.29.1, Marmor Parium *FGrH* 239 §19, see also Ch. 6.
84 Diod. XIX.105; for 'freedom and autonomy', see Ch. 5; Saitta, op. cit., pp. 70–1.
85 Diod. XX.25.1; suggested by Saitta, op. cit., p. 71, opposed by E. Will, *Histoire politique du monde hellénistique*, Nancy, University of Nancy, 1979, p. 309; Diod. XX.25.1–2, Diod. XX.22–5, for Spartocid euergetism, see e.g. Tod., op. cit., no. 167, *IG* II² 1485a.
86 For indemnities, see Ch. 5.
87 See e.g. G. Mihailov, 'La Thrace au IVᵉ et IIIᵉ siècle avant notre ère', *Athenaeum*, 1961, vol. 39, p. 38, Pippidi, 1971, op. cit., p. 93, Hoddinott, 1975, op. cit., p. 52; P. Alexandrescu, 1967, op. cit., pp. 85–91, based on mid-fourth century BC coins minted at Callatis and stamped *ATAIAS*. Pippidi objects (1971, op. cit., p. 91), citing a lack of Scythian finds at Callatis and Just. IX.2.5–16 (which puts Philip II's campaign straight after Atheas' arrival), but Scythian–type arrowheads have been found in the Callatis necropolis (Preda, op. cit., p. 302), while Justin's role as epitomator may have led him to compress events; Pippidi, 1963, op. cit., pp. 158–67, D. M. Pippidi, 'Istros et les Gètes au IIᵉ siècle av. notre ère', *Studii Clasice*, 1961, vol. 3, pp. 53–66; Pippidi, 1967, op. cit., pp. 554–6; Poenaru Bordea, 1974, op. cit., p. 121.
88 K. Jordanov, 'Les formations d'état gètes de la fin du VIᵉ siècle avant notre ère', in Vulpe, 1980, op. cit., vol. I, pp. 331–2, 335, Hoddinott, 1981, op. cit., p. 131, N. Conovici, 'Les relations entre les Gètes des deux rives du Bas-Danube à la lumière des données archéologiques et numismatiques (IVᵉ–IIᵉ siècles av. n.e.), in Vulpe, 1980, op. cit., vol. II, pp. 44–5; Arr. *Anab.* I.4.1, Strabo VII.3.14, Diod. XXI.F.12.

89 Conovici, op. cit., p. 44, E. Moscalu and I. Voievozanu, 'Le tombeau princier gète et le trésor de Peretu', in Vulpe, 1980, op. cit., vol. I, p. 389; Diana Gergova gave a preliminary report on the Sboryanovo excavations at the Institute of Classical Studies in London in November 1989.

90 See p. 20; Arr. *Anab*. I.4-5, Hoddinott, 1981, op. cit., p. 131.

91 For W. Pontic/Getic trade, see I. Irimaia, 'Nouvelles découvertes concernant la population de la dobroudja (V-ème-I-er s. av. JC)', *Pontica*, 1973, vol. 6, pp. 68-71, Conovici, op. cit., p. 50; Diod. XIX.73.5, see pp. 28-9.

92 Diod. XXI.F.12, Plut. *Demet*. 39, Mor. 555D, Memn. *FGrH* 434 F.5.1, Polyaen. VI.12, Paus. I.9.6, Strabo VII.3.8, 14, Polyb. F.102; B. Niese, *Geschichte der Griechischen und Makedonischen Staaten seit der Schlact bei Chaeronea*, vol. I, Gotha, Friedrich Andreas Perthes, 1893, p. 367, Saitta, op. cit., p. 117; Saitta, op. cit., p. 74, Pippidi, 1971, op. cit., p. 93.

93 See pp. 38, 43; Pippidi, 1971, op. cit., p. 93, H. Bengtson, *Die Diadochen*, Munich, C. H. Beck, 1987, p. 128.

94 Plut. *Pyrrh*. 6, Just. XVI.1.9., Porph. *FHG* III F.3.3; see also Ch. 4.

95 Niese, op. cit., vol. I, pp. 367-8, Beloch, 1925, op. cit., p. 225, Saitta, op. cit., p. 88; Diod. XXI.F.11; Paus. I.9.6, Diod. XXI.F.12.

96 Saitta, op. cit., p. 83, Plut. *Demet*. 32, *OGIS* 10, see also Ch. 4; Niese, op. cit., vol. I, pp. 367-8, Beloch, 1925, op. cit., p. 225 - Niese cites Paus. 1.9.6., but the only pact mentioned there is the alliance between Ptolemy and Lysimachus on his return from the Danube; Paus. I.9.6, Diod. XXI.F.11 (Agathocles), Diod. XXI.F.12 (Lysimachus).

97 Saitta, op. cit., p. 117, rejects Pausanias' account in favour of the 'superior' Hieronymus; Plut. *Demet*. 39 for Hieronymus as governor of Thebes at this date.

98 See Map 1, Strabo VII.3.14 describes the 'desert' as 'facing that part of the Pontic sea which extends from Ister to Tyras'; C. Daicovicu, 'Il paese di Dromichaete', in C. Daicovicu (ed.) *Dacica*, Cluj, Bibliotheca Musei Napocensis, 1973, pp. 97-100.

99 A suggestion made verbally by Dr Z. H. Archibald; Polyaenus' figure (VI.12) of 100,000 may be suspiciously neat, but certainly a force of considerable size is implied; as suggested by Beloch, 1925, op. cit., p. 225; Diod. XXI.F.11,12, see pp. 19-20, Hoddinott, 1981, op. cit., p. 131.

100 Diod. XXI.F.12, Plut. *Mor*. 555D, Strabo VII.3.14; Polyaen. VI.12.

101 Jordanov, op. cit., p. 333, A. D. Alexandrescu, 1983, op. cit., pp. 71, 89; Arr. *Anab*. I.4.4-5; V. Parvan, *Dacia*, Cambridge, Cambridge University Press, 1928, p. 62, R. Lane Fox, *Alexander the Great*, London, Allen Lane, 1973, p. 75.

102 Polyaen. VI.12, Diod. XXI.F.12, Plut. *Mor*. 555D; Memn. *FGrH* 434 F.5.1; Diod. XXI.F.12; Daicovicu, 1973, op. cit., p. 97; e.g. the Macedonian assembly could, on occasion, determine the succession - see Cawkwell, op. cit., pp. 27-8.

103 Diod. XXI.F.12; Daicovicu, 1973, op. cit., p. 97; for Getic treasures, see pp. 43-4.

104 Memn. *FGrH* 434 F.5.1; Paus. I.9.6; Pippidi, 1971, op. cit., p. 93.

105 See Chs 3 and 4.

106 P. Alexandrescu, 1967, op. cit., pp. 85-93; Just. XXIV.5.1-12, E. Will,

'The succession to Alexander', in A. E. Astin *et al.* (eds) *Cambridge Ancient History*, 2nd edn, vol. VII, Cambridge, Cambridge University Press, 1984, p. 115, argues that Ceraunus' failure to make a pact with the Dardanians led to their co-operation with the invaders.

107 As suggested by Parvan, op. cit., pp. 102–3, Mihailov, 1961, op. cit., p. 38, Hoddinott, 1975 op. cit., p. 137; for the rule of Ptolemy Ceraunus and its aftermath, see H. Heinen, *Untersuchungen zur Hellenistischen Geschichte des 3. Jahrhunderts v. Chr.*, Wiesbaden, *Historia* Einzelschriften 20, 1972, pp. 3–94; for the Celts, see H. D. Rankin, *Celts and the Classical World*, London and Sydney, Croom Helm, 1987, pp. 83–102.

3 THE ACQUISITION OF EMPIRE

1 E. Will, 'The succession to Alexander', in A. E. Astin *et al.* (eds) *Cambridge Ancient History*, 2nd edn, vol. VII, Cambridge, Cambridge University Press, 1984, p. 110; Plut. *Demet.* 48.

2 For use of Hieronymus in our extant literary sources, see Ch. 1.

3 e.g. V. Tscherikower, *Die Hellenistischen Stadtegrundungen von Alexander dem Grossen bis auf der Romerzeit*, Leipzig, *Philologus* Supplement 19, 1927, pp. 156, 163, G. Longega, *Arsinoe II*, Rome, L'erma di Bretschneider, 1968, p. 39, H. Bengtson, *Die Diadochen*, Munich, C. H. Beck, 1987, p. 70; E. Will, *Histoire politique du monde hellénistique*, vol. I, Nancy, University of Nancy, 1979, p. 80; e.g. P. Roussel, 'Le Démembrement de l'empire d'Alexandre', in G. Glotz *et al.*, *Histoire grecque*, vol. IV, Paris, Presses Universitaires de France, 1938, p. 333, Will, 1984, op. cit., p. 29.

4 Diod. XVIII.50.2, XX.106.4, Plut. *Demet.* 28; the criticism of this tendency by P. Cloché, *La Dislocation d'un empire*, Louvain and Paris, Editions Nauwelaerts and Brouwer et Cie, 1959, p. 16, strikes a rare dissonant note.

5 Diod. XVIII.36.6, 39.5, 43.1; Diod. XVIII.54.2.

6 e.g. Diod. XX.37.4, Diod. XX.51.1l; Diod. XX.106.2 (Loeb translation).

7 The classic example is Demetrius' seizure of the Macedonian throne in 294 BC, see Ch. 4; see Chs 6 and 7.

8 S. M. Burstein, 'Lysimachus and the Greek cities: the early years', *Ancient World*, 1986b, vol. 14, p. 24, see also Ch. 2; see Will, 1984, op. cit., p. 35, Bengtson, op. cit., p. 120.

9 Bengtson, op. cit., p. 119; see Chs 1 and 2; Burstein, 1986b, op. cit., p. 24; P. Briant, 'D'Alexandre le Grand aux diadoques: le cas d'Eumène de Kardia', *REA*, 1972, vol. 54, pp. 32–74 for Eumenes' task in Cappadocia; Just. XV.3.15.

10 With Seuthes and the Greek states respectively; Diod. XVIII.14, Arr. *Succ.* *FGrH* 156 F.1.10, Diod. XVIII.9–18.

11 On marriage alliance, see J. Seibert, *Historische Beitrage zu die Dynastische Verbindungen in hellenistischer Zeit*, Wiesbaden, *Historia* Einzelschriften 10, 1967, pp. 129–31, G. M. Cohen, 'The Diadochs and the new monarchies', *Athenaeum*, 1974, vol. 52, p. 177; it is usually assumed (e.g. K. J. Beloch, *Griechsche Geschichte*, vol. IV^2, Berlin, Walter de

Gruyter & Co., 1925, p. 127) that Nicaea married Lysimachus as Perdiccas' widow; Arr. *Succ. FGrH* 156 F.1.37; Bengtson, op. cit., p. 122.

12 Diod. XVIII.18.4–5, Roussel, op. cit., p. 270.

13 Roussel, op. cit., p. 284; a route via Thrace is suggested by Perdiccas' dispatch of Eumenes to the Hellespont to prevent the regent's crossing (Diod. XVIII.29.1); Arr. *Succ. FGrH* 156 F.11.45.

14 Antipater's loyalty to Philip's house, whatever his feelings about Alexander, is generally accepted, e.g. Will, 1984, op. cit., p. 26; Diod. XVIII.33.3. for Perdiccas' aspirations to royalty.

15 Plut. *Phoc.* 30 (compare Diod. XVIII.48.2), Diod. XVIII.49.1; e.g. M. Thompson, 'The mints of Lysimachus', in C. Kraay and G. K. Jenkins (eds), *Essays in Greek Coinage Presented to Stanley Robinson*, Oxford, Clarendon Press, 1968, p. 164, Bengtson, op. cit., p. 134; M. Fortina, *Cassandro, re di Macedonia*, Turin, Società Editrice Internazionale, 1965, p. 102, merely cites Cassander's 'invariable' habit of summoning Lysimachus in a crisis (Diod. XX.106.4).

16 Diod. XVIII.49.3; Diod. XVIII.50.2; Diod. XVIII.54.2.

17 Diod. XVIII.72.9; see Diod. XIX.77.6–7 and Ch. 2.

18 Will, 1984, op. cit., p. 41; Diod. XVIII.50.2, though this may be the product of Hieronymus' hindsight; Diod. XXI.F.7, Just. XVI.1.19, 2.4; E. Aucello, 'La politica dei Diadochoi e l'ultimatum del 314 av. Cr.', *Riv. Fil.*, 1957, vol. 35, p. 382, for Lysimachus in spring 315 BC as 'secured on the Macedonian side by the victory of Cassander'.

19 Will, 1984, op. cit., p. 40; Fortina, op. cit., pp. 8–9, Plut. *Alex.* 74; Diod. XVIII.75.2; Diod. XVIII.55.2.

20 On the dating, see R. M. Errington, 'Diodorus Siculus and the chronology of the early Diadochoi, 320–311 BC', *Hermes*, 1977, vol. 105, p. 494; Diod. XIX.19.52, 61.2–5.

21 Diod. XX.106.4; see pp. 60, 69.

22 Thompson, op. cit., pp. 164–5; a suggestion made verbally by Dr Price – see also C. Erhardt, 'A catalogue of issues of tetradrachms from Amphipolis 318–294 BC', *JNFA*, March 1976, vol. 4 no. 4, p. 86; Olympias held Pella and Amphipolis through the winter of 316/5 BC (Diod. XIX.50.1); C. M. Kraay, 'Greek coinage and war', in W. Heckel and R. Sullivan (eds), *Ancient Coins of the Graeco-Roman World*, Waterloo, Ont., Wilfred Laurier University Press, 1984, pp. 3–18, for the frequent link between issue of coinage by cities or rulers and the need to hire mercenary troops.

23 Diod. XVIII.58.1–2, Plut. *Eum.* 8; Diod. XIX.42–3, Plut. *Eum.* 16–18, *Heid. Epit. FGrH* 155 F3.2; for Antigonus' territorial gains, Will, 1984, op. cit., p. 46, Bengtson, op. cit., p. 50; the ultimatum of 315 BC might suggest an agreement to share the spoils, but since some of its demands clearly exceeded what was just or reasonable (see pp. 58–9) it cannot safely be regarded as reliable; Diod. XIX.46.1–4, 48.5.

24 Arr. *Succ. FGrH* 156 F.1.34; E. R. Bevan, *The House of Seleucus*, London, Edward Arnold, 1902, pp. 31–6, A. Mehl, *Seleukos Nikator und Sein Reich*, Lovanii, Studia Hellenistica 28, 1986, pp. 19–28; Diod. XIX.48.6; Diod. XIX.55–6.

25 Diod. XIX.57.1–2, Just. XV.15.1.2.; they demanded a share in Antigonus'

booty from the war with Eumenes, Cappadocia and Lycia (?) for Cassander (or Asander?), Hellespontine Phrygia for Lysimachus, Syria for Ptolemy, Babylonia for Seleucus; see e.g. Aucello, op. cit., pp. 382–404, who perhaps takes the allies' claims on Antigonus too seriously, P. Cloché, 'La Coalition de 315–311 av. J.-C. contre Antigone le Borgne', *CRAI*, 1957, pp. 130–8, Cloché, 1959, op. cit., pp. 143–6, Fortina, op. cit., pp. 51–7.

26 Cloché, 1957, op. cit., pp. 132–3; e.g. the demand for Lycia (legitimately bestowed on Antigonus) and Hellespontine Phrygia (taken by him outside the context of the war against Eumenes); Diod. XIX.57.1, Diod. XVIII.51–2.

27 G. Saitta, 'Lisimaco di Tracia', *Kokalos*, 1955, vol. 1, pp. 66–7; Will, 1984, op. cit., p. 46, for the ultimatum as 'a poor disguise for ambition and understandably rejected'.

28 Diod. XIX.58.1–5, 61.4, Fortina, op. cit., pp. 63–4; Diod. XIX.57.1, 60.2, 62.5, 63–6, 68.5–7, *Syll*³ 320.

29 Diod. XIX.73.6–10, Saitta, op. cit., p. 68; H. Hauben, 'On the chronology of the years 313–311 B.C.', *A. J. Phil.*, 1973, vol. 94, pp. 258–9 for Cassander's operations in Epirus (Diod. XIX.89.1–2) as simultaneous with Antigonus' presence with a large army near the Hellespont (XIX.77.5–7); he stresses Lysimachus' role as guardian of the Hellespont and defender of Thrace and Macedon.

30 Diod. XIX.75.6, *OGIS* 5 ll.5–8; R. H. Simpson, 'The historical circumstances of the Peace of 311', *JHS*, 1954, vol. 74, p. 27; Diod. XX.106.2–3; Saitta, op. cit., p. 69 – though the identity of these 'meddlers' (*OGIS* 5 ll.7–8) remains uncertain, Lysimachus, with perhaps the most to lose from a separate peace, is certainly a plausible candidate.

31 Cassander lost Apollonia, Epidamnus, Chalcis, Thebes and the Phocian cities; his attempted recovery of Apollonia towards the end of 312 BC failed dismally – see Cloché, 1957, op. cit., p. 134, Fortina, op. cit., pp. 74–7.

32 Diod. XIX.80–8, Plut. *Demet.* 5, J. Seibert, *Untersuchungen zu Geschichte Ptolemaios I*, Munich, C. H. Beck, 1969, pp. 164–75; Diod. XIX.90–1, Plut. *Demet.* 7, App. *Syr.* 64, A. K. Grayson, *Assyrian and Babylonian Chronicles*, Locust Valley, NY, J. J. Augustin, 1975, pp. 25–6 – though Diodorus dates Seleucus' 'recovery of Babylon' to 312 BC, Chronicle 10 ll.1–43 shows that fighting continued in the satrapy until 308–7 BC; Simpson, 1954, op. cit., p. 29, Bengtson, op. cit., p. 46.

33 *OGIS* 5 ll.1–8, Simpson, 1954, op. cit., pp. 29–30, argues persuasively against a separate treaty with Seleucus; Grayson, op. cit., p. 26, Chron. 10 ll.26–7, 39–40, Will, 1984, op. cit., p. 53; the elimination of Seleucus was Antigonus' first priority in 311 BC (Will, 1984, op. cit., Simpson, 1954, op. cit.).

34 Diod. XIX.105.1, *OGIS* 5 ll.1–8.

35 C. B. Welles, *Royal Correspondence in the Hellenistic Period*, New Haven, Yale University Press, 1934, p. 8; Diod. XVIII.54.1, XIX.105.1, Aucello, op. cit., pp. 382, 390; Fortina, op. cit., p. 78, Roussel, op. cit., p. 319, Bengtson, op. cit., p. 47; Diod. XIX.105.3–4, Welles, op. cit., p. 7, for Alexander IV's death as 'no more unforeseen by Antigonus than . . . it was unwelcome'; Diod. XIX.61.3, 105.1.

36 Saitta, op. cit., p. 71; see Ch. 5; Simpson, 1954, op. cit., p. 28; Diod. XX.25.1, for Lysimachus' resumption of hostilities with Callatis in 310 BC.
37 Diod. XX.19.3, Will, 1984, op. cit., p. 54; Diod. XX.19.2–4, Roussel, 1938, op. cit., p. 323, Fortina, op. cit., p. 85; Will, 1984, op. cit., p. 53; Saitta, op. cit., p. 72.
38 Diod. XIX.105.2; Cassander's fears regarding potential support in Macedon for the pretender Heracles in 309 BC (see p. 65) suggest that loyalty to the Argead dynasty was still strong; Diod. XX.28.1.
39 Diod. XX.25.1, see Ch. 2; Diod. XX.29.1, Marmor Parium *FGrH* 239 §19; Saitta, op. cit., p. 73, Bengtson, op. cit., pp. 121–2.
40 Tscherikower, op. cit., pp. 163, 156; for Hieronymus' focus on Eumenes and the Antigonids and his understated treatment of Lysimachus, see Ch. 1; for Lysimachus' capacity for daring, see Ch. 1.
41 Cassander's experiences in Caria may have proved a salutary lesson; for Lysimachus' need for reinforcements for the Asian campaign of 302 BC, see pp. 71, 73.
42 Diod. XX.19.3, XX.27.1–3; Diod. XX.37.2; e.g. Saitta's explanation for Lysimachus' failure to fight in the Four Years War (see pp. 68–9); Diod. XX.106.2.
43 Diod. XX.19.2, Fortina, op. cit., p. 84; Diod. XX.28.2–3, Bengtson, op. cit., p. 54; Diod. XX.37.2.
44 Plut. *Demet.* 8–9, 10.1, 4–5.
45 Diod. XX.107.5; Phoenix' position in Hellespontine Phrygia may have become more difficult with Polemaeus' death in 309 BC (Diod. XIX.27.3).
46 *IG* II² 1,485a ll.5–6 for the dating to 307–6 BC; S. M. Burstein, 'IGII² 1485a and Athenian relations with Lysimachus', *ZPE*, 1978, vol. 31, pp. 181–5; for fuller discussion, see H. S. Lund, 'Bridging the Hellespont: the Successor Lysimachus – a study in early Hellenistic kingship', University of London Ph.D. thesis, Senate House Library, 1992, pp. 144–5.
47 For Philippides, see Plut. *Demet.* 12, *Syll*³ 374, Ch. 6; for Spartocid benefactions, P. Gauthier, *Les Cités grecques et leurs bienfaiteurs*, Paris, *BCH* Supplement XII, 1985, p. 43, A. Aymard, 'Le protocole royal grec et son évolution', in A. Aymard, *Etudes d'histoire ancienne*, Paris, Presses Universitaires de France, 1965, p. 89, for the frequent omission of the royal title in Greek city inscriptions dealing with the rulers of these peripheral kingdoms; *IG* II² 1492b ll.99–103 – compare *IG* II² 1492 ll.47–53 (*Basileus* is scrupulously appended to Alexander's name in the context of dedications made by his wife Roxane).
48 Notably in Epirus and Corcyra, see p. 69; Polyb. XVIII.50–1, XXI.15, Livy XXXII.39; Simpson, 1954, op. cit., p. 30.
49 Diod. XX.19, 27, 37; Diod. XX.37.4; Diod. XX.37.5–6.
50 Diod. XX.52, Plut. *Demet.* 15–16, Bengtson, op. cit., pp. 56–8; for the Diadochs' adoption of the kingly title, see Ch. 6; Diod. XX.73.5, Plut. *Demet.* 19, Fortina, op. cit., p. 94, Will, 1984. op. cit., p. 56.
51 Diod. XX.84.1; see pp. 68–9, 76.
52 Diod. XX.81.1, Fortina, op. cit., p. 96, Bengtson, op. cit., pp. 64–6; Diod. XX.84.1; Diod. XX.96, 98, Plut. *Demet.* 21–2; R. M. Berthold, *Rhodes in the Hellenistic Age*, Ithaca and London, Cornell University Press, 1984, p.

77; Diod. XX.100.2; Diod. XX.99.3, Plut. *Demet.* 22 – Rhodes was to be Demetrius' ally, but without obligation to take up arms against Ptolemy.

53 See Ch. 6; Saitta, op. cit., pp. 73–5; Diod. XX.102–3, Plut. *Demet.* 23, *SEG* 26, no. 89.

54 For Lysimachus' policy towards Greece, see Ch. 4; since Prepelaus held Corinth for Cassander in that year (Diod. XX.102.1); Roussel, 1938, op. cit., p. 337.

55 Plut. *Demet.* 23, Diod. XX.102–3, H. Hauben, 'IG II² 492 and the siege of Athens in 304 BC', *ZPE*, 1974, vol. 14, p. 10; Plut. *Demet.* 25, *Pyrrh.* 4; Diod. XX.105.1.

56 Diod. XX.102.1; *SEG* 2 no.339 = *IG* IV² 68; *SEG* 14 no.58; Diod. XX.106; Just. XV.2.16.

57 Saitta, op. cit., p. 75, Diod. XX.106.2 says simply that Cassander summoned Lysimachus from Thrace; Bengtson, op. cit., p. 66; Diod. XVIII.54.1; Cassander's defeats in Caria (Diod. XIX.68.5–7) may have contributed to this reluctance; Diod. XX.107.1 – the source used by Justin (XV.2.16) and Orosius (*Adv. Pag.* III.23.42) stresses Cassander's preoccupation with *finitimum bellum* in 302 BC; Plut. *Demet.* 28.

58 Fortina, op. cit., p. 102, Will, 1984, op. cit., pp. 58–9; Bengtson, op. cit., p. 124.

59 Diod. XX.106.2–3; Cloché, 1959, op. cit., pp. 211–12, C. Wehrli, *Antigone et Demetrios*, Geneva, Librairie Droz, 1968, p. 67, Just. XV.2.16, Oros. *Adv. Pag.* III.23.42.

60 Saitta, op. cit., p. 76, Wehrli, op. cit., p. 67; Will, 1979, op. cit., p. 75, for Antigonus' plan to use the League as the basis for conquest of Macedon.

61 Diod. XX.107.2; for Prepelaus' career, see Lund, op. cit., Appendix III.

62 Diod. XX.107.2, Arr. *Anab.* I.18.1.

63 Diod. XX.107.3–4, see Ch. 5 for Lysimachus' treatment of Erythrae.

64 Diod. XX.107.3; for Sardis, see G. M. A. Hanfmann and W. E. Mierse, *Sardis from Prehistoric to Roman Times*, Cambridge, Mass., and London, Harvard University Press, 1983, p. 125; Arr. *Anab.* I.17.5 for the 'extremely strong' acropolis fortress.

65 R. H. Simpson, 'A possible case of misrepresentation in Diodorus XIX', *Historia*, 1957b, vol. 77, pp. 504–5, for Docimus' defection from Perdiccas to Antigonus under shady circumstances; M. M. Austin, 'Hellenistic kings, war and the economy', *CQ*, 1986, vol. 36 (New Series), pp. 457–60, for the cycle of victory → money → purchase of more troops → victory; Diod. XX.107.2, see Ch. 5 for Lysimachus and the Greek cities.

66 Diod. XX.108.1–3; see Strabo XIV.5.10, R. H. Simpson, 'A note on Cyinda', *Historia*, 1957a, vol. 77, pp. 503–4; Saitta, op. cit., p. 77, M. Cary, *A History of the Greek World from 323-146 BC*, London, Methuen, 1951, p. 40, notes the unique nature of this campaign in Greek history; Diod. XX.108.4–5.

67 Just. XV.2.16; Strabo XV.724, A. Bouché-Leclerq, *Histoire des Séleucides*, Paris, Ernest Leroux, 1913, pp. 28–9, Mehl, op. cit., pp. 166–81; Plut. *Demet.* 25, Bouché-Leclerq, op. cit., p. 30, H. Hauben, 'A royal toast in 302 BC', *Ancient Society*, 1974, vol. 5, pp. 106–14; Bevan, op. cit., p. 59, Bengtson, op. cit., p. 123.

68 W. W.Tarn, 'The proposed new date for Ipsus', *CR*, 1926, pp. 13–14, A. J.

Sachs, *Late Babylonian Astronomical and Related Texts*, Providence, Brown University Studies 18, 1955, no. 1,216, F. X. Kugler, *Sternkunde und Sterndienst in Babel*, vol. II, Munster, 1924, p. 438; Mehl, op. cit., pp. 196–8, follows Tarn in accepting the historicity of Antigonus' 'second capture' of Babylon as does R. A. Billows, *Antigonus the One-Eyed and the Creation of the Hellenistic State*, Berkeley, Los Angeles and London, University of California Press, 1990, p. 178; Arr. *Ind.* 43.4.5.

69 Tarn is surely over-optimistic in assuming that Arrian's source must be Hieronymus and therefore that this incident 'may . . . be accepted as fact'; Sachs, op. cit., Kugler, op. cit., p. 438; for a full discussion, see A. T. L. Kuhrt's review of Mehl's book, *Bibliotheca Orientalis*, 1989, vol. 46, pp. 507–12.

70 Diod. XX.108.1, Plut. *Demet.* 28; Diod. XX.113.2–3, Roussel, op. cit., p. 343, Wehrli, op. cit., p. 69; Diod. XX.113.4 – 20,000 infantry, 12,500 cavalry, 480 elephants, 100+ scythed chariots; Plut. *Demet.* 28 (for numbers at Ipsus, see p. 78), Bengtson, op. cit., p. 123.

71 Diod. XX.108.4, Bengtson, op. cit., p. 123.

72 Diod. XX.109.1, Saitta, op. cit., p. 77; Diod. XX.109.2–4 – bad weather finally forced Antigonus to abandon his pursuit; Frontinus I.V.11; Diod. XX.109.7, Memn. *FGrH* 434 F.4.9.

73 Memn. *FGrH* 434 F.4.4, Diod. XX.109.7; Saitta, op. cit., p. 77, Wehrli, op. cit., p. 67; Arr. *Anab.* VII.4.5, for Alexander as heir to the Achaemenids, see Ch. 6; Memn. *FGrH* 434 F.4.9.

74 Diod. XX.109.4–5, 111.1.

75 *Syll*[3] 352, Diod. XX.111.3; Polyaen. IV.12.1; *IG* XII 354 = *Inschr. von Lampsakos*, 1978, no. 1, dated by G. Daux, 'Inscriptions de Thasos', *BCH*, 1928, vol. 52, p. 46, to *c.* 300 BC; M. Cary, 'An inscription from Lampsacus', *JHS*, 1930, pp. 253–4, for a context in 302 BC – the lettering style does seem to favour a date nearer the turn of the century than the mid-fourth-century context suggested by P. Frisch, *Inschriften von Lampsakos*, Bonn, Rudolf Habelt Verlag GMBH, 1978, pp. 5–6.

76 Diod. XX.112.3–4, Saitta, op. cit., p. 78, Roussel, op. cit., p. 343.

77 Diod. XX.113.1, XX.43.1, Will, 1979, op. cit., pp. 137–86 for Coele-Syria's importance for Egypt's security; Seibert, 1969, op. cit., pp. 231–2.

78 Diod. XVIII.3.1 for Cassander's resettlement of the Autariatae; Diod.XX.19.1, Polyaen. IV.12.1; Saitta, op. cit., p. 78 n. 49; compare Diod. XX.75.1–3 – defectors from Antigonus in Egypt in 306 BC make their way over to Ptolemy with arrows whistling round their ears; those recaptured are severely tortured.

79 This phraseology may suggest an Autariataean attempt to make good their losses by a convenient fiction, though it cannot be pressed too far; compare Diod. XIX.43.8–9 – Eumenes' troops likewise defect to Antigonus after the loss of their *aposkeue*.

80 Wehrli, op. cit., p. 69.

81 For the site, see E. Honigmann, 'Sur quelques évêchés d'Asie Mineure', *Byzantion*, 1935, vol. 10, pp. 647–50; Plut. *Demet.* 28; Antigonus had 70,000+ infantry, the coalition 64,000. Seleucus' 20,000 may have been mostly indigenous troops from his Asian satrapies; the inferior reputation of such troops as infantry is reflected by Achaemenid employment of

Greek mercenary hoplites in the fifth and fourth centuries BC (G. T. Griffith, *The Mercenaries of the Hellenistic World*, Cambridge, Cambridge University Press, 1935, pp. 3, 7).

82 It is plausible that Hieronymus might wish his patron to be seen as in part, like all tragic heroes, the victim of the gods; for portents in royal propaganda, see Ch. 6.

83 Plut. *Demet.* 28; Antigonus had 10,000 cavalry, the coalition had 10,500; the latter figure is unlikely to be correct since according to Diodorus (XX.113.4) Seleucus alone brought 12,500; for elephants as the tanks of the ancient world, see Bengtson, op. cit., p. 69; W. W. Tarn, 'Two notes on Seleucid History: 1. Seleucus' 500 elephants', *JHS*, 1940, vol. 60, pp. 85–8; Plut. *Demet.* 25, *Athen.* VI.66, Phylarch. *FGrH* 81 F.31.

84 For understatement in Hieronymus' treatment of Lysimachus, see Ch. 1; Tarn, 1940, op. cit., p. 87, sees the military understanding of Plutarch's account of Ipsus as derived from Hieronymus; Plut. *Demet.* 29–30, Wehrli, op. cit., p. 71.

4 AFTER IPSUS: THE EMPIRE EXTENDED

1 The ownership of Lycia and Pamphylia, for example, is the subject of considerable dispute, see p. 81, n.5.

2 See Ch. 3 and p. 89; see Diod. XX.112.2 and Ch. 2 for Pleistarchus' shipwreck – perhaps his later actions were more distinguished!

3 Plut. *Demet.* 32; the Halys had formed the eastern border of Antigonus' kingdom in 311 BC (E. Meyer, *Die Grenzen der Hellenistischen Staaten in Kleinasien*, Leipzig, 1925, p. 22) and, earlier, the boundary between the Mermnad and Assyrian kingdoms (J. M. Balcer, *Sparda by the Bitter Sea*, Chico, Calif., Scholar's Press, 1984, p. 95); App. *Syr.* 55 – Appian's ascription of Phrygia to Seleucus is generally accepted as a strategic and geographical nonsense (e.g. Meyer, op. cit., p. 28, G. Corradi, *Studi ellenistici*, Turin, Società Editrice Internazionale, 1929, p. 29).

4 Meyer, op. cit., p. 28; E. Will, 'The succession to Alexander', in A. E. Astin *et al.* (eds) *Cambridge Ancient History*, 2nd edn, vol. VII, Cambridge, Cambridge University Press, 1984, p. 110.

5 Meyer, op. cit., p. 19, Diod. XVIII.50.2–3; Diod. XX.113.3. If Lycia and Pamphylia 'went with' Greater Phrygia, then logically they must have gone to Lysimachus, not Seleucus (as claimed by M. Segre, 'Decreto di Aspendos', *Aegyptus*, 1934, vol. 14, p. 255); Diod. XVIII.51, XX.107.5, see p. 72.

6 D. Magie, *Roman Rule in Asia Minor*, Princeton, Princeton University Press, 1950, p. 47, Strabo XIII.4.5; E. T. Newell, *The Coinage of the Western Seleucid Mints from Seleucus I to Antiochus II*, New York, American Numismatic Society, 1941, pp. 242–69 – Sardis' history as a major administrative centre makes it a likely mint for Lysimachus, though Price doubts whether the issues linked with Sardis by M. Thompson, 'The mints of Lysimachus', in C. M. Kraay and G. K. Jenkins (eds) *Essays in Greek Coinage Presented to Stanley Robinson*, Oxford, Clarendon Press, 1968, p. 165, are the correct ones (see p. 83); Magie, op. cit., pp. 43–5, 50.

7 Magie, op. cit., pp. 50, 125, 127–8, V. Tscherikower, *Die Hellenistischen Stadtegrundungen von Alexander des Grossen bis auf die Römerzeit*, Leipzig, *Philologus* Supplement 19, 1927, p. 155.
8 Memn. *FGrH* 434 F.4.9; for tribute levied by Alexander at Sardis and in Cappadocia, Arr. *Anab.* 1.17.7, App. *Mith.* 8.
9 Diod. XIX.60.2; Plut. *Demet.* 4, App. *Mith.* 9.
10 H. Bengtson, *Die Diadochen*, Munich, C. H. Beck, 1987, p. 74, Magie, op. cit., pp. 74–5; for Abydus as the best crossing point between Europe and Asia, Magie, op. cit., p. 82, *Heid. Epit. FGrH* 155 F.10.45.
11 Thompson, op. cit., pp. 163–82; H. R. Baldus, 'Zum Siegel des Königs Lysimachos von Thrakien', *Chiron*, 1978, vol. 8, pp. 195–201, for the lion as Lysimachus' emblem; Dr Price imparted this information verbally – see H. S. Lund, 'Bridging the Hellespont: the Successor Lysimachus – a study in early Hellenistic kingship', University of London Ph.D. thesis, Senate House Library, 1992, pp. 177–8, for fuller discussion.
12 *I.Priene* 37 ll.65–73, 80–1, 111–12; Polyaen. IV.7.4; for Lysimachus and Hiero, see Ch. 5.
13 *I.Priene* 37 ll.65, 80–1, 123–30 for the chronology; *I.Priene*, 11 and 12, L. Robert, 'Hellenica¹ – XX decrets de Priène', *Rev. Phil.*, 1944, vol. 18, pp. 6–9, 10; Athen. VI. 62, Plut. *Demet.* 19, *SEG* 26, no. 89.
14 Plut. *Demet.* 30, 31, E. T. Newell, *The Coinages of Demetrius Poliorcetes*, London, Oxford University Press and Humphrey Milford, 1927, pp. 27–31; *Syll*³ 352; Polyaen. IV.7.4; Magie, op. cit., p. 90 – Demetrius' rush from Caria to save Ephesus personally is dated to 298 BC by Corradi, op. cit., p. 38, but over-hasty action by Lysimachus, hoping to exploit Demetrius' absence, and Demetrius' return from Caria is equally possible.
15 Diod. XX.107.5, W. Dittenberger, *Orientis Graeci Inscriptiones Selectae*, vol. I, Lipsiae, S. Hirzel, 1903, commenting on no. 9, p. 31 (= *Inschr. Eph.* 1452/*Inschr. Claz.* 505) – there is no archon date.
16 Meyer, op. cit., p. 29.
17 Plut. *Demet.* 20, 25, 27 – Demetrius calls her Penelope, presumably implying her possession of many suitors!
18 Plut. *Demet.* 30; G. Saitta, 'Lisimaco di Tracia', *Kokalos*, 1955, vol. 1, p. 80, G. Longega, *Arsinoe II*, Rome, L'erma di Bretschneider, 1968, p. 29 – see also Ch. 7.
19 *Syll*³ 374, Plut. *Demet.* 12, J. M. Edmonds, *Comici: The Fragments of Attic Comedy*, vol. IIIA, Leiden, E. J. Brill, 1961, p. 179 F.25; W. S. Ferguson, *Hellenistic Athens*, New York, Macmillan & Co., 1911, p. 123, see also Ch. 6; *Syll*³ 374 ll.17–29.
20 Plut. *Demet.* 30; *Syll*³ 362, Marmor Parium *FGrH* 239 l.26; for Cassander and Lachares, see Paus. 1.25.7, M. Fortina, *Cassandro, rè di Macedonia*, Turin, Società Editrice Internationale, 1965, p. 118 – Philippides of Paiania, proposer of *Syll*³ 362, is another possible protégé.
21 *Syll*³ 374. ll.12–15; Plut. *Demet.* 12, Edmonds, op. cit., p. 179 F.25.
22 Corradi's date (op. cit., p. 37); Plut. *Demet.* 31; as Saitta suggests (op. cit., pp. 80–1).
23 Plut. *Demet.* 31.
24 Saitta, op. cit., p. 81 suggests a breach between the two; Ferguson, op. cit., pp. 124, 137; for Demochares and Lysimachus, see Ch. 6; Bengtson's view

(op. cit., p. 103) of Philippides as 'the most important man in Athens' after Ipsus seems overstated, and the assumption of his return to Athens before 286–5 BC unsupported.

25 Saitta, op. cit., p. 81, P. Roussel, 'Le démembrement de l'empire d'Alexandre', in G. Glotz *et al.*, *Histoire grecque*, vol. IV, Paris, Presses Universitaires de France, 1938, p. 348, Bengtson, op. cit., p. 104; for Coele-Syria, see Diod. XXI.F.1.5, Polyb. V.67, App. *Syr.* 5, Plut. *Demet.* 31; Diod. XIX.80–5, XX.50–2, Plut. *Demet.* 4.15–17.

26 Saitta, op. cit., p. 81; for Ptolemy, see pp. 89, 90.

27 A Lycian text (*Titul. Lyc.* 35) dated to 'Year 4 of King Ptolemy' might support Ptolemy's occupation of parts of Lycia before Ipsus, but T. R. Bryce in T. R. Bryce and J. Zahle, *The Lycians*, vol. I, Copenhagen, Museum Tusculanum Press, 1986, pp. 49–50, is sceptical about this reading; Meyer, op. cit., p. 33, argues that without a strong fleet, keeping control of Lycia would be hard for Lysimachus. For Lagid control of the Pamphylian coast between 301 BC and 298 BC, see Segre, op. cit., pp. 253–68, and more cautiously, R. S. Bagnall, *The Administration of the Ptolemaic Possessions outside Egypt*, Leiden, E. J. Brill, 1976, pp. 112–14. Otherwise Ptolemy's occupation of these coastal cities must be seen as a provocative and hostile move later on.

28 Plut. *Demet.* 31, Memn. *FGrH* 434 F.4.9; Memn. *FGrH* 434 F.5.1.

29 Corradi, op. cit., p. 37; that Cassander was not a possibility supports the view that he and Lysimachus were still on good terms, see Will, 1984, op. cit., p. 104; Plut. *Demet.* 31; Plut. *Demet.* 32. For Cyinda, see R. H. Simpson, 'A note on Cyinda', *Historia*, 1957a, vol. 77, pp. 503–4, J. D. Bing, 'A further note on Cyinda/Kundi', *Historia*, 1973, vol. 22, pp. 346–8.

30 Bing, op. cit., p. 347; Bengtson, op. cit., p. 105; Plut. *Demet.* 20, Corradi, op. cit., p. 39, Saitta, op. cit., p. 82; L. Robert, *Le Sanctuaire de Sinuri près de Mylasa*, vol. I, Paris, De Boccard, 1945, p. 161, thus overthrowing the view that Pleistarchus held Cilicia and Caria concurrently as a 'buffer state' (e.g. Meyer, op. cit., p. 28).

31 Corradi, op. cit., p. 39; Saitta, op. cit., p. 82.

32 S. M. Burstein, 'Lysimachus and the Greek cities of Asia: the case of Miletus', *Ancient World*, 1980, vol. 3, p. 78, n.54.

33 *OGIS* 10 = *Inschr. Eph.* 1453; *OGIS* 213 = *I.Didyma* 479 (Antiochus' gift of a stoa at Didyma *c.* 299 BC) – see also Ch. 5.

34 Plutarch's account (*Demet.* 32) is clearly highly compressed; this treaty is generally dated to 297–6 BC (Saitta, op. cit., p. 82, Burstein, 1980, op. cit., p. 78); Corradi, op. cit., p. 39, based on dating Demetrius' attack on Samaria (Euseb. *Chron.* II.118) in 298 BC rather than 296 BC; *I.Milet.* 139 = *RC* 14 ll.4–9, *I.Milet.* 123 l.22, Burstein, 1980, op. cit., pp. 78–80.

35 Saitta, op. cit., p. 82 ; see Ch. 3, also T. L. Shear, *Kallias of Sphettos and the Revolt of Athens in 286 B.C.* Princeton, *Hesperia* Supplement XVII, 1978, p. 17 ll.18–23 and below, for Ptolemy's active involvement in Athenian affairs in 287 BC; his restoration of Pyrrhus (Plut. *Pyrrh.* 4, 5) as king of Epirus in 298–7 BC also reflects an interest in mainland Greece; Plut. *Demet.* 35.

36 Plut. *Demet.* 32, Corradi, op. cit., p. 43; Will, 1984, op. cit., p. 104, stresses

the serious threat which Demetrius' ownership of Tyre and Sidon, and his new naval bases in Cilicia, posed for Seleucus; Bengtson, op. cit., p. 105; Roussel, 1938, op. cit., p. 352, Corradi, op. cit., p. 44.

37 S. M. Burstein (ed.) *The Hellenistic Age from the Battle of Ipsos to the Death of Kleopatra VII*, Cambridge, Cambridge University Press, 1985, no. 5 = *P.Oxy.* 2082, for Cassander's death; Philip died four months later, *P.Oxy.* 2082, Euseb. *Chron.* I. 241, Paus. IX.7.3, Just. XV.4.24; on the chronology, see C. Habicht, *Untersuchungen zur politischen Geschichte Athens im 3 Jahrhundert v. Chr.*, Munich, C. H. Beck, 1979, p. 12.

38 Antipater seems to have deliberately divided the empire, entrusting Asia to Antigonus, while the kings returned to Macedon (Diod. XVIII.39.6–7, Arr. *Succ. FGrH* 156 F.44, Just. XIV.1); Diod. XVIII.54.3; Plut. *Demet.* 35 (Demetrius held on to Salamis), Roussel, 1938, op. cit., p. 352, Saitta, op. cit., p. 85.

39 Plut. *Demet.* 35, 36 – the news reached Demetrius at Sparta, and it was from the Peloponnese that he marched on Macedon in autumn 294 BC.

40 Strabo XIV.1.4 lists them as Ephesus, Miletus, Myus, Lebedus, Colophon, Priene, Teos, Erythrae, Phocaea, Chios, Clazomenae, Samos; *Syll*² 363; *Syll*³ 363; J. G. Milne, 'The autonomous coinage of Smyrna', *Num. Chron.*, 1923, vol. 3 (series 5), pp. 3–4 dates the series *c.* 288 BC–281 BC, but his reasons are not sound – see Lund, op. cit., p. 195, n.109; *SEG* 1985, no. 926, W. G. Forrest, 'Some inscriptions of Chios', *Horos*, 1985, vol. 3, pp. 94–5; *Syll*³ 368 1.24, Tscherikower, op. cit., p. 163; B. V. Head, *On the Chronological Sequence of the Coins of Ephesus*, London and Paris, Rollin & Feuardent, 1880, p. 43, dates the series from 288 BC to 280 BC; Pliny *N.H.* VII.3.5.

41 Burstein, 1980, op. cit., pp. 78–9; *Syll*³ 364; Plut. *Demet.* 46; *RC*, no.7, S. M. Sherwin-White, 'Ancient archives: the edict of Alexander to Priene, a reappraisal', *JHS*, 1985, vol. 105, p. 8; for Lysimachus and Duris, see Ch. 5.

42 See Ch. 6 for the kings' personal involvement in city foundations; Porph. *FHG* III F.3.3, Just. XVI.2.4 for Antipater's marriage to Eurydice – if Antipater's coup in summer 294 BC coincides with his majority (see p. 94), a date between 297 BC and 294 BC is perhaps more plausible than the last years of Cassander's reign.

43 Paus. 1.25.7, 29.10, Polyaen. IV.7.5, *P.Oxy.* 2082; Habicht, op. cit., p. 8, for Lachares' assumption of the tyranny in Elaphebolion, 295 BC; Plut. *Demet.* 33–4, Habicht, op. cit., pp. 4, 6, for peace as agreed by 9 Elaphebolion 294 BC; Plut. *Demet.* 34, *P.Oxy.* 2082, Paus. 1.25.7, Roussel, 1938, op. cit., p. 352; Polyaen. III.7.2 and 3 (though compare Paus. 1.25.7).

44 Plut. *Demet.* 33, 35 (news of Cyprus' capture reaches Demetrius in the Peloponnese); *Syll*³ 381, with Dittenberger's commentary (p. 615) – particularly if Demaratus acts primarily in the capacity of king's friend rather than Sparta's representative.

45 Plut. *Demet.* 34; N. G. L. Hammond and F. W. Walbank, *A History of Macedonia*, vol. III, Oxford, Clarendon Press, 1988, p. 211; Habicht, op. cit., pp. 7–8, 22–6, for evidence for the oligarchy; Plut. *Demet.* 34, Habicht, op. cit., p. 29.

46 See Ch. 2.

47 Plut. *Demet.* 37, R. M. Errington, 'Alexander in the Hellenistic world', in

Alexandre le Grand: image et réalité, Geneva, Fondation Hardt, 1975, pp. 145–7, for the still potent influence of Philip's memory in early Hellenistic Macedon; Porph. *FHG* III F.3.5; for Lysimachus and Antipater, see below, Ptolemy's interest in Macedon is reflected in his restoration of Pyrrhus as king of Epirus (P. Lévêque, *Pyrrhos*, Paris, De Boccard, 1957, p. 127).

48 Porph. *FHG* III F.3.3, Plut. *Demet.* 36, *Pyrrh.* 6, Lévêque, op. cit., pp. 126–7.

49 Bengtson, op. cit., p. 110, perhaps lays too much emphasis on manpower as Macedon's most valuable resource – see A. B. Bosworth, 'Alexander the Great and the decline of Macedon', *JHS*, 1986, vol. 106, pp. 1–12; for Seleucus' aspirations to Macedon, see Ch. 7; Plut. *Pyrrh.* 6, Just. XVI.1.5; Lévêque, op. cit., p. 129.

50 Plut. *Pyrrh.* 6; Saitta, op. cit., p. 125; see Ch. 2; Just. XVI.1.9, Porph. *FHG* III F.3.3, Plut. *Demet.* 36.

51 Plut. *Demet.* 36 – this seems more convincing than Diod. XXI.F.7, who makes Demetrius the murderer of both brothers; e.g. Macedon had been unable to prevent Demetrius' recovery of Athens.

52 Events after Lysimachus' death reinforced the wisdom of this stance (see Ch. 2); Just. XVI.1.9., Lévêque, op. cit., p. 132, Bengtson, op. cit., p. 108; Paus. 1.9.7. (Paus. 1.10.3, which puts this wedding before the death of Lysandra's previous husband, is presumably wrong).

53 Plut. *Demet.* 39, Hammond and Walbank, op. cit., p. 222.

54 Plut. *Demet.* 39, Bengtson, op. cit., p. 111.

55 *Syll*³ 337, M. Holleaux, 'Sur une inscription de Thèbes', *REG*, 1895, vol. 8, p. 44; *Syll*³ 366, R. Flacelière, *Les Aitoliens à Delphes*, Paris, De Boccard, 1937, p. 58, sets this in the context of expected aggression from Cassander; G. T. Griffith, *The Mercenaries of the Hellenistic World*, Cambridge, Cambridge University Press, 1935, p. 81, Diod. XVIII.8.6, 9.5, 11.1; Flacelière, op. cit., pp. 50–2.

56 Flacelière, op. cit., p. 58; *Syll*³ 337, Fortina, op. cit., p. 115, sees Cassander renouncing a policy of military aggression in mainland Greece soon after Ipsus; the death of Philip IV (Euseb. *Chron.* 1.241) at Elateia (liberated in 301 BC – *SEG* 18 no.197) suggests its recapture by Cassander.

57 Diog. Laert. II 140; L. Robert, 'Sur une loi d'Athènes relative au petites Panathenées', in *Hellenica*, vol. XI–XII, Paris, Imprimerie A. Bontemps, 1960, p. 201, interpreted Menedemus' visit thus; *Syll*³ 337, Holleaux, op. cit., pp. 44–5.

58 Polyaen. III.7.2, Paus. 1.25.7, Plut. *Demet.* 39, Flacelière, op. cit., pp. 69, 71.

59 Plut. *Demet.* 39, Flacelière, op. cit., pp. 71–2 – Cleonymus' only possible route was via Aetolia; Plut. *Demet.* 39, Polyaen. III.7.2; see p. 93 for Lachares' isolation in 294 BC.

60 Plut. *Demet.* 39, P. Cloché, *Thèbes de Beotie*, Louvain and Paris, Editions Nauwelaerts and Brouwer et Cie, 1952, p. 209; Plut. *Demet.* 40 for Pyrrhus' invasion of Thessaly which forced Demetrius to divert resources from Boeotia.

61 Athen. VI.63 (citing Duris), Plut. *Demet.* 40, Flacelière, op. cit., pp. 75–6; Lévêque, op. cit., p. 140, sees Pyrrhus as responding to the strategic threat

of Demetrius' possession of Corcyra, gained, to add insult to injury, by marriage to Pyrrhus' ex-wife Lanassa; Plut. *Demet.* 41, *Pyrrh.* 8 (though the likelihood of Epirote propaganda here is high), Bengtson, op. cit., p. 112; Plut. *Demet.* 43, Plut. *Pyrrh.* 10.

62 Plut. *Demet.* 43, *Pyrrh.* 10, Newell, 1927, op. cit., pp. 87–91, 108–11.
63 See Ch. 5.
64 Diod. XX.77.1, Trog. *Prol. Lib.* 16, Just. XVI.3.1, Memn. *FGrH* 434 F.5.3; Saitta, op. cit., pp. 127–30 – possibly he has confused the two Clearchuses; S. M. Burstein, *Outpost of Hellenism: The Emergence of Heracleia on the Black Sea*, Berkeley and Los Angeles, University of California Publications, 1976, pp. 93–4, for this date and a solution to the supposed clash in Diodorus' chronology.
65 Plut. *Demet.* 43 (500 ships), *Pyrrh.* 10 (100,000 soldiers, 500 ships), Lévèque, op. cit., p. 151; Plut. *Demet.* 44, Roussel, 1938, op. cit., p. 362; Lévèque, op. cit., p. 153.
66 Plut. *Demet.* 44, *Pyrrh.* 11, Lévèque, op. cit., pp. 153–4.
67 Plut. *Demet.* 44. C. F. Edson Jr., 'The Antigonids, Heracles and Beroea', *HSCP*, 1934, vol. 45, pp. 239–41, for Beroia's symbolic significance as the Antigonid dynasty's birthplace, though Lévèque, op. cit., p. 156, is sceptical; Will, 1984, op. cit., p. 108, argues that Demetrius saw rule in Macedon largely as a springboard for Asia's recovery; Plut. *Demet.* 42 – one story at least is conventional – see Lund, op. cit., p. 210, n.186; Plut. *Demet.* 44, *Pyrrh.* 11.
68 Plut. *Demet.* 44; Amphipolis – Paus. I.10.2, Saitta, op. cit., p. 128, Lévèque, op. cit., p. 157; Plut. *Demet.* 44, Plut. *Pyrrh.* 11, Shear, op. cit., ll.18–23 for Ptolemy's fleet in action at Athens and in the Cyclades; the border is usually placed at the River Axios.
69 *Syll*[3] 380; Just. XXIV.2.1, 3.3 for Cassandreia's value as a stronghold to Arsinoe in 280 BC, Thuc. IV.102 for Amphipolis' strategic and commercial value; Polyaen. IV.12.2.
70 Just. XVI.2.4 – though Porph. *FHG* III F.3.3 dates Antipater's death to 294 BC, this is probably the result of compression (Saitta, op. cit., p. 130); Ferguson, op. cit., p. 137, dates it later, identifying Antipater with Plutarch's contributor of funds to Athens in 286–5 BC (*Vit. X. Orat.* 851E).
71 Plut. *Pyrrh.* 11, *Demet.* 44, Shear, op. cit., p. 50, Will, 1984, op. cit., p. 108; Paus. 1.26.1, *Syll*[3] 386; Habicht, op. cit., p. 54, argues persuasively against Shear's date of spring 286 BC (op. cit., p. 50).
72 Plut. *Demet.* 46; Shear, op. cit., ll.32–6; Habicht, op. cit., p. 62.
73 Paus. I.29.1, Polyaen. V.17, Habicht, op. cit., p. 63; Plut. *Vit. X. Orat.* 851 E–F; *Syll*[3] 374 ll.34–5; a new inscription from Cassandreia (M. B. Hatzopoulos, 'Une donation du Roi Lysimaque', *ΜΕΛΗΘΗΜΑΤΑ*, Paris, De Boccard, 1988, pp. 38–9) confirms the identification, see also Ch. 6.
74 Shear, op. cit., pp. 49–50, *Syll*[3] 374 ll.46–50; Plut. *Vit. X. Orat.* 851 E; see L. C. Smith, 'Demochares of Leuconoe and the dates of his exile', *Historia*, 1962, vol. 11, pp. 114–15, Ferguson, op. cit., p. 137, for his previous connection with Lysimachus; Habicht, op. cit., p. 78, *Syll*[3] 361 = *SEG* 14.461.A.
75 The confident tone of the Euthius decree (B. D. Meritt, 'Greek inscriptions', *Hesperia*, 1938, p. 100, no.18) suggests bribery (P. Gauthier, 'La

réunification d'Athènes en 281 et les deux archontes Nicias', *REG*, 1979, vol. 92, pp. 369–71) rather than military assault (Shear, op. cit., pp. 28–9); Gauthier, op. cit., pp. 367–8; see Ch. 7 for the date of Corupedium.

76 Plut. *Demet.* 46; for Lysimachus' naval strength, see Ch. 7; Plut. *Demet.* 46, Shear, op. cit., l.20 for Andros as Ptolemaic, Habicht, op. cit., p. 65 thinks it possible that by now he had most of the Cyclades.

77 Habicht, op. cit., pp. 64–5; Plut. *Demet.* 46; for Berenice and Eurydice, see M. Cary, *A History of the Greek World from 343-146 B.C.*, London, Methuen, 1951, p. 55.

78 Shear, op. cit., p. 50, dismissed by Habicht, op. cit., p. 64; *IG* II² 663, 662 – for Artemidorus' nationality, C. Habicht, 'Beitrage zur Prosopographie der altgriechischen welt', *Chiron*, 1972, vol. 2, p. 107; Shear himself, op. cit., p. 50, connects Artemidorus' 'usefulness to an Athenian embassy' with the second embassy of Demochares (see p. 101).

79 *I.Milet* 138 ll.6–7, Burstein, 1980, op. cit., p. 78; Polyaen. V.7. Demetrius' last Asian campaign is the most likely context for this action; Plut. *Demet.* 46.

80 *I.Priene* 14, 15 (= *RC* 6), 16 (= *RC* 8); Sherwin-White, 1985, op. cit., pp. 69-89, for these texts as part of an archive; C. B. Welles, *Royal Correspondence in the Hellenistic Period*, New Haven, Yale University Press, 1934, p. 43.

81 Plut. *Demet.* 46; Polyaen. III.7.3 for Lachares' flight to Lysimacheia when 'the enemy were prevailing at Sestos'; Sardis was again in Lysimachus' hands when Seleucus invaded in 282/1 BC (Polyaen. IV.9.4); Plut. *Demet.* 46, for Agathocles, see also Ch. 7; Roussel, 1938, op. cit., p. 365.

82 Plut. *Demet.* 46–7.

83 Plut. *Demet.* 49.

84 Diod. XXI F.1.20, Plut. *Demet.* 48, 51; Cary, op. cit., p. 52 – for Seleucus and Macedon, see Ch. 7; Lévèque, op. cit., p. 167; Plut. *Pyrrh.* 12, Lévèque, op. cit., p. 162, for the resultant great increase in Pyrrhus' revenues.

85 Edmonds, op. cit., p. 247, Phoenic. F.1; Lévèque, op. cit., p. 168, Hammond and Walbank, op. cit., p. 235; *Syll*³ 380, Lévèque, op. cit., p. 165, for honours for Prepelaus at Aetolian-controlled Delphi *c.* 287 BC.

86 Cary, op. cit., p. 55; Ferguson, op. cit., p. 153, Cary, op. cit., p. 51; Lévèque, op. cit., p. 165; Habicht, op. cit., pp. 80–1. For the marriage, Schol. Theoc. 17.128.

87 Plut. *Demet.* 41, 44, *Pyrrh.* 11, 12; Hammond and Walbank, op. cit., p. 234 – for a similar omission in Plutarch (Lysimachus' defeat at Amphipolis in 287 BC) see Ch. 1; Bengtson, op. cit., p. 130, cites disruption in communications, trade and a break in family ties as reasons for popular discontent with the kingdom's division; Plut. *Pyrrh.* 12; Paus. 1.9.7 – Lévèque, op. cit., p. 171, and J. Hornblower, *Hieronymus of Cardia*, Oxford, Oxford University Press, 1981, Appendix I, pp. 246–8, both see this story as the result of confusion with Plut. *Pyrrh.* 26 and Diod. XXII.12 where Pyrrhus' mercenaries sack Macedon's royal tombs.

88 Just. XVI.3.1, Pomp. Trog. *Prol. Lib.* 16, Burstein, 1976, op. cit., pp. 84, 93 identifies this war in *Thraciae* with operations against Zipoites; Memn. *FGrH* 434 F.6.3, Diod. XIX.60.3, Paus. V.12.7 for Zipoites' victories

against Lysimachus; Memn. *FGrH* 434 F.8.4–5, Burstein, 1976, op. cit., p. 84.

89 Memn. *FGrH* 434 F.5.3.

90 I. L. Merker, 'The ancient kingdom of Paionia', *Balkan Studies*, 1965, vol. 6, p. 48; *IG* II² 654; Polyaen. IV.12.3; Merker, op. cit., p. 49.

91 For the wealth of Pella's mint, see Newell, 1927, op. cit., pp. 79–80; Strabo VII.F.34 for the Crenides gold mines and Paeonian wealth; Thessaly was famed for its pastureland and horses (see G. Cawkwell, *Philip of Macedon*, London, Faber & Faber, 1978, p. 58); for Heracleia's resources, see Burstein, 1976, op. cit., pp. 4–5; it is generally agreed that evidence for Lysimachus' plans for a military conquest of Greece is lacking, e.g. W. W. Tarn, *Antigonus Gonatas*, Oxford, Clarendon Press, 1913, p. 121, Cloché, 1952, op. cit., p. 210, Will, 1984, op. cit., p. 112.

92 Will, 1984, op. cit., p. 110; for Lysimachus as Alexander's heir, see also Chs 1, 6 and 7.

5 GOVERNOR OF THE GREEKS

1 e.g. E. Will, 'The succession to Alexander', in A. E. Astin *et al.* (eds) *Cambridge Ancient History*, 2nd edn, Cambridge, Cambridge University Press, 1984, p. 112, P. Roussel, 'Le démembrement de l'empire d'Alexandre', in G. Glotz *et al.*, *Histoire grecque*, vol. IV, Paris, Presses Universitaires de France, 1938, p. 367, H. Bengtson, *Die Diadochen*, Munich, C. H. Beck, 1987, p. 127; Plut. *Demet.* 25; A. Andreades, 'L'administration financière du roi Lysimaque', in *Mélanges P. Thomas*, Bruges, Imprimerie Sainte Catherine, 1930, p. 9; G. Shipley, *A History of Samos 800–188 B.C.*, Oxford, Clarendon Press, 1987, pp. 176–7, Roussel, op. cit., pp. 367–8; R. A. Billows, Antigonus the One-Eyed and the Creature of the Hellenistic State, Berkeley, Los Angeles and London, University of California Press, 1990, p. 203, n.39; G. Saitta, 'Lisimaco di Tracia', *Kokalos*, 1955, vol. 1, pp. 98–9, Shipley, op. cit., p. 174.

2 e.g. F. Geyer, 'Lysimachos', in G. Wissowa (ed.) *PW*, vol. XIV₁, Stuttgart, J. B. Metzlerscher, 1928, cols. 23–7, W. W. Tarn, 'The succession to Alexander', in J. B. Bury *et al.* (eds), *Cambridge Ancient History*, 1st edn, vol. VI, Cambridge, Cambridge University Press, 1927, pp. 90–1, S. M. Burstein, 'Lysimachus and the Greek cities of Asia: the case of Miletus', *Ancient World*, 1980, vol. 3, pp. 73–9, S. M. Burstein, 'Lysimachus the Gazophylax – a modern scholarly myth?', in W. Heckel and R. Sullivan (eds) *Ancient Coins of the Graeco-Roman World*, Waterloo, Ont., Wilfred Laurier University Press, 1984, pp. 57–68, S. M. Burstein, 'Lysimachus and the Greek cities: the early years', *Ancient World*, 1986b, vol. 14, pp. 19–24, S. M. Burstein, 'Lysimachus and the Greek cities: a problem in interpretation', in *Ancient Macedonia IV*, Thessaloniki, Institute for Balkan Studies, 1986a, pp. 133–8; e.g. Will, 1984, op. cit., p. 112, Bengtson, 1987, op. cit., pp. 127, 134–5, Shipley, op. cit., pp. 174–7; for Lysimachus and the West Pontic Greek cities, see Ch. 2.

3 Shipley, op. cit., pp. 174–6; for poetic laments for cities like Colophon and Ephesus, see Paus. I.9.7, *FHG* II 466; Arr. *Anab.* V.29.3, IV.4.1,

V.17.4, *Ps.-Callisth.* I.31.2, S. Hornblower, *Mausolus*, Oxford, Clarendon Press, 1982, pp. 78–102; C. B. Welles, *Royal Correspondence in the Hellenistic Period*, New Haven, Yale University Press, 1934, nos. 3 and 4 and p. 30 for a possible obstructionist tactic by Teos.

4 *I Milet.* 138, 139, e.g. Roussel, op. cit., p. 367; see below for Burstein's reinterpretation.

5 W. Orth, *Königlicher Machtanspruch und Stadtische Freiheit*, Munich, C. H. Beck, 1977, pp. 12–13, for royal favours designed to win sympathy as an alternative method to brute force.

6 *IG* XII Suppl. 1939 no. 355, Ch. Picard, 'Fouilles de Thasos (1914–1920)', *BCH*, 1921, vol. 45, p. 153; L. Robert, 'Inscriptions de Thasos', *Rev. Phil.*, 1936, vol. 8, p. 131.

7 e.g. Andreades, op. cit., p. 11; Burstein, 1984, op. cit., p. 62, for Lysimachus' mineral resources in Asia Minor and Macedon, see Ch. 4; P. Briant, *Rois, tributs, paysans*, Paris, University de Besançon, 1982, pp. 103–5 – for further discussion, see pp. 146–52.

8 C. Wehrli, *Antigone et Demetrios*, Geneva, Librairie Droz, 1968, p. 128; e.g. Diod. XVIII.69.3–4, XIX.61.4, 105.1, XX.111.2; *RC* 1. ll.53–6, *RC* 15 = *Inschr. Eryth.*, no. 30 l.34, B. D. Meritt, 'Inscriptions de Colophon', *A. J. Phil.*, 1935, vol. 56, no. 1.l.6, V. Ehrenberg, *Alexander and the Greeks*, Oxford, Basil Blackwell, 1938, p. 35; R. H. Simpson, 'Antigonus the One-Eyed and the Greeks', *Historia*, 1959, vol. 8, p. 385, T. R. Martin, *Sovereignty and Coinage in Classical Greece*, Princeton, Princeton University Press, 1985, p. 7.

9 A. H. M. Jones, 'Civitates liberae et immunes', in W. M. Calder and J. Keil (eds) *Anatolian Studies Presented to William Hepburn Buckler*, Manchester, Manchester University Press, 1939, p. 104.

10 S. M. Sherwin-White, 'Ancient archives: the edict of Alexander to Priene, a reappraisal', *JHS*, 1985, vol. 105, pp. 69–89; R. E. Allen, *The Attalid Kingdom*, Oxford, Clarendon Press, 1983, p. 57; E. Bikermann, 'La cité grecque dans les monarchies hellénistiques', *REG*, 1939, vol. 47, p. 344.

11 Saitta, op. cit., pp. 98–101, Shipley, op. cit., p. 177 takes a similar line; G. Orwell, *Nineteen-Eighty-Four*, London, Secker & Warburg, 1949, p. 62 – a reduced chocolate ration represented as an increased one is widely celebrated!

12 e.g. by the Great King, Sparta, Athens and Thebes, finally Alexander, see Wehrli, op. cit., p. 128; D. M. Lewis, *Sparta and Persia*, Leiden, E. J. Brill, 1977, p. 147; R. Meiggs, *The Athenian Empire*, Oxford, Clarendon Press, 1972, pp. 234–54; App. *Syr.* 12.

13 For the Ionian cities as part of the Achaemenid tribute and satrapal system, see e.g. Hdt. III.89, R. Frye, *The Heritage of Persia*, London, Weidenfeld & Nicolson, 1962, p. 81, J. M. Balcer, *Sparda by the Bitter Sea*, Chico, Calif., Scholar's Press, 1984, pp. 169–71, R. Déscat, 'Mnésimachos, Hérodote et le système tributaire achéménide, *REA*, 1985, vol. 87, pp. 97–112; Hdt. I.6, VII.53 (Croesus and Cyrus); Briant, 1982, op. cit., p. 116 for *phoros* as a sign of subjection, Hdt. IV.98, 136, VI.95, VII.93, VIII.18; Hdt. I.142; e.g. M. O. B. Caspari, 'The Ionian confederacy', *JHS*, 1915, vol. 35, p. 176 – for the sceptical view, S. Hornblower, op. cit., p. 17; Hdt. VI.42; Xen. *Hell.* III.4.25.

14 e.g. Demosth. *Chers.* 6–10, 24, 30, Ps.-Arist. *Oec.* II.2.30, Aen. Tact. 24.3, Polyaen. III.14, Ps.-Arist. *Oec.* II.2.23; for tyrants and oligarchs, e.g. Hdt. IV.136, Xen. *Hell.* III.4.3, III.1.10–15 – see also A. T. Olmstead, *History of the Persian Empire*, Chicago, Chicago University Press, 1948, pp. 421–2, J. M. Cook, *The Persian Empire*, London, J. M. Dent & Sons, 1983, pp. 219–20, T. R. Bryce in T. R. Bryce and J. Zahle, *The Lycians*, vol. 1, Copenhagen, Museum Tusculanum Press, 1986, pp. 101, 108–9, 111–12.

15 Ps.-Arist. *Oec.* 1348a–1348b; the starting date for Priene's Athena Polias temple remains uncertain, see J. C. Carter, *The Sculpture of the Sanctuary of Athena Polias at Priene*, London, Society of Antiquaries, 1983, pp. 25–43, Sherwin-White, 1985, op. cit., p. 70; Olmstead, op. cit., p. 483; perhaps only the oligarchs whom S. Hornblower, op. cit., pp. 107, 110–12 sees as favoured by Mausolus.

16 e.g. The Batinetis dispute (Priene versus Samos) (*I.Priene* 37 ll.73–80, 86–7, 101–2, 107–8, 118, 122, *RC* 7 ll.8–9) drew on records going back to the sixth century BC.

17 See Ch. 6; Arr. I.29.3 for Antigonus' government of Greater Phrygia; as Alexander's friend, Lysimachus was well placed to observe and/or advise on policy decisions at the top (see Ch. 6 for friends as advisers); see, e.g., S. M. Sherwin-White, 'Seleucid Babylonia: a case-study for the installation and development of Greek rule', in A. T. L. Kuhrt and S. M. Sherwin-White (eds) *Hellenism in the East*, London, Duckworth, 1987, pp.1–30.

18 This tradition, propounded by Droysen, Kaerst, Wilcken, Berve and Tarn, is reviewed and challenged by E. Badian, 'Alexander the Great and the Greeks of Asia', in E. Badian (ed.) *Ancient Society and Institutions*, Oxford, Basil Blackwell, 1966, pp. 37–8; E. Bikermann, 'Alexandre le Grand et les villes d'Asie', *REG*, 1934, vol. 47, pp. 346, 354–5, Ehrenberg, op. cit., p. 33.

19 Arr. *Anab.* I.17.8, Badian, op. cit., pp. 44–5; compare the propaganda of 334–3 BC – liberation (Diod. XVII.24.1) – with that of 335–4 BC at Corinth – revenge for Persian offences against Greece (Diod. XVII.4.9).

20 Bikermann, 1934, op. cit., pp. 369, 371, 373, 358, Ehrenberg, op. cit., pp. 12, 34, 41, 15, Badian, op. cit., p. 46, A. B. Bosworth, *A Historical Commentary on Arrian's* History of Alexander, Oxford, Clarendon Press, 1980, p. 136 – for a similarly flexible approach by the Achaemenid and Assyrian kings, see A. T. L. Kuhrt, 'Earth and water', in A. T. L. Kuhrt and H. Sancisi-Weerdenburg (eds) *Achaemenid History III*, Leiden, Nederlands Instituut voor Het Nabije Oosten, 1988, pp. 87–98; Arr. *Anab.* II.20.5 – see also Arr. *Anab.* I.23.6–8 (Caria), I.26.3, 27.1–4 (Aspendus), II.5.5 (Soli); Arr. *Anab.* I.17.1, Paus. VI.18.2, Arr. *Anab.* I.18.1–2, Diod. XVII.24.1, Bikermann, 1934, op. cit., p. 358.

21 Arr. *Anab.* I.18.2 – the grant was not universal (Bosworth, op. cit., p. 135); Allen, op. cit., pp. 50–3, Sherwin-White, 1985, op. cit., pp. 85–6 for *syntaxeis* as a term used interchangeably with *phoros* to denote regular royal taxes by Alexander's day, rather than a war tax (e.g. Badian, op. cit., pp. 49, 59, Bosworth, op. cit., p. 166); *Syll*³ 283 ll.9–10, Ehrenberg, op. cit., p. 24; for garrisons (Chios and Priene (?)), *Syll*³ 283 ll.17–18, *I.Priene* 1 l.15; Badian, op. cit., p. 49; satrapal control (Soli and Aspendus), Bikermann, 1934, op. cit., p. 371; gifts, Plut. *Phoc.* 18 –

compare Plut. *Them.* 29; Eresus, *OGIS* 8 ll.60, 127, 143, *RC* 2 ll.12–14; Plut. *Phoc.* 18, Ehrenberg, op. cit., p. 33, Badian, op. cit., p. 59.

22 Ehrenberg, op. cit., p. 34; Arr. *Anab.* VI.27.3–4, VI.29.2, VII.23.6, Badian, op. cit., p. 59 sees Philoxenus' task as specifically to prevent revolution in the cities; Orontes – Diod. XV.91.1, Olmstead, op. cit., pp. 414–21, Cook, 1983, op. cit., p. 221.

23 Badian, op. cit., p. 61; Diod. XIX.61.4; for benefactions, see Ch. 6.

24 Diod. XVIII.18.7, 55.2; Diod. XIX.62.2.

25 *I.Milet.* 123 ll.2–4, E. Meyer, *Die Grenzen der hellenistischen Staaten in Kleinasien*, Leipzig, 1925, pp. 20–1; *RC* 15 ll.34–5; B. D. Meritt, 'Inscriptions of Colophon', *A. J. Phil*, 1935, vol. 56, pp. 358–71; *I.Priene* 1–4(1), 6, 7; F. Hiller, *Inschriften von Priene*, Berlin, 1906, pp. 4–13 sees the 'autonomy' formula ending *c.* 328–7 BC (nos. 4(2), 8), but his reconstruction of the stephanephorate table rests on the uncertain assumption that Alexander personally dedicated the Athena Polias temple in 335–4 BC; Diod. XIX.105.1, *RC* 1, ll.1, 53–6; Diod. XX.45.5, Plut. *Demet.* 8–9, Diod. XX.102.1, A. G. Woodhead, 'Athens and Demetrius Poliorketes at the end of the fourth century B.C.', in H. J. Dell (ed.) *Ancient Macedonian Studies in Honour of Charles F. Edson*, Thessaloniki, Institute for Balkan Studies, 1981, pp. 357–67; Diod. XX.111.2.

26 Ptolemy, Diod. XIX.62.1, XX.37.1–2, *Inschr. Iasos* no. 2; Lysimachus, see pp. 72, 118–19, Seleucus, see Ch. 7; V. Tscherikower, *Die Hellenistischen Stadtegrundungen von Alexander dem Grossen bis auf die Römerzeit*, Leipzig, *Philologus* Supplement 19, 1927 p. 161, Billows, op. cit., pp. 200–5; Wehrli, op. cit., p. 103 for further examples; e.g. *RC* 1 l.44; Saitta, op. cit., pp. 98–9, Simpson, 1959, op. cit., p. 388, Shipley, op. cit., p. 177.

27 Wehrli, op. cit., pp. 99, 126, Bikermann, 1939, op. cit., p. 346; Diod. XVIII.55.2.

28 *RC* 1, l.43; see below for Seibert and Burstein's reassessment of *I.Milet.* 139 ll.5–6, also Wehrli, op. cit., p. 100.

29 e.g. Jones, op. cit., p. 106, Simpson, 1959, op. cit., p. 388.

30 Diod. XIX.74.1–2, 78.2; *Syll*³ 328 honours the Euripus garrison commander in 306/5 BC; Diod. XX.19.3, XX.111.3, Polyaen. IV.7, Diod. XX.107.3, *Inschr. Iasos* 2, pre-305 BC.

31 e.g. Diog. Laert. II.140 – Demetrius accuses the Eretrians of 'plotting with Ptolemy' when they send embassies to Egypt; for the link between democracy and autonomy, Simpson, 1959, op. cit., p. 385, Wehrli, op. cit., p. 129, Bosworth, 1980, op. cit., p. 135; *RC* 3 and 4, Wehrli, op. cit., p. 88; Welles, 1934, op. cit., pp. 26, 29–30, *RC* 3 ll.69–71, 72–88; Strabo XIII.33.

32 Wehrli, op. cit., pp. 151–2, 185–6, 193–9 (see also Ch. 4); Diog. Laert. II.140 – compare Athens' total annual revenue from allied tribute in her imperial heyday (*c.* 400T).

33 Plut. *Demet.* 27, though the source may well be hostile (Duris or his brother Lynceus); see Ch. 4 for the oligarchy; *IG* XII 7, 68, 69, 70, F. Durrbach, *Choix d'inscriptions de Delos*, vol. I, Paris, Ernest Leroux, 1921, p. 27, no. 18, Wehrli, op. cit., pp. 100–1.

34 e.g. Simpson, 1959, op. cit., p. 385; see Ch. 2.

35 As Burstein (1986b, op. cit., p. 20) points out; Arr. *Anab.* I.18.1.
36 Diod. XX.107.2,5, Burstein, 1980, op. cit., p. 74, though Colophon was not, as he suggests, among the cities which resisted in 302 BC; it was 'won over' by Prepelaus (Diod. XX.107.5); the Colophonian resistance of Paus. VII.3.4–5 comes later; Erythrae, *RC* 1934 no.15 ll.34–5.
37 Diod. XX.107.4, *Syll*³ 353 ll.4–5.
38 Simpson, 1959, op. cit., p. 405; Diod. XX.107.5,3; Diod. XX.111.3.
39 Shipley, op. cit., p. 177.
40 e.g. Hdt. V.70–3 (Athens), Thuc. III.71–82 (Corcyra), VIII.21 (Samos), Xen. *Hell.* IV.8.20 (Rhodes); IV.8.29 (Lesbos).
41 Memn. *FGrH* 434 F.4.6; Memn. *FGrH* 434 F.5.3.
42 Memn. *FGrH* 434 F.1.2, S. M. Burstein, *Outpost of Hellenism: The Emergence of Heracleia on the Black Sea*, Berkeley and Los Angeles, University of California Publications, 1976, p. 78.
43 e.g. Xanthippus (see Ch. 6), Olympiodorus (C. Habicht, *Untersuchungen zur politischen Geschichte Athens im 3 Jahrhundert v. Chr.*, Munich, C. H. Beck, 1979, pp. 27–30); *OGIS* 10, L. Robert, 'Sur des inscriptions d'Ephèse', *Rev. Phil*, 1967, vol. 41, no. 4, pp. 37–40.
44 e.g. the Samian tyranny of Kaios and Duris (see pp. 123–5) makes no impact on the epigraphic record, but Demetrius' oligarchy at Athens (294 BC to 287 BC) is reflected in the changed nomenclature of officials; Burstein, 1980, op. cit., p. 76 n. 34.
45 Shipley, op. cit., p. 178.
46 W. Dittenberger, *Orientis Graeci Inscriptiones Selectae*, vol. I, Lipsiae, S. Hirzel, 1903, pp. 332–9, no. 218 = P. Frisch, *Die Inschriften von Ilion*, Bonn, Rudolf Habelt Verlag GMBH, 1975, no. 25 ll.19–131 and p. 72.
47 *OGIS* 221 = *RC* nos. 10–12; A. Bruckner, 'Geschichte von Troja et Ilion', in B. Doerpfeld, *Troja und Ilion*, Athens, Beck & Barth, 1902, pp. 581–2; Dittenberger, op. cit., p. 333; R. Dareste *et al.*, *Recueil des inscriptions juridiques grècques*, Paris, Ernest Leroux, 1898, pp. 25–7; B. Haussoulier, 'Les Séleucides et le temple d'Apollon Didyméen', *Rev. Phil*, 1901, vol. 25, p. 13.
48 See Ch. 7 for Seleucus' tough line when Heracleia Pontica took his promise of independence at face-value; on the city walls, see A. R. Bellinger, *Troy: The Coins*, Princeton, Princeton University Press, 1961, p.5, n. 25, D. Magie, *Roman Rule in Asia Minor*, Princeton, Princeton University Press, 1950, p. 923, n. 16, Liv. XXXVII 37.2; Sigeum, J. M. Cook, *The Troad*, Oxford, Clarendon Press, 1973, p. 179.
49 Stressed by Bellinger, 1961, op. cit., pp. 1–3; Dareste *et al.*, op. cit., pp. 25–7; *OGIS* 219; Priene, see Ch. 4 and pp. 122–3; e.g. Arr. *Anab.* I.17.10, Polyaen. VI.9 (Ephesus); *RC* 2 (Eresus); Bosworth, op. cit., pp. 132–3, 178–9; Haussoulier, 1901, op. cit., p. 13, for Hiero (see pp. 122–3).
50 *Syll*³ 1220 = *IG* XII 3 87; *Inschr. Ilion* 25 ll.120–30.
51 Paus. VII.2.10; *I.Priene* 37 ll.65, 80–1, 123–30; *Syll*³ 363 = *I.Priene* 494 – M. Holleaux' attempt to redate this text to 286 BC ('Ephèse et les Priénians du Charax', *REG*, 1916, vol. 29, pp. 29–45) is not convincing; *I.Priene* 11 and 12.
52 e.g. Will, 1984, op. cit., p. 88, followed by Shipley, op. cit., p. 177.
53 On the basis of Polyaen. V.19; as suggested in Ch. 4; *I.Priene* 37 l.73.

54 As suggested by R. Kebric, *In the Shadow of Macedon: Duris of Samos*, Wiesbaden, *Historia* Einzelschriften no. 29, 1977, p. 8, Burstein, 1986a, op. cit., p. 135.

55 *I.Priene* 37 l.73, Shipley, op. cit., p. 177; H. Berve, *Die Tyrannis bei den Griechen*, vol. I, Munich, C. H. Beck, 1967, p. 423, interpreted the decree as a plea from Hiero, but thought that it received no response; Shipley, op. cit., p. 177 n. 6; Polyaen. V.19, see also Ch. 4; e.g. Roussel, op. cit., p. 353, E. Will, *Histoire politique du monde hellénistique*, vol. I, Nancy, University of Nancy, 1979, p. 88, Bengtson, 1987, op. cit., p. 127.

56 Plut. *Demet.* 36; *I.Priene* 37 ll.77–80; control of the Hellespont and important strategic points like Abydus may have taken priority at this time.

57 For a defence of Duris the historian, see Kebric, op. cit., pp. 20–3, 30–1; Athen. VIII.18 = *FGrH* 76 T2; J. P. Barron, 'The tyranny of Duris at Samos', *CR*, 1962, vol. 12, no. 3, p. 191, Kebric, op. cit., p. 6; J. P. Barron, *The Silver Coins of Samos*, London, Athlone Press, 1966, p. 132, C. Habicht, 'Samische Volks beschlusse der hellenistischen Zeit', *Ath. Mitt.*, 1957, vol. 72, p. 33; Shipley, op. cit., p. 177; Will, 1979, op. cit., pp. 90–2, for this dating.

58 Barron, 1962, op. cit., p. 191, for Kaios and Duris as father and son, see also Kebric, op. cit., p. 8; Paus. VI.13.5, Habicht, 1957, op. cit., no. 23, Barron, 1962, op. cit., pp. 190–2 – he restores the lacuna in Pausanias' text to read, *ton de Kaion [tyrraneusai legousin epanagagonta] epi ta oikeia ton demon*.

59 Shipley, op. cit., p. 179; Kebric, op. cit., pp. 7–8.

60 Shipley, op. cit., p. 179; Habicht, 1957, op. cit., pp. 154–209, assigns thirty-three inscriptions to the Antigonid period; the democratic forms continue to appear in the fifteen(?) assigned to Lysimachus.

61 As Barron suggests (1966, op. cit., p. 136).

62 Shipley, op. cit., p. 173; Habicht, 1957, op. cit., no. 20; Habicht, 1957, op. cit., no. 22, for Samians serving in the royal armies, though they may be mercenaries rather than conscripts; Barron, 1966, op. cit., p. 140, links a large emergency issue of Samian coins with Antigonid operations at Rhodes in 305–4 BC.

63 Burstein, 1980, op. cit., pp. 76–7, Burstein, 1986a, op. cit., p. 138 for a high degree of local autonomy at Miletus and Priene under Lysimachus' rule; Kebric, op. cit., p. 9; even Shipley, op. cit., p. 180, admits that evidence for the unpopularity of this Samian tyranny is lacking.

64 Strabo XIV.21; *Syll*³ 353 = *Inschr. Eph.* no. 1449, *BMI* III no. 470; e.g. by B. V. Head, *On the Chronological Sequence of the Coins at Ephesus*, London and Paris, Rollin & Feuardent, 1880, p. 40, Tscherikower, op. cit., p. 164, C. J. Cadoux, *Ancient Smyrna*, Oxford, Basil Blackwell, 1938, p. 99.

65 Diod. XX.111.3, see pp. 72,76.

66 Antigonus' capture of the city by the fifth column method in 319 BC reflects earlier factional division at Ephesus (Diod. XVIII.52.7); for the Ephesian debt law, see Ch. 4.

67 See p. 120; for Echeanax, see Head, op. cit., p. 41; e.g. W. S. Ferguson, *Hellenistic Athens*, New York, Macmillan & Co., 1911, pp. 125, 136–7,

Habicht, 1979, op. cit., p. 27 for contrasting views on the political stance of the Athenians Olympiodorus and Philippides, son of Philomelos.

68 Strabo XIV.21; see also Paus. VII.3.4–5 for active Colophonian resistance to the project.

69 *Syll*[3] 353; D. Van Berchem, 'La gérousie d'Ephèse', *Mus. Helv.*, 1980, vol. 37, p. 27; J. H. Oliver, *The Sacred Gerousia*, Athens, *Hesperia* Supplement VI, 1941, pp. 15, 19; Van Berchem, 1980, op. cit., p. 29.

70 *Syll*[3] 353, though Oliver, op. cit., p. 19 does suggest that this may be a pure formality; J. Keil, 'Ephesische Burgerrechts- und Proxeniedekrete aus dem vierten und dritten Jahrhundert v. Chr.', *JOAI*, 1913, vol. 16, IIIc; H. Engelmann and D. Knibbe, 'Aus ephesischen Skizzenbuchern', *JOAI*, 1980, vol. 52, p. 19 n. 2, *I.Milet.* 138 1.57.

71 Oliver, op. cit., p. 17; Van Berchem, 1980, op. cit., p. 28, argues that, given Strabo's tendency 'to juxtapose and combine what he finds interesting or characteristic from his sources, without great attention to logic or chronology', the statement 'there was an enrolled council' which follows the account of Lysimachus' foundation need not have any connection with it.

72 Diod. XX.107.4; *RC* 15 = *Inschr. Eryth.* 30; Welles, 1934, op. cit., p. 120 – compare e.g. erasure of Demetrius' name from the Theban building inscription (M. Holleaux, 'Sur une inscription de Thèbes', *REG*, 1895, vol. 8, p. 30), the defacement of Mausolus' statue (*Syll*[3] 167), the recent defacement of Lenin's statues all over the Soviet Union (e.g. *The Economist*, 20 October 1990, p. 3).

73 *Syll*[3] 284 = *Inschr. Eryth.* 503; *Syll*[3] 284 ll.2–6, P. Gauthier, 'Notes sur trois décrets honorant des citoyens bienfaiteurs', *Rev. Phil.*, 1982, vol. 56, no. 1, pp. 215–21; A. J. Heisserer, 'The Philites stele (SIG[3] 284 = IEK 503)', *Hesperia*, 1979, vol. 43, pp. 284, 287–9; neither the letter forms nor the pronounced apices are unparalleled in an early third-century texts (see Welles, 1934, op. cit., pp. li–liii, and S. M. Sherwin-White, 'Ancient archives: the edict of Alexander to Priene, a reappraisal', *JHS*, 1985, vol. 105, p. 73 and Pls. II and III; Heisserer, op. cit., pp. 290–2.

74 *I.Milet.* 139, 138, Andreades, op. cit., pp. 11–12, Shipley, op. cit., p. 176; Plut. *Demet.* 25, *Athen.* VI.246, XIV.614–15, Phylarch. *FGrH* 81 F.65, Plut. *Apophth. Lac.* 233 C.

75 Andreades, op. cit., pp. 6–14.

76 W. W. Tarn, *Antigonus Gonatas*, Oxford, Clarendon Press, 1913, p. 101 – see Ch. 6 for the sort of amounts regularly involved in royal benefactions; Keil, 1913, op. cit., p. 237 no. IIIC, Tarn, 1927, op. cit., p. 91; Meritt, 1935, op. cit., nos. 1 and 2, pp. 358–78; ll.7–11 establish a close link between Antigonus' efforts to emulate Alexander's euergetism, Colophonian safety and the decision to build walls; Meritt, 1935, op. cit., no. 2 ll.31–2; *Inschr. Eryth.* 22.

77 Burstein, 1980, op. cit., pp. 73–9, Burstein, 1984, op. cit., p. 62, Burstein, 1986a, op. cit., p. 133; J. Seibert, 'Ptolemaios I und Milet', *Chiron*, 1971, vol. 1, p. 165.

78 Burstein, 1984, op. cit., p. 62.

79 Phylarch. *FGrH* 81 F.12 = Athen. XIV.3 (slaves at court); F.31 = Athen. VI.66 (*gazophylax*); 65 = Athen. III.3 (salt-tax); see F.6 = Athen. X.51,

F.64 = Athen. II.21, F.20 = Athen. XII.51 for royal drunkenness and luxury; for affinities with Duris, see Kebric, op. cit., p. 10 and Ch. 1; Aristodemus – *FHG* III 307 = *FGrH* 22.

80 Plut. *Mor.* 182D, 531E, 182E; Athen. III.3, Burstein, 1984, op. cit., p. 60; Athen. III. 73; e.g. Ps.-Arist. *Oec.* 1347b, 1350b (Mausolus), Arr. *Succ. FGrH* 156 F.11.45 (Antipater), Xen. *Anab.* VII.1.7 (Anaxibius); Cook, 1983, op. cit., p. 220 for Persian kings as 'notoriously bad pay-masters'.

81 Burstein, 1980, op. cit., p. 75, see also Ch. 6; Andreades, op. cit., p. 14; Plut. *Demet.* 12.

82 e.g. Plut. *Mor.* 180 6,7, *Phoc.* 18, *Alex.* 15; Plut. *Demet.* 51, Diod. XXI.F.12; Plut. *Pyrrh.* 6, Just. XVI.1.5.

83 Plut. *Demet.* 27, P. Briant, 'Dons de terres et de villes: l'Asie Mineure dans le contexte Achéménide', *REA*, 1985, vol. 87, p. 60, sees this as analogous to the Achaemenid practice of designating a city's revenues 'for the queen's shoes' or 'the queen's girdle'; Plut. *Demet.* 39 – Hieronymus' authorship is assured by the apologetic tone and the reference to his own appointment as governor; Diog. Laert. II.140.

84 Namely at Pergamum (Strabo XIII.4), Sardis (Polyaen. IV.9.4) and Tirizis (Strabo VII.6.1); Andreades, op. cit., p. 7, plausibly infers the existence of at least two more, one near Lysimacheia and one in Macedon.

85 Cyinda, see Diod. XVIII.58.1, 62.2, XIX.56.5 and Ch. 4; Susa, Diod. XIX.12.3, 15.5, 48.6; Ecbatana, Diod. XIX. 46.6; Media, Diod. XIX.20.4; Synnada and Hellespontine Phrygia, Diod. XX.107.3–4.

86 e.g. Burstein, 1980, op. cit., p. 74 n. 14; M. Thompson, 'The mints of Lysimachus', in C. Kraay and G. K. Jenkins (eds) *Essays in Greek Coinage Presented to Stanley Robinson*, Oxford, Clarendon Press, 1968, pp. 164–78 – see Ch. 4 for the objections raised by Price to her methods of classifying the Lysimachus coins.

87 A. R. Bellinger, *Essays in the Coinage of Alexander the Great*, New York, American Numismatic Society, 1963, pp. 57–8, for Alexander's mints at Sardis, Magnesia, Lampsacus, Abydus, Colophon, Miletus and Teos; again, the methodology underlying this precise and detailed picture may be suspect (see M. J. Price, *Coins of Alexander the Great*, London, British Museum, forthcoming); E. T. Newell, *The Coinages of Demetrius Poliorcetes*, London, Oxford University Press and Humphrey Milford, 1927, pp. 60–2, 67–70; E. Bikermann, *Institutions des Séleucides*, Paris, Libraire Orientaliste Paul Geuthner, 1938, p. 229.

88 e.g. Bikermann, 1938, op. cit., p. 229, Bellinger, 1963, op. cit., p. 50; for coinage seen primarily as a symbol of autonomy, M. Finley, *The Ancient Economy*, London, Chatto & Windus, 1973, pp. 168–9.

89 Head, op. cit., pp. 31–2, 37, 41–2, Newell, op. cit., p. 70 (Ephesus); Cadoux, op. cit., p. 101, J. G. Milne, 'The autonomous coinage of Smyrna', *Num. Chron.*, 1923, vol. 3 (series 5), p. 3; M. Rostovtzeff, 'Notes on the economic policy of the Pergamene kings', in W. H. Buckler and W. M. Calder (eds) *Anatolian Studies Presented to Sir William Mitchell Ramsay*, Manchester, Manchester University Press, 1923, p. 282 (Priene); W. Leaf, 'Scepsis in the Troad', in Buckler and Calder, op. cit., p. 279 (Scepsis); K. Lehmann, *Samothrace: A Guide to the Excavations and*

the Museum, Locust Valley, NY, J. J. Augustin, 1983, pp. 108–9; J. G. Milne, 'The mint of Kyme in the third century BC', *Num. Chron.*, 1940, vol. 20 (series 5), p. 129; A. R. Bellinger, 'The earliest coins of Ilium', *ANSMN*, vol. 34, 1956, p. 47 and Bellinger, 1961, op. cit., p. 189 (Alexandria Troas).

90 e.g. Shipley, op. cit., p. 176.

91 Newell, op. cit., p. 70; Bikermann, 1938, op. cit., p. 230.

92 T. R. Martin, *Sovereignty and Coinage in Classical Greece*, Princeton, Princeton University Press, 1985, e.g. pp. 11, 214–16 – the link between sovereignty and coinage originates in medieval political philosophy; ibid., pp. 6, 13, 48, 57.

93 ibid., pp. 128–9, 221, 246.

94 ibid., pp. 233–4; see Ch. 6 and pp. 110, 116–17.

95 Rostovtzeff, 1923, op. cit., pp. 359–90; H. Seyrig, 'Monnaies hellénistiques de Byzance et Calcédoine', in Kraay and Jenkins, op. cit., pp. 184–5, 187–90; for the continued circulation of posthumous Lysimachi in the Roman period, see F. W. Walbank, 'Sources for the period', in A. E. Astin *et al.* (eds) *Cambridge Ancient History*, vol. VII, 2nd edn, Cambridge, Cambridge University Press, 1984, pp. 18–19.

96 Bikermann, 1938, op. cit., p. 152; Arr. *Anab.* I.17.10.

97 e.g. Keil, 1913, op. cit., I. f, l, m, and n, Engelmann and Knibbe, op. cit., no. 2, *Syll*³ 372 l.3; *Syll*³ 353, Robert, 1967, op. cit., no. 4, Keil, 1913, op. cit., III c and e; Oliver, op. cit., p. 14.

98 Oliver, op. cit., pp. 14–15, 17; see pp. 125–6.

99 T. R. S. Broughton, 'New evidence on temple-estates in Asia Minor', in P. R. Coleman-Norton (ed.) *Studies in Roman Economic and Social History*, Princeton, Princeton University Press, 1951, pp. 236–40, for Attalid and Bithynian kings as benefactors rather than predators at Aezani's temple of Zeus; e.g. Phocis' occupation of Delphi from 356 BC to 346 BC (see G. Cawkwell, *Philip of Macedon*, London, Faber & Faber, 1978, pp. 64–6, 103, 107–8, 110), Lachares at Athens *c.* 296–5 BC, (Paus. 1. 25.7–8 and Ch. 4).

100 For royal *eusebeia*, see Ch. 6; Rostovtzeff, 1923, op. cit., pp. 385–9, compare 2 Maccabees 3.4–40 for priestly corruption at Jerusalem in the reign of Antiochus IV; as Oliver himself admits (op. cit., p. 13), Burstein, 1980, op. cit., p. 7.

101 *RC* no. 9; *I.Didyma.* 479, 480, Orth, op. cit., pp. 20–3.

102 *OGIS* 214, *I.Milet* 123 l.29; *Syll*³ 368; Burstein, 1980, op. cit., p. 74 n. 3 for bibliography.

103 Welles, 1934, op. cit., p. 37, Orth, op. cit., p. 29; Plut. *Demet.* 48, 51, for clear hostility between Seleucus and Lysimachus by 286 BC; Plut. *Demet.* 46.

104 Burstein, 1980, op. cit., p. 77; *OGIS* 214 ll.19–20, Orth, op. cit., p. 30; Welles, 1934, op. cit., p. 38; E. Abbott and E. D. Mansfield, *A Primer of Greek Grammar*, London, Rivingtons, 1971, §2, pp. 5, 26–7, § 19, 101 v. and 105 for participles used adverbially to express cause.

105 Y. Garlan, *War in the Ancient World*, London, Chatto & Windus, 1975, p. 64, *I.Priene* 14 l.10, *OGIS* 219 ll.17, 20–3.

106 *OGIS* 23, P. M. Fraser, *The Inscriptions on Stone*, vol. II of K. Lehmann

(ed.) *Samothrace*, New York, Pantheon Books, 1960, p. 6; R. S. Bagnall, *The Administration of the Ptolemaic Possessions outside Egypt*, Leiden, E. J. Brill, 1976, p. 103; Allen, op. cit., p. 17.

107 For royal *eusebeia* and discussion of Greek attitudes to religion in this period, see Ch. 6.

108 App. *Syr.* 61, Plut. *Mor.* 330E; Badian, op. cit., p. 39, Allen, op. cit., p. 175; *RC* 67 l.16.

109 See p. 117; *RC* 2; *OGIS* 7 ll.1–2, Athen. XV.697D, though the exact function of this Seleucid judge is uncertain; Bikermann, 1938, op. cit., p. 207.

110 The king himself seemingly judged only the most important cases, such as those involving high treason (Bikermann, 1938, op. cit., p. 186); Polyaen. VI.49, Paus. II.37.4, Plut. *Phoc.* 18, Ael. *V. H.* I.25; L. Missitzis, 'A royal decree of Alexander the Great on the lands of Philippi', *Ancient World*, 1985, vol. 12, no.1, pp. 3–14, Allen, op. cit., pp. 18, 103–4, *RC* 53 ll.6–8 = *I.Perg.* no. 63; Burstein, 1986b, op. cit., p. 136, see also pp. 150–1.

111 J. R. McCredie, 'Samothrace: preliminary campaigns of 1965–7', *Hesperia*, 1968, vol. 37, pp. 220–1 ll.10–11; *I.Priene* 16, see Ch. 4 and pp. 150–1; *Syll*³ 372 ll.15–16.

112 *RC* 7, see also Ch. 7; Burstein, 1986a, op. cit., p. 137.

113 Plut. *Demet.* 42, *Mor.* 179C.

114 e.g. Saitta, op. cit., p. 99, J. D. Grainger, *Seleukos Nikator*, London and New York, Routledge, 1990, p. 161; see pp. 116–18.

115 H. Bengtson, *Die Strategie in der Hellenistischen Zeit*, vol. II, Munich, C. H. Beck, 1937, pp. 198–207, Diod. XX.19.2, 107.4, 5.

116 *RC* 10 ll.1–6, 9–10, *RC* 11 ll.1, 6–7, 9–12, 19–20, *RC* 12 ll.1, 7–8, 15–20; *OGIS* 220 = *Inschr. Ilion* 34; *Syll*³ 502, P. Roussel, 'La Perée Samothracienne au IIIᵉ siècle avant J.-C.', *BCH*, 1939, vol. 63, pp. 135–40, Fraser, op. cit., p. 8; M. Holleaux, 'Inscription trouvée à Brousse', *BCH*, 1924, vol. 48, pp. 1–57, Allen, op. cit., p. 88–9, 100; *Inschr. Eph.* 201; App. *Syr.* 55; Bikermann, 1938, op. cit., p. 201; Habicht, 1957, op. cit., no. 57, F. J. Frost, 'Ptolemy II and Halicarnassus: an honorary decree', *Anatolian Studies*, 1971, vol. 21, p. 171, Bagnall, op. cit., p. 90.

117 Bikermann, 1938, op. cit., p. 207.

118 *Syll*³ 368, for the Ionian *koinon* see Caspari, op. cit., p. 173–87; *SEG*, 1985, no. 926, W. G. Forrest, 'Some inscriptions of Chios', *Horos*, 1985, vol. 3, p. 95.

119 Bengtson, 1937, op. cit., p. 191, for the direct genitive or *epi* as designating the *strategos* as governor, while *en* signifies a military post; e.g. E. Meyer, *Die Grenzen der hellenistischen Staaten in Kleinasien*, Leipzig, 1925, p. 36, Tarn, 1927, op. cit., p. 91, Roussel, op. cit., p. 368.

120 Bengtson, 1937, op. cit., pp. 215–16, sees Hippostratus' appointment as inspired by that of Philoxenus; Plut. *Alex.* 22; Saitta, op. cit., pp. 98–9.

121 *Syll*³ 368 ll.7–8,19; §2 l.2; Bengtson, 1937, op. cit., p. 216; Bengtson, 1937, op. cit., p. 208; e.g. S. Hornblower, op. cit., p. 142, Frye, op. cit., p. 99 for Achaemenid debts to Lydia and Assyria, see also Ch. 6; Robert, 1945, op. cit., p. 161, S. Hornblower, op. cit., pp. 64 n. 90, 319–20, 368, R. Merkelbach, 'Ein Zeugnis aus Tralles über Pleistarchus', *ZPE*, 1975, vol. 16, p. 163, *Inschr. Tralles* no. 34.

122 Bengtson, 1937, op. cit., p. 215; I. L. Merker, 'The Ptolemaic officials and the League of Islanders', *Historia*, 1970, vol. 19, p. 152; for judicial and financial intervention, see *IG* XII 7, Durrbach, op. cit., no. 18; *IG* IV² 68.ll.21–2, Cawkwell, op. cit., pp. 170–1, L. Robert, 'Adeimantos et la Ligue de Corinthe', in *Hellenica*, vol. I, Limoges, Imprimerie A. Bontemps, 1940, pp. 22–8.

123 Diod. XVIII.51–2, XIX.62.2–3.

124 See above; suggested by Caspari, op. cit., p. 184; *OGIS* 9, Habicht, 1957, op. cit., no. 22; *I.Priene* 14, 15, 37, *RC* no. 7.

125 Hippodamus also receives *ateleia*, but the fragmentation of the text leaves it unclear as to whether he gets identical honours to Hippostratus; *Syll³* 368 ll.1–8, 12–15; Burstein, 1986b, op. cit., p. 20, Burstein, 1986b, op. cit., p. 137.

126 Bengtson, 1937, op. cit., p. 217.

127 ibid., pp. 210–14, 216; ibid., p. 211; for Alcimachus, see Arr. *Anab.* I.18.1, Bosworth, 1980, op. cit., p. 134, Badian, op. cit., p. 58.

128 Bengtson, 1937, op. cit., p. 223, *I.Priene* 15 ll.11–12; *I.Priene* 15 l.6 – Lysimachus corrects Priene's omission of his *philoi* from their congratulations (*I.Priene* 14 l.10).

129 *Syll³* 368 ll.1–8;

130 Pomp. Trog. *Prol. Lib.* 16, Geyer, *PW* XIV₁ 1928, col. 16.

131 For the extent of royal land, Bikermann, 1938, op. cit., p. 169; Xen. *Cyrop.* IV.4.5; R. T. Hallock, *Persepolis Fortification Tablets*, Chicago, Chicago University Press, 1969, p. 37, Briant, 1982, op. cit., pp. 479–80; see Ch. 4 for a brief survey of industrial activity in the *poleis* of western Asia Minor; e.g. *RC* 3 ll.83–4, Briant, 1982, op. cit., p. 476; Bikermann, 1938, op. cit., p. 169, Rostovtzeff, 1923, op. cit., p. 376.

132 *I.Priene* 15 ll.13–14, *I.Priene* 16 = *RC* 8 ll.11–14; Plut. *Phoc.* 29. See Sherwin-White, 1987, op. cit., pp. 5–6; S. Hornblower, op. cit., p. 142; Cook, 1973, op. cit., p. 367, Briant, 1982, op. cit., p. 104, 151–5; Bikermann, 1938, op. cit., p. 116.

133 P. Briant, 'Pouvoir central et polycentrisme culturel dans l'empire achéménide: quelques reflexions et suggestions', in H. Sancisi-Weerdenberg (ed.) *Achaemenid History I*, Leiden, Nederlands Instituut voor Het Nabije Oosten, 1987, p. 13, Briant, 1982, op. cit., pp. 103–4, 150, 467; the Mnesimachus inscription (W. H. Buckler and D. M. Robinson, *Sardis*, vol. VII, Leyden, E. J. 1932, no. I.I) shows villages, *kleroi, laoi* and slaves coexisting on one estate; Briant, 1987, op. cit., p. 14, A. K. Grayson, *Assyrian and Babylonian Chronicles*, Locust Valley, NY, J. J. Augustin, 1975, pp. 277–8, Chron. 13b for Seleucid offerings to Babylon's Esagila sanctuary, see also Ch. 6; Briant, 1987, op. cit., pp. 1–31 for central power and local autonomy as complementary rather than mutually exclusive; Sherwin-White, 1987, op. cit., pp. 6–7, for non-Greeks in high military and administrative positions under Seleucid rule.

134 *RC* 10–12, Cook, 1973, op. cit., pp. 365–7; Rostovtzeff, 1923, op. cit., p. 368; *OGIS* 335 l.134; *RC* 18 l.3; *OGIS* 748, Rostovtzeff, 1923, op. cit., p. 363; Plut. *Phoc.* 29, Briant, 1982, op. cit., p. 105; *RC* 3 ll.83–4; *I.Priene* 16 = *RC* no. 8, Burstein, 1986a, op. cit., p. 137.

135 *RC* 10–12, Buckler and Robinson, 1932, op. cit., no. I.I, *RC* 18; *OGIS* 335 ll.134–5.

136 Briant, 1982, op. cit., p. 106; though M. B. Hatzopoulos, 'Une donation du Roi Lysimaque', *ΜΕΛΗΘΗΜΑΤΑ*, Paris, De Boccard, 1988, pp. 31, 34–5 disputes this, citing land grants by Cassander and Lysimachus in Macedonia which are *em patrikois* (granted to the recipient and his descendants), this phrase does not invariably appear in land grant texts (e.g. *RC* 10–12); Briant, 1985, op. cit., pp. 63–4, makes the point that while royal 'gifts' of land *could* be transmitted from generation to generation, as long as the family remained loyal to the ruling dynasty, the king retained the right to revoke his 'gift' at any time; *RC* 18. ll.27–8, Briant, 1982, op. cit., p. 102; Bikermann, 1938, op. cit., p. 209, for other Seleucid archives at Uruk and Seleuceia-on-Tigris.

137 M. Rostovtzeff, *The Social and Economic History of the Hellenistic World*, 2 vols, Oxford, Clarendon Press, 1941, pp. 507–8, 1,185–6, 1,195–7, see Briant, 1982, op. cit., pp. 98–9 for full bibliography; Bikermann, 1938, op. cit., pp. 177–9; Briant, 1982, op. cit., pp. 103–7, 116–18, 155, Briant, 1985, op. cit., pp. 53–72.

138 W. H. Buckler and D. M. Robinson, 'Greek inscriptions from Sardis', *AJA*, 1912, vol. 16 (2nd series), pp. 11–82, Buckler and Robinson, 1932, op. cit., no. I.I; W. E. Mierse in G. M. A. Hanfmann and W. E. Mierse, *Sardis from Prehistoric to Roman Times*, Cambridge, Mass., and London, Harvard University Press, 1983, p. 125 dates its *inscription* to *c.* 250 BC, though since 'Antigonus' is named as donor, the *grant* may pre-date 305 BC (Déscat, 1985, op. cit., p. 97); Briant, 1982, op. cit., p. 104.

139 H. Malay, 'A royal document from Aigai in Aeolis', *GRBS*, 1983, vol. 24, pp. 349–52, §A.ll.1–9, 12–16, 16–18; Briant, 1982, op. cit., p. 102, Xen. *Anab.* III.2.1, V.2.2, V.5.6 for the unpopularity of billeting.

140 Malay, op. cit., p. 352; e.g. *RC* no. 20 l.6, Bikermann, 1938, op. cit., p. 129, *SEG* 1925 no. 580, Allen, op. cit., p. 54; the general conclusions of R. P. Austin, *The Stoichedon Style in Greek Inscriptions*, Oxford, Oxford University Press, 1938, p. 124, suggest that the stoichedon style is increasingly rare in the third century BC.

141 *RC* 11. ll.23–5; Malay, op. cit., pp. 349–52; *I.Priene* 3.

142 *I.Priene* 14 ll.5–6, 15 ll.13–14, 16 = *RC* 8 ll.1–9, 11–16, Sherwin-White, 1985, op. cit., pp. 77, 79–80.

143 Welles, 1934, op. cit., pp. 52–3; W. G. Forrest, *A History of Sparta*, 2nd edn, London, Duckworth, 1980, pp. 30–1; Welles, 1934, op. cit., p. 53, Burstein, 1986a, op. cit., p. 136 and n. 24.

144 Sherwin-White, 1985, op. cit., p. 79 n. 79 following Hiller, op. cit., *I.Priene* 16 pp. 22–3.

145 Sherwin-White, 1985, op. cit., pp. 79, 82; ibid., 81–2, for the 'Alexander edict' as a section of a longer decree, published contemporaneously with the texts below as part of an archive.

146 As Burstein supposes (1986b, op. cit., p. 136).

147 Plut. *Phoc.* 29; S. Mitchell, 'Requisitioned transport in the Roman empire: a new inscription from Pisidia', *JRS*, 1976, vol. 66, p. 129; Grayson, op. cit., Chron. 10 Rev. 39 for 'weeping and lamentation' in Babylonia under the impact of Antigonus' army; Xen. *Anab.* III.2.1,

V.2.2, V.5.6. for the unpopularity of scavenging armies; Briant, 1982, op. cit., p. 143; Briant, 1982, op. cit., p. 116.

6 KINGSHIP, CULT AND COURT

1 D. Cannadine, 'Introduction: divine rites of kings', in D. Cannadine and S. R. F. Price (eds) *Rituals of Royalty*, Cambridge, Cambridge University Press, 1987, p. 19.

2 ibid., pp. 3, 6; S. R. F. Price, *Rituals and Power*, Cambridge, Cambridge University Press, 1984, pp. 7-8, 29, R. R. R. Smith, *Hellenistic Royal Portraits*, Oxford, Clarendon Press, 1988, p. 19.

3 A. T. L. Kuhrt, 'Usurpation, conquest and ceremonial: from Babylon to Persia' in Cannadine and Price, op. cit., 1987b, p. 43 for the frequent emphasis in history on tradition and stability in unstable times.

4 e.g. by A. Aymard, 'Le protocole royal grec et son évolution', *REA*, 1948, vol. 61, p. 232, who saw the Macedonian monarchic revival as coinciding with a favourable climate of opinion in the Greek *poleis*; for a more realistic view, see E. Will, *Le Monde grec et l'orient*, vol. II, Paris, Presses Universitaires de France, 1975, p. 422; for continuity in kingship ritual see A. T. L. Kuhrt, 'Berossus' *Babyloniaka* and Seleucid Rule in Babylonia', in A. T. L. Kuhrt and S. M. Sherwin-White (eds) *Hellenism in the East*, London, Duckworth, 1987a, pp. 49-50, and Kuhrt 1987b, op. cit., pp. 39, 48-50, A. T. L. Kuhrt and S. M. Sherwin-White, 'Aspects of Seleucid royal ideology: the cylinder of Antiochus I from Borsippa', *JHS*, 1991, vol. 111, pp. 71-87.

5 Euhemerus = Diod. VI.1.1-11; Hecataeus = Diod. I.46.8, 47.1-49.3, 53. 1-58.3, O. Murray, 'Hecataeus of Abdera and Pharaonic kingship', *JEA*, 1970, vol. 12, pp. 141-71; Kuhrt, 1987a, op. cit., pp. 53-5, for Berossus as a Seleucid protégé.

6 R. M. Errington, 'From Babylon to Triparadeisos', *JHS*, 1970, vol. 90, p. 57; J. Goody, *Succession to High Office*, Cambridge, Cambridge University Press, 1966, pp. 10-12; the choice of gun-men and sword-bearers as stakeholders among the African Ashanti may suggest a parallel with the role taken here by Alexander's Bodyguards.

7 J. Hornblower, *Hieronymus of Cardia*, Oxford, Oxford University Press, 1981, p. 103, dates the composition of Hieronymus' history to the 270s BC; M. M. Austin, 'Hellenistic kings, war and the economy', *CQ*, 1986, vol. 36, (New Series) pp. 451-8.

8 Arr. *Succ. FGrH* 156 F.178; Q.C. X.5.4, Diod. XVIII.23.1-3, G. M. Cohen, 'The Diadochs and the new monarchies', *Athenaeum*, 1974, vol. 52, p. 178; Diod. XIX.52.1.

9 Diod. XVIII.75.2; Diod. XVIII.14.2, 33.3-5.

10 Diod. XIX.48.1, Plut. *Demet.* 18; H. W. Ritter, *Diadem und Königsherrschaft*, Munich, C. H. Beck, 1965, p. 127, though seemingly not in Babylon, where regnal dating on astronomical texts continues in the name of Alexander IV, with Seleucus described as 'General' and first called King in 305-4 BC (A. J. Sachs and H. Hunger, *Astronomical Diaries and Related Texts from Babylonia*, vol. I, Vienna, Osterreichische

Akademie der Wissenschaften, 1988, pp. 230–1 no.-309 obv. l.14, pp. 232–3 no.-308 ll.1,17).

11 Diod. XX.37.4; Diod. XIX.57.1; Ritter, op. cit., p. 106, see also Ch. 3; see Ch. 1 and pp. 159–61, Plut. *Demet.* 44.

12 Diod. XIX.53.4, 105.2, 3–4; Plut. *Demet.* 18.1; *I.Priene* 14 l.10, 15 ll.6–7, *OGIS* 219 ll.9–10.

13 Plut. *Demet.* 18.2–3, App. *Syr.* 34, *FGrH* 155 F.6, H. Hauben, 'A royal toast in 302 B.C.', *Ancient Society*, 1974, vol. 5, pp. 105–6; A. J. Sachs and D. J. Wiseman, 'A Babylonian king list of the Hellenistic period', *Iraq*, 1954, vol. 16, pp. 202–11; Ritter, op. cit., p. 106, sees Cassander and Lysimachus as kings by the time they were honoured at Rhodes in summer 304 BC; Goody, op. cit., p. 12, for royal regalia's legitimising power.

14 Aymard, op. cit., pp. 232–43; for Alexander's measures to create an impression of continuity with Achaemenid rule, see Plut. *Alex.* 69, H. R. Baldus, 'Die Siegel Alexanders des Grossen. Versuch einer Rekonstruktion auf literarischer und numismatischer Grundlage', *Chiron*, 1987, vol. 17, pp. 396–7, see also S. M. Sherwin-White, 'Seleucid Babylonia: a case-study for the installation and development of Greek rule', in Kuhrt and Sherwin-White, 1987, op. cit., p. 9.

15 Ritter, op. cit., pp. 125–6: E. A. Fredericksmeyer, 'Alexander the Great and the Macedonian *kausia*', *TAPhA*, 1986, vol. 116, pp. 215–27, for Alexander's Macedonian/Persian royal dress, though his conclusion that 'the Macedonian-Greek component prevailed' seems misconceived; Aristob. *FGrH* 49 F.55, App. *Syr.* 64.

16 e.g. Ritter, op. cit., pp. 125–6, Aymard, op. cit., pp. 252–3, Hauben, op. cit., p. 106.

17 See Ch. 3; Plut. *Demet.* 25.4 = Phylarch. *FGrH* 81 F.31, Athen. VI.261B, Hauben, op. cit., pp. 105–17; App. *Syr.* 34, *Heid. Epit. FGrH* 155 F.6, Diod. XX.53.2, Plut. *Demet.* 18.37, Aymard, op. cit., p. 255 on the royal title in documentation.

18 Ritter, op. cit., p. 106.

19 See Kuhrt, 1987b, op. cit., p. 24; R. Burghart, 'Gifts to the gods: power, property and ceremonial in Nepal', in Cannadine and Price, 1987, op. cit., p. 247 for the fortified capital as one of the seven 'limbs of state' in nineteenth-century Nepal; Kuhrt, 1987b, op. cit., p. 29, M. C. Root, *The King and Kingship in Achaemenid Art*, Leiden, *Acta Iranica* vol. 19, 1979, pp. 303–8 for this idea expressed visually with the Achaemenid motif of royal hero versus wild beast at Persepolis; Isoc. *Ad. Nic.* 9, Murray, op. cit., p. 156, Burghart, op. cit., pp. 242–3, 255, 261, 265.

20 Kuhrt, 1987b, op. cit., pp. 41–3, 50, Root, op. cit., pp. 73, 169–70.

21 Isoc. *Nic.* 27; Kuhrt, 1987a, op. cit., pp. 43, 48–9; Sherwin-White, 1987, op. cit., pp. 10–11, for the Seleucids as the 'good successors' to the Achaemenids after a 'bad' period of war and chaos (Alexander's conquest and the early Diadoch wars) in the Babylonian 'Dynastic Prophecy'.

22 W. W. Tarn, 'Two notes on Ptolemaic history', *JHS*, 1933, vol. 52, pp. 57–9, C. F. Edson, Jr, 'The Antigonids, Heracles and Beroea', *HSCP*, 1934, vol. 45, p. 224; W. W. Tarn, 'Queen Ptolemais and Apama', *CQ*, 1929, vol. 23, p. 139, Sherwin-White, 1987, op. cit., pp. 7–8.

23 M. P. Nilsson, *Cults, Myths, Oracles and Politics in Ancient Greece*, Lund, C. W. K. Gleerup, 1951, pp. 101–4, O. Palagia, 'Imitation of Heracles in ruler portraiture: a survey from Alexander to Maximinus Daza', *Boreas*, 1986, vol. 9, p. 140; Theoc. *Id.* 17 I.26, Nilsson, op. cit., p. 109; Edson, op. cit., pp. 214, 217–18, 221.

24 See Ch. 1; P. Goukowsky, *Essai sur les origines du mythe d'Alexandre*, Nancy, University of Nancy, 1978, p. 118; E. T. Newell, *The Coinages of Demetrius Poliorcetes*, London, Oxford University Press and Humphrey Milford, 1927, p. 168, cites Demetrius' replacement of Alexander's coin types with his own *c.* 292 BC as typically arrogant; Plut. *Demet.* 41–2, 44, *Pyrrh.* 12; apart from the Hydaspes crossing episode (Arr. *Anab.* V.13.1 and Ch. 1), there is only the diadem story mentioned above (Aristob. *FGrH* 49 F.55).

25 See Ch. 1; Isoc. *Ad Phil.* 110; App. *Syr.* 57, Edson, op. cit., p. 214 for wild bulls slain by Seleucus and Philip V, Ch. 1 for the lion-slaying exploits of Perdiccas and Craterus; J. J. Pollitt, *Art in the Hellenistic Age*, Cambridge, Cambridge University Press, 1986, pp. 38–42, see also the Alexander and Satrap sarcophagi from Sidon (Istanbul Museum, Cat. nos. 368, 367); see n. 19.

26 H. R. Baldus, 'Zum Siegel des Königs Lysimachos von Thrakien', *Chiron*, 1978, vol. 8, pp. 191, 196–8; G. F. Hill, 'Some coins of southern Asia Minor', in W. H. Buckler and W. M. Calder (eds) *Anatolian Studies Presented to Sir William Mitchell Ramsay*, Manchester, Manchester University Press, 1923, §3, p. 211–12; Baldus, 1987, op. cit., pp. 402–6; Memn. *FGrH* 434 F.8.5; B. Killerich, 'Physiognomics and the iconography of Alexander', *Symbolae Osloenses*, 1988, vol. 43, pp. 56–7, for Alexander as lion-like.

27 E. Atalay and S. Turkoglu, 'Ein fruhhellenistischer Portratkopf des Lysimachos aus Ephesos', *JOAI*, 1972–5, vol. 50, pp. 124–49; for Scopas' style, see A. F. Stewart, *Skopas of Paros*, New Jersey, Noyes Press, 1977, pp. 71, 107, 114, 121.

28 For Lysimachus' cult at Ephesus and his stance on personal portrait coins, see pp. 173; 162, 164; Killerich, op. cit., p. 57; for fuller discussion, see H. S. Lund, 'Bridging the Hellespont: the Successor Lysimachus – a study in early Hellenistic kingship', University of London Ph.D. thesis, Senate House Library, 1992, pp. 334–7.

29 Diod. XIX.90.4, R. Hadley, 'Hieronymus of Cardia and early Seleucid mythology', *Historia*, 1969, vol. 18, pp. 142–3, 152; H. W. Parke, *The Oracles of Apollo in Asia Minor*, London, Croom Helm, 1985, p. 46; N. Davis and C. Kraay, *The Hellenistic Kingdoms: Portrait Coins and History*, London, Thames & Hudson, 1973, p. 270; Just. XV.4.3; *OGIS* 219 I.23–7; Newell, 1927, op. cit., pp. 29, 38, 58, 71.

30 Palagia, op. cit., pp. 140–1 and n. 37; R. Hadley, 'Seleucus, Dionysus or Alexander?', *Num. Chron.*, 1974b, vol. 14 (series 7), p. 11; R. R. R. Smith, op. cit., p. 13, see also p. 164.

31 e.g. Hadley, 1974b, op. cit., p. 12; R. R. R. Smith, op. cit., p. 13.

32 C. M. Kraay, 'Greek coinage and war', in W. H. Heckel and R. Sullivan (eds) *Ancient Coins of the Graeco-Roman World*, Waterloo, Ont., Wilfred Laurier University Press, 1984, pp. 3–18, R. R. R. Smith, op. cit.,

p. 14; Diod. XIX.43.7–9, XX.75.1–3, XX.113.2; R. Hadley, 'Royal propaganda of Seleucus I and Lysimachus', *JHS*, 1974a, vol. 94, pp. 50–65, O. H. Zervos, 'Debate: on "The earliest coins of Alexander the Great" ', *Num. Chron.*, 1982, vol. 142, pp. 173–4.

33 e.g. L. Morawiecki, *Political Propaganda in the Coinage of the Late Roman Republic*, Wroclaw, Zaklad Narodowy im Ossolinskich, 1983, passim, M. H. Crawford, 'Roman imperial coin types and the formation of public opinion' in C. N. L. Brooke *et al.* (eds) *Studies in Numismatic Method Presented to Philip Grierson*, Cambridge, Cambridge University Press, 1983, p. 51, for Brutus' 'Liberator' coins as 'perhaps the most dramatic coin types of antiquity'; Crawford, op. cit., pp. 47–64.

34 As suggested by M. Thompson, 'The mints of Lysimachus', in C. M. Kraay and G. K. Jenkins, *Essays in Greek Coinage Presented to Stanley Robinson*, Oxford, Clarendon Press, 1968, p. 165; Edson, op. cit., p. 224; App. *Syr.* 64.

35 Thompson, op. cit., p. 165; see also B. R. Brown, 'Styles in the Alexander portraits on the coins of Lysimachus', in L. Casson and M. J. Price (eds) *Coins, Culture and History*, Detroit, Wayne State University, 1981, pp. 17–27; H. Seyrig, 'Monnaies hellénistique de Byzance et Calcédoine', in Kraay and Jenkins, op. cit., pp. 183–200; C. Seltman, *Greek Coins*, London, Methuen, 1955, p. 219; Plut. *De Fort. Alex.* 331; Plut. *Demet.* 41, *Pyrrh.* 8 and Pollitt, op. cit., pp. 33–7 for the Lysippan Alexander's influence on later ruler portraits; Pollitt, op. cit., p. 25.

36 Hadley, 1974a, op. cit., pp. 56–7, Plut. *Demet.* 29; Seltman, op. cit., p. 219.

37 Hadley, 1974b, op. cit., pp. 10–13.

38 M. J. Price, *Coins of the Macedonians*, London, British Museum, 1974, pp. 26–7; Strabo XIII.1.26 for Alexander's promise of games and the sanctuary's embellishment; *Syll*³ 330 for the benefactions of Antigonus' friend and envoy Gargareus the Malusian.

39 e.g. Thompson, op. cit., p. 165, R. R. R. Smith, op. cit., p. 13; O. Brendel, 'Ein Bildnis des Königs Lysimachos', *Die Antike*, 1928, pp. 314–16, G. M. A. Richter, *The Portraits of the Greeks*, vol. III, London, Phaidon Press, 1965, Fig. 1755.

40 Davis and Kraay, op. cit., p. 274, for royal coin legends promoting distinction, divinity, justice, piety, military prowess, ideal family relations; Paus. I.9.4., Diod. XX.100.3–4; *OGIS* I. l.11, Richter, op. cit., p. 257.

41 R. R. R. Smith, op. cit., pp. 1, 9, 15, 17, 21–2.

42 See pp. 158, 166–7; Kuhrt, 1987b, op. cit., pp. 24, 53, for kings in Babylon and India as providers/protectors of vital resources (rain, water and women!).

43 Euhemerus = Diod. VI.1.2; see p. 158, n.19, also A. T. L. Kuhrt, 'The Achaemenid empire: a Babylonian perspective', *PCPS*, 1988, vol. 14, p. 62; Hom. *Od.* VIII.389–93; Aristot. *Pol.* 3.1286b 11, V.1310b 35, 1311a 22; for Alexander, see Ch. 5; Murray, op. cit., p. 161.

44 Diod. XX.96.1–3, 100.2–3; see pp. 68, 100–1, 168; e.g. *I.Milet.* 139 ll.5–6, Kuhrt, 1988, op. cit., pp. 63–4 for Cyrus blackening Nabonidus' reputation.

45 P. Gauthier, *Les Cités grecques et leurs bienfaiteurs*, Paris, *BCH* Supplement XII, 1985, p. 42, for the Diadochs as rival benefactors in an imaginary 'cosmopolis', for examples see Ch. 5; Diod. XIX. 53.2, see p. 167; S. R. F. Price, op. cit., pp. 39–40, R. R. R. Smith, op. cit., p. 18; Gauthier, op. cit., p. 48.

46 Hom. *Il.* XVI.2, XXII.277; A. K. Grayson, *Assyrian and Babylonian Chronicles*, Locust Valley, NY, J. J. Augustin, 1975, p. 26, Chron. 10 Rev. ll.39–40; e.g. Plut. *Demet.* 8; J. J. Gabbert, 'Piracy in the early Hellenistic period: a career open to talents', *Greece and Rome*, 1986, vol. 33, pp. 156–63, P. McKechnie, *Outsiders in the Greek Cities in the Fourth Century B.C.*, London and New York, Routledge, 1989, pp. 101–41; for Lysimachus as *soter*, see pp. 167–8.

47 e.g. *Syll*³ 206; Diod. XX.25.1–2; Gauthier, op. cit., pp. 38–42, 49; Diod. XX.96.1–3, 100.2–3; for hardship, e.g. Plut. *Demet.* 34, Diod. XIX.49. 2–4; R. R. R. Smith, op. cit., pp. 15, 17; see pp. 169–71.

48 Diod. XX.100.2–3; *Syll*³ 374 ll.10–13, 15–16, Plut. *Mor.* 851e–f, see p. 181 for Bithys and the new Limnaeus inscription from Cassandreia, *IG* II² 1458a, Paus. I.9.4; Strabo XIII.1.26, A. R. Bellinger, *Troy: The Coins*, Princeton, Princeton University Press, 1961, pp. 15–16; *Syll*³ 372 ll.2–17, *OGIS* 15 (P. M. Fraser, *The Inscriptions on Stone*, vol. II of K. Lehmann, *Samothrace*, New York, Pantheon Books, 1960, p. 10, for the Arsinoeion's dedication while Arsinoe was queen of Thrace), J. R. McCredie, 'Samothrace: preliminary campaigns of 1965–7', *Hesperia*, 1968, vol. 37, pp. 220–1; *I.Priene* 14 ll.5–8, 15 ll.10–15, 16 ll.12–15, C. B. Welles, *Royal Correspondence in the Hellenistic Period*, New Haven, Yale University Press, 1934, pp. 43–4, *I.Priene* 15 ll.19–20, S. M. Sherwin-White, 'Ancient archives: the edict of Alexander to Priene, a reappraisal', *JHS*, 1985, vol. 105, pp. 77–8; *Syll*³ 381; *Syll*³ 337, M. Holleaux, 'Sur une inscription de Thèbes', *REG*, 1895, vol. 8, pp. 14–15.

49 Diod. XX.96.3 – Ptolemy, 300,000 medimnoi, Cassander, 10,000 medimnoi, Lysimachus, 80,000 medimnoi – Ptolemy gave another 300,000 medimnoi and promised as much again but simultaneously urged peace (Diod. XX.98.1, 99.2); Plut. *Mor.* 851e–f – Athens gets 130T from Lysimachus, 50T from Ptolemy; Gauthier, op. cit., p. 45; Diod. XX.100.3, Plut. *Demet.* 10, 12, *OGIS* 212 ll.5–25.

50 See Ch. 5; Plut. *Demet.* 25 = Athen. VI.246; Hauben, op. cit., pp. 106–15; J. D. Grainger, *Seleukos Nikator*, London and New York, Routledge, 1990, pp.107–8, sees Chandragupta as 'the clear winner' in this campaign.

51 Hauben, op. cit., p. 114; see Ch. 5; Murray, op. cit., p. 161.

52 Hauben, op. cit., pp. 108–13, for the dating of this episode to 302 BC; S. M. Burstein, 'Lysimachus the Gazophylax – a modern scholarly myth?', in Heckel and Sullivan, op. cit., p. 59, S. M. Burstein, 'Lysimachus and the Greek cities: the early years', *Ancient World*, 1986b, p. 20.

53 Hecataeus = Diod. 1.46.8 – 49.6.1, Murray, op. cit., p. 160 assumes that Diod. 1.53–8 also derives from Hecataeus; Euhemerus = *FGrH* 63, Diod. VI.1.1–11; Diod. VI.F.1.6; F.1.8, Diod. XVIII.75.

54 Burghart, op. cit., pp. 237–8, *The Economist*, 10 November 1991; A. D. Nock, 'Notes on ruler cult I–IV', *JHS*, 1928, vol. 48, p. 145, Hom. *Od.*

VIII. 467–8, see also Aesch. *Suppl.* 980; J. R. Balsdon, 'The divinity of Alexander', *Historia*, 1950, vol. 70, p. 365, Nock, op. cit., p. 152.

55 The sharp distinction drawn by S. R. F. Price (op. cit., pp. 29, 34–5) between hero and ruler cult is perhaps overstated; the line taken by e.g. F. W. Walbank, 'Monarchies and monarchic ideas' in A. E. Astin *et al.* (eds) *Cambridge Ancient History*, 2nd edn, vol. VII, Cambridge, Cambridge University Press, 1984, p. 88, Gauthier op. cit., p. 46; S. R. F. Price, op. cit., p. 35.

56 E. Bikermann, *Institutions des Séleucides*, Paris, Librairie Orientaliste Paul Geuthner, 1938, p. 247; *Syll*³ 390 ll.39–57, R. S. Bagnall, *The Administration of the Ptolemaic Possessions outside Egypt*, Leiden, E. J. Brill, 1976, p. 104. Compare the temple built by Antiochus I for his father at Seleuceia-on-Orontes (Bikermann, op. cit., p. 255); Bikermann, op. cit., p. 256, F. E. Adcock, 'Greek and Macedonian kingship', in *Proceedings of the British Academy*, 1953, vol. 39, p. 175, S. R. F. Price, op. cit., p. 36.

57 e.g. *OGIS* 212, *I.Priene* 14 15–22; Plut. *Demet.* 10, 12, Ch. Habicht, *Gottmenschentum und Griechische Stadte*, 2nd edn, Munich, C. H. Beck, 1970, pp. 87, 91.

58 J. Gould, 'On making sense of Greek religion', in P. E. Easterling and J. V. Muir (eds) *Greek Religion and Society*, Cambridge, Cambridge University Press, 1985, pp. 2–5, 7, S. R. F. Price, op. cit., pp. 2, 10–19; P. Cartledge, 'The Greek religious festivals', in Easterling and Muir, op. cit., p. 98, for Greek religion as 'a question of doing, not of believing'; Gould, op. cit., p. 15; R. Lane Fox, *Pagans and Christians*, Harmondsworth, Viking, 1986, p. 38, for the gods' great potential to help and harm.

59 For minimal interference under Achaemenid rule, see Ch. 5. S. R. F. Price's explanation (op. cit., p. 26) for the lack of cult honours for the Great King as due to Greek resentment of Persian rule, contrasted with that of Macedon which was 'at least partially Greek', does not altogether convince; Gould, op. cit., p. 8; Lane Fox, op. cit., pp. 34–5; S. R. F. Price, op. cit., p. 29.

60 Though R. R. R. Smith, op. cit., pp. 15–16, sees honorary statues as a tacit expression of the city's dependence on the king's power and wealth, cult honours do not, however, invariably reflect direct political dependence (Bikermann, op. cit., p. 256, S. R. F. Price, op. cit., p. 164); Plut. *Demet.* 10, K. Scott, 'The deification of Demetrius Poliorcetes', *A. J. Phil.* 1934, vol. 55, pp. 147, 164; *Syll*³ 372 ll.25–6.

61 S. R. F. Price, op. cit., pp. 14–15, for a bibliography on this tradition.

62 Plut. *Demet.* 10, 11, 18, 23; Athen. VI.63. Duris or his brother Lynceus are likely sources; see Ch. 1 for Duris' attitude towards the Antigonids.

63 e.g. Diog. Laert. VI.63, Hyperides *Contra Dem.* col. 31, *Fun. Or.* 21; Balsdon, op. cit., p. 383 for the late and derivative nature of most of the sources, Lane Fox, op. cit., pp. 64, 66 for intellectual thought as frequently atypical; Plut. *Demet.* 8, *Syll*³ 372 ll.5–12, 14–17.

64 *OGIS* 229 ll.10–11, L. Robert, 'Sur un décret d'Ilion et sur un papyrus concernant des cultes royaux', in *Essays in Honour of C. Bradford Welles*, New Haven, American Society of Papyrologists, 1966b, pp. 205–8 for private worship of Arsinoe as Aphrodite Euploia, R. R. R. Smith, op. cit.,

p. 11; Cartledge, op. cit., p. 101, Lane Fox, op. cit., p. 70 for festivals as good for business and 'enormous fun', Kuhrt, 1987b, op. cit., p. 39 for the free flow of alcohol at the Babylonian New Year Festival; Aristot. *Pol.* 1321A 31.

65 Bikermann, op. cit., pp. 238–42; accusations of Antigonid hubris from Lysimachus' friend Philippides, for example, are unlikely to be impartial.

66 Plut. *De Fort. Alex.* 338; there are many examples, usually involving philosophers – e.g. Plut. *Mor.* 458B, Diog. Laert. II.115; *Syll*³ 372 ll.25–6, *I.Priene* 14 ll.5–8, 15 ll.10–15; 16 ll.12–15, Welles, op. cit., pp. 43–4; *OGIS* 480, Plut. *Demet.* 25, Habicht, op. cit., no. 18 pp. 40–1 – the cult's revival suggests a later appreciation, not felt at the time, of the prosperity which their new site brought them; *Syll*³ 380, *Syll*³ 332, Habicht, op. cit., pp. 37–8, M. B. Hatzopoulos, 'Une donation du Roi Lysimaque', *ΜΕΛΗΘΗΜΑΤΑ*, Paris, De Boccard, 1988, pp. 17–18, 22, 28.

67 Habicht, op. cit., pp. 42–81, 82–108, 109–23.

68 *Syll*³ 390 especially ll.39–57, Bagnall, op. cit., p. 104, Davis and Kraay, op. cit., pl. no. 19; Habicht, op. cit., pp. 106–7 nos. 42 b and e.

69 *OGIS* 6 ll.22–7, Welles, op. cit., pp. 8–9; App. *Syr.* 64 .

70 V. Tscherikower, *Die Hellenistischer Stadtegrundungen von Alexander Dem Grossen bis auf die Römerzeit*, Leipzig, *Philologus* Supplement 19, 1927, concentrates almost exclusively on these aspects; Kuhrt, 1987a, op. cit., p. 51, for Seleuceia-on-Tigris as founded in conformity with Mesopotamian tradition; Root, op. cit., pp. 16–17, Kuhrt and Sherwin-White, 1991, op. cit., pp. 79–80 for active involvement in building programmes by Assyrian, Egyptian, Achaemenid and Seleucid kings; App. *Syr.* 58, Kuhrt and Sherwin-White, 1991, op. cit., p. 82 (Seleuceia-on-Tigris and divine approval for the wise king), compare Arr. *Anab.* III.2.1–2; Hdt. I.97, 101.

71 G. Cawkwell, *Philip of Macedon*, London, Faber & Faber, 1978, pp. 43–4, Plut. *Alex.* 9; Plut. *De Alex. Fort.* I.328E, App. *Syr.* 38, Tscherikower's total (op. cit., pp. 140–5) is thirty-four, C. Préaux, *Le Monde Hellénistique*, vol. II, Paris, Presses Universitaires de France, 1978, p. 401 cites thirty certain foundations and twenty more possibilities.

72 Diod. XIX.52.1–2, 4; Tscherikower, op. cit., p. 162.

73 W. W. Tarn, 'The heritage of Alexander', in J. B. Bury *et al.* (eds) *Cambridge Ancient History*, 1st edn, vol VI, Cambridge, Cambridge University Press, 1927, p. 429, for dynastic glory as a motive for city foundations; Tscherikower, op. cit., pp. 156, 165, Plut. *Demet.* 25, Newell, op. cit., pp. 144–6; Newell, op. cit., pp. 131–5 for Antigonid city nomenclature.

74 Tscherikower, op. cit., pp. 162–3 (the Aetolian cities are generally seen as Aetolian work, not that of Lysimachus himself); positive relations between Lysimachus and Aetolia (e.g. *Syll*³ 380) and Aetolian Lysimacheia seem to link this Arsinoeia with Arsinoe's years as queen of Thrace rather than Egypt – G. Longega, *Arsinoe II*, Rome, L'erma di Bretschneider, 1968, pp. 33–5 for bibliography; J. G. Milne, 'The autonomous coinage of Smyrna', *Num. Chron.*, 1923, vol. 3 (series 5), p.

3; L. Robert, 'Les inscriptions grecques de Bulgarie', *Rev. Phil.*, 1959, vol. 38, pp. 177–8, see also Ch. 7.

75 Strabo XIII.1.26; Seleucus I likewise created several Alexandrias, but razed another Antigoneia to the ground in founding Antioch (App. *Syr.* 57; Préaux, op. cit., p. 405).

76 Paus. VII.5.1; Parke, op. cit., p. 127 for the idea of a local invention.

77 Both W. Leaf, 'Skepsis in the Troad' in Buckler and Calder, 1923, op. cit., p. 279, and J. M. Cook, *The Troad*, Oxford, Clarendon Press, 1973, p. 364, praise Lysimachus' decision to restore Scepsis; L. Robert, *Etudes de numismatique grecque: monnaies et villes de Troade*, Paris, Collège de France, 1951, pp. 11, 20, G. E. Bean, 'New inscriptions', in Cook, op. cit., p. 338 no. 27.

78 Tscherikower, op. cit., pp. 155–6, 163 – his evident admiration for Antigonus may lead him to underestimate Lysimachus' achievement; e.g. Plut. *Demet.* 44, 48, *Pyrrh.* 11, *RC* 9 ll.54–60, see also Ch. 7.

79 Tscherikower, op. cit., pp. 162–4; J. L. Ferrary and P. Gauthier, 'Le traité entre le Roi Antiochus et Lysimacheia', *Journal des Savants*, 1981, pp. 327–45 for a redating of this text to the reign of Antiochus I or the early years of Antiochus II, Liv. XXXII.39, XXXIV.59, Polyb. XVIII.50–1, XXI.15, Appian's suggestion (*Syr.* 1) that Thracians destroyed Lysimacheia soon after Lysimachus' death may be the result of compressing events.

80 Bellinger, op. cit., p. 133 for Ilium's 'splendid wall of large hewn stones' attributed to Lysimachus, Cadoux, op. cit., pp. 101–3 for Lysimachus' towered walls at Smyrna, F. G. Maier, *Griechische Mauerbauinschriften* vol. I, Heidelberg, Quelle & Meyer, 1959, no. 71 ll.236–42 for the Lysimachean walls at Ephesus; e.g. App. *Syr.* 58, Liv. XXXII.39; Diod. XX.147.5 (Antigoneia on the Orontes), App. *Syr.* 58 (Seleuceia-on-Tigris), see also Kurht and Sherwin-White, 1991, op. cit., pp. 79–80.

81 W. Alzinger, 'Die Altertumer von Belevi. Versuch einer topographischen, archäologischen und historischen Einordnung', in C. Praschniker and M. Theuer (eds) *Das Mausoleum von Belevi*, Vienna, Osterreichisches Archäologisches Institut, 1979, p. 192, draws parallels with tombs at Vergina and Leucadia, C. Praschniker, 'Die Datierung', in Praschniker and Theuer, op. cit., p. 117; G. B. Waywell, 'Mausolea in South-west Asia Minor', *YAYLA*, Third Report of the Northern Society for Anatolian Archaeology, 1980, pp. 5, 9, sees the variations in design from those of the Mausoleum as reflecting a time-lapse of *c.* fifty years; Alzinger, op. cit., p. 193, R. Fleischer, 'Ergänzungen zum Abschnitt: Der Figurliche Schmuck', in Praschniker and Theuer, op. cit., p. 159; for the cult, see p. 173, Polyaen. VIII.57; Fleischer, op. cit., p. 158, Alzinger, op. cit., p. 193 – J. C. Carter, *The Sculpture of the Sanctuary of Athena Polias at Priene*, London, Society of Antiquaries, 1983, p. 34, suggests that the ceiling coffers were carved some time before they were actually set in place; for fuller discussion, see Lund, op. cit., 1992, pp. 370–3.

82 e.g. Isoc. *Ad Nic.* 21, 27–8.

83 e.g. Bikermann, op. cit., p. 48, S. Le Bohec, 'Les *philoi* des Rois antigonides', *REG*, 1985, vol. 98, p. 93; Root, op. cit., pp. 74, 186, 209, J. M. Cook, *The Persian Empire*, London, J.M. Dent & Sons, 1983, p. 71,

Hdt. III.70.1–3, 78; R. Frye, *The Heritage of Persia*, London, Weidenfeld & Nicolson, 1962, p. 290.

84 Murray, op. cit., p. 163; Arr. *Succ. FGrH* 156 F.1.7, Athen. IV.146, Plut. *Alex.* 40; Diod. XVIII.49, 50, XIX.56, 57.

85 G. Herman, 'The 'friends' of the early Hellenistic rulers: servants or officials', *Talanta*, 1981, vol. 13, p. 115; *Syll*³ 374, J. M. Edmonds, *Comici: The Fragments of Attic Comedy*, vol. IIIA, Leiden, E. J. Brill, 1961, p. 179; J. Hornblower, op. cit., pp. 12–14, 147–51, Diod. XVIII.50.1, XIX.69.1, 81.1, 99.3, 100.1, Plut. *Demet.* 39.

86 Austin, op. cit., pp. 462–63; Isoc. *Ad Nic.* 19, see also Dionys. Halic. XIX.14; Plut. *Demet.* 12, Athen. IV.1.165, Welles, *RC*, 1934, nos. 10–12, Bikermann, op. cit., pp. 34–36, Hatzopoulos, op. cit., ll.3–8, 11–14, 17–20; 9–10.

87 Athen. VI.63, Diog. Laert. XI.40; *Syll*³ 373, T. L. Shear, *Kallias of Sphettos and the Revolt of Athens in 286 B.C.*, Princeton, *Hesperia* Supplement XVII, 1978, pp. 2–4; e.g. *SEG* 26 no. 89, *SEG* 1 no. 358, *OGIS* 10.

88 Diod. XXI.F.11, compare Jos. *Antt.* XIII 368 for Seleucus VI's death alongside his *philoi*; e.g. Plut. *Demet.* 49; e.g. Plut. *Demet.* 46, Diod. XIX.87.1, XX.107.3–4 – Hieronymus stresses Eumenes' rare quality of *pistis* (trustworthiness) (J. Hornblower, op. cit., pp. 204–5); Tscherikower, op. cit., p. 155, R. H. Simpson, 'A possible case of misrepresentation in Diodorus XIX', *Historia*, 1957b, vol. 77, pp. 504–5.

89 Herman, op. cit., p. 113, following C. Habicht, *Die herrschende Gesellschaft in dem hellenistischen Monarchien*, Wiesbaden, Vierteljahrschrift fur Sozial- und Wirtschaftgeschichte 45, 1958, pp. 1–16; e.g. Dionys. Halic. XIX.14; Hdt. I.207–8, Plut. *Them.* 29; Arr. *Anab.* III.23.7–8.

90 Herman, op. cit., pp. 108–12, 115; see Ch. 1.

91 Herman, op. cit., p. 115, sees a decline in courtiers recruited from the Macedonian/Persian nobility or the Greek *polis*; Diod. XX.19.5, 20.112; Plut. *Demet.* 31; Diod. XIX.74.3–6; Plut. *Demet.* 46; Memn. *FGrH* 434 F.5.1; *Syll*³ 373.

92 Isoc. *Ad Phil.* 18; Herman, op. cit., p. 113; G. Dunst, 'Ein neues chiisches Dekret aus Kos', *Klio*, 1959, vol. 37, pp. 63–8, *SEG* 14. no. 58, *IG* II² 498; Athen. XIV.614–15.

93 S. M. Burstein, *The Hellenistic Age from the Battle of Ipsos to the Death of Kleopatra VII*, Cambridge, Cambridge University Press, 1985, no. 14, Plut. *Mor.* 1097B, 1126E; L. Robert, *Noms indigènes dans l'Asie Mineure gréco-romaine*, vol. I, Paris, Librairie Adrien Maisonneuve, 1963, pp. 82, 217, 291, 519, for examples of the name Mithres as Iranian in origin; the idea of the 'all-Greek' character of the Diadochs' courts (most recently advanced by McKechnie, op. cit., pp. 207, 212) ignores this evidence from Lysimachus' court: see also P. Briant, *Alexandre le Grand*, 3rd edn, Paris, Presses Universitaires de France, 1974, pp. 101–3, Sherwin-White, 1987, op. cit., pp. 6–7.

94 For the name Bithys on Thracian inscriptions, see G. Mihailov, *IGBR*, vol. IV, Sofia, 1966, p. 315, nos. 2196, 1962, 2337, 2322; Hom. *Il.* VI ll.280, 503, VII. l.83; Herman, op. cit., pp. 108–12.

95 *IG* II² 808, most recently by S. M. Burstein, 'Bithys son of Cleon from

Lysimacheia: a reconsideration of the date and significance of *IG* II² 808',
CSCA, 1980, vol. 12, pp. 39–50; Plut. *Arat.* 34, M. Osbourne, 'The decree
for Bithys of Lysimacheia *IG* II² 808', *Ancient Society*, 1974, vol. 5, pp.
97–104; Hatzopoulos, op. cit., pp. 38–9, ll.8–10; Burstein, 1980, op. cit.,
pp. 41, 45–6.

96 Plut. *Demet.* 12., *Syll*³ 374, Shear, op. cit., p. 49, Diod. XXI.F.11.

97 Plut. *Mor.* 851e–f, L. C. Smith, 'Demochares of Leuconoe and the dates of
his exile', *Historia*, 1962, vol. 11, pp. 114–18, Shear, op. cit., p. 20; W.
Dittenberger, *Sylloge Inscriptionum Graecarum*, 3rd edn, vol. I, Lipsiae,
S. Hirzel, 1915, no. 381, followed by L. Olshausen, *Prosopographie der
Hellenistischen Königsgesandten*, Louvain, Studia Hellenistica 19, 1974,
no. 6, Plut. *Them.* 29, Hdt. VII.101; *Inschr. Eph.* 1464, *IG* II² 662 and 663,
Ch. Habicht, *Beitrage zur Prosopographie der altgriechischen Welt*,
Chiron, 1972, vol. 2, pp. 107–8; *Syll*³ 368, *SEG* 1985 no. 926, W. G.
Forrest, 'Some inscriptions of Chios', *Horos*, 1985, vol. 3, p. 95.

98 Assuming that the two different spellings of the patronymic
(*Hippodamus* (Chios), *Hippodemus* (Miletus)) reflect only a difference
in dialect.

99 *Syll*³ 361, W. W. Tarn, *Antigonus Gonatas*, Oxford, Clarendon Press,
1913, p. 118.

100 Isoc. *Nic.* 41; Just. XVII.2.1, Oros. *Adv. Pag.* 57, Memn. *FGrH* 434 F.5.7;
for the king as warrior, see Isoc. *Ad Nic.* 25, *OGIS* 219 ll.7–9, *OGIS* 332,
Austin, op. cit., pp. 458–9, Burghart, op. cit., pp. 267–8 (the king's
prowess is an important factor in determining battle's outcome –
compare Arr. *Anab.* II.11.4); Isoc. *Ad Nic.* 37; Plut. *Demet.* 52 ascribes
the Besieger's death to 'inactivity and over-indulgence'!

7 SCHEMING WOMEN AND SENILE DECAY?

1 M. J. Fontana, *Le lotte per la successione di Alessandro Magno dal 323 al
315*, Palermo, Boccone de Povero, 1960, p. 187, for the Trogus/Justin
moralising tendency; see pp. 187–91.

2 Plut. *Demet.* 46–8, Just. XVII.1.4; see Ch. 2 for his part in the Getic
expedition; Memn. *FGrH* 434 F.5.7.

3 Just. XVII.1.7 for Seleucus as *iam pronum* [to make war] . . . *ex
aemulatione gloriae.*, Memn. *FGrH* 434 F.5.7.

4 W. W. Tarn, *Antigonus Gonatas*, Oxford, Clarendon Press, 1913, p. 106,
I. L. Merker, 'The Ptolemaic officials and the League of Islanders',
Historia, 1970, vol. 19, p. 150, E. Will, *Histoire politique du monde
hellénistique*, vol. I, Nancy, Nancy University Press, 1979, p. 94; Diod.
XX.112.1–2; for Alexander's Chian ships, see Ch. 5; Plut. *Demet.* 43,
Tarn, op. cit., p. 117; Memn. *FGrH* 434 F.8.4–6, S. M. Burstein, *Outpost of
Hellenism: The Emergence of Heracleia on the Black Sea*, Berkeley and
Los Angeles, University of California Publications, 1976, p. 84; this figure
is surely exaggerated.

5 *Syll*³ 381, S. M. Burstein, 'Arsinoe Philadelphos II', in W. L. Adams and E.
N. Borza (eds) *Philip II, Alexander the Great and the Macedonian
Heritage*, Washington, DC, University Press of America, 1982, p. 209, for

Merker's redating of the inscription to the 280s BC; Burstein himself (1982, op. cit., p. 209) sees the context for this diplomacy as friendly relations between Egypt and Thrace); Memn. *FGrH* 434 F.8.2, Paus. I.16.2, H. Heinen, *Untersuchungen zur Hellenistischen Geschichte des 3. Jahrhunderts v. Chr.*, Wiesbaden, *Historia* Einzelschriften 20, 1972, §1. pp. 14–16; Schol. Theoc. XVII 128, K. J. Beloch, *Griechische Geschichte*, vol. IV², Berlin, Walter de Gruyter & Co., 1925, p. 130, G. Macurdy, *Hellenistic Queens*, Baltimore, Johns Hopkins Press, 1932, p. 110.

6 Plut. *Demet.* 46, Just. XVII.1.4, Memn. *FGrH* 434 F.5.6; Just. XVII.1.1, Pomp. Trog. *Prol. Lib.* 17, Memn. *FGrH* 434 F.5.6; Strabo XIII.4.1–2.

7 Memn. *FGrH* 434 F.5.6, Pomp. Trog. *Prol. Lib.* 17; Paus. I.10.3–4, Just. XVII.1.1 for Arsinoe as Lysimachus' *ministra*, Porph. *FHG* III F.4.4; Memn. *FGrH* 434 F.5.4, 5.6, Paus. I.10.3–4, Just. XVII.1.1, 7–8, Oros. *Adv. Pag.* III.23.56.

8 Strabo XIII.4.1, Paus. I.10.4; Paus. I.10.3, App. *Syr.* 64; *Syll*³ 373 – for Ptolemy's Boeotian trip, see pp. 197–8.

9 G. Corradi, *Studi ellenistici*, Turin, Società Editrice Internazionale, 1929, p. 59; e.g. Tarn, op. cit., p. 124; Burstein, 1982, op. cit., p. 200; e.g. Will, op. cit., p. 100, H. Bengtson, *Die Diadochen*, Munich, C. H. Beck, 1987, p.134; Burstein, 1976, op. cit., p. 4, for Nymphis as Memnon's source; Tarn, op. cit., p. 125.

10 G. Longega, *Arsinoe II*, Rome, L'erma di Bretschneider, 1968, pp. 44–54; Memn. *FGrH* 434 F.5.4–5.6.

11 Heinen, op. cit., pp. 8–11; Memn. *FGrH* 434 F.5.2 – similar phraseology in Plut. *Demet.* 51 (*miaron kai barbaron*) is usually thought to reflect a hostile source. F. Jacoby, *FGrH* vol. IIIb, Leiden, E. J. Brill, 1955, pp. 258–61.

12 Longega, op. cit., p. 50; Memn. *FGrH* 434 F.1.1–2; F.2.1–2; F.3.1–3; F.4.1–7; Burstein, 1976, op. cit., p. 3; Memn. *FGrH* 434 F.7.3, F.16.3.

13 See Ch.1.

14 G. Forni, *Valore storico e fonti di Pompeio Trogo*, vol. I. Urbino, University of Urbino, 1958, pp. 50, 101; Pomp. Trog. *Prol. Lib.* 17; Porph. *FHG* III F.4.4; Memn. *FGrH* 434 F.5.6, Longega, op. cit., pp. 50–1; see pp. 190–1.

15 Paus. I.10.3, Eurip. *Hippol.* ll.525–65; it has, however, prompted its share of scholarly discussion, notably by Macurdy, op. cit., p. 113.

16 Memn. *FGrH* 434 F.5.4; e.g. P. Roussel, 'Le démembrement de l'empire d'Alexandre', in G. Glotz *et al.*, *Histoire grecque*, vol. IV, Paris, Presses Universitaires de France, 1938, p. 371.

17 For the beauty suggested by Arsinoe's coin portraits, see N. Davis and C.M. Kraay, *The Hellenistic Kingdoms: Portrait Coins and History*, London, Thames & Hudson, 1973, pls 20–2; Memn. *FGrH* 434 F.5.3.

18 e.g. Diod. II.5.2, 6.5, 6.9, 13.1; Hdt. II.100, III.132–6, VII.2–3, IX.109; Tac. *Ann.* I.4, 1.5.1, X.1.15, XI.2.5–3, 12, 26.1–28, 28, 30; Procop. *Anecdota* I.11–21, 26–8, III.6–13, IX.11–27, XV.1–10, 20–24, XXX. 31–6; Memn. *FGrH* 434 F.5.4, 5.6, Paus. I.10.3, Plut. *Demet.* 25, Just. XVII.1.4, Pomp. Trog. *Prol. Lib.* 17, Porph. *FHG* III F.3.3.

19 E. A. Fisher, 'Theodora and Antonina in the *Historia Arcana*: history and/ or fiction?', in J. Peradotto and J. P. Sullivan (eds) *Women in the Ancient*

World, New York, State University of New York, 1984, pp. 291, 293, 294; compare the Soviet rumour which blamed Raisa Gorbachev for the September 1991 coup, accusing her of an affair with Boris Pugo (*Guardian*, 18 September 1991, p. 21); Diod. II.5.2, Catherine the Great attracts similar stories (I. De Madariaga, *Russia in the Age of Catherine the Great*, London, Weidenfeld and Nicholson, 1981, pp. 355–6, 579).

20 H. Sancisi-Weerdenburg, 'Exit Atossa: images of women in Greek historiography on Persia', in A. Cameron and A. Kuhrt (eds) *Images of Women in Antiquity*, London and Canberra, Croom Helm, 1983, pp. 20–32; R. Kebric, *In the Shadow of Macedon: Duris of Samos*, Wiesbaden, *Historia* Einzelschriften 29, 1977, p. 18, for Duris as self-styled heir to the tradition of 'tragic history' started by Herodotus.

21 Ovid *Metam.* I 1.14; Tac. *Ann.* I.3, 4, 6, 10 – B. Walker, *The Annals of Tacitus*, Manchester, Manchester University Press, 1952, p. 482, suggests that Tacitus 'weighed the scales against Livia'; Memn. *FGrH* 434 F.5.6.

22 Plut. *Demet.* 3; Porph. *FGH* III F.3.3, Just. XVI.2.4; Memn. *FGrH* 434 F.5.3.

23 Heinen, op. cit., pp. 3–94, see also end of Ch. 2; Arsinoe's son Ptolemy was at most 16 years old *c.* 283 BC; his brothers, Lysimachus and Philip, were 16 and 13 when Arsinoe married Ceraunus in 280 BC (Just. XXIV.3.5).

24 See Ch. 4.

25 A helpful suggestion made by Dr J. Patterson at a reading of a preliminary paper on this subject; Memn. *FGrH* 434 F.7.3, W. Orth, *Königlicher Machtanspruch und Stadtische Freiheit*, Munich, C. H. Beck, 1977, pp. 39–42; Nymphis indeed held a leading position in Heraclea at a time when the city took a determined stand against Seleucid domination.

26 Longega, op. cit., p. 51.

27 Just. XVII.1.6, XXIV.3.7–9; Plut. *Demet.* 46–7.

28 M. Lefkowitz, 'Influential women', in Cameron and Kuhrt, op. cit., pp. 51–7, observes that women in literature and history who seem to play a major role in political life almost invariably act on behalf of male kinsmen.

29 Longega, op. cit., pp. 42–4; W. Dittenberger, *Sylloge Inscriptionum Graecarum*, 3rd edn, Lipsiae, S. Hirzel, 1915, p. 615, no. 381, Longega, op. cit., p. 27; Heraclea (Memn. *FGrH* 434 F.5.4), Ephesus (*Syll³* 368 ll.25–6, Macurdy, op. cit., p. 117, A. Mehl, *Seleukos Nikator und Sein Reich*, Lovanii, Studia Hellenistica 28, 1986, p. 294), Cassandreia (Macurdy, op. cit., p. 117, S. M. Burstein, 'Lysimachus and the Greek cities of Asia: the case of Miletus', *Ancient World*, 1980, vol. 3, p. 74 n. 16).

30 *Syll³* 381, *OGIS* 730 ll.5, 13, 19, Polyb. V.83–4, Longega, op. cit., pp. 27–9. For fuller discussion, see H. S. Lund, 'Bridging the Hellespont: the Successor Lysimachus – a study in early Hellenistic kingship', University of London Ph.D. thesis, Senate House Library, 1992, pp. 406–11.

31 See p. 186, Ch. 4 and Ch. 6; *I.Priene* 14 = *RC* 7; *Syll³* 372; see Chs. 3, 4 and 6.

32 B. V. Head, *On the Chronological Sequence of the Coins of Ephesus*, London and Paris, Rollin & Feuardent, 1880, pp. 43–4, J. G. Milne, 'The autonomous coinage of Smyrna', *Num. Chron.*, 1923, vol. 3 (series 5), p. 3; Polyaen. VIII.57; Just. XXIV.2.1, 3.4, Pomp. Trog. *Prol. Lib.* 24, Tarn, op. cit., p. 128 for Cassandreian sympathy for Lysimachus; a verbal suggestion

NOTES

from Amélie Kuhrt, see Hdt. II.98, Xen. *Anab.* I.49, Plato *Alcib.* 122–3, P. Briant, 'Dons de terres et de villes: l'Asie Mineure dans le contexte achéménide', *REA*, 1985, vol. 87, pp. 59–60.

33 L. Robert, 'Sur un décret d'Ilion et sur un papyrus concernant des cultes royaux', in *Essays in Honour of C. Bradford Welles*, New Haven, American Society of Papyrologists, 1966b, pp. 205–8, for worship of Arsinoe as Aphrodite Euploia; Burstein, 1982, op. cit., pp. 201–2, for 'unprecedented' posthumous honours for Arsinoe – he does, however, challenge the idea of her as *de facto* ruler of Egypt (pp. 197–212).

34 Memn. *FGrH* 434 F.5.3, see p. 190; *RC* 7, *c.* 283–2 BC, *I.Priene* 37 ll.81, 126 for the dating; C. B. Welles, *Royal Correspondence in the Hellenistic Period*, New Haven, Yale University Press, 1934, pp. 49, 51.

35 See e.g. J. Goody, 'Introduction' in J. Goody, *Succession to High Office*, Cambridge, Cambridge University Press, 1966, pp. 1–56, and M. Southwold, 'Succession to the throne in Buganda', in Goody, op. cit., pp. 82–126.

36 Head, op. cit., p. 43, B. Niese, *Geschichte der Griechischen und Makedonischen Staaten seit der Schlacht bei Chaeronea*, vol. I. Gotha, Friedrich Andreas Perthes, 1893, p. 402; *I.Priene* 14, S. M. Sherwin-White, 'Ancient archives: the edict of Alexander to Priene, a reappraisal', *JHS*, 1985, vol. 105, pp. 79–80; H. Bengtson, *Die Strategie in der Hellenistischen Zeit*, vol. II, Munich, C. H. Beck, 1937, pp. 227–9.

37 See Ch. 6; Plut. *Demet.* 38 – the motive for this marriage was probably political, aiming to create an impression of continuity and to express publicly Seleucus' confidence in his heir; *RC* 9 l.1; A. K. Grayson, *Assyrian and Babylonian Chronicles*, Locust Valley, NY, J. J. Augustin, 1975, Chron. 11 Obv. 5,7,9, Rev. 3,6,11, R. A. Parker and W. H. Dubberstein, *Babylonian Chronology 626 BC-AD 75*, Providence, Brown University, 1956, p. 21.

38 L. Robert, 'Les inscriptions grecques de Bulgarie', *Rev. Phil*, 1959, vol. 38, pp. 172–9; W. W. Tarn, *Alexander the Great*, vol. II, Cambridge, Cambridge University Press, 1948, p. 249, saw an eponymous foundation by Alexander while Philip lived as 'a declaration of independence, the clearest act of rebellion known to the ancient world'; Diod. XX.107.4, see Ch. 6.

39 Robert, 1959, op. cit., pp. 172–9; see e.g. J. Zahle, 'Persian satraps and Lycian dynasts: the evidence of the Diadems' in T. Hackens and R. Weiller (eds) *Actes du 9ᵉ Congrès International de Numismatique, Berne 1979*, Louvain-la-Neuve, Association Internationale des numismates professionels, 1981,pp. 101–9; Hdt. IV.166 (Aryandes), T. R. Martin, *Sovereignty and Coinage in Classical Greece*, Princeton, NJ, Princeton University Press, 1985, p. 119; H. W. Ritter, *Diadem und Königsherrschaft*, Munich, C. H. Beck, 1965, pp. 125–6, Arr. *Anab.* VII.22.2–5 suggests that if anyone but the king wore the diadem it was an unlucky portent for the ruler.

40 L. Robert, 'Notes d'épigraphie Hellénistique', *BCH*, 1933, vol. 57, §XI. pp. 485–90.

41 A recently published dedication to Pleistarchus from Tralles (*Inschr. Nysa und Tralles* I no. 34) provides a parallel for the broken cross-bar alpha in

257

an early third-century BC text; for fuller discussion of the Ptolemy text, see Lund, 1992, op. cit., pp. 416–18.

42 Strabo XIII.4.1–2.

43 Memn. *FGrH* 434 F.5.7; Just. XVII.1.7; Paus. I.10.3.

44 A. Mehl's detailed analysis (op. cit., pp. 284–9) adds little to what the sources say; ibid., pp. 289, 291–2, rightly questions this assumption.

45 See e.g. J. Keil, 'Ephesische Burgerrechts- und Proxeniedekrete aus dem vierten und dritten Jahrhundert v. Chr.', *JOAI*, 1913, vol. 16, p. 235, nos 1 l, n, p for Ephesus' shift from Perdiccas to Antipater and Craterus, Arr. *Anab.* I.18.4 for Milesian wavering between Alexander and Memnon in 333 BC.

46 Compare Plut. *Them.* 26 where Themistocles, on the run with a Persian price on his head, receives aid from his *xenos* Nicogenes of Aegae.

47 Cassander's Macedon in 294 BC is the obvious parallel (see Ch. 4); see Ch. 6; apart from Philetaerus and Alexander, their identity is unknown; Mithres' imprisonment by Antigonus Gonatas at Corinth and Athens *c.* 280 BC (S. M. Burstein, *The Hellenistic Age from the Battle of Ipsos to the Death of Kleopatra VII*, Cambridge, Cambridge University Press, 1985, no. 11) has led him to be dubbed another Harpalus, but the date of his defection is far from clear (see P. Gauthier, 'La réunification d'Athènes en 281 et les deux archontes Nicias', *REG*, 1979, vol. 92, pp. 375–8).

48 Polyaen. VIII.57.

49 Strabo XIII.4.1, E. V. Hansen, *The Attalids of Pergamum*, 2nd edn, Ithaca and London, Cornell University Press, 1971, p. 17; Polyaen. VIII.57; see Appendix 1; *OGIS* 213, 214, Plut. *Demet.* 46, *I.Milet.* 138 l.7; Burstein, 1980, op. cit., pp. 73, 78–9, *I.Milet* 123 l.37; *RC* 7, *I.Priene* 37 l.126.

50 Grayson, op. cit., p. 27 Chron. 12 Obv. ll.3–4, A. J. Sachs and D. J. Wiseman, 'A Babylonian king list of the Hellenistic period', *Iraq*, 1954, vol. 16, pp. 202–6; Heinen, op. cit., pp. 26–7.

51 A solution suggested verbally by Amélie Kuhrt.

52 Heinen, op. cit., p. 27, admits this possibility; Just. XVII.1.7, Paus. I.10.3; A. B. Bosworth, 'Alexander the Great and the decline of Macedon', *JHS*, 1986, vol. 106, p. 10, for the drain on Macedonian manpower.

53 Polyaen. VIII.57; Paus. I.10.3.

54 Grayson, op. cit., Chron. 12 Rev. l.3. for Seleucus' march, in summer 281 BC, on Macedon – 'his land'; see also S. M. Sherwin-White, 'Babylonian Chronicle fragments as a source for Seleucid history', *JNES*, 1983, vol. 42, pp. 266–7.

55 Polyaen. VI.12, App. *Syr.* 64, Paus. I.10.3. A context after Corupedium (Mehl, op. cit., p. 292) is less likely since stratagem implies the expectation of resistance; Heinen, op. cit., p. 27, J. D. Grainger, *Seleukos Nikator*, London and New York, Routledge, 1990, p. 182 favours the latter of these routes.

56 Corradi, op. cit., p. 77; Memn. *FGrH* 434 F.7.1 for Heracleia Pontica's alliance with Byzantium, Calchedon and Mithridates of Pontus against Seleucid domination; *RC* 9 ll.5–8, 10.

57 Mehl, op. cit., p. 297, rightly emphasises the uncertainty of a 'wave of defection' as Seleucus marched west; Polyaen. IV.9 – Sardis' resistance and a position east of Corupedium seem to set this action before the battle

(Heinen, op. cit., p. 31); Polyaen. VIII. 57, Heinen, op. cit., p. 38, Mehl, op. cit., p. 297; Seleucus' courtship of Athens in summer 281 BC (see pp. 203–4) has been linked with a need for naval support (*IG* II² 672, Heinen, op. cit., p. 44).

58 Attested at Erythrae, Colophon, Magnesia-on-Maeander, Priene, Ilium and Lemnnos; Heinen, op. cit., pp. 42–4, C. Habicht, *Gottmenschentum und Griechische Stadte*, 2nd edn, Munich, C. H. Beck, 1970, pp. 82–91; Arr. *Anab.* I.16; 18.1–2,4; 27.4 (see also Ch. 5); Habicht, op. cit., pp. 82–9, sees the cults at Ilium, Erythrae, Colophon, Priene and Lemnos as *probably* originating in 281 BC, after Corupedium.

59 See Ch. 5; for Colophon's continued existence, see *Syll*³ 368, *I.Priene* 57, B. D. Meritt, 'Inscriptions of Colophon', *A. J. Phil.*, 1935, vol. 56, no. 1; see Ch. 5 and Appendix I.

60 Phylarch. *FGrH* 81 F.29 = Athen. VI 255; Orth, op. cit., p. 37, followed by Burstein, 1980, op. cit., p. 74 n. 5; *IG* II² 672, E. Schweigert, 'Two third century inscriptions', *Hesperia*, 1941, vol. 10, §1. pp. 338–9; see above, n. 56.

61 Welles, op. cit., p. 56 and *RC* 9 ll.5–10; A. T. L. Kuhrt, 'The Achaemenid empire: a Babylonian perspective', *PCPS*, 1988, vol. 14, pp. 64–6.

62 For selectivity, see Sherwin-White, 1985, op. cit., pp. 74–5, 80; e.g. *RC* 14. ll.5–7, 15 ll.22–3; Mehl, op. cit., p. 308; see Ch. 6 for cult honours as acknowledging the king's 'godlike' powers.

63 Justin. XVII.1.10–2.1.

64 Corradi, op. cit., pp. 79–81, criticises his insistence on the submission of powers like Heracleia and the Bithynian and Cappadocian dynasts; Grayson, op. cit., Chron. 12 Rev. l.4 for mutiny among Seleucus' troops en route to Europe, l.3 for 'Macedon, his land'; Memn. *FGrH* 434 F.8.1 XX for Seleucus' wish to end his days in Macedon; e.g. App. *Syr.* 12, Liv. XXXV.16, Polyb. XVIII.51.4.

65 Just. XVII.2.1; Memn. *FGrH* 434 F.5.7; Mehl, op. cit., p. 299 – Arsinoe's control of Heracleia precludes a formal contingent; Sachs and Wiseman, op. cit., pp. 202–5; Mehl, op. cit., p. 298; A. T. Clay, *Babylonian Records in the Library of J. Pierpoint Morgan*, New York, 1913, no. 5, Parker and Dubberstein, op. cit., p. 21; for posthumous regnal dating in Babylon, see Parker and Dubberstein, op. cit., pp. 17–18 (Artaxerxes I), 20, A. J. Sachs and H. Hunger, *Astronomical Diaries and Related Texts from Babylonia*, vol. I, Vienna, Osterreichische Akademie der Wissenschaften, 1988, p. 233 no. 308 (Alexander IV); in Egypt, M. Atzler, 'Ein ägyptischen Reliefbruchst des Königs Alex. IV', *Antike Kunst*, 1972, vol. 15, p. 120.

66 G. Mendel, 'Inscriptions de Bithynie', *BCH*, 1900, vol. 24, p. 380, W. Peek, *Griechische Versinschriften*, Berlin, Akadamie Verlag, 1955, no. 1965; Polyaen. IV.9, Heinen, op. cit., p. 30; Mehl, op. cit., p. 298.

67 Duris *FGrH* 76 F.55, App. *Syr.* 64, Plut. *Mor.* 28, *De Soll. Anim.* 14, Ael. *V. H.* VI.25; Plut. *Them.* 10; Soph. *Antig.* ll.25–30, Eurip. *Suppl.* ll.120–30; Paus. I.10.4 – presumably feelings of filial piety had overcome Alexander's resentment; for Lysimachus and the Belevi tomb, see Ch. 6; Paus. I.10.4, App. *Syr.* 64.

APPENDIX 1 LYSIMACHUS AND THE PROBLEM OF PRIENEAN AUTONOMY

1 *I.Priene* 1, 2, 3, 4(1), 6, 7.
2 Sext. Emp. *Adv. Gramm.* 1.13.
3 As argued by E. Bikermann, *Institutions des Séleucides*, Librairie Orientaliste Paul Geuthner, Paris, 1938, p. 137.
4 See p. 168.
5 S. M. Sherwin-White, 'Ancient archives: the edict of Alexander to Priene, a reappraisal', *JHS*, 1985, vol. 105, pp. 69, 73–5, 78.
6 S. M. Burstein, 'Lysimachus and the Greek cities: a problem in interpretation', in *Ancient Macedonia IV*, Thessaloniki, Institute for Balkan Studies, 1986a, pp. 137–8.
7 S. M. Burstein, 'Lysimachus and the Greek cities of Asia: the case of Miletus', *Ancient World*, 1980, vol. 3, p. 74 n. 15.
8 C. B. Welles, *Royal Correspondence in the Hellenistic Period*, New Haven, Yale University Press, 1934, p. 44; Sherwin-White, op. cit., p. 78.
9 Sherwin-White, op. cit., p. 78.
10 Welles, op. cit., no. 7, see also Chs 4 and 7.
11 W. Orth, *Königlicher Machtanspruch und Griechische Freiheit*, Munich, C. H. Beck, 1977, p. 105, *I.Priene* 18 = *OGIS* 215; Sherwin-White, op. cit., p. 80, makes the point that the decision was not totally adverse for Priene, which was awarded the Karion fort and its *chora*; Sherwin-White, op. cit., p. 87, n. 145, for Prienean acceptance of Lysimachus' decision.

BIBLIOGRAPHY

Abbott, E. and Mansfield, E. D., *A Primer of Greek Grammar*, London, Rivingtons, 1971.

Adcock, F. E., 'Greek and Macedonian kingship', in *Proceedings of the British Academy*, 1953, vol. 39, pp. 164–79.

Alexandrescu, A. D., 'Tombes de chevaux et pièces du harnais dans le nécropole Gète de Zimnicea', *Dacia*, 1983, vol. 27, pp. 45–66.

Alexandrescu, P., 'Ataias', *Studii Clasice*, 1967, vol. 9, pp. 85–91.

—— 'Le groupe de trésors Thraces du nord du Balkans, *Dacia*, 1983, vol. 27, pp. 45–66.

Allen, R. E., *The Attalid Kingdom*, Oxford, Clarendon Press, 1983.

Alzinger, W., 'Die Altertumer von Belevi. Versuch einer topographischen, archäologischen und historischen Einordnung', in C. Praschniker and M. Theuer (eds) *Das Mausoleum von Belevi*, Vienna, Österreichisches Archäologisches Institut, 1979.

Andreades, A., 'L' administration financière du Roi Lysimaque', in *Mélanges P. Thomas*, Bruges, Imprimerie Sainte Catherine, 1930.

Archibald, Z. H., 'Greek imports – some aspects of the Hellenistic impact on Thrace', in A. G. Poulter (ed.) *Ancient Bulgaria*, vol. 1, Nottingham, University of Nottingham, 1983.

—— 'The Greeks in Thrace c. 500–270 BC', Oxford University D.Phil. thesis, Bodleian Library, 1984.

Ariescu, A., 'Mitteilung über ein bisher unveroffentliches Hellenistischen dekret aus den Beständen des Arhäologischen regionalmuseums der Dobrudschens', *Studii Clasice*, 1963, vol. 5, pp. 315–18.

Atalay, E. and Turkoglu, S.,'Ein fruhhellenistischer Portratkopf des Lysimachos aus Ephesos', *JOAI*, 1972–5, vol. 50, pp. 124–49.

Atzler, M., 'Ein ägyptischen Reliefbruchst des Königs Alex. IV', *Antike Kunst*, 1972, vol. 15, pp. 120–1.

Aucello, E., 'La politica dei Diadochoi e l'ultimatum del 314 av. Cr.', *Riv. Fil.*, 1957, vol. 35, pp. 382–404.

Austin, M. M., 'Hellenistic kings, war and the economy', *CQ*, 1986, vol. 36 (New Series), pp. 450–66.

Austin, R. P., *The Stoichedon Style in Greek Inscriptions*, Oxford, Oxford University Press, 1938.

Aymard, A., 'Le protocole royal grec et son évolution', in A. Aymard, *Etudes*

261

d'histoire ancienne, Paris, Presses Universitaires de France, 1965.

Badian, E., 'Alexander the Great and the Greeks of Asia', in E. Badian (ed.) *Ancient Society and Institutions*, Oxford, Basil Blackwell, 1966.

Bagnall, R. S., *The Administration of the Ptolemaic Possessions outside Egypt*, Leiden, E. J. Brill, 1976.

Balcer, J. M., *Sparda by the Bitter Sea*, Chico, Scholar's Press, Calif., 1984.

Baldus, H. R., 'Zum Siegel des Königs Lysimachos von Thrakien', *Chiron*, 1978, vol. 8, pp. 195–201.

—— 'Die Siegel Alexanders des Grossen. Versuch einer Rekonstruction auf literarischer und numismatischer Grundlage', *Chiron*, 1987, vol. 17, pp. 395–448.

Balsdon, J. R., 'The divinity of Alexander', *Historia*, 1950, vol. 71, pp. 363–88.

Balkanska, A., 'Tirisis-Tirisa-Akra: Die Thrakisch und römisch-byzantinische stadt am Kap Kaliakra (Scythia Minor)', *Klio*, 1980, vol. 62, pp. 27–45.

Barladeanu Zavatin, E., 'Terracotta statuettes from a tomb discovered in Callatis', *Pontica*, 1985, vol. 18, p. 98.

Barron, J. P., 'The tyranny of Duris at Samos', *CR*, 1962, vol. 12, no. 3, pp. 189–90.

—— *The Silver Coins of Samos*, London, Athlone Press, 1966.

Bean, G. E., 'New inscriptions', in J. M. Cook, *The Troad*, Oxford, Clarendon Press, 1973.

Bellinger, A. R., 'The earliest coins of Ilium', *ANSMN*, vol. 34, 1956, pp. 43–9.

—— *Troy: The Coins*, Princeton, NJ, Princeton University Press, 1961.

—— *Essays in the Coinage of Alexander the Great*, New York, American Numismatic Society, 1963.

Beloch, K. J., *Griechische Geschichte*, vol. III, Leipzig, Walter de Gruyter & Co., 1904; vol. IV², Berlin, Walter de Gruyter, & Co., 1925.

Bengtson, H., *Die Strategie in der Hellenistischen Zeit*, Munich, C. H. Beck, 1937.

—— 'Neues zur Geschichte des Hellenismus in Thrakien und in der Dobrudscha', *Historia*, 1962, vol. 11, pp. 18–28.

—— *Die Diadochen*, Munich, C. H. Beck, 1987.

Berthold, R. M., *Rhodes in the Hellenistic Age*, Ithaca and London, Cornell University Press, 1984.

Berve, H., *Das Alexanderreich auf prosopographischer Grundlage*, Munich, C. H. Beck, 1926.

—— 'Nikaia' in *PW*, vol. XVII₁, Stuttgart, 1936, §2 cols 220–1.

—— *Die Tyrannis bei den Griechen*, vol. I, Munich, C. H. Beck, 1967.

Best, J. G. P., *Thracian Peltasts and their Influence on Greek Warfare*, Groningen, Wolters-Noordhoff, 1969.

Bevan, E. R., *The House of Seleucus*, London, Edward Arnold, 1902.

Bikermann, E., 'Alexandre le Grand et les villes d'Asie', *REG*, 1934, vol. 47, pp. 346–73.

—— *Institutions des Séleucides*, Librairie Orientaliste Paul Geuthner, Paris, 1938.

—— 'La cite grecque dans les monarchies hellénistiques', *REG*, 1939, vol. 47, pp. 335–49.

Billows, R. A., Antigonos the One-Eyed and the Creation of the Hellenistic State, Berkeley and Los Angeles and London, University of California Press, 1990.

Bing, J. D., 'A further note on Cyinda/Kundi', *Historia*, 1973, vol. 22, pp. 346–50.

Bosworth, A. B., *A Historical Commentary on Arrian's* History of Alexander, Oxford, Clarendon Press, 1980.

—— 'Arrian and the Alexander Vulgate', in *Alexandre le Grand: image et réalité*, Geneva, Fondation Hardt, 1975.

—— 'Alexander the Great and the decline of Macedon', *JHS*, 1986, vol. 106, pp. 1–12.

Bouché-Leclerq, A., *Histoire des Séleucides*, Paris, Ernest Leroux, 1913.

Brendel, O., 'Ein Bildnis des Königs Lysimachos', *Die Antike*, 1928, vol. 4, pp. 314–16.

Briant, P., 'D'Alexandre le Grand aux diadoques: le cas d' Eumène de Kardia', *REA*, 1972, vol. 54, pp. 32–73.

—— *Alexandre le Grand*, 3rd edn, Paris, Presses Universitaires de France, 1974.

—— *Rois, tributs, paysans*, Paris, University de Besançon, 1982.

—— 'Dons de terres et de villes: l'Asie Mineure dans le contexte achéménide', *REA*, 1985, vol. 87, pp. 53–72.

—— 'Pouvoir central et polycentrisme culturel dans l'empire achéménide: quelques reflexions et suggestions', in H. Sancisi-Weerdenburg (ed.) *Achaemenid History I*, Leiden, Nederlands Instituut voor Het Nabije Oosten, 1987, pp. 1–31.

Broughton, T. R. S., 'New evidence on temple-estates in Asia Minor', in P. R. Coleman-Norton (ed.) *Studies in Roman Economic and Social History*, Princeton, NJ, Princeton University Press, 1951.

Brown, B. R., 'Styles in the Alexander portraits on the coins of Lysimachus', in L. Casson and M. J. Price (eds) *Coins, Culture and History*, Detroit, Wayne State University, 1981, pp. 17–27.

Brown, T. S., 'Callisthenes and Alexander', *A. J. Phil.*, 1949, vol. 70, pp. 235–48.

Bruckner, A., 'Geschichte von Troja et Ilion', in B. Doerpfeld, *Troja und Ilion*, Athens, Beck & Barth, 1902, pp. 549–93.

Brunt, P. A. (transl.), *Arrian*, vol. II, Cambridge, Mass., and London, Loeb, 1983.

Bryce, T. R. and Zahle, J., *The Lycians*, vol. I, Copenhagen, Museum Tusculanum Press, 1986.

Buckler, W. H. and Robinson, D. M., 'Greek inscriptions from Sardis', *AJA*, 1912, vol. 16 (2nd series), pp. 11–82.

—— *Sardis*, vol. VII, Leyden, E. J. Brill, 1932.

Burghart, R., 'Gifts to the Gods: power, property and ceremonial in Nepal', in D. Cannadine and S. R. F. Price (eds) *Rituals of Royalty*, Cambridge, Cambridge University Press, 1987.

Burstein, S. M., *Outpost of Hellenism: The Emergence of Heracleia on the Black Sea*, Berkeley and Los Angeles, University of California Publications, 1976.

—— 'IGII^2 1485a and Athenian relations with Lysimachus', *ZPE*, 1978, vol. 31, pp. 181–5.

—— 'Lysimachus and the Greek cities of Asia: the case of Miletus', *Ancient World*, 1980, vol. 3, pp. 74–9.

—— 'Arsinoe Philadelphos II', in W. L. Adams and E. N. Borza (eds) *Philip II, Alexander the Great and the Macedonian Heritage*, Washington, DC, University Press of America, 1982.

—— 'Lysimachus the Gazophylax – a modern scholarly myth?', in W. Heckel and R. Sullivan (eds) *Ancient Coins of the Graeco-Roman World*, Waterloo, Ont., Wilfred Laurier University Press, 1984.

—— (ed.) *The Hellenistic Age from the Battle of Ipsos to the Death of Kleopatra VII*, Cambridge, Cambridge University Press, 1985.

—— 'Lysimachus and the Greek cities: a problem in interpretation', in *Ancient Macedonia IV*, Thessaloniki, Institute for Balkan Studies, 1986a.

—— 'Lysimachus and the Greek cities: the early years', *Ancient World*, vol. 14, 1986b, pp. 19–24.

—— 'Bithys son of Cleon from Lysimacheia: a reconsideration of the date and significance of IGII^2 808', *CSCA*, 1980, vol. 12, pp. 39–50.

Cadoux, C. J., *Ancient Smyrna*, Oxford, Basil Blackwell, 1938.

Cannadine, D., 'Introduction: divine rites of kings', in D. Cannadine and S. R. F. Price (eds) *Rituals of Royalty*, Cambridge, Cambridge University Press, 1987.

Carter, J. C., *The Sculpture of the Sanctuary of Athena Polias at Priene*, London, Society of Antiquaries, 1983.

Cartledge, P., 'The Greek religious festivals', in P. E. Easterling and J. V. Muir (eds) *Greek Religion and Society*, Cambridge, Cambridge University Press, 1985, pp. 98–127.

Cary, M., 'An inscription from Lampsacus', *JHS*, 1930, vol. 50, pp. 253–4.

—— *A History of the Greek World from 323–146 B.C.*, London, Methuen, 1951.

Caspari, M. O. B., 'The Ionian confederacy', *JHS*, 1915, vol. 35, pp. 173–95.

Cawkwell, G., *Philip of Macedon*, London, Faber & Faber, 1978.

Cicikova, M., 'The Thracian city of Seuthopolis' in A. G. Poulter (ed.) *Ancient Bulgaria*, vol. I, Nottingham, University of Nottingham, 1983.

Clay, A. T., *Babylonian Records in the Library of J. Pierpoint Morgan*, New York, 1913.

Cloché, P., *Thèbes de Beotie*, Louvain and Paris, Editions Nauwelaerts and Brouwer et Cie, 1952.

—— 'La coalition de 315–311 av. J.-C. contre Antigone le Borgne', *CRAI*, 1957.

—— *La Dislocation d'un empire*, Louvain and Paris, Editions Nauwelaerts and Brouwer et Cie, 1959.

Cohen, G. M., 'The Diadochs and the new monarchies', *Athenaeum*, 1974, vol. 52, pp. 177–9.

Condurachi, E. and Daicovicu, C., *The Ancient Civilisation of Roumania*, London, Barrie & Jenkins, 1971.

Conovici, N., 'Les relations entre les Gètes des deux rives du Bas-Danube à la lumière des données archéologiques et numismatiques (IVe–IIe siècles av.

n.e.), in R. Vulpe (ed.) *Actes du IIe Congrès International de Thracologie*, vol. II, Bucharest, Editura Academiei Republicii Socialiste Romania, 1980.

Cook, J. M., The Troad, Oxford, Clarendon Press, 1973.

—— *The Persian Empire*, London, J. M. Dent & Sons, 1983.

Corradi, G., *Studi ellenistici*, Turin, Società Editrice Internationale, 1929.

Crawford, M. H., 'Roman imperial coin types and the formation of public opinion', in C. N. L. Brooke, B. H. I. Stewart, J. G. Pollard and T. R. Volk (eds) *Studies in Numismatic method presented to Philip Grierson*, Cambridge, Cambridge University Press, 1983.

Daicovicu, C., 'Il paese di Dromichaete', in C. Daicovicu (ed.) *Dacica*, Cluj, Bibliotheca Musei Napocensis, 1973.

Danoff, Ch., 'Zur Geschichte des westpontische *koinon*', *Klio*, 1938, vol. 31, pp. 436–9.

Dareste, R., Haussoulier, B. and Reinach, Th. (eds) *Recueil des inscriptions juridiques grecques*, Paris, Ernest Leroux, 1898.

Daux, G., 'Inscriptions de Thasos', *BCH*, 1928, vol. 52, pp. 46–50.

Davis, N. and Kraay, C., *The Hellenistic Kingdom: Portrait Coins and History*, London, Thames & Hudson, 1973.

De Madariaga, I., *Russia in the Age of Catherine the Great*, London, Weidenfeld & Nicholson 1981.

Déscat, R., 'Mnésimachos, Hérodote et le système tributaire achéménide', *REA*, 1985, vol. 87, pp. 97–112.

Diehl, E., 'Tyras' in *PW*, vol. VII A₂, Stuttgart, 1948, cols 1,850–63.

Dimitrov, D. P. and Cicikova, M., *The Thracian City of Seuthopolis*, Oxford, B. A. R. Supplement Series no. 38, 1978.

—— and Dimitrov, K., 'Le monnayage de Seuthes III selon les donnéés de Seuthopolis', in R. Vulpe (ed.) *Actes du IIe Congrès International de Thracologie*, vol. II, Bucharest, Editura Academiei Republicii Socialiste Romania, 1980.

Dittenberger, W., *Orientis Graeci Inscriptiones Selectae*, vol. I, Lipsiae, S. Hirzel, 1903.

—— *Sylloge Inscriptionum Graecarum*, 3rd edn, vol. I, Lipsiae, S. Hirzel, 1915.

Domaradzki, M., 'Présence celte en Thrace au début de l'époque hellénistique', in R. Vulpe (ed.) *Actes du IIe Congrès International de Thracologie*, vol. II, Bucharest, Editura Academiei Republicii Socialiste Romania, 1980.

—— 'Les données numismatiques et les études de la culture Thrace du Second Age du Fer', *Numizmatika*, 1987, vol. 21, no. 4, pp. 5–18.

Dunst, G., 'Ein neues chiisches Dekret aus Kos', *Klio*, 1959, vol. 37, pp. 63–9.

Durrbach, F., *Choix d'inscriptions de Delos*, vol. I, Paris, Ernest Leroux, 1921.

Edmonds, J. M., *Comici: the Fragments of Attic Comedy*, vol. IIIA, Leiden, E. J. Brill, 1961.

Edson, C. F., Jr., 'The Antigonids, Heracles and Beroea', *HSCP*, 1934, vol. 45, pp. 213–47.

Ehrenberg, V., *Alexander and the Greeks*, Oxford, Basil Blackwell, 1938.

Engelmann, H. and Knibbe, D., 'Aus ephesischen Skizzenbuchern', *JOAI*, 1980, vol. 52, pp. 19–61.

Erhardt, C., 'A catalogue of issues of tetradrachms from Amphipolis 318–294 BC', *JNFA*, March 1976, vol. 4, no. 4, p. 85–9.

Errington, R. M., 'Bias in Ptolemy's *History of Alexander*', *CQ*, 1969, vol. 18, pp. 233–42.

—— 'From Babylon to Triparadeisos', *JHS*, 1970, vol. 90, pp. 49–77.

—— 'Alexander in the Hellenistic world', in *Alexandre le Grand: image et réalité*, Geneva, Fondation Hardt, 1975.

—— 'Diodorus Siculus and the chronology of the early Diadochoi, 320–311 B.C.', *Hermes*, 1977, vol. 105, pp. 478–504.

Ferguson, W. S., *Hellenistic Athens*, New York, Macmillan & Co., 1911.

Ferrary, J. L. and Gauthier, P., 'Le traité entre le Roi Antiochus et Lysimacheia', *Journal des Savants*, 1981, pp. 327–45.

Finley, M., 'The Black Sea and Danubian regions and the slave trade in antiquity', *Klio*, 1962, vol. 40, pp. 51–60.

—— *The Ancient Economy*, London, Chatto & Windus, 1973.

Fisher, E. A., 'Theodora and Antonina in the *Historia Arcana*: history and/or fiction?', in J. Peradotto & J. P. Sullivan (eds) *Women in the Ancient World*, New York, State University of New York Press, 1984.

Flacelière, R., *Les Aitoliens à Delphes*, Paris, De Boccard, 1937.

Fleischer, R., 'Ergänzungen zum Abschnitt: Der Figurliche Schmuck', in C. Praschniker and M. Theuer (eds) *Das Mausoleum von Belevi*, Vienna, Österreichisches Archäologisches Institut, 1979.

Fol, A. and Mazarov, I., *Thrace and the Thracians*, London, Cassell, 1977.

—— and Hoddinott, R. F., Nikolov, B., *The New Thracian Treasure from Rogozen*, London, British Museum, 1986.

Fontana, M. J., *Le Lotte per la successione di Alessandro Magno dal 323 al 315*, Palermo, Boccone de Povero, 1960.

Forni, G., *Valore storico e fonti di Pompeio Trogo*, vol. I., Urbino, University of Urbino, 1958.

Forrest, W. G., *A History of Sparta*, 2nd edn, London, Duckworth, 1980.

—— 'Some inscriptions of Chios', *Horos*, 1985, vol. 3, pp. 95–104.

Fortina, M., *Cassandro, rè di Macedonia*, Turin, Società Editrice Internationale, 1965.

Fraser, P. M., *The Inscriptions on Stone*, vol. II of K. Lehmann (ed.) *Samothrace*, New York, Pantheon Books, 1960.

Fredericksmeyer, E. A., 'Alexander the Great and the Macedonian *kausia*', *TAPhA*, 1986, vol. 116, pp. 215–27.

Frisch, P., *Die Inschriften von Ilion*, Bonn, Rudolf Habelt Verlag GMBH, 1975.

—— *Die Inschriften von Lampsakos*, Bonn, Rudolf Habelt Verlag GMBH, 1978.

Frost, F. J., 'Ptolemy II and Halicarnassus: an honorary decree', *Anatolian Studies*, 1971, vol. 21, pp. 167–72.

Frye, R., *The Heritage of Persia*, London, Weidenfeld & Nicolson, 1962.

Gabbert, J. J., 'Piracy in the early Hellenistic period: a career open to talents', *Greece and Rome*, 1986, vol. 33, pp. 156–62.

Garlan, Y., *War in the Ancient World*, London, Chatto & Windus, 1975.

Gauthier, P., 'La réunification d'Athènes en 281 et les deux archontes Nicias', *REG*, 1979, vol. 92, pp. 348–99.

—— 'Notes sur trois décrets honorant des citoyens bienfaiteurs', *Rev. Phil.*, 1982, vol. 56, no. 1, pp. 215–31.

—— *Les Cités grecques et leurs bienfaiteurs*, Paris, *BCH* Supplement XII, 1985.

Gerasimov, Th., 'Rare coins of Thrace', *Num. Chron.*, 1957, vol. 17 (series 6), pp. 1–5.

Geyer, F., 'Lysimachos', in G. Wissowa (ed.) *PW*, vol. XIV₁, Stuttgart, J. B. Metzlerscher, 1928, col. 1–31.

Glotz, G., Roussel, P. and Cohen, R., *Histoire grecque*, vol. IV, Paris, Presses Universitaires de France, 1938.

Goody, J., 'Introduction', in J. Goody, *Succession to High Office*, Cambridge, Cambridge University Press, 1966.

Gould, J., 'On making sense of Greek religion', in P. E. Easterling and J. V. Muir (eds) *Greek Religion and Society*, Cambridge, Cambridge University Press, 1985.

Goukowsky, P., *Essai sur les origines du mythe d'Alexandre*, vol. I, Nancy, Nancy University Press, 1978.

Grainger, J. D., *Seleukos Nikator*, London and New York, Routledge, 1990.

Grayson, A. K., *Assyrian and Babylonian Chronicles*, Locust Valley, NY, J. J. Augustin, 1975.

Griffith, G. T., *The Mercenaries of the Hellenistic World*, Cambridge, Cambridge University Press, 1935.

Habicht, C., 'Samische Volks beschlusse der hellenistischen Zeit', *Ath. Mitt.*, 1957, vol. 72, pp. 154–274.

—— 'Die herrschende Gesellschaft in dem hellenistischen Monarchien', Wiesbaden, *Vierteljahrschrift fur Sozial- und Wirtschaftgeschichte* vol. 45, 1958, pp. 1–16.

—— *Gottmenschentum und Griechische Stadte*, 2nd edn, Munich, C. H. Beck, 1970.

—— 'Beitrage zur Prosopographie der altgriechischen welt', *Chiron*, 1972, vol. 2, pp. 107–9.

—— *Untersuchungen zur politischen Geschichte Athens im 3 Jahrhundert v. Chr.*, Munich, C. H. Beck, 1979.

Hadley, R., 'Hieronymus of Cardia and early Seleucid mythology', *Historia*, 1969, vol. 18, pp. 142–52.

——'Royal propaganda of Seleucus I and Lysimachus', *JHS*, 1974a, vol. 94, pp. 50–65.

——'Seleucus, Dionysus or Alexander?', *Num. Chron.*, 1974b, vol. 14 (series 7), pp. 9–13.

Hallock, R. T., *Persepolis Fortification Tablets*, Chicago, Chicago University Press, 1969.

Hamilton, J. R., *Alexander the Great*, London, Hutchinson & Co., 1973.

Hammond, N. G. L., *Three Historians of Alexander the Great*, Cambridge, Cambridge University Press, 1983.

—— and Griffith, G. T., *A History of Macedonia*, vol. II, Oxford, Clarendon Press, 1979.

—— and Walbank, F. W., *A History of Macedonia*, vol. III, Oxford, Clarendon Press, 1988.

Hanfmann, G. M. A. and Mierse, W. E., *Sardis from Prehistoric to Roman Times*, Cambridge, Mass., and London, Harvard University Press, 1983.

Hansen, E. V., *The Attalids of Pergamum*, 2nd edn, Ithaca and London, Cornell University Press, 1971.

Hatzopoulos, M. B., 'Une donation du Roi Lysimaque', *ΜΕΛΗΘΗΜΑΤΑ*, Paris, De Boccard, 1988.

Hauben, H., 'On the chronology of the years 313–311 B.C.', *A. J. Phil.*, 1973, vol. 94, pp. 256–67.

—— 'A royal toast in 302 B.C.', *Ancient Society*, 1974, vol. 5, pp. 108–14.

—— 'IGII² 492 and the siege of Athens in 304 B.C.', *ZPE*, 1974, vol. 14, p. 10.

Haussoulier, B., 'Les Séleucides et le temple d'Apollon Didyméen', *Rev. Phil.*, 1901, vol. 25, pp. 1–39.

Head, B. V., *On the Chronological Sequence of the Coins of Ephesus*, London and Paris, Rollin & Feuardent, 1880.

Heckel, W., 'The *Somatophylakes* of Alexander the Great: some thoughts', *Historia*, 1978, vol. 29, pp. 224–8.

—— *The Last Days and Testament of Alexander the Great*, Stuttgart, *Historia* Einzelschriften 56, 1988.

Heinen, H., *Untersuchungen zur Hellenistischen Geschichte des 3 Jahrhunderts v. Chr.*, Wiesbaden, *Historia* Einzelschriften 20, 1972.

Heisserer, A. J., 'The Philites stele (SIG³ 284 = IEK 503)', *Hesperia*, 1979, vol. 43, pp. 281–93.

Herman, G., 'The "friends" of the early Hellenistic rulers: servants or officials', *Talanta*, 1981, vol. 13, pp. 103–49.

Hill, G. F., 'Some coins of southern Asia Minor', in W. H. Buckler and W. M. Calder (eds) *Anatolian Studies Presented to Sir William Mitchell Ramsay*, Manchester, Manchester University Press, 1923.

Hiller, F., *Inschriften von Priene*, Berlin, Georg Reiner, 1906.

Hind, J. G. F., 'Istrian faces and the river Danube. The type of the silver coins of Istria', *Num. Chron.*, 1970, vol. 10 (series 7), pp. 7–17.

Hoddinott, R. F., *Bulgaria in Antiquity*, London and Tonbridge, Ernest Bean Ltd., 1975.

—— *The Thracians*, London, Thames & Hudson, 1981.

Holleaux, M., 'Sur une inscription de Thèbes', *REG*, 1895, vol. 8, pp. 7–48.

—— 'Ephèse et les Priénians du Charax', *REG*, 1916, vol. 29, pp. 29–45.

—— 'Inscription trouvée à Brousse', *BCH*, 1924, vol. 48, pp. 1–57.

Honigmann, E., 'Sur quelques évêchés d'Asie Mineure', *Byzantion*, 1935, vol. 10, pp. 647–50.

Hornblower, J., *Hieronymus of Cardia*, Oxford, Oxford University Press, 1981.

Hornblower, S., *Mausolus*, Oxford, Clarendon Press, 1982.

Irimaia, I., 'Nouvelles découvertes concernant la population de la dobroudja (V-ème –I-er s.av. JC)', *Pontica*, 1973, vol. 6, pp. 68–72.

Jacoby, F. *FGrH* vol. IIIb, Leiden, E. J. Brill, 1955, pp. 258–61.

Jones, A. H. M., 'Civitates liberae et immunes', in W. M. Calder and J. Keil (eds) *Anatolian Studies Presented to William Hepburn Buckler*, Manchester, Manchester University Press, 1939.

Jordanov, K., 'Les Formations d'état gètes de la fin du VIᵉ siècle avant notre ère', in R. Vulpe (ed.) *Actes du II ᵉ Congrès International de Thracologie*, vol. I, Bucharest, Editura Academiei Republicii Socialiste Romania, 1980.

Kebric, R., *In the Shadow of Macedon: Duris of Samos*, Wiesbaden, *Historia* Einzelschriften 29, 1977.

Keil, J., 'Ephesische Burgerrechts- und Proxeniedekrete aus dem vierten und dritten Jahrhundert v. Chr.', *JOAI*, 1913, vol. 16, pp. 231–44.

Killerich, B., 'Physiognomics and the iconography of Alexander', *Symbolae Osloenses*, 1988, vol. 43, pp. 51–63.

Kraay, C. M., 'Greek coinage and war', in W. Heckel and R. Sullivan (eds) *Ancient Coins of the Graeco-Roman World*, Waterloo, Ont., Wilfred Laurier University Press, 1984.

Kroymann, J., 'Phylarchos' in *PW* Supplement vol. VIII, Stuttgart, 1956, cols 471–89.

Kugler, F. X., *Sternkunde und Sterndienst in Babel*, vol. II, Munster, 1924.

Kuhrt, A. T. L., 'Berossus' *Babyloniaka* and Seleucid rule in Babylonia', in A. T. L. Kuhrt and S. M. Sherwin-White (eds) *Hellenism in the East*, London, Duckworth, 1987a.

—— 'Usurpation, conquest and ceremonial: from Babylon to Persia', in D. Cannadine and S. R. F. Price (eds) *Rituals of Royalty*, Cambridge, Cambridge University Press, 1987b.

—— 'The Achaemenid empire: a Babylonian perspective', *PCPS*, 1988, vol. 14, pp. 60–76.

—— 'Earth and water', in A. T. L. Kuhrt and H. Sancisi-Weerdenburg (eds) *Achaemenid History III*, Leiden, Nederlands Institut voor Het Nabije Oosten, 1988.

—— 'Andreas Mehl, Seleukos Nikator und sein Reich' (Review), Bibliotheca Orientalis, 1989, vol. 46, pp. 507–12.

Kuhrt, A. T. L. and Sherwin-White, S. M., 'Aspects of Seleucid royal ideology: the cylinder of Antiochus I from Borsippa', *JHS*, 1991, vol. 111, pp. 71–87.

Lane Fox, R., *Alexander the Great*, London, Allen Lane, 1973.

—— *Pagans and Christians*, Harmondsworth, Viking, 1986.

Le Bohec, S., 'Les *philoi* des rois antigonides', *REG*, 1985, vol. 98, pp. 93–124.

Leaf, W., 'Scepsis in the Troad', in W. H. Buckler and W. M. Calder (eds) *Anatolian Studies Presented to Sir William Mitchell Ramsay*, Manchester, Manchester University Press, 1923.

Lefkowitz, M., 'Influential women', in A. Cameron and A. Kuhrt (eds) *Images of Women in Antiquity*, London and Canberra, Croom Helm, 1983.

Lehmann, K., *Samothrace: A Guide to the Excavations and the Museum*, Locust Valley, NY, J. J. Augustin, 1983.

Lévèque, P., *Pyrrhos*, Paris, De Boccard, 1957.

Lewis, D. M., *Sparta and Persia*, Leiden, E. J. Brill, 1977.

Longega, G., *Arsinoe II*, Rome, L'erma di Bretschneider, 1968.

Lund, H. S., 'Bridging the Hellespont: the Successor Lysimachus – a study in early Hellenistic kingship', University of London Ph.D. thesis, Senate House Library, 1992.

Maier, F. G., *Griechische Mauerbauinschriften*, vol. I, Heidelberg, Quelle & Meyer, 1959.

McCredie, J. R., 'Samothrace: preliminary campaigns of 1965-7', *Hesperia*, 1968, vol. 37, pp. 200–35.

McKechnie, P., *Outsiders in the Greek Cities in the Fourth Century B.C.*, London and New York, Routledge, 1989.

Mackendrick, P., *The Dacian Stones Speak*, Chapel Hill and London, University of North Carolina Press, 1975.

Macurdy, G., *Hellenistic Queens*, Baltimore, Johns Hopkins University Press, 1932.

Magie, D., *Roman Rule in Asia Minor*, Princeton, NJ, Princeton University Press, 1950.

Malay, H., 'A royal document from Aigai in Aeolis', *GRBS*, 1983, vol. 24, pp. 349–54.

Manni, E., *Plutarchi: Vita Demetri Poliorcetis*, Florence, La Nuova Italia Editrice, 1953.

Martin, T. R., *Sovereignty and Coinage in Classical Greece*, Princeton, NJ, Princeton University Press, 1985.

Mehl, A., *Seleukos Nikator und Sein Reich*, Lovanii, Studia Hellenistica 28, 1986.

Meiggs, R., 'Timber' in N. G. L. Hammond and H. H. Scullard (eds) *Oxford Classical Dictionary*, 2nd edn, Oxford, Clarendon Press, 1970, cols 1074–5.

—— *The Athenian Empire*, Oxford, Clarendon Press, 1972.

Mendel, G., 'Inscriptions de Bithynie', *BCH*, 1900, vol. 24, pp. 361–426.

Merkelbach, R., 'Ein Zeugnis aus Tralles über Pleistarchus', *ZPE*, 1975, vol. 16, p. 163.

Merker, I. L., 'The ancient kingdom of Paionia', *Balkan Studies*, 1965, vol. 6, pp. 35–54.

—— 'The Ptolemaic officials and the League of Islanders', *Historia*, 1970, vol. 19, pp. 141–60.

—— 'Lysimachus – Macedonian or Thessalian', *Chiron*, 1979, vol. 9, pp. 31–6.

Meritt, B. D., 'Inscriptions of Colophon', *A. J. Phil*, 1935, vol. 56, pp. 358–79.

—— 'Greek inscriptions', *Hesperia*, 1938, vol. 7, pp. 77–160.

Meyer, E., *Die Grenzen der hellenistischen Staaten in Kleinasien*, Leipzig, 1925.

Mihailov, G., 'La Thrace au IVe et IIIe siècle avant notre ère', *Athenaeum*, 1961, vol. 39, pp. 33–44.

—— *Inscriptiones Graecae in Bulgaria Repertae*, vols. I–IV, Sofia, Academia Litterarum Bulgarica, 1961–6.

—— 'Il tesoro di Rogozen: le iscrizioni', *Epigraphica*, 1988, vol. 50, pp. 9–40.

Miller, J., 'Pixodaros' in *PW*, vol. XX$_2$, Stuttgart, 1950, cols 1893–4.

Milne, J. G., 'The autonomous coinage of Smyrna', *Num. Chron.*, 1923, vol. 3 (series 5), pp. 1–30.

—— 'The mint of Kyme in the third century B.C.', *Num. Chron.*, 1940, vol. 20 (series 5), pp. 129–37.

Missitzis, L., 'A royal decree of Alexander the Great on the lands of Philippi', *Ancient World*, 1985, vol. 12, no. 1, pp. 3–14.

Mitchell, S., 'Requisitioned transport in the Roman empire: a new inscription from Pisidia', *JRS*, 1976, vol. 66, pp. 106–31.

Morawiecki, L., *Political Propaganda in the Coinage of the Late Roman Republic*, Wroclaw, Zaklad Narodowy im Ossolinskich, 1983.

Moretti, I., *Iscrizione storiche ellenistiche*, vol. II, Florence, La Nuova Italia Editrice, 1975.

Moscalu, E. and Voievozanu, I., 'Le tombeau princier gète et le trésor de

Peretu', in R. Vulpe (ed.) *Actes du IIe Congrès International de Thracologie*, vol. I, Bucharest, Editura Academiei Republicii Socialiste Romania, 1980.

Muller, C., *Fragmenta Historicorum Graecorum*, vol. III, Paris, Didot & Co., 1883.

Murray, O., 'Hecataeus of Abdera and Pharaonic kingship', *JEA*, 1970, vol. 12, pp. 141–71.

Newell, E. T., *The Coinages of Demetrius Poliorcetes*, London, Oxford University Press and Humphrey Milford, 1927.

—— *The Coinage of the Western Seleucid Mints from Seleucus I to Antiochus II*, New York, American Numismatic Society, 1941.

Nicolov, D., 'Caracteristique économique et démographique des colonies grecques du littoral de la Mer Noire', in A. Fol (ed.) (with collaboration of I. Karayotov, P. Pelex, V. Popov, K. Porogeanov and M. Tzaneva) *Thracia Pontica I*, Sofia, L'Academie Bulgare de Sciences, 1982.

Niese, B., *Geschichte der Griechischen und Makedonischen Staaten seit der Schlact bei Chaeronea*, vol. I, Gotha, Friedrich Andreas Perthes, 1893.

Nilsson, M. P., *Cults, Myths, Oracles and Politics in Ancient Greece*, Lund, C. W. K. Gleerup, 1951.

Nock, A. D., 'Notes on ruler cult I–IV', *JHS*, 1928, vol. 48, pp. 134–59.

—— Σεννǎος Θεος' in *HSCP*, vol. XLI, 1930, pp. 1–62.

'Ognenova-Marinova, L., 'Quis autem erat Epimenes?', *Klio*, 1980, vol. 62, pp. 47–9.

Oliver, J. H., *The Sacred Gerousia*, Athens, *Hesperia* Supplement VI, 1941.

Olmstead, A. T., *History of the Persian Empire*, Chicago, Chicago University Press, 1948.

Olshausen, L., *Prosopographie der Hellenistischen Königsgesandten*, Louvain, Studia Hellenistica 19, 1974.

Orth, W., *Königlicher Machtanspruch und Stadtische Freiheit*, Munich, C. H. Beck, 1977.

Orwell, G., *Nineteen-Eighty-Four*, London, Secker & Warburg, 1949.

Osbourne, M., 'The decree for Bithys of Lysimacheia IG II² 808', *Ancient Society*, 1974, vol. 5.

Palagia, O., 'Imitation of Heracles in ruler portraiture: a survey from Alexander to Maximinus Daza', *Boreas*, 1986, vol. 9, pp. 137–52.

Parke, H. W., *The Oracles of Apollo in Asia Minor*, London, Croom Helm, 1985.

Parker, R. A. and Dubberstein, W. H., *Babylonian Chronology 626 BC-AD 75*, Providence, RI, Brown University Studies, 1956.

Parvan, V., *Dacia*, Cambridge, Cambridge University Press, 1928.

Pearson, L., *The Lost Histories of Alexander the Great*, New York, New York Philological Association, 1960.

Peek, W., *Griechische Versinschriften*, Akademie Verlag, Berlin, 1955.

Picard, Ch., 'Fouilles de Thasos (1914-1920)', *BCH*, 1921, vol. 45, pp. 144–73.

Pippidi, D. M., 'Istros et les Gètes au IIe siècle av. notre ère', *Studii Clasice*, 1961, vol. 3, pp. 53–66.

—— 'Note sur l'organisation militaire d'Istros a l'époque hellénistique', *Klio*, 1963, vol. 41, pp. 158–67.

—— *Contributii la Istoria Veche Romanei*, Bucharest, Editura Stiintifica, 1967.

—— *I Greci nel Basso Danubio*, Milan, Il Saggiatore, 1971.

Pippidi, D. M. and Popescu, Em., 'Les relations d'Istros et d'Apollonia du Pont a l'époque hellénistique', *Dacia*, 1959, vol. 3, pp. 235–59.

Poenaru Bordea, G. H., 'Note epigrafice', in C. Daicovicu (ed.) *Noi monumente epigrafice din Scythia Minor*, Constanta, 1964.

—— 'Le trésor de Marasesti', *Dacia*, 1974, vol. 18, pp. 103–20.

Pollitt, J. J., *Art in the Hellenistic World*, Cambridge, Cambridge University Press, 1986.

Popov, D., 'L'institution royale dans la maison dynastique des Odryses', in R. Vulpe (ed.) *Actes du IIe Congrès International de Thracologie*, vol. II, Bucharest, Editura Academiei Republicii Socialiste Romania, 1980.

Praschniker, C., 'Die Datierung' in C. Praschniker and M. Theuer (eds) *Das Mausoleum von Belevi*, Vienna, Österreichisches Archäologisches Institut, 1979.

Préaux, C., *Le Monde hellénistique*, vol. II, Paris, Presses Universitaires de France, 1978.

Preda, C., 'Archaeological discoveries in the Greek cemetery of Callatis-Mangalia', *Dacia*, 1961, vol. 5, pp. 275–304.

Price, M. J., *Coins of the Macedonians*, London, British Museum, 1974.

—— *Coins of Alexander the Great*, London, British Museum, forthcoming.

Price, S. R. F., *Rituals and Power*, Cambridge, Cambridge University Press, 1984.

Rankin, H. D., *Celts and the Classical World*, London and Sydney, Croom Helm, 1987.

Regling K., 'Lysimacheia', in *PW*, vol. XIII$_2$, Stuttgart, 1927, cols 2254–5.

Richter, G. M. A., *The Portraits of the Greeks*, vol. III, London, Phaidon Press, 1965.

Ritter, H. W., *Diadem und Königsherrschaft*, Munich, C. H. Beck, 1965.

Robert, L., 'Notes d'épigraphie héllenistique', *BCH*, 1933, vol. 57, §XI. pp. 485–90.

—— 'Inscriptions de Thasos', *Rev. Phil.*, 1936, vol. 8, pp. 127–37.

—— 'Adeimantos et la Ligue de Corinthe', in *Hellenica*, vol. I, Limoges, Imprimerie A. Bontemps, 1940.

—— 'Hellenica^1 – XX décrets de Priene', *Rev. Phil.*, 1944, vol. 18, pp. 5–10.

—— *Le Sanctuaire de Sinuri près de Mylasa*, vol. I, Paris, De Boccard, 1945.

—— *Etudes de numismatique grecque: monnaies et villes de Troade*, Paris, College de France, 1951.

—— 'Les inscriptions grecques de Bulgarie', *Rev. Phil.*, 1959, vol. 38, pp. 172–9.

—— 'Sur une loi d'Athènes relative au petites Panathenées', in *Hellenica*, vol. XI–XII, Paris, Imprimerie A. Bontemps, 1960.

—— *Villes d'Asie Mineure*, 2nd edn, Paris, De Boccard, 1962.

—— *Noms indigenes dans l'Asie Mineure gréco-romaine*, vol. I, Paris, Librairie Adrien Maisonneuve, 1963.

—— 'Sur un décret d'Ilion et sur un papyrus concernant des cultes royaux', in *Essays in Honour of C. Bradford Welles*, New Haven, American Society of Papyrologists, 1966b.

—— 'Sur des inscriptions d'Ephèse', *Rev. Phil*, 1967, vol. 41, no. 4, pp. 37–40.

Roisman, J., 'Ptolemy and his rivals in his history of Alexander', *CQ*, 1984, vol. 33 (New Series), pp. 373–85.

Root, M. C., *The King and Kingship in Achaemenid Art*, Leiden, *Acta Iranica* vol. 19, 1979.

Rostovtzeff, M., 'Notes on the economic policy of the Pergamene kings', in W. H. Buckler and W. M. Calder (eds) *Anatolian Studies Presented to Sir William Mitchell Ramsay*, Manchester, Manchester University Press, 1923.

—— *The Social and Economic History of the Hellenistic World*, 2 vols, Oxford, Clarendon Press, 1941.

Roussel, P., 'Le démembrement de l'empire d'Alexandre', in G. Glotz, P. Roussel, and R. Cohen, *Histoire grecque*, vol. IV, Paris, Presses Universitaires de France, 1938.

—— 'La Perée Samothracienne au IIIe siècle avant J.-C.', *BCH*, 1939, vol. 63, pp. 133–41.

Sachs, A. J., *Late Babylonian Astronomical and Related Texts*, Providence, RI, Brown University Studies 18, 1955.

Sachs, A. J., and Hunger, H., *Astronomical Diaries and Related Texts from Babylonia*, vol. I, Vienna, Osterreichische Akademie der Wissenschaften, 1988.

Sachs, A. J. and Wiseman, D. J., 'A Babylonian king list of the Hellenistic period', *Iraq*, 1954, vol. 16, pp. 202–11.

St Marin, D., 'Il foedus Romano con Callatis', *Epigraphica*, 1948, vol. 10, pp. 106–30.

Saitta, G., 'Lisimaco di Tracia', *Kokalos*, 1955, vol. 1, pp. 62–152.

Saller, R., 'Anecdotes as historical evidence for the Principate', *Greece and Rome*, 1980, vol. 27 (2nd series), pp. 69–82.

Sancisi-Weerdenburg, H., 'Exit Atossa: images of women in Greek historiography on Persia', in A. Cameron and A. Kuhrt (eds) *Images of Women in Antiquity*, London and Canberra, Croom Helm, 1983.

Schubert, R., *Die Quellen zur Geschichte der Diadochenzeit*, Leipzig, Theodor Weicher, 1914.

Schweigert, E., 'Two third century inscriptions', *Hesperia*, 1941, vol. 10, §1, pp. 338–41.

Scott, K., 'The deification of Demetrius Poliorcetes', *A. J. Phil.*, 1934, vol. 55, pp. 137–66.

Segre, M., 'Decreto di Aspendos', *Aegyptus*, 1934, vol. 14, p. 253–68.

—— 'Decreto di Apollonio sul Ponto', *Athenaeum*, 1934, vol. 12, pp. 3–9.

Seibert, J., *Historische Beitrage zu Die Dynastische Verbindungen in hellenistischer Zeit*, Wiesbaden, *Historia* Einzelschriften 10, 1967.

—— *Untersuchungen zu Geschichte Ptolemaios I*, Munich, C. H. Beck, 1969.

—— 'Ptolemaios I und Milet', *Chiron*, 1971, vol. 1, pp. 159–66.

Sekunda, N., 'The rhomphaia: a Thracian weapon of the Hellenistic period', in A. G. Poulter (ed.) *Ancient Bulgaria*, vol. 1, Nottingham , University of Nottingham, 1983.

Seltman, C., *Greek Coins*, London, Methuen, 1955.

Seyrig, H., 'Paron au 3e siècle avant notre ère', in H. Ingolt (ed.) *Centennial Publication of the American Society*, New York, American Numism. Soc., 1958, pp. 603–26.

—— 'Monnaies héllenistiques de Byzance et Calcédoine', in C. M. Kraay and

G. K. Jenkins (eds) *Essays in Greek Coinage Presented to Stanley Robinson*, Oxford, Clarendon Press, 1968.

Shear, T. L., *Kallias of Sphettos and the Revolt of Athens in 286 B.C.* Princeton NJ, *Hesperia* Supplement XVII, 1978.

Sherwin-White, S. M., 'Babylonian Chronicle fragments as a source for Seleucid history', *JNES*, 1983, vol. 42, pp. 265–70.

—— 'Ancient archives: the edict of Alexander to Priene, a reappraisal', *JHS*, 1985, vol. 105, pp. 69–89.

—— 'Seleucid Babylonia: a case-study for the installation and development of Greek rule', in A. T. L. Kuhrt and S. M. Sherwin-White (eds) *Hellenism in the East*, London, Duckworth, 1987.

Shipley, G., *A History of Samos 800–188 B.C.*, Oxford, Clarendon Press, 1987.

Simpson, R. H., 'The historical circumstances of the peace of 311', *JHS*, 1954, vol. 74, pp. 25–31.

—— 'A note on Cyinda', *Historia*, 1957a, vol. 6, pp. 503–4.

—— 'A possible case of misrepresentation in Diodorus XIX', *Historia*, 1957b, vol. 77, pp. 504–6.

—— 'Antigonus the One-Eyed and the Greeks', *Historia*, 1959, vol. 8, pp. 385–409.

Smith, L. C., 'Demochares of Leuconoe and the dates of his exile', *Historia*, 1962, vol. 11, pp. 114–18.

Smith, R. R. R., *Hellenistic Royal Portraits*, Oxford, Clarendon Press, 1988.

Southwold, M., 'Succession to the throne in Buganda', in J. Goody *Succession to High Office*, Cambridge, Cambridge University Press, 1966.

Stefan, A., 'Graffite callatien du IV ͤ siecle av. N. E.' in D. M. Pippidi and Em. Popescu (eds) *Epigraphica. Travaux dedités au VII ͤ Congrès d'Epigraphie grecque et latine*, Bucharest, Editura Academiei Republicii Socialiste Romania, 1977.

Stewart, A. F., *Skopas of Paros*, New Jersey, Noyes Press, 1977.

Stoian, I., 'Echos de la lutte des classes à Istros', in I. Stoian *Etudes Histriennes*, Brussels, Latomus, 1972.

Tarn, W. W., *Antigonus Gonatas*, Oxford, Clarendon Press, 1913.

—— 'The proposed new date for Ipsus', *CR*, 1926, vol. 40, pp. 13–14.

—— 'The succession to Alexander', in J. B. Bury, S. A. Cook and F. E. Adcock (eds) *Cambridge Ancient History*, 1st edn, vol. VI, Cambridge, Cambridge University Press, 1927.

—— 'Queen Ptolemais and Apama', *CQ*, 1929, vol. 23, pp. 138–42.

—— 'Two notes on Ptolemaic history', *JHS*, 1933, vol. 52, pp. 57–9.

—— 'Two notes on Seleucid history: 1. Seleucus' 500 elephants', *JHS*, 1940, vol. 60, pp. 84–9.

—— *Alexander the Great*, vol. II, Cambridge, Cambridge University Press, 1948.

Thompson, M., 'The mints of Lysimachus', in C. M. Kraay and G. K. Jenkins (eds) *Essays in Greek Coinage Presented to Stanley Robinson*, Oxford, Clarendon Press, 1968.

Tod, M. N., *Greek Historical Inscriptions*, vol. II, Oxford, Clarendon Press, 1948.

Tscherikower, V., *Die Hellenistischen Stadtegrundungen von Alexander dem Grossen bis auf der Römerzeit*, Leipzig, *Philologus* Supplement 19, 1927.

Van Berchem, D., 'La gérousie d'Ephèse', *Mus. Helv.*, 1980, vol. 37, pp. 25–40.

Velkov, V., 'The Thracian city of Cabyle', in A. G. Poulter (ed.) *Ancient Bulgaria*, vol. I, Nottingham, University of Nottingham, 1983.

Vulpe, R., 'La succession des rois Odryses', in R. Vulpe (ed.) *Studia Thracologica*, Bucharest, Editura Academiei Republicii Socialiste Romania, 1976.

Walbank, F. W., 'Sources for the period' and 'Monarchies and monarchic ideas' in A. E. Astin, M. W. Frederiksen, R. M. Ogilvie and F. W. Walbank (eds) *Cambridge Ancient History*, 2nd edn, vol. VII, Cambridge, Cambridge University Press, 1984.

Walker, B., *The Annals of Tacitus*, Manchester, Manchester University Press, 1952.

Waywell, G. B., 'Mausolea in South-west Asia Minor', *YAYLA*, Third Report of the Northern Society for Anatolian Archaeology, 1980, pp. 4–11.

Wehrli, C., *Antigone et Demetrios*, Geneva, Librairie Droz, 1968.

Welles, C. B., *Royal Correspondence in the Hellenistic Period*, New Haven, CT, Yale University Press, 1934.

Will, E., *Le Monde grec et l'orient*, vol. II, Paris, Presses Universitaires de France, 1975.

—— *Histoire politique du monde héllenistique*, vol. I, Nancy, University of Nancy Press, 1979.

—— 'The succession to Alexander', in A. E. Astin, M. W. Frederiksen, R. M. Ogilvie and F. W. Walbank (eds) *Cambridge Ancient History*, 2nd edn, vol. VII, Cambridge, Cambridge University Press, 1984.

Woodhead, A. G., 'Athens and Demetrius Poliorketes at the end of the fourth century B.C.', in H. J. Dell (ed.) *Ancient Macedonian Studies in Honour of Charles F. Edson*, Thessaloniki, Institute for Balkan Studies, 1981.

Wörrle, M., 'Epigraphische Forschungen zur Geschichte Lykiens II' in *Chiron*, vol. 8, 1978, pp. 201–46.

Youroukova, Y., *Coins of the Ancient Thracians*, Oxford, B.A.R. Supplement Series no. 4, 1976.

Zahle, J., 'Persian satraps and Lycian dynasts: the evidence of the diadems', in T. Hackens and R. Weiller (eds) *Actes du 9ᵉ Congrès International de Numismatique, Berne 1979*, 1982.

Zervos, O. H. in O. H. Zervos and M. J. Price, 'Debate: on "The earliest coins of Alexander the Great" ', *Num. Chron.*, 1982, vol. 142, pp. 166–90.

Ziegler, K., 'Proxenos', in G. Wissowa (ed.) *PW*, vol. XXXIII, Stuttgart, J. B. Metzlerscher, 1957, cols 1,033–4.

INDEX

INDEX

1f.600 Lex.   2302834040|28